SECULARIZATION AND THE WORLD RELIGIONS

SECULARIZATION
AND
THE WORLD RELIGIONS

Edited by Hans Joas and Klaus Wiegandt
Translated by Alex Skinner

Liverpool University Press

First English edition published 2009 by
Liverpool University Press
4 Cambridge Street
Liverpool
L69 7ZU

Originally published as *Säkularisierung und die Weltreligionen* (Frankfurt am Main: Fischer, 2007)

British Library Cataloguing-in-Publication data
A British Library CIP record is available

ISBN 978–1–84631–187–1 cased
      978–1–84631–188–8 limp

Typeset in Perpetua by Carnegie Book Production, Lancaster
Printed and bound by Bell and Bain Ltd, Glasgow

Contents

Notes on Contributors

Winfried Brugger, Professor of Public Law and Philosophy of Law at the University of Heidelberg, Fellow of the Max Weber Centre for Advanced Cultural and Social Studies, Erfurt

José Casanova, Professor of Sociology and Senior Fellow in the Berkley Center for Religion, Peace, and World Affairs at Georgetown University, Washington, DC

Ernst Peter Fischer, Professor of History of Science at the University of Constance

Joachim Gentz, Senior Lecturer in Chinese Studies and Research Fellow in Cultural Studies at the University of Edinburgh

Friedrich Wilhelm Graf, Professor of Systematic Theology at the University of Munich

Hans Joas, Director of the Max Weber Centre for Advanced Cultural and Social Studies, Erfurt and Professor of Sociology and Social Thought at the University of Chicago

Hans Gerhard Kippenberg, Professor Emeritus of Religious Studies at the University of Bremen and Fellow of the Max Weber Centre for Advanced Cultural and Social Studies, Erfurt

Gudrun Krämer, Professor of Islamic Studies at the Free University of Berlin

Cardinal Karl Lehmann, Bishop of Mainz and President of the German Bishops' Conference (1987–2008)

David Martin, Professor Emeritus of Sociology of Religion at the London School of Economics

Eckart Otto, Professor of Old Testament Studies at the University of Munich and Honorary Professor at the University of Pretoria (South Africa)

Heinrich von Stietencron, Professor Emeritus of Indology and Comparative Religion at the University of Tübingen

Rudolf G. Wagner, Professor of Sinology at the University of Heidelberg

Foreword

Hans Joas and Klaus Wiegandt

From 31 March to 5 April 2006, the fifth conference of the Forum für Verantwortung foundation, entitled 'Secularization and the World Religions', was held at the European Academy, Otzenhausen (Saarland). The foundation invited scholars in various fields, among them Cardinal Lehmann, to cast light on the topic in a way comprehensible to the approximately 180 attendees, whose interests cover a broad spectrum. The discussions with the audience that followed the lectures showed that they had fully achieved this aim. We would like to take this opportunity to again thank all the speakers.

The lectures delivered in Otzenhausen have been brought together in the present volume in order to make them accessible to a broader public beyond the conference participants. As with the volumes arising from the earlier conferences, all published in German by S. Fischer Verlag and tackling the subjects of evolution; humanity and the cosmos; the cultural values of Europe (with a volume of the same title published by Liverpool University Press in 2008) and the future of the earth, for reasons of space it was necessary to forego reproducing the incisive discussions of the individual lectures. The podium discussion moderated by Hans Joas on 'Religion and Politics at the Beginning of the Twenty-First Century', which concluded the fifth conference, is also left out of account here.

We would like to thank the attendees for their deep engagement and critical questions, which not only invigorated the conference but also inspired later modifications to the written forms of the lectures and have thus entered into the contributions published here.

We owe a debt of gratitude to Ulrike Holler of S. Fischer Verlag, who not only performed her tasks with her usual skill and reliability, but also had to contend with tardy manuscripts, a challenge to which she rose with aplomb.

And last but not least we would like to thank Monika Presting, who is responsible for the *Teleakademie* of the broadcasting company Südwestrundfunk

(SWR), and who filmed seven of the lectures held in Otzenhausen for a televised lecture series. These were broadcast in autumn 2006 (SWR and 3sat).

Chicago and Seeheim-Hugenheim, autumn 2006

Society, State and Religion: Their Relationship from the Perspective of the World Religions: An Introduction

Hans Joas

The question of religion, its contemporary and future significance and its role in society and state is currently perceived as an urgent one by many and is widely discussed within the public sphere. But it is also – and has long been – one of the core topics of the historically oriented modern social sciences, indeed, of the modern disciplines of history and philosophy of history since their emergence in the eighteenth century. Increased public interest opens up an opportunity to think in new ways about the immense stock of knowledge furnished by the history of religion and religious studies, theology, sociology and history, and to introduce it into the public conscience. It is of course beyond dispute that a contemporary treatment of these issues cannot remain limited to Europe or the North Atlantic world, but must adopt a truly global perspective. This means that we must take full account of religious traditions other than those of Christianity and consider other parts of the world – beyond Europe and North America. It has, in any event, become quite impossible to draw clear boundaries between territories with respect to concepts of religion – as the notion of the 'Christian West', for example, attempts to do. The drawing of such boundary lines has always been problematic historically, as it underestimates the reality of religious pluralism, with respect, for example, to European religious history.[1] Christianity has spread across the world to such an extent that, at least from a quantitative point of view, a

---

[1]   An excellent account with a focus on the Middle Ages can be found in Michael Borgolte, *Christen, Juden, Muselmanen. Die Erben der Antike und der Aufstieg des Abendlandes 300–1400 n.Chr.*, Munich, Siedler, 2006.

shift of emphasis away from Europe is becoming increasingly probable. In Europe especially, processes of secularization have loosened people's identification with Christianity, and Islam too has become a global phenomenon through migration and the modern media. The present volume attempts to bring clarity to this rapidly changing and confusing situation. The goal of this introduction, after reflecting briefly on the historical situation from which our questions arise, and provisionally clarifying the key terms 'secularization' and 'world religions', is to develop the problem which it is this book's task to investigate. I then briefly summarize the answers to which I believe some of the contributions point.

The present-day relevance of the topic of 'religion', it seems to me, is anchored in four different contexts. Two of these contexts are quite obvious and receive frequent mention, while the other two seem to me less obvious and point to fundamental changes in contemporary culture.

The two most oft-cited factors are political in nature. The terrorist attacks of 11 September 2001 have shocked many people into an awareness that there are globally active terrorist networks whose self-understanding is based on a specific politicization of one of the great world religions, Islam. The spectacular acts of violence of 2001 were by no means the first crimes committed by Islamist fanatics; an attack was in fact carried out on the World Trade Center itself some years previously. Such terrorism, moreover, does not represent the only form of an intensive politicization of Islam, unmistakable since the Iranian revolution of 1979 at the latest. But it is only since 2001 that these forms of the politicization of religion have shaken the assumptions of those who formerly tended to dismiss religion as a thing of the past. Islam and the various forms of Islamism have thus moved to the centre of public debates; at the same time, it is only now that religious justifications of political action on other sides of the Middle East conflict have received greater attention. It is true that the foundation of the state of Israel was above all the result of a secular-nationalist movement, but the Jewish settlement of areas conquered and occupied in 1967 is also a religious project. And American foreign policy under President George W. Bush at least takes account of the worldview characteristic of certain strands of a Protestant fundamentalism that links an apocalyptic perspective with the settlement of what was once Jewish land.[2]

The second political context which must be mentioned here relates to the integration of Muslim immigrants in Europe and the issue of the limits of the expansion of the European Union. Of course, on closer consideration, these are two quite different issues, but ones which are constantly confused within public debate, which turns the relationship with Turkey in particular into an emotional trouble spot. In Europe, the integration of large minorities of Muslim

---

[2]   See the chapter by Hans Gerhard Kippenberg in this volume.

immigrants confronts all the arrangements of state and religion that have arisen over the course of its history with new challenges; this is quite unavoidable, but is often perceived as a danger of regressing to the bloody conflicts between religious communities that have plagued Europe in the past. At the same time, the eastwards expansion of the European Union and the debates on a European constitution, particularly the issue of a reference to God in its preamble, have made Europe's religious identity an issue again. When the processes of European unification were still in their early stages after the Second World War, there would have been no doubt about Europe's Christian (or Judaeo-Christian) identity, but the processes of secularization in Europe have now become so strong that not only this early phase of post-war politics, but Europe's religious history in general have been forgotten. This gives rise to argumentative constellations of an often paradoxical nature. The Christian character of Europe, for example, is advanced as a reason why Turkey should not be allowed to join the EU, even by those who otherwise want nothing to do with this Christian character. In parallel with this, pupils in eastern Germany, some of them fully secularized, are developing an interest in the history of their own culture and its religious roots only after being confronted with religiously self-aware Muslim classmates. In view of this, we must inevitably ask whether Europe should understand itself in light of Christianity or by distancing itself from it, whether Christianity is merely a legacy or also a source of contemporary guidance, whether it is only Christianity that can represent such a source or whether other religions also belong within this identity-founding consensus.

Less obvious than these contemporary political contexts are two profound changes. In my view, we should have the courage to speak of the 'end of postmodernity'. By this I mean that a strand of intellectual life, which dominated the cultural life of the West in many ways from the late 1970s on, has run out of steam. It had succeeded in picking up on the disappointment felt about both the euphoric faith in state planning of the 1960s and early 1970s and the impossibility of realizing the utopian dreams of 1968, expressing this disappointment in memorable phrases. Its scepticism about schemes of progress and grand historical narratives dovetailed with the *Zeitgeist* and the celebration of unbounded pluralism as a guarantee of freedom and creativity. But since the appearance of Zygmunt Bauman's important book on modernity and the Holocaust from 1989[3] it has been apparent that this is a problematic way of thinking, one which implicitly endorsed an ethos of tolerance and non-violent coexistence, but which was unable to provide a foundation for such an ethos. An understanding of the limits of

---

[3] Zygmunt Bauman, *Modernity and the Holocaust*, Cambridge, Polity, 1989; see Hans Joas and Wolfgang Knöbl, *Social Theory*, Cambridge, Cambridge University Press, 2009, pp. 475–84.

tolerance and the necessity of anchoring it in a positive foundation whenever there is a need to counter the enemies of pluralism or preserve and pass on this ethos was bound to place the issue of values and their transmission back on the agenda sooner or later. This has occurred to a profound degree in recent years. Such a revival of interest in 'values' is inevitably bound up with a new interest in the historical origins of ideas of tolerance and religious freedom themselves, however sceptical we may be about metahistorical constructions. It is no coincidence that impressive works have recently been produced on this subject;[4] the question of whether tolerance and religious freedom arose, and have a permanent potential to arise, primarily by distancing themselves from religion or on the basis of religious motives has become a question of burning interest.

The fourth context is the one closest to the concerns of the present volume. We might call this the crisis or the end of secularization theory. What I am thinking of here is the assumption, which was extraordinarily widespread for a long time, that processes of modernization must lead, with a kind of inherent inevitability, to the weakening of religion on all levels, a weakening, moreover, which is irreversible and will sooner or later cause religion to disappear entirely. Admittedly, this assumption was only rarely expressed so crassly; but in a milder form it dominated the thinking of non-believers, who could thus see themselves as modern people, but to some extent even that of believers, who inevitably felt akin to an endangered species as a result or saw themselves as the vanguard of those who must resist modernization as a whole, this being the only way to defend religion against the forces of secularization. This is not the place[5] to examine in more depth the difficulties which have always beset this explanatory schema with respect to individual European countries (such as Poland and Ireland) and, above all, the USA.[6] Now though, since the rapid economic ascent of East Asia, as well as South Asia and large parts of Latin America in recent years, we are witnessing extensive modernization outside the North Atlantic area for the first time. And though it is impossible to sum up the religious developments in these areas in

---

[4]   Rainer Forst, *Toleranz im Konflikt*, Frankfurt am Main, Suhrkamp, 2003; Perez Zagorin, *How the Idea of Religious Toleration Came to the West*, Princeton, Princeton University Press, 2003.

[5]   The most important studies critiquing this notion have been produced by British sociologist David Martin, who has contributed a chapter on Africa and Latin America to the present volume. See his *A General Theory of Secularization*, Oxford, Blackwell, 1978; idem, *On Secularization: Towards a Revised General Theory*, Aldershot, Ashgate, 2005; idem, 'Secularization and the Future of Christianity', *Journal of Contemporary Religion*, 20 (2005), pp. 145–60.

[6]   I say more about this in my chapter on the religious situation in the USA (in this volume).

a few words, this huge open-air experiment, together with examination of the religious history of the non-European world in the long nineteenth century,[7] gives us every reason to affirm at least one negative conclusion: the thesis of secularization formulated with reference to Europe has not proved helpful in explaining these developments. Rather, with this expectation, Europeans have expressed their own sense not only of being different from others, but of being in the vanguard of historical progress. Increasingly, therefore, the USA no longer seems a strange exception, in which secularization is absent under modern conditions, but a prototype for the non-European world. This itself is probably another overstatement, as many specific features of the USA are also absent in other cases. But we do not need a fitting explanation for every case in order to assert that it is only by taking leave of secularization theory that we can probe the real reasons for secularization, which has in fact occurred on a spectacular scale in parts of Europe. Those who believe in the thesis of secularization have no serious questions to ask about advancing secularization. They merely see their expectations being fulfilled. Only if we take seriously the fact that secularization has occurred, but avoid assuming that we already have the explanation for it in the general character of modernization processes, can we grasp in a sensitive and open-minded way that the history of secularization is one variant of modern history in all its contingency and instability.

But what exactly do we mean when we refer to secularization? Unfortunately, the term has so many meanings and is used in so many different ways that there is a great danger of misunderstanding. Painstaking historical studies of the concept[8] show clearly that it started out in the sixteenth century as a legal term. Initially, it was used to refer to the transition of a member of an order to the status of 'secular' priest. But even in a legal sense the term is ambiguous, because it later referred not only to the changing status of clergy, but to the nationalization or at least expropriation and seizure of church property. In Germany, the 'secularization' of 1803, featuring expropriation and the abolition of religious principalities and monasteries, is remembered as a key date in history. It was only later that this legal term took on a meaning rooted, as it were, in the philosophy of history. It lent itself to the discussion of genealogical connections between

---

7 For an excellent account, see C. A. Bayly, *The Birth of the Modern World 1789–1914*, Oxford, Blackwell, 2004, pp. 325–65.

8 The most valuable being Hermann Lübbe, *Säkularisierung. Geschichte eines ideenpolitischen Begriffs*, Freiburg, Alber, 1965; Giacomo Marramao, *Die Säkularisierung der westlichen Welt*, Frankfurt am Main, Insel, 1996; Werner Conze, Hans Wolfgang Strätz and Hermann Zabel, 'Säkularisation, Säkularisierung', in Otto Brunner, Werner Conze and Reinhart Koselleck (eds.), *Geschichtliche Grundbegriffe*, vol. 5, Stuttgart, Klett/Cotta, 1984, pp. 789–829.

modern culture and Christian tradition. The evaluation of such connections sometimes differed radically. Some voices within nineteenth-century German Protestant theology (such as Richard Rothe), for example, expected the modern state to be pervaded by a Christian ethos to such an extent that the church would be rendered superfluous as a separate institution. Secularization in this sense, which was also found in the twentieth century, would then mean the realization rather than the weakening of religion. Conversely, some perceived the traces of Judaism and Christianity within the modern state and in modern society as signs of a process of as yet incomplete emancipation from religion, one which must eventually succeed fully. The weakening of the driving forces of religion within a social form which would not have come about without them was also perceived at times – as in the case of Max Weber – as a tragic fate, in contrast to both the optimism of cultural Protestantism and the radical critique and utopianism of Marxism. In the second half of the twentieth century, German philosophy saw major controversy[9] over the question of whether the idea of progress itself should be understood as a product of secularization, as the secularization of the idea of *Heilsgeschichte* (history of salvation), or whether such a view deprives modern culture of its legitimacy as an independent form, making secularization a discursive weapon, a 'category of historical illegitimacy' (Hans Blumenberg).

Further, we must not only distinguish between the legal and philosophical-theological uses of the term 'secularization', but also consider its use within the social sciences. Here again, it is used in a variety of ways. We owe the clearest distinction between the three social scientific uses of the term 'secularization' to the Spanish-American sociologist of religion José Casanova,[10] one of the contributors to this volume. First, the term may refer to a decline in the importance of religion; second to the withdrawal of religion into the private sphere; and third to the emancipation of societal spheres from direct religious control. Misunderstandings are bound to result if we fail to distinguish clearly between these three uses. But as helpful as it is, this clarification can only be described as a first step towards fathoming the concept, as further uncertainties immediately arise. It is not really clear, for example, whether the assertion that 'religion' is declining in importance refers to a decline in the significance of religious practices (such as praying or going to church), a fall in the number of those belonging to churches and religious communities, or a diminishing number

---

[9]   Karl Löwith, *Meaning in History: The Theological Implications of the Philosophy of History*, Chicago, University of Chicago Press, 1949; Hans Blumenberg, *The Legitimacy of the Modern Age* (1966), Cambridge, MA, MIT Press, 1985.

[10]   José Casanova, *Public Religions in the Modern World*, Chicago, University of Chicago Press, 1994.

of people who adhere to certain articles of faith (such as the divine nature of Jesus). Such distinctions would be superfluous only if developments in these different dimensions always ran in parallel, but this is *not* the case: people may remain members of a church despite having lost their faith; they may believe yet not belong to a religious community. If secularization is taken to mean privatization, it is unclear where the private sphere is in fact to be found. Does the retreat of religion mean only that it no longer exercises power at the level of the state, or does it imply its disappearance from public political and cultural life in general? Does privatization mean a withdrawal into the family and circle of friends, or does it perhaps mean a withdrawal into the inner life of the individual, who feels a sense of shame when talking about religious topics even among his or her closest confidants, a feeling which seems to be stronger today than in the case of the intimate sphere as traditionally understood? Finally, the liberation of societal spheres such as the economy and science, art and politics from direct religious control may be understood as resistance to all religious and moral accountability on the part of these spheres or as mere differentiation, in which case all these spheres may assert their own rights without being entirely decoupled from public objectives and ties to common values.

In the chapters of the present volume, the term 'secularization' is used in a wide variety of ways. The term becomes even more problematic when we leave the Christian cultural area. It incorporates the word *saeculum*, a category of worldly time, whose meaning is derived from the contrast with the sacred temporal dimension characteristic of the history of salvation.[11] The chapters by Rudolf Wagner and Joachim Gentz in particular, which deal respectively with Buddhism and Confucianism and with the contemporary religious situation in East Asia, bring out the difficulties of approaching the realities of regions such as this one by means of an originally Christian category.

The second key term used in this volume, that of 'world religion', also requires brief historical reflection.[12] While the term was occasionally used in the seventeenth and eighteenth centuries, its meaning fluctuated. It might refer in a neutral way to all the religions of the world or (in the case of Kant) to a kind of natural religion or (in the work of Goethe) to a religiosity that flows outwards into the world rather than remaining locked up within the individual. But none of these are the meanings which we associate with this term today. Contemporary usage dates back to the religious studies of the nineteenth century, though here again the picture was not entirely uniform. The term 'world religion'

---

[11]   Robert A. Markus, *Christianity and the Secular*, Notre Dame, IN, University of Notre Dame Press, 2006.

[12]   See for example G. Lanczkowski, 'Weltreligionen', in *Historisches Wörterbuch der Philosophie*, vol. 12, Basle, Schwabe, 2007, pp. 510f.

may for example simply refer to the major religions, ones, that is, which are found throughout the world and which have a large number of adherents. Or it may be used as a counter-concept to 'primitive' religions and thus indicates that some religions are superior to others, however this superiority may be understood. Finally, one may have in mind those religions which feature an inherent aspiration to expand, which actively seek out new followers, and which are prepared to admit anyone, regardless of ethnicity and previous religion. Only the first-mentioned, purely quantitative meaning seems value-free. The second is entirely dependent on where the criterion of assessment itself is taken from, and it would be surprising if this criterion were completely unconnected with the contents of a particular faith. And a universalist aspiration alone is certainly not sufficient qualification for the status of world religion, because it may also be found in an as yet tiny sect. Hence, if other structural features (such as a unified organization, the presence of a holy scripture or similar) are incorporated into the definition, it becomes more plausible to use the term, but also raises the suspicion that a specific image is being surreptitiously derived from a particular religion and fashioned into a yardstick by which all other religions are judged.

Thus, as willing as we may be to concede the problematic nature of the concept of world religions, it is practically indispensable, at least in the quantitative sense. Three religions are always presented as world religions in different surveys: Christianity, Islam and Buddhism. All other candidates are subject to controversy. In the case of Confucianism, views differ as to whether it is a religion in the first place rather than a secular doctrine of wisdom. Whether Judaism truly sees itself, or is capable of seeing itself, as a missionary religion is subject to dispute. In the case of Hinduism, we must ask whether it is in fact a unified religion or a family of very different but peacefully coexisting systems of belief;[13] Daoism seems too limited to East Asia to be included in the list of 'world religions'.

The present volume takes a pragmatic approach to these conceptual difficulties. Neither in the case of 'secularization' nor in that of 'world religions' can we impose clarity of usage by decree. Thus, what is required is sensitivity to the different ways in which the term is used and a willingness to see the diversity of the designated objects in the diversity of meanings itself. The question of what it means for a religion when it recognizes another religion as in principle of equal status, or if not then at least of great value, is one of the central problems of interreligious dialogue, but may be left to one side here. This volume is concerned not with religions' claims to truth from a religious perspective, but with the connections between religion and the social world and with the extent, limits and future of secularization.

---

[13]   See the detailed account by Heinrich von Stietencron in this volume.

The book comprises two major thematic sections and, placed between these, a number of contributions dealing with other facets of the subject. The first section deals with the world religions: Catholic Christianity, Protestant Christianity, Judaism, Islam, Hinduism and Buddhism and Confucianism. The focus of the other major thematic section is on geographical entities and the religious situation within them, namely Europe, the USA, East Asia, Latin America, Africa and the Middle East. Neither thematic block can lay claim to completeness. There are obvious lacunae: we do not examine Orthodox Christianity or Daoism, nor do we deal separately with the Sunni and Shia variants of Islam. There are also conspicuous gaps with respect to geography (Canada, Russia and Iran, to give just three examples). On the other hand, there is thematic overlap between the chapters, as the intention is not only to consider the 'world religions' internally, but also in their relationships to their 'bearers', in other words the large numbers of the faithful and the religious virtuosi and specialists. Between the two sections are studies anchored in a legal and history of science perspective. Modern natural science is often described as one of the main factors in secularization; the historical investigation of their relationship is thus of great value (see the contribution by Ernst Peter Fischer). And in the political debate on the legal organization of the relationship between state and church, theocracy and laicism often seem to face one another as irreconcilable opponents, with no third party existing beyond their confrontation. A comprehensive typology of legal arrangements across the world, however, reveals a quite different picture (see the chapter by Winfried Brugger).

The contributors to the first thematic section were presented with a common set of problems which I gleaned from one of the most important works of historical social science ever written. I am referring to the thousand-page study 'The Social Teachings of the Christian Churches and Groups' produced in 1912 by the great Protestant theologian, historian of religion and philosopher Ernst Troeltsch.[14] Today, the term 'social teaching' is redolent of social policy, a branch of policy. But Troeltsch's aim was not to compile a compendium of statements on social policy, but to examine fundamental ideas about the social realm within the Christian tradition. This description might arouse the suspicion that, as is indeed the case with many secular social scientists, his study fails to capture the essence of religion, taking from it, as it were, only those elements accessible to him and regarding the religious as no more than camouflage, if not a cloak for material interests. But Troeltsch was trained as a theologian and had rejected this false view at an early stage in an important essay on 'The Independence of

---

[14]   Ernst Troeltsch, *Die Soziallehren der christlichen Kirchen und Gruppen*, Tübingen, Mohr, 1912. The title of the English translation of this book differs from the German original (*The Social Teaching of the Christian Churches*, London, Allen & Unwin, 1931).

Religion' ('Die Selbständigkeit der Religion').[15] Moreover, profoundly influenced by the best aspects of nineteenth-century German historicism, he was also aware of the historical and cultural relativity of all the concepts with which we attempt to characterize historical and cultural phenomena. Hence, he could not simply refer to 'society' and 'state' as if these were transhistorical phenomena. For these reasons, Troeltsch wished to uncover the religious core of a religious tradition, its deepest inspiration. With respect to Christianity, for him this lies in the idea of a 'love which flows from God and returns to Him'.[16] He also asked what might be the ethical consequences of this inspiration, particularly in terms of political ethics, and which conclusions had been drawn in respect to this over the course of history.

For him, this gives rise to four major complexes of issues. The first thing to investigate is what idea of the individual and of human community this religious core, in this case the message of the Gospel, entails. We must then explain how the community of believers ought to be arranged to correspond to the basic religious inspiration. In this regard, even one religious tradition, such as Christianity, often features quite different models, and with his distinction between church, sect and (individualist) mysticism,[17] Troeltsch provided a conceptual apparatus intended to capture this diversity. The third question is concerned with an ideal of human coexistence within state and society that transcends the community of believers and which thus relates, virtually unavoidably, to religiously grounded ideas about the relationship between the community of believers and non-believers, as individuals or in the form of competing communities. The fourth question is a double-sided one about causality: how has a specific religious tradition, such as Christianity, *really influenced* the structures of society and state, and how, on the other hand, has the religious tradition been shaped by economic, political, military and cultural forces? In itself, this dual question concerning causality already suggests that no single historical form of a religious tradition should be seen as the true, fully internally homogeneous realization of a religious inspiration, from which subsequent generations have merely fallen away, and to which, therefore, believers should strive to return. Troeltsch of all people was aware of the tremendous variety of political orders justified as Christian

---

[15]   Ernst Troeltsch, 'Die Selbständigkeit der Religion', *Zeitschrift für Theologie und Kirche*, 5 (1895), pp. 361–436 and 6 (1896), pp. 71–110 and pp. 167–218.

[16]   Troeltsch, *Social Teaching*, p. 33. For a systematic presentation of Troeltsch's insights, see Max Scheler, 'Ernst Troeltsch als Soziologe' (1923/24), in idem, *Schriften zur Soziologie und Weltanschauungslehre* (Gesammelte Werke, vol. 6), Bern/Munich, Francke, 1963, pp. 377–90.

[17]   Troeltsch, *Social Teaching*, p. 993.

throughout history.[18] This often involved justificatory ideologies merely overlain with a patina of Christianity, ideologies borrowed, for example, from (Stoic) natural law, Aristotle or Roman law. And the historic experiments in deriving state structures directly from Christianity certainly hold no appeal for the contemporary world. 'The lessons provided by the state of the Anabaptists, the Cromwellian saints and, in a different but equally Christian way, by the Jesuit state in Paraguay must not be forgotten.'[19]

Even if, as is the case here, we leave largely to one side the fourth question with its causal aspirations, Troeltsch's study suggests a massive programme of research. He dealt 'only' with Christianity. Even within the context of such Christianity-focused research, it is of course an open question whether all of Troeltsch's views were right, how current research differs from his statements with respect to specific issues, and what shifts in emphasis might result from an in-depth engagement with Orthodox Christianity and with the so-called 'Counter-Reformation'. No-one, however, would deny that in today's world all religions, at least all 'world religions' as defined above, must be subject to similar and comparative study. It stands to reason that such a programme of research can be pursued only through a division of labour, by drawing on a broad range of expertise.

One attempt was already made in Troeltsch's day to realize a similar research programme, in this case, in fact, by a single scholar with a propensity for gigantomaniac endeavours. I am referring here to Max Weber, Troeltsch's longstanding friend and housemate. In a famous letter to his publisher Siebeck from 30 December 1913 he wrote with reference to his manuscript 'The Economy and the Social Orders and Powers' that he had 'drawn up a cohesive theory and account that relates the major forms of community to the economy: from the family and household to the firm, kin group, ethnic community, religion' – and here comes the crucial passage: '(taking in all the major religions of the world: sociology of doctrines of redemption and of religious ethics, – doing what Troeltsch did but for *all* religions and in considerably fewer words), at last a comprehensive sociological theory of the state and domination. I can claim that *nothing* of this kind has been produced so far, not even a "precursor".'[20]

Weber's study remained a fragment. The world war that broke out in 1914 changed Weber's priorities; he also recognized how lacking in knowledge about the great religions he still was, and while the war was still raging he immersed

[18]   Ernst Troeltsch, *Politische Ethik und Christentum*, Göttingen, Vandenhoeck & Ruprecht, 1904.

[19]   Troeltsch, *Politische Ethik*, p. 23.

[20]   Weber's letter is cited in Wolfgang Schluchter, *Religion und Lebensführung*, vol. 2, Frankfurt am Main, Suhrkamp, 1988, p. 570.

himself in their study. Once the war was over, little time remained to him before he succumbed to his fatal illness in 1920. Nevertheless, this fragment, together with the three volumes of comparative studies on the economic ethics of the world religions, have been major sources of inspiration for the social sciences. This remains the case even if it is impossible to avoid the conclusion that many of Weber's specific assertions are incorrect and dependent on out-of-date research. In a way, what matters is the questions Weber asked rather than the specific answers he came up with. As far as these questions are concerned, however, it seems to me that Weber fell victim to a potential self-misunderstanding, particularly as regards the questions of interest to us here. His interest in the 'economic ethics' of the world religions and his investigation of the connections between the ideas inherent to a religion and economic behaviour, particularly the kind of behaviour which is a prerequisite for and demanded by a rational capitalism, is of the greatest significance – but it is not an extension of Troeltsch's programme to the non-Christian religions. It represents both a more restricted focus than Troeltsch's examination of 'political ethics' and a greater emphasis on causal connections. For many, these differences will indicate Weber's superiority. For others, though, who concede this difference, the argument will arise that Weber by no means remained consistently within the narrower boundaries of his economically focused concerns, but – particularly in his 'systematic study of religion'[21] – repeatedly went beyond them.

This is certainly not the place to examine in detail such questions of interpretation and history of science, especially given that, because Max Weber is a charismatic figure for so many people, discussion of these issues can easily become an emotionally charged conflict rather than being carried out with the necessary composure and objectivity.[22] The reason why I mention these issues in the first place is that returning to the questions that underpinned Troeltsch's study of the history of Christianity seems to me to offer a way out of the impasses resulting from the discussion of Weber's ideas on the Protestant ethic and the spirit of capitalism within the history of Europe and North America, and above all on the question of the cultural and religious prerequisites for economic growth outside the Christian-influenced North Atlantic cultural area, impasses which *also* bedevilled later so-called modernization theory.[23] There were three

---

[21]   Max Weber, 'Religious Groups (The Sociology of Religion)', in *Economy and Society*, vol. 2, New York, Bedminster, 1968, pp. 399–634; originally *Religiöse Gemeinschaften* (Max-Weber-Gesamtausgabe, vol. 22.2, ed. Hans G. Kippenberg), Tübingen, Mohr, 2001.

[22]   See my essay on Joachim Radkau's biography of Weber, *Merkur*, 61 (2007), pp. 62–68.

[23]   See the outstanding critical account of modernization theory in Wolfgang Knöbl, *Spielräume der Modernisierung. Das Ende der Eindeutigkeit*, Weilerswist, Velbrück, 2001.

key reasons why I based this volume more on the complex of questions tackled by Ernst Troeltsch than on that with which Max Weber was concerned. First, as our aim is to diagnose the global religious situation, questions about the causal relationship between economic development and religion can in fact be largely bracketed off. Second, when we are dealing with the prospects of democratization beyond Europe and North America and the dangers of the religious legitimation of undemocratic conditions or even, as some think, with new forms of a religiously backed twenty-first-century totalitarianism, it is the links between religion and political ethics rather than those between religion and economic ethics that are of most interest at present. This does not entail an ignorance of the economic preconditions for democracy, but merely a distance from the idea, from which Max Weber also dissociated himself in the strongest possible terms,[24] that a capitalist economic boom in itself has much affinity with democracy. Third and finally, the fact that Troeltsch was less bound than Weber to the notion that modernization inevitably leads to secularization also plays an important role. His perspective was characterized by an interest in forms of religiosity suitable for the modern world, by the future prospects of Christianity, and, without wishing to prejudge its outcome, this volume also sees itself as a contribution from this perspective, but now on a global scale and not limited to the prospects of Christianity.

Naturally, each chapter follows its own logic. The set of problems presented to the contributors is not intended as a straitjacket. But it is possible to summarize here how their efforts have illuminated these problems.

Christianity is represented in two of its variants. Catholicism is dealt with by Cardinal Karl Lehmann. As a leading theologian and longstanding chairman of the German Bishops' Conference, he is uniquely equipped to tackle this subject. He begins by making it very clear that he has no wish to speak of Catholicism as if this represents a distinct religion, separated from Protestantism for example by insurmountable differences; for him, we can speak of Catholic Christianity only if we speak about Christianity in general. Thus, the focus is on that which is common to Christianity as a whole rather than differentiating or exclusive factors. But he is well aware that the definition of what is shared may also vary widely and provoke controversy. Rather than attempting to define the 'essence

---

[24] Particularly in his writings on Russia; in 1906 for example he wrote: 'It is absolutely ridiculous to attribute to the high capitalism which is today being imported into Russia and already exists in America – this "inevitable" economic development – any elective affinity with "democracy" let alone with "liberty" (in *any* sense of the word). The question should be: how can these things exist at all for any length of time under the domination of capitalism?' See 'Bourgeois Democracy in Russia', in *The Russian Revolutions*, Cambridge, Polity, 1995, pp. 41–147, here p. 109.

of Christianity', his chapter is chiefly concerned with the understanding of the institution of the church within Catholic Christianity. This he characterizes with reference to the four hallmarks also identified by the Creed itself: *una sancta catholica et apostolica.* In his view, the unity of the Church is guaranteed by the Creed, the sacraments and a united ecclesiastical government, though for him this unity allows rich internal diversity and should in no way be confused with uniformity. Most liable to misunderstanding is the second element in the definition of the Church, which refers to its sacredness. In accordance with recent theological currents, Lehmann too underlines that it is not only – how could it be otherwise? – the people of the Church, in other words individual believers, that are sinners, but that even the Church itself is sinful; for him, though, this does not mean that its sacredness, which he sees as arising from its relationship with God, is to be denied. The Church's sacredness is thus at once indicative and imperative, a definition of its character and an exhortation to engage in a ceaseless process of self-renewal. In the same way, the 'Apostolic' character of the Church is both a historical claim, a reference to the foundation laid by the Apostles of Jesus Christ, and a call to continue the historical Mission. It is the fourth aspect, the Church's Catholic nature, which Lehmann tackles in greatest depth. This too is more of a mission than a possession acquired for all time, namely the mission to pursue concrete universalism. This mission entails going beyond all that is national; a constant spur to transcend the identification of faith with the specific characteristics of a particular culture; and a commitment to global understanding – but all of this not merely in the sense of a secular proposal for ever greater universalization, but in the sense of a deep respect for cultural diversity coupled with an emphasis on the penetration of all cultures by the Christian message of salvation. Only after this in-depth explanation of how the Church is understood, and almost with a certain reluctance, Lehmann returns to the attempt to list the principles of Catholicism. Here, it is the breadth of Catholicism, rather than any attempt to demarcate, let alone exclude, that drives his reflections. These determinations also entail an answer to the question of political ethics. On this view, no single historical-social form may be sacralized. This applies even to specific Church structures, but yet more to the political or economic order, with respect to which the Church, and thus the faithful as well, must always retain a final 'eschatological' caveat.

Protestant Christianity is tackled by Friedrich Wilhelm Graf, one of the most brilliant, markedly Protestant intellectuals in Germany. It is fascinating to observe how he too initially emphasizes that his guiding concept, 'Protestantism', covers a broad range of theological doctrines and phenomena of religious culture. He even goes so far as to ask, in view of this diversity, whether we can speak of one central idea common to all these 'Protestantisms' in the first place. The standpoint from which he does in fact go on to identify such common ground is

obtained by underlining the 'special character of Protestantism in both religio-
cultural and theological terms [...] in contradistinction to the Roman Catholic
global church and Orthodox Christianity'.[25] Hence, this very diversity, but above
all an understanding of faith which leads to a constant 'critical relativization of
the religious institution', emerges as the core of this commonality. On the basis
of Paul Tillich's formulation of the 'Protestant principle', a distance from every
'absolute claim made for a relative reality' (Tillich), even when it is a church
– including Protestant ones – that is making it, is identified as the principle of
orientation guiding Protestant Christians.

The methodological approach taken by Graf, himself a leading interpreter
of the writings of Ernst Troeltsch, enables him to orient his chapter towards
the complex of problems which all the contributors were asked to consider
with particular precision, and to produce highly nuanced answers within this
framework. Like Troeltsch, he knows that we must be extremely cautious about
crediting Protestantism with the authorship of every positive achievement of
modernity. Following Troeltsch, he is in no doubt that 'the Reformation and
early Protestantism remained profoundly indebted to medieval concepts of order
and that their religious impulses towards freedom with their inherent critique
of tradition contributed to the achievement of political and social freedom only
in a multiply fractured way, through extremely complex processes of mediation'.
He is aware that Max Weber's thesis on the link between the 'Protestant ethic'
and the spirit of capitalism is untenable in this form, but he also recognizes
the analytical potential of an intellectual approach concerned with the non-
religious consequences of religious faith, thought and action. Above all, with
great circumspection and stylistic verve, and mostly but not only with reference
to Germany, he shows what a wide spectrum of fundamental political ideas
Protestantism has generated and how, because of their devaluation of the status
of the church, Protestants in particular tend to direct their 'mental energies'
towards the political sphere. Apparent in his account is his deep knowledge of the
tradition of German paternalistic social Protestantism, which involved the linkage
of Protestantism, Prussian-German nationalism and an 'anti-capitalism anchored
in a romantic view of society', a tradition that still moulded the Protestantism
of East Germany. 'Protestants were both emphatic modernizers and utterly
distraught by modernity.' And these differences internal to Protestantism can by
no means simply be traced back to denominational differences – such as those

---

[25]   The price of this methodological decision is, however, a tendency to understand
Catholic Christianity in an 'essentialist' manner. For an alternative view of the link
between Reformation and individualization, see Wolfgang Reinhard, 'The Affirmation
of Everyday Life', in: Hans Joas and Klaus Wiegandt (eds.), *The Cultural Values of Europe*,
Liverpool, Liverpool University Press, 2008, pp. 187–216.

between a Lutheranism with a blind faith in the state and an activist Calvinist Protestantism.

Eckart Otto, the distinguished Protestant Old Testament specialist and leading expert in the re-evaluation of Max Weber's view of ancient Judaism,[26] approaches his account of the Jewish religion in a quite different way than the two contributors on Christianity. He is primarily interested in the dynamic interplay between religion, state and society in the history of Judaism, describing this interaction as a 'dialectic of secularization and theologization'. Here, secularization does not mean the diminishing importance of religion, but an increasingly sharp separation between the world of everyday experience and the divine world accessible through faith. But this sharper division virtually demands a new type of intellectual mediation between the separate spheres, that is, of 'God' and 'world', generating a theologization that counteracts secularization so understood – and this has happened repeatedly throughout history, by no means only during the time of the emergence of Jewish monotheism or in the present. In the Fifth Book of Moses (Deuteronomy), the text of the oath of loyalty required of the rich and powerful of the Assyrian empire and that obligated them to absolute allegiance to the king or his successors, indeed, to denounce all criticism of the king or even to kill all traitors, had been incorporated and transformed. The core of Otto's exposition is the fascinating evidence of how, in the second half of the seventh century BC, this text was interpreted by Jews in such a way that God took over from the king. However, marking a new era in world history, this removed from the worldly ruler the final word on the legitimacy of his rule. No longer could an earthly authority appear legitimate in itself, and no ruler could claim the status of God; at the very least he had to present himself as one who has entered into a covenant with God on behalf of his people. This 'Axial Age' breakthrough[27] entails the specifically Jewish characteristic that the Jewish people itself entered into a covenant with God 'while disregarding the king'. Following this breakthrough, the true cohesion of the Jewish people was decoupled from statehood and founded in a cultic community for which state-like institutions could play only a secondary role. After the destruction of the Jewish state by the Babylonians as well as later in history, this mental separation of state and religious community proved central to saving the identity of Judaism. In addition, there was a growing tendency to worship the one and only God – and

---

[26]   Eckart Otto, *Max Webers Studien des Antiken Judentums. Historische Grundlegung einer Theorie der Moderne*, Tübingen, Mohr, 2002.

[27]   Karl Jaspers, *The Origin and Goal of History* (1949), New Haven, CT, Yale University Press, 1953; Shmuel N. Eisenstadt, 'The Axial Age in World History', in Hans Joas and Klaus Wiegandt (eds.), *The Cultural Values of Europe*, Liverpool, Liverpool University Press, 2008, pp. 22–42.

this in the temple of Jerusalem as the *one* solely legitimate central shrine. Otto relates how an ethic rooted in the kin group was transferred to the community of the Jewish 'People of God' through these processes and what the Prophets' role here appears to have been (in light of today's research). It was assumed for a long time – by Max Weber for example – that the prophetic sayings in the Bible are expressions of the ecstatic experiences of charismatics, reminding people to live according to God's commandments and His Word. Yet the texts of the Bible have not passed these prophetic sayings down to us in an authentic way, but are in fact the interpretations 'of scribes who adopted the mantle of the prophets by updating the prophetic books'. The relationship between prophecy and tradition here is the equivalent of Greek philosophy's break with myth – though, in contrast to Athens, in Jerusalem this dialectic remained an internal religious one. Here, 'internal religious' does not mean decoupled from everyday experience – quite the reverse. As Otto brings out, the dynamism of a radical relationship with God opened up the world to practical action; the belief that acting in accordance with the divine commandments would also result in a successful life was constantly put to the test through this experience, but this intensified hopes of redemption through divine intervention, particularly in a messianic sense. While Otto is primarily interested in intra-religious dynamics, his account also takes a realistic view of the extent to which the specific social situations of the Jews permitted them to live in conformity with the commandments.

No religion has attracted more attention within contemporary political debates than Islam. Yet it is discussed by a remarkably large number of unqualified commentators with a meagre knowledge of Islam, often with extreme ideas about its character and alleged boundaries. In the present volume, Gudrun Krämer, a leading authority on the history of Islam and the Middle East, rectifies many distorted notions about this highly sensitive subject with her judicious account. Central to these notions is the thesis that, in contrast to the Judaeo-Christian tradition, Islam has great, perhaps insurmountable difficulties in separating religion and state. Krämer's reflections focus not on the religious content of Islam, but on the evidence that this thesis is based on an unreflective application to Islam of categories which simply cannot be so applied. In recent times, this unreflective application of categories has of course been inspired above all by the critique of Islamism, a politicization of religion which claims sole authority to speak for Islam and which does in fact set the tone within certain spheres. As important as the critique of Islamism is, it is equally important to avoid simply taking at face value its claim to be the contemporary articulation of Islam.

The difficulties involved in analysing Islam with concepts obtained by abstraction from the Christian tradition is immediately apparent in the concept of the church – which does not exist within Islam. There is 'no church in Islam in the form of a hierarchically structured institution with established doctrinal authority and thus no "institution of salvation" offering, or possibly even monopolizing, services relevant to redemption'. Yet this solely negative characterization is also too simple. In the course even of its earliest history, Islam certainly produced specialists to record and impart its religious and legal teachings. Only after several centuries did religious colleges then emerge to educate them, such that it is also possible to refer, approximately, to an Islamic clergy, but *not* in the sense of a hierarchical and all-embracing church-like institution. With regard to the state, Gudrun Krämer comes to the conclusion that 'until the nineteenth century, religion and government were no more closely associated in Islamic societies than in European ones'. She scrutinizes in a nuanced way the different forms of religious legitimation of domination and rulers' religious influence on their own subjects, leading her to conclude that what we find in this field is great diversity but no evidence of social differentiation or secularization of Islamic societies. Such evidence is to be found in a quite different context, namely whenever 'the validity of the Sharia as the foundation and framework of individual conduct, social order and political action' is at issue. Here again, though, things are more complex than they appear at first sight. For the understanding of the status of the Sharia and its regulations varies tremendously; to acknowledge this interpretive diversity and reliance on interpretation is itself controversial. Gudrun Krämer refers to the *de facto* pluralization of religious authority in contemporary Islam, but one which is concealed by a 'fiction of self-evidence' characteristic of the sacred texts. Even greater than the plurality of interpretations is the plurality of the political order in countries with a Muslim population. According to her analysis, the two key questions here would be how the political instrumentalization of Islam might be overcome and how the prohibition of non-Muslim missionary work and of the right to change religion without restriction might be repealed, from both a theological and a legal perspective, in 'Islamic lands'.

Our account of Hinduism is provided by Heinrich von Stietencron, the doyen of German Indology. From a purely numerical perspective, Hinduism could be described as the third largest religion in the world (after Christianity and Islam). However, the tremendous heterogeneity concealed by the term 'Hinduism', which relates not only, as in all world religions, to doctrinal differences, but to fundamentally different types of religion, gives grounds for caution. It is therefore better to refer to Hinduism as a 'civilization' in which these very different religions coexist in what is, historically speaking, an unusually tolerant way. With tremendous sensitivity, Stietencron elaborates the innermost core of this source of religious inspiration: a doctrine of the cosmic order and the threats facing it, the cyclical nature of all processes, panpsychism and rebirth. He describes how, within this context, the doctrine of reincarnation is related to ethical behaviour within the world. Here, the desire to escape this cycle explains a deep affinity with renunciation of the world, meditation and asceticism, which, however, are by no means the only determining factors, as throughout history a counter-movement has inevitably set in that emphasizes the selfless discharge of one's duties within society rather than renunciation. It is again apparent, as in the case of Islam, that categories derived from the history of Christianity cannot simply be transferred – but also that it enhances our understanding if we determine more precisely why these categories are inappropriate. It is characteristic of India that the implicit prerequisites for using the concept of secularization – the existence of a 'church' and the state's emancipation from it – are found, and only in incipient form, during the long periods of foreign domination, that is, under Islamic rule (from the thirteenth to the eighteenth centuries) and during British colonial rule in the nineteenth and twentieth centuries and, as a consequence, today. Prior to this period, there was no centralized religious control, no holy scripture or binding tradition, though there were 'a number of textbooks on correct behaviour written from a Brahmanic perspective and commissioned by the state'. The Hindu religions, in Stietencron's vivid formulation, 'resembled a sea, one which certainly has borders and into which numerous rivers flow, but within whose waters no stable forms take shape'. Though not fixed for all time, ever new forms of ritual practice and philosophical thought developed. Here, the continuity of ritual and social obligations was more important to social life than such thought. The social teachings of Hinduism are described here as a form of traditionalism with a strong focus on the family; the state is expected to provide the conditions for individuals and families to live together in peace, and this means unmolested and free from fear, providing them with 'a suitable environment for meditation and contemplation'. While the British, as colonial masters, initially wished merely to take over the role of the previous rulers and thus left the Hindu religions intact, clashes eventually occurred. The British public and the Christian missionaries saw all social injustices in the subcontinent as consequences of religion; they were outraged by (what they saw as) barbaric practices (such as widow-burning), which in turn triggered a movement for religious reform: neo-Hinduism. In the wake of the liberation movement against the colonial masters, religion was then politicized, while the old conflicts with the Muslims were also revived, resulting in an appalling loss of lives. In the twentieth century, in the shape of Hindu nationalism, Hinduism too has generated a form of the politicization of religion, which must probably be interpreted as a mere instrumentalization of religion to political ends.

Our account of Confucianism and Buddhism as the determining religious forces in East Asia is provided by leading contemporary Sinologist Rudolf Wagner. In an essay replete with scintillating ideas, he describes with respect to China the supreme importance of the long tradition of highly developed statehood. For him, ensuring the order of the state was the chief concern of the class of educated civil servants even before the Common Era. The 'Ru', as this political class was called, took their lead from an intellectual progenitor whose name was later Latinized by Jesuits and whose doctrine was increasingly stylized into a religion by followers and opponents: Confucius and Confucianism. Wagner uses this current of state-centred thought, whose impact extends to Communist China, as a foil against which Buddhism stands out; its origins lying in the north of India, it arrived in China around two thousand years ago via the Silk Road. An ethos of state order, of course, lacks answers to existential questions. The newly arriving Buddhist monks, meanwhile, offered such answers in a variety of ways: 'the institution of the monastery with its frugal and ascetic lifestyle far removed from the state and the family; a radical philosophical analysis of consciousness as the creator of a world which in itself is empty and devoid of all essence; and on top of all this and most importantly, a meditational route to enlightenment as the end of attachment to this empty world'. While Wagner describes the key characteristics of Confucianism with marked irony, he provides a highly sympathetic account of Buddhism in light of the threat of monotheistic intolerance. Crucially, Buddhism did not eliminate existing local religions as it spread, but could accept them if they 'could be seen as the first steps towards encouraging behaviour in accordance with basic Buddhist values'. Central to the social teaching of Mahayana Buddhism, which was not restricted to an elite, is the ideal of the Bodhisattva. While this refers to someone who has reached the highest level in his pursuit of enlightenment, this individual must be concerned with more than merely his own enlightenment. Should the pursuit of enlightenment take this ego-centred form, then, in contradictory fashion, the attachment to the ego as a part of the world remains in place. Only if the enlightened one devotes himself to other people and living beings and helps liberate them from attachment to the world is he living in accordance with the ideal of the Buddha. Strong institutionalization would be at variance with the inspirational core of this religion. But the bringing together of monks, i.e. those striving to liberate themselves from the world and whose efforts are directed towards this end in a monastic community, is undoubtedly a form of institutionalization. This also gives rise to the ideal of 'worldly' rule. The best ruler is the one who himself lives in accordance with this ideal and promotes Buddhism both materially and non-materially. This is scarcely a sufficient definition of a political ethics. It is thus only consistent if Buddhism makes no claims to exclusivity either religiously or ethically. Wagner provides a highly vivid account of how people in East Asia draw on very different sources and practices of religious and ethical orientation as they go about their lives, without seeing this as contradictory. A quite new dimension entered into this set of circumstances when, under the impact of the (lack of) modernization in the nineteenth century, questions were raised about the causes of China's difficulties and its loss of importance. This led to claims that Chinese traditions or 'imported' religions were impeding modernization

– and such claims were made repeatedly, culminating in the Chinese communists' struggle against all religion. Today, however, in light of the tremendous economic progress achieved by China, and before it by other parts of East Asia, we should be very cautious about any claims about the conditions for economic success or failure centred on religion. Max Weber would surely modify his view of Confucianism considerably today. Wagner, incidentally, does not speculate about the collapse of the Communist regime or the large-scale religious revitalization of China. For him, a Leninist party doctrine is highly compatible with central aspects of Confucianism, particularly the emphasis on state order and secularism. In his view, despite all the dramatic changes, China thus remains in unmistakable continuity with itself.

To varying degrees, all these contributions on the world religions have also examined the contemporary religious situation in different world regions, which are moulded by these religions. This is inevitable, for the religions do not exist in a supra-empirical world, but in the lives of the faithful. Historical figures or sacred texts or ancient traditions may claim a timeless validity, but this validity must always be lived anew. It is not inherently clear what they require of the current generation. If it is correct to understand religion in a way that focuses on the fact that individuals, groups, organizations and institutions always take fresh action in the present, then two things follow. First, this generates guidelines for the arduous but productive attempts to encourage debate between these religions, to create a global, interreligious dialogue.[28] Second, with respect to the diagnosis of religion, we must start from the beginning a second time, not on the basis of the analysis of the 'essence' of a religion, but in light of the empirical knowledge of contemporary social realities. The last five chapters of the present volume take up this task. Alongside the already mentioned analysis of the religious aspects of the Middle East conflict by Hans Gerhard Kippenberg, outlines are provided of the religious situation of Europe, the USA, East Asia, Latin America and Africa. José Casanova's key concern is to bring out the tremendous heterogeneity of Europe; he shows that it is not differences in modernity that best explain different degrees of secularization in different European countries and describes typical tendencies of change in religious life, which has by no means disappeared from Europe. The chapter on the USA gives special emphasis to the country's religious vitality, its explanation and specific character. In a sense, the chapter by Joachim Gentz on East Asia starts where Rudolf Wagner's contribution left off. He describes the religious-political situation in China, Japan and South Korea individually and, with tremendous knowledge and impressive sensitivity, uses secularization as a *leitmotif* in order to bring out the specific features of the religious situation of

---

[28]   For an initial outline, see Hans Joas, 'Werte und Religion', in Liz Mohn et al. (eds.), *Werte. Was die Gesellschaft zusammenhält*, Gütersloh, Bertelsmann, 2006, pp. 19–32.

the region. Drawing on his extensive research on the Pentecostalist movement, a rapidly expanding current of global Christianity, David Martin shows why European models of secularization are not being repeated in Africa and Latin America. In Africa, the strongly developed state central to these models is missing altogether. For a time, Latin America sometimes seemed similar to the countries of southern Europe as regards the arrangement of state, Catholic Church and secular intellectuals. But it is not this constellation, which applies only to certain countries, that dominates there today, but the transition to a model of lively religious pluralism which more closely resembles the USA than Europe.

As far as the Troeltsch-inspired research programme sketched out here is concerned, this volume represents just one step. It is intended to inform readers of the current state of knowledge in an accessible way; far from being a problem, lacunae should act as a spur to further study. As with all fruitful research and creative work, the questions also change as we attempt to answer them. The book will have achieved its goal if it helps promote greater awareness of the tremendous complexity of the contemporary global religious situation and its links with politics and economics – and thus helps counter rash syntheses such as the 'clash of civilizations'.[29] Without such awareness, there is a danger that distorted concepts of self and other will turn such objectively untenable analyses into self-fulfilling prophecies.

---

[29]   See the chapter by Dieter Senghaas, 'The Realities of Cultural Struggles', in Hans Joas and Klaus Wiegandt (eds.), *The Cultural Values of Europe*, Liverpool, Liverpool University Press, 2008, pp. 320–37.

Catholic Christianity

Cardinal Karl Lehmann

I

Even from a methodological point of view, references to Catholic Christianity are far from straightforward. Such references are possible only if we have already referred to Christianity in general, for it is only within the genus 'Christianity' that we can deal meaningfully with the Catholic component in the sense of a specific difference. It is, however, certainly possible to dispute this, for there are those who believe, specifically with respect to Christianity in general, that the specific activities in which the denominations are engaged are underpinned by a fundamental hermeneutic difference, such as the Protestant principle.

We may attempt to escape this difficulty in a number of ways. We may attempt to draw up basic models of the individual world religions and, within Christianity for example, outline the denominational variations. This may be done, as we often find today, in a way understandable to the general reader.[1] It is not unusual for it to be done in a fairly vulgar fashion.[2] A more sophisticated variant is the attempt – with more stringent philosophical means, and above all with the aid of the phenomenology of religion – to convey the specific ways in which the Christian faith has been elaborated.[3] Here again, differing emphases are to be found, because there are of course very different forms and types of philosophy of religion, not to mention predominantly sociological or psychological

---

[1] See for example Peter Antes (ed.), *Die Religionen der Gegenwart. Geschichte und Glauben*, Munich, Beck, 1996; Manfred Hutter, *Die Weltreligionen*, Munich, Beck, 2005; idem (ed.), *Große Religionsstifter*, Munich, Beck, 1992.

[2] See for example Teja Fiedler and Peter Sandmeyer, *Die sechs Weltreligionen. Alles über Buddhismus, Judentum, Hinduismus, Islam, Taoismus, Christentum*, Berlin, Stern, 2005.

[3] See Axel Michaels and Michael Bergunder, 'Religionsphänomenologie' and Hermann Deuser, 'Religionsphilosophie', in *Religion in Geschichte und Gegenwart*, vol. 7, Tübingen, Mohr Siebeck, 4th edn, 2004, pp. 352–55, pp. 355–71.

foci. While scholars have generally been wary of producing denomination-specific accounts, some respectable attempts have been made in this direction.[4]

There can be no doubt, however, that many attempts to reduce the diversity of religious propositions and forms to something like the 'essence of Christianity'[5] rapidly reveal their tailoring to particular perspectives, which relate not only to Catholic, Protestant and Orthodox Christianity, but which often reflect even more strongly a specific theological approach.[6]

In formulating my approach here, I may no doubt draw on the previous endeavours of the 'Forum für Verantwortung'.[7] At the same time, however, I also want to try something slightly different.

II

There is no denying that understanding a particular branch of Christianity always involves the concept of the Church. The term 'Christianity', even if elaborated upon, risks remaining no more than an abstract proposition. It is always realized in a particular church. From the outset, of course, one's understanding of the Church plays a crucial role here.

The problem already begins with the question of whether Jesus wished to found a church. Formerly, it seemed a matter of course to assume that the church was founded by Jesus of Nazareth. Since the turn of the twentieth century, however, a number of theologians have stated provocatively that Jesus did not found a church during his lifetime. What is meant by this? Such observations are often anchored in a strictly historical interpretation, for – it is suggested – there is neither deed of foundation nor evidence of any act of establishment by Jesus in his lifetime, at least not of an explicit and formal kind that can be dated with certainty and legally guaranteed. Some therefore refer only to the 'emergence of the church', though the usefulness of this term is more apparent than real.

Now, it is not at all the aim of the New Testament to answer such historical questions directly. Rather than seeing 'foundation' as an entirely self-contained

---

[4]   See for example Willem Hendrik van de Pol, *Das reformatorische Christentum*, Zurich, Benziger, 1956; idem, *Probleme und Chancen der Ökumene*, Vienna, Manz, 1962; idem, *The End of Conventional Christianity*, New York, Pauls & Newman, 1968; idem, *Die Zukunft von Kirche und Christentum*, Freiburg, Herder, 1970.

[5]   This can readily be seen in Adolf von Harnack, *What is Christianity?* (1900), Philadelphia, Fortress Press, 1986.

[6]   See also the response to Harnack's portrayal of Judaism by Leo Baeck, *The Essence of Judaism*, New York, Schocken, 1948.

[7]   See Hans Joas and Klaus Wiegandt (eds), *The Cultural Values of Europe*, Liverpool, Liverpool University Press, 2008.

act, we must understand it as a historical process, which certainly exhibits internal consistency, but which should not be understood merely as the unwavering execution of a plan clear from the very beginning. The risks of a historical path, with all its consequences, constitute one component of such an event. To shed light on the meaning of this process, we must distinguish between specific phases and stages. No stage represents the whole. Hence, no isolated passage, such as Matthew 16:18ff., can provide us with an unambiguous and adequate answer to our question. However, careful consideration of the individual stages yields a meaningful connection between them, a reasonable, plausible means of distinguishing between them and, finally, also something of a general tendency characteristic of each specific phase.

We can identify these key stages, at least in outline form, as follows:

- Jesus' general call to discipleship;

- The rejection of Jesus and his Gospel by his people;

- The lasting movement, gathering disciples around Jesus, continuing the instruction and preaching of the Gospel;

- Jesus' death for the many, that is, for everyone, as the precondition for a new gathering of the faithful;

- The resurrection of Jesus Christ and associated revival of the broken community;

- Concrete instruction and practice in the forms of ecclesial community through the appearances of the resurrected Christ;

- The new understanding of Scripture and the Eucharistic Meal as key elements in the construction of the Church;

- More in-depth instruction of the disciples.

Much of this culminates in the so-called Great Commission: 'Go therefore and make disciples of all nations' (Mt. 28:19a). The descent of the Holy Spirit at Pentecost – at least according to the theology of Luke (see Acts 2:1–13) – completes the birth of the Church.

If we consider this overall context and the general theme identifiable within it, it is apparent that the Church is not the Kingdom of God, but that it cannot be entirely separated from it. The Church is thus a real, concrete sign of the reign of God, a trace of His Kingdom laid down in history by God and a genuine vanguard of eschatological hope for all. In this sense, the Church is part of the proclaimed nearness of the Kingdom of God. We cannot, therefore, simply respond to the question of whether Jesus founded a church with a straightforward 'no'. Upon careful reflection, it is still quite possible to answer with a clear conscience in the affirmative: in proclaiming the nearness of the Kingdom of God, Jesus wished to gather together the Covenant People. Jesus' intention is evident in the course and overall direction of his life and is not revoked by his death. No one can be in any doubt that Jesus associated with the community of his disciples the hope, indeed the certainty, that this community would endure. Following Easter and the division between Judaism and the new Israel, this gave rise to the Church.

III

One elementary characterization of the Church can be found fairly early on in the first statements of faith, which are still evident in the contemporary Credo: 'We believe [...] [the] one holy catholic and apostolic church'. We rightly refer to the essential features or characteristics of the Church. These amount to an overall structure which, through its internal coherence and density of meaning, has, and is able to convey, a special persuasiveness. This is why we may summarize the 'nature' of the Church by reference to these four dimensions. This is an important common legacy amidst the division of the churches, though it is often interpreted in different ways.

The *unity* of the Church is anchored fundamentally in the fact that there is *one* mediator, Jesus Christ. In this sense, the Church is not something which would first have to be created artificially. In Jesus Christ, as the fruit of the Spirit, this unity is already a reality. There is therefore only one Church (uniqueness). Also, in line with Jesus' final wishes (see Jn 17:21–23), the Church is internally united (unity). But this unity is not only a lasting gift, but always a mission as well; the Epistle to the Ephesians urges us to walk 'with all humility and gentleness, with patience, bearing with one another in love, eager to maintain the unity of the Spirit in the bond of peace. There is *one* body and *one* Spirit – just as you were called to the *one* hope that belongs to your call – *one* Lord, *one* faith, *one* baptism, *one* God and Father of all, who is over all and through all and in all' (4:2–6). This sevenfold bond ultimately establishes unity. According to the Holy Scripture (see Acts 2:42) and according to the constant teaching of the Church – now expressed in somewhat narrower and more concentrated form – this unity consists of a threefold commonality: the bond of the profession of faith, of the sacraments and of the ecclesiastical government and community (see *Lumen Gentium* 14).

But this unity is not uniformity. It is diversity in unity and can therefore become all things to all people (see 1 Cor. 9:19–23). In light of this, there is a multifaceted exchange between individuals of all nations, races, cultures, languages and ways of thinking in the context of mutual recognition. However, while there may certainly be fruitful, vital tensions, there can be no irreconcilable differences. Heresy and schism are expressions of an irreconcilable multiplicity. *Schism* abolishes the unity of the lived community, particularly with respect to common worship, while the more fundamental *heresy* abandons the unity of one faith. These malformations occur above all when a one-sided, highly exaggerated, erroneous view clings stubbornly to its position and finally grows rigid. This is one of the key reasons why the unity of the Church must always be a unity in truth. We shall return later to the divisions and reconciliation within the Church and to the ecumenical movement.

No one can deny that there is sin in the Church. Yet faith recognizes a deeper dimension and professes that *holiness* characterizes the Church's most profound essence. This in turn is closely bound up with God Himself in His triune nature. The well-spring of the Church, God Himself, is absolutely holy (see Isa. 6:3). He created a 'holy nation' (see Ex. 19:6; 1 Pet. 2:9). Jesus Christ himself is 'the Holy One of God' (Mk 1:24). He gave his life out of love for the Church, to 'sanctify her, having cleansed her' (Eph. 5:26). Thus, as the temple of the Holy Spirit, the Church itself is called holy (see 1 Cor. 3:17). In this context, the early Christians are also referred to as 'saints' in the New Testament (see Acts 9:13, 32, 41; Rom. 8:27; 1 Cor. 6:1). Nevertheless, the Bible does not deny that there were from the outset shortcomings and fatigue, disputes and even scandals, as we are told particularly with reference to the congregation in Corinth. How can this be reconciled with holiness? Holiness undoubtedly requires flawless ethics. But the primary mark of holiness is the final election to the people of God, to the body of Christ and to the temple of the Holy Spirit. In light of this, the Church is separated out from the realm of the worldly and belongs wholly to God. The Church is holy because it comes from God and strives towards Him. It is holy because the holy God keeps faith with it and does not abandon it entirely to perdition. Through his salvific giving of himself for all and through his presence, Jesus Christ is indivisibly linked with it (see Mt. 28:20). The powerful presence of the Holy Spirit is forever promised to it (see Jn 14:26; 16:7–9). The Church may also be described as holy because through the sacraments, His Word and exemplary individuals of the discipleship of Jesus, God has provided it with trustworthy, living signs and witnesses of holiness. In addition, the Scripture points out that while the Church is in the world, it is not of the world (see Jn 17:11, 14–15).

The holiness of the Church and the holiness of the individual believer determine and depend on one another. 'Objective' holiness is followed by the ethical realization of this holiness in individual subjects. 'Be holy, for I am holy' (Lev. 11:44, 45; 1 Pet. 1:16; 1 Jn 3:3). Time and again, in light of the holy gift of salvation granted to human beings by God, Paul urges Christians to transform themselves. The *indicative*, which means the real, initial existence of grace, which is of course incomplete and remains imperilled, belongs together with the *imperative*, which expresses the task that remains to be done (see Rom. 6:6–14; 8:2–17). 'If we live by the Spirit, let us also walk by the Spirit' (Gal. 5:25). Or: 'For freedom Christ has set us free; stand firm therefore' (Gal. 5:1). All Christians are called to embody this holiness. Paul's maxim applies to everybody: 'For this is the will of God, your sanctification' (1 Thess. 4:3). Here, the realization of the love of God and of one's neighbour is crucial (see Mk 12:30–31; Jn 13:34; 15:12; 1 Cor. 13): to love Him above all else and one's neighbour as oneself.

The sinfulness of the Church stands in contrast with this God-given holiness (see *Lumen Gentium* 8). The Church, and its members, must pray every day: 'forgive us our debts' (see Mt. 6:12). The sin within it may darken the Church's holiness, but the purity and fidelity with which God has endowed it through salvation cannot simply be extinguished. However distorted this ultimate inner origin and alignment with God may be, it cannot be completely destroyed. This is one of the main reasons why modern theology is prepared to speak of the sinfulness of the Church ('sinful Church'), and not only of a Church which includes sinners ('Church of sinners'). However, this does not mean that its holiness can simply be taken from it or denied. In the classical era of theology, theologians expressed this concurrence of holiness and sin within the Church more freely, facing these tensions head-on. Hence, the tradition described in Hans Urs von Balthasar's compelling account refers to the Church as a 'casta meretrix', a 'chaste whore'. However, particularly in the modern, post-Reformation age, the official language of the Church tends to shy away from such a charged and paradoxical characterization.

One piece of evidence of consistent application of the concept of sin is the fact that the Church has repeatedly rejected rigorist currents that aspire to create a Church of the 'pure' *now*. Baptized sinners also belong to the Church. Only at the consummation of the ages will the Church be 'without spot or wrinkle' (see Eph. 5:27). Hence, the Church and its members are in constant need of conversion and repentance. 'While Christ, holy, innocent and undefiled (Heb. 7:26) knew nothing of sin, (2 Cor. 5:21) but came to expiate only the sins of the people, (see Heb. 2:17) the Church, embracing in its bosom sinners, at the same time holy and always in need of being purified, always follows the way of penance and renewal' (*Lumen Gentium* 8). This recalls Luther's conviction that the human being is 'righteous and a sinner at the same time'; considering the sovereignty of divine grace, this can certainly be said from a Catholic standpoint as well.

Because the countenance of the Church may be, and is, greatly disfigured by the power of sin within it, it is fundamental to any account of the total reality of the Church that it must engage ceaselessly in a process of self-renewal. The Church is the 'una sancta', but at the same time it is always the 'ecclesia semper reformanda'. In terms of way of life, preaching the Gospel and its basic structures, it must constantly take its lead from the Word of God and renew itself in light of it (see also *Unitatis Redintegratio* 6). In this sense, in its own way, Catholic theology can also cautiously endorse the call for an 'ecclesia semper reformanda' found in the Calvinist theology of the seventeenth century. Again and again throughout its history, particularly in the monastic movements, there have been processes of such reflection and cleansing that have drawn on God's Word. The monastic movements themselves later had once again to take up the challenge of fundamental reform. Here, however, it is also important that the understanding of renewal is not directed exclusively or initially towards structures and institutional elements alone, as much as the concrete, bodily individual is always in need of renewal in his social situation. What counts is that the individual personally repents by renewing his life in light of the spirit of the Gospel.

We also profess that the Church is *apostolic*. It is built on the foundation of the Apostles and forever bound to this witness (see Mt. 16:18; Eph. 2:20; Rev. 21:14; *Lumen Gentium* 19). The Church is fundamentally beholden to this apostolic foundation and, as the centuries pass by, must maintain its identity with this apostolic beginning. But this also means that the Church must pursue its mission to the world, both near and far, and that doing so is part of the nature of the Church. Thus, the apostolic mission must be continued in the post-apostolic era. This also explains why, during their own lifetimes, the Apostles themselves appointed helpers, but also called men to continue their work after their death, so that the mission with which they had been entrusted may continue until the completion of history.

In the Acts of the Apostles and in the so-called Pastoral Epistles, we find much evidence of the continuation of the apostolic mission; one of the main ways in which this occurs is through the prayer of the Church with the symbol of the laying on of hands (ordination). In this way, the idea of the apostolic succession came alive, as it rapidly developed during the transition from the apostolic to the post-apostolic era. The office of Apostle itself is of course a one-off phenomenon, but certain apostolic powers must be continued beyond the time of the Apostles. Hence there is the unique office of Apostle and the enduring apostolic command in corresponding services and ministries. Only in this respect are the bishops, for example, successors of the Apostles. What counts here is not the superficial notion of a mechanical chain of layings on of hands or the mere external evidence that an Episcopal see has been occupied in an unbroken line; what counts is the overall context of the transmission of the apostolic faith. Here, it is certainly possible to distinguish between, but not to separate, the form and the content of the apostolic mission. The apostolic succession – including with respect to specific personal witnesses – is the form of the tradition, and the tradition is the content of the succession. Today, the ecumenical debate is grappling in a fundamental way with the question of what concrete form the apostolic nature of ecclesial ministry should take.

This brings us naturally to the final characteristic of the Church, which requires more precise elucidation: its catholic nature. Here, it goes without saying that this word, which first appears in the writings of Ignatius of Antioch around the year 100 (Epistle to the Smyrnaeans 8:2), does not refer to the Roman Catholic Church in the sense of a modern denomination but to the entire, worldwide and universal community of believers. But as we have seen, the Church is not reserved to a particular people, culture, class or even language, but always has a universal orientation and thus always a missionary mandate. Despite all the changes that have occurred over the course of the centuries, the Church, in this sense of a worldwide community of faith, has remained fundamentally true to itself. This does not exclude the possibility of distortions – often of long duration – such as a 'Eurocentrism'.

IV

As we wish here to shed light on the structure of 'Catholic Christianity', it makes sense to look more closely at the understanding of the term 'Catholic'. The word, of course, has a pre-Christian history; in Greek antiquity, it referred to the qualities of wholeness, completeness and fullness in the sense of an organic, all-embracing unity. Hence, it refers in any case first and foremost to the overall Church, as distinct from specific congregations. The basic meaning of fullness and universality, partly in the sense of geographical spread ('found throughout the world', 'numerically the largest church'), still applies. At the same time, the word is also used as a synonym for true, genuine, orthodox. Vincent of Lérins formulates the term more precisely, emphasizing the temporal and holistic continuity of the self-identity of the Church throughout history, namely 'that which has been believed everywhere, always, by all'. Three elements thus play an important role in this conception. They constitute something like the basic elements of Catholicism: *universitas*, *antiquitas* and *consensio*. The Middle Ages adopted these ideas of the catholicity of space, time and individuals.

After early attempts in the work of Irenaeus and Cyprian, a more precise notion of the 'catholic', attained through addition of the prefix 'Roman', appears to have taken hold in the context of Gregorian reform in the twelfth century, as a means of countering ecclesiological errors among the Cathars and Waldensians. Of course, this process has long been shaped by the special status conferred on Rome at an early stage. When the intention was to set the 'catholic Church' apart from sects and separate ecclesiastical communities, there was an increasing tendency to refer to the 'ecclesia Romana'. Here, particularly in the narrower sense, 'Roman' has a double meaning: first, within the apostolic structure of the

Church, particularly through the two Apostles Peter and Paul and the Office of St Peter, Rome has a position of pre-eminence; second, this quality is linked with the specific geographical location of Rome. This, of course, provokes criticism, but we shall not be examining this here.[8] It goes almost without saying that in the modern age, not least for apologetic reasons, the 'una sola catholica' has been given particular emphasis. Yet it is revealing that, in returning to the original meaning of 'catholic', the Second Vatican Council, while it does not use the term 'Roman Catholic' in this form, maintains the idea of a close connection between the Catholic Church and the primacy of Rome and the Pope.[9] The merely cultural and sociological sense of 'Roman' is generally declining in importance today, as emphasis is now placed on enculturation for all peoples and cultures and on opening a dialogue with other churches, as well as with the non-Christian religions.

Catholic theologians take account of this development in many ways. In the wake of the confessionalization in the early modern period and the formation of a new relationship between state and church, the term 'Roman Catholic' certainly exists, but the Catholic Church itself does not see itself as a denomination in the theological sense. 'Catholic' is not a theologically legitimated term for a denomination; this applies far more to 'Roman Catholic', particularly with respect to state church law.

It must not be forgotten that the major denominations have manifested the catholicity of the Church in their respective confessions, though this has been interpreted in different ways. Recent common endeavours within an ecumenical framework have taken up an older tradition in a new form whenever they understand the Church in terms of its essential characteristics: the one, holy, catholic and apostolic Church.

Long before the Second Vatican Council, the theology of various countries had rediscovered the original meaning of catholicity. The key work here is the famous book by Henri de Lubac, *Catholicisme*, which first appeared in French in 1938, and was translated into English in 1950 by Lancelot Sheppard. Others have of course also played a major role in this rediscovery, such as J. A. Möhler, Y. Congar, R. Guardini, E. Przywara, K. Adam and G. Thils, as well as writers such as C. Péguy and P. Claudel. Y. Congar in particular expressed much the same idea at the same time from an ecumenical perspective.[10] Translating de Lubac's book was in itself a difficult task, for 'Catholicisme' had taken on such

---

[8]   See Yves Congar, in *Mysterium Salutis* 4/1, Einsiedeln, Benziger, 1972, pp. 357–594, esp. pp. 478ff.; idem, *Eglise et Papauté*, Paris, Editions du Cerf, 1994, pp. 31–64.

[9]   See *Lumen Gentium* 8, 18, 22–25.

[10]   See for example Yves Congar, *Divided Christendom: A Catholic Study of the Problem of Reunion* (1937), London, Geoffrey Bles, 1939, p. 139.

denominational overtones, particularly in the German language, that it made it difficult to conceive of it in new ways.[11]

The definition of catholicity in this original sense is very comprehensive theologically. It is not primarily a merely ecclesiological characterization, but is derived from the Trinitarian life of God through its revelation in Creation and in history; it is an attempt to convey the message of the salvation in Jesus Christ by taking up the mission and spreading it across the entire world to the benefit of humanity as a whole. The Church is catholic because – holding within it the mystery of God's living truth – it is called to communicate this mystery of salvation to one and all by transmitting it to the entire world. Hence, on this basis, the entire fullness and richness of God's gifts are being rediscovered within the Church.[12]

Here, then, we are best advised to go back to the early Church, returning to its origins and avoiding the later, narrower variants of the term 'catholic'. The entire Art. 13 of *Lumen Gentium* exemplifies this. Here, catholicity is first and foremost a gift from the Lord Himself.[13] The people of God fosters and takes to itself the abilities, riches and customs of different peoples, 'insofar as they are good'.[14] Catholicity is realized within the specific peoples and cultures through a tremendous process of give and take. About the Church itself, whose rich diversity is envisaged, it is said:

> In virtue of this catholicity each individual part contributes through its special gifts to the good of the other parts and of the whole Church. Through the common sharing of gifts and through the common effort to attain fullness in unity, the whole and each of the parts receive increase. [...] within the Church particular Churches hold a rightful place; these Churches retain their own traditions, without in any way opposing the primacy of the Chair of Peter, which presides over the whole assembly of charity and protects legitimate differences, while at the same time assuring that such differences do not hinder unity but rather contribute toward it. [...] For the members of the people of God are called to share these goods in common, and of each of the Churches the words of the Apostle hold good: 'According to the gift that each has received,

---

[11]   See Eugen Maier, *Einigung der Welt in Gott. Das Katholische bei Henri de Lubac*, Einsiedeln, Johannes, 1983.

[12]   On de Lubac, see Hans Urs von Balthasar, *The Theology of Henri de Lubac: An Overview* (1976), San Francisco, Ignatius, 1991, pp. 35–43; idem, *Katholisch* (1975), Einsiedeln, Johannes, 3rd edn, 1993.

[13]   See *Lumen Gentium* 13.

[14]   *Lumen Gentium* 13.

administer it to one another as good stewards of the manifold grace of God' (1 Pet. 4:10).[15]

In this connection, it also goes without saying that catholicity is not a self-contained gift, which it is now merely a question of administering. It is not a self-evident state of affairs or an unquestionable 'possession'. Above all, it is a duty that calls us into mission. In this sense, catholicity must always first be realized between the undoubtedly real, but also initial, gift – and its fulfilment, which has yet to come. True catholicity constantly shows the Church how far it lags behind this gift. Here as well, as de Lubac's book clearly shows, lie the origins of a theology of mission, of the witness of Christians and of the Church in the various spheres of life, of ecumenical opening, of dialogue with the religions of different peoples and of the process of coming to terms with atheism.[16] From this perspective, the local churches are esteemed more highly in terms of their own values. In this way, all uniformity is opened up in the direction of greater variability. Catholicity means: the fullness of salvation and the grace of God through the diversity of gifts.

These words may at times seem rather imprecise, perhaps even nebulous. And indeed, this catholicity cannot simply be pinned down somehow as a fixed state or at a particular moment. It is always moving from its origin to its goal, as gift and duty. But the Second Vatican Council leaves us in no doubt about that which Ignatius of Antioch had already concluded: catholicity means *comprehensive* fullness, which is the origin of the Church and which it strives to accomplish, but at the same time this catholicity always has a *particular form*, with its changeable and unchanging elements. In this sense, the catholicity of the Church is *not* a nebulous entity, but is concretely upheld, realized in history and constantly actualized through calling and mission. Structures are one of the elements involved here. In this sense, catholicity is to be found, for example, whenever the successor of Peter governs the Church in communion with the bishops.[17]

It is also apparent here that catholicity remains a theological phenomenon, a part of the Church's profession of faith. We are not dealing primarily with a transnational organization, with the tendency towards cultural standardization,

---

[15]   *Lumen Gentium* 13.

[16]   See Maier, *Einigung der Welt in Gott*, pp. 203ff., pp. 238ff., pp. 244ff., pp. 257ff.

[17]   See the well-known passage from *Lumen Gentium* 8: 'This Church constituted and organized in the world as a society, subsists [*subsistit*] in the Catholic Church, which is governed by the successor of Peter and by the Bishops in communion with him, although many elements of sanctification and of truth are found outside of its visible structure. These elements, as gifts belonging to the Church of Christ, are forces impelling toward catholic unity.'

with global understanding or the idea of one humanity. Catholicity is not simply a secular proposal for ever greater universalization. We should keep this in mind when the Catholic Church is readily described as a 'global player'.

Time and again, catholicity has been limited, violated and marred by the sins of individuals within the Church. Divisions in the Church and schisms or heresies have darkened its original catholicity. Above all, the divisions among Christians have prevented the fullness of catholicity from taking full effect.[18] Diversity in itself does not prevent unity,[19] but it is impeded by the tendency to engage in self-assertion of a kind that closes one off from others, and to establish a rounded identity that is no longer able to identify, in the spirit of solidarity, with that which is injured and suffers.

From an ecumenical perspective, this requires further clarification. There is a trend in some Protestant theological models to interpret the category of catholicity in a basically eschatological sense. As a consequence, in concrete terms, catholicity is understood as the anticipation of eschatological fullness amidst a history awaiting its completion (W. Pannenberg). Finally, catholicity appears as an expression of the movement of the Church towards the eschatological goal. Catholicity is thus related to universal salvation. It is for this reason that prayer and solidarity with the poor are ways of expressing this catholicity, perfected only in the Kingdom of God (J. Moltmann).

Catholic theology can absorb many elements which, incidentally, are also to be found in the teachings of the early Church. There is also an eschatological component in *Lumen Gentium*, though this has been paid too little attention so far. Yet there can be no doubt that the Council does not see true catholicity in the eschatological distance. Thus, the Dogmatic Constitution on the Church states that the Church of Christ subsists in the Catholic Church and here takes on 'concrete form'.[20] While the Decree on Ecumenism[21] clearly acknowledges that the other churches may also be used by the Spirit as 'giving access to salvation', it affirms that 'it is only through Christ's Catholic Church, which is "the all-embracing means of salvation", that they can benefit fully from the means of salvation'.

V

In this context, it is obvious that the question of what constitutes the 'typically Catholic' or the 'typically Protestant' represents a significant problem for Catholic theologians. We can raise this question in this way only if the differentiating,

---

[18]   See *Unitatis Redintegratio* 4.

[19]   See *Unitatis Redintegratio* 17; *Lumen Gentium* 8, 23.

[20]   *Lumen Gentium* 8: 'subsistit in ecclesia catholica ...'.

[21]   *Unitatis Redintegratio* 3.

and to some extent also the exclusive, takes precedence. In examining the issue of catholicity, we approach the problem from the opposite direction, placing comprehensive fullness and the whole of reality centre stage. Here again, admittedly, the thorny problem arises of how all of God's gifts may be integrated to the greatest possible extent into the one Catholic Church, given that this is also a specific form which cannot simply assimilate anything and everything. The Church cannot be a motley collection of all possible random elements, the market, as it were, of all religious possibilities.

It is at precisely this point that the question arises of the status and implications of difference. Though I am unable to go into this in depth here, there are differences which may appear at first sight to be fundamental in nature, but which are not truly opposed in any exclusive sense. In any event, in the struggle over the purity and truth of faith, there are methods and procedures generally geared towards clarificatory delineation. This discernment is indispensable. In this context, it may then appear that different concepts and terminologies are mutually exclusive in a factual sense. However, upon closer and more rigorous examination, they may in fact complement one another, superficial polemics notwithstanding. The doctrine of justification in particular offers numerous examples of this.[22] There is no need to run through the entire toolkit of ecumenical hermeneutics, which serves to assess, interpret and safeguard this finding.

When we refer to the 'typically Protestant' or 'typically Catholic', we run a great risk of focusing inappropriately on a difference, which may undoubtedly exist, but which is raised to the false status of fundamental distinction. One need think only of the opposition between word and sacrament, of the universal priesthood (we Catholics prefer to say 'the common priesthood') and the ministerial priesthood, of forensic and effective justification, etc.

The key question is not whether differences exist in the first place, but whether they are so extensive that they have a church-dividing effect. Differences may also, for example, represent different styles and forms of expression of a theology, of piety, of church order, etc. They may mould the particular character of a church, its 'typical' form, in dramatic and profound fashion, yet they are not automatically an expression of division between churches. Such differences certainly exist, in the evaluation of the papacy for example, but we must always examine closely whether a difference truly is of a church-dividing nature.

But it is not a question only of obvious differences. Identical structures do not in themselves constitute evidence that they mean the same thing. There are theological conceptions that work on the assumption that a radical difference may open up behind identical wordings. Gerhard Ebeling for example, at least

---

[22]   See Karl Lehmann and Wolfhart Pannenberg, *The Condemnations of the Reformation Era – Do They Still Divide?*, trans. Margaret Kohl, Minneapolis, Fortress Press, 1990.

in his earlier work,[23] is of the opinion that profound denominational-hermeneutic differences apply to the understanding of the same statements in the Bible. Over the last few decades, some have asked whether there exists a basic difference or fundamental disagreement pervading all that appears common and which would, in a way, undermine all attempts to pursue substantial unity. In the message of justification, particularly when applied critically to the Church, the sacraments and the offices, some still see such a barrier. To postulate such a final, basic difference would in my opinion be the final reinforcement of the 'typically Protestant' or 'typically Catholic'. Ultimately, this would also be the death of ecumenicalism. For there could then only be unconditional conversion, but no truly serious dialogue. In the absence of such fundamental difference, there is a possibility that contrasting positions may complement one another on common ground, constituting something of a 'reconciled diversity'. This is not, however, the last word on the matter, as the following section in particular will demonstrate.

VI

We shall now try again to understand the remaining differences. In order to get to grips with these, we must ask whether, beyond specific controversies, there are non-deducible and thus ultimate principles which are demonstrably not identical with the specific, theologically controversial issues discussed so far. These ultimate principles would determine the concrete, that is, specific form of 'Protestantism' and/or 'Catholicism'. Here, they must not be understood only in terms of their dogmatic, theoretical content; they must also be understood as regulative of the Christian witness. These are formative principles which mould the basic character of Catholic or Protestant phenomena. We thus find some who advocate the idea that Protestantism owes its fundamental character to the principle of freedom, while, up to and including its saving activity, Catholicism is determined primarily by belonging to a community. Such ideas are found in various forms from G. W. F. Hegel to P. Tillich, in G. Ebeling and W. Pannenberg.

The search for such elementary formative principles of Protestantism and Catholicism is an entirely legitimate endeavour. In the first place, in no way does it have to be undertaken for dogmatic reasons, but may initially represent a phenomenological concern, namely with grasping the particular form of a denomination in its origins and basic structures. We should not exclude the possibility that the search for such radically formative principles may inspire

---

[23]   See for example Gerhard Ebeling, *The Word of God and Tradition*, London, Collins, 1968.

further reflections. It is, incidentally, no coincidence that such a search for principles is more prevalent within the Protestant sphere. The concepts of 'sola gratia', 'sola scriptura' and 'sola fide' imply a radical, exclusive approach, which also entails a certain critical, combative, sometimes even militant pathos. Here, the exclusivity can easily be overstated; this approach thus often sees irreconcilable differences where there is no need for them. In this sense, there are ways of thinking which seem to us Catholics 'typically Protestant' with the emphasis on the element of 'protest'. By contrast, emphasis is placed on the Catholic 'And' and especially on analogy, which admittedly require greater elaboration as ways of thinking.

No doubt, with respect to specific theological propositions, the Catholic Church expresses views that exclude certain possibilities from time to time. For the most part, however, there is no systematic connection between these views that is obvious or inescapable. In this sense, at a fundamental level, Catholicism is less concerned with establishing a delineating exclusivity. Hence, the listing of principles of Catholicism must not lead to any false systematization of Catholicism that might have a constraining effect. In this sense, it is in fact characteristic of 'heretical' thought, that is, thought intent on selection, to engage in such exhaustive systematization. To the extent that catholicity has a correct understanding of itself, its openness and expansiveness must not be put at risk. While the Church has undoubtedly often offended against this, it must not, of course, become the mere notary of prevailing views: when challenges arise, it must discern between the spirits and serve the truth of the Gospel effectively by making a decision.

VII

Thus, as our discussion so far has laid bare, the postulate that there are 'principles of Catholicism' entails certain risks with respect to our understanding of the Catholic Church itself. The aim can in fact only be to help us better grasp catholicity's open expansiveness and universality, its safeguarding of fullness and its particular form. On this condition, I would like to put forward the following 'principles of Catholicism':

1. The catholicity of the Church is rooted in the fullness of the triune God, in the Creator's generosity with a tremendous wealth of gifts, in God's universal salvific will with respect to every human being, in His coming into the world through the incarnation of Jesus Christ, in Jesus' Good News of God's boundless love, in Jesus' death 'for everyone' and in the descent of the Pentecostal Spirit, which edifies the Church through the fullness of gifts.

2. These are the foundations on which the catholic nature of the Church rests. However, it honours this catholicity fully only when, rid of limitations and schisms and redeemed of all sin, it is cleansed of all imperfections through the death of Jesus Christ and, ultimately, God's Judgement.

3. Catholicity prevents the Church from tying itself to a specific historical and social form, because such identification must not occur; at the same time, catholicity binds the Church to each earthly society, because it must involve itself fully in the concrete situation and the people living within it. This is closely bound up with the relationship between catholicity and history: simply in light of its mission, the Church is at all times referred to concrete history, but this is never its true homeland. This is why the image and understanding of the Church must never lack an eschatological component.

4. The Catholic faith is aware of the indissoluble tension between a creative fidelity to the traditional faith of the Church, insofar as it is binding, *and* the unavoidable obligation to produce interpretations appropriate to the present day. Only in this way can historical legacy be preserved as truth for a changed time.

   In the same way, this principle of catholicity avoids ahistorical fixity and a discontinuous progressivism. Steadfast affirmation of the fundamental truths enables and allows extensive suppleness and flexibility with regard to all other issues.

5. The nature of Catholic mobility, especially in the modern period, is bound up with this. Catholicism changes more than one might think and often more than it itself can know in advance (this can frequently only be determined after the event!). Catholicism is conservative in the sense that it is at pains to retain and integrate that which has been acquired over the course of history and has proved worth preserving, and in the sense that it assimilates the new more slowly and more hesitantly, more critically and more sceptically. But when it appropriates the new, transforming it even as it absorbs it, this occurs more fundamentally and enduringly. Thus, while it always lags somewhat behind historical and social developments, in general, particularly with respect to its unchanging characteristics, it succumbs less often to passing fashions. There is a general scepticism towards trendsetters. This includes rather than excludes the possibility of pioneers and vanguards, charisma and holy reformers. They know, and live, the discernment of spirits.

6. It is essentially Catholic to embrace all that is truly human in the biblical sense. Its integrative capacity is tremendous, in line with Phil. 4:8:

'whatever is true, whatever is honorable, whatever is just, whatever is pure, whatever is lovely, whatever is commendable, if there is any excellence, if there is anything worthy of praise, think about these things'. Or in accordance with the principle 'test everything; hold fast what is good' (1 Thess. 5:21). This is why the Catholic Church has had from the outset a fundamental relationship to the unity, multiplicity and richness of human history, extending to attempts to come to terms with myth, other religions and popular beliefs. This always occurs through a process of continuation and contradiction, and is never merely a matter of reception.

7. True catholicity shows itself in the overcoming of any claim to absoluteness put forward by any of the specific groupings within the Church (races, languages, cultures, classes, nations, social strata, etc.) and in an awareness of the unlimited scope this opens up for the reign of God's love in our time.

8. A fundamental principle of Catholicism is the safeguarding of Spirit-given unity amidst the diversity of specific expressions of life and religious witness within the community of the Church. As this unity does not come about of its own accord and the Gospel must not become vague, feeble and inconsistent, the realization and preservation of this unity also requires external forms, such as liturgical regulations, and enduring modes of representation, as found in the services and ministries of the Church. Catholicism too is aware of the Gospel's power of initiative and sovereignty, but it distrusts the thesis of its absolute power of self-assertion, emphasizing instead, in full awareness of the priority of the Word of God, the significance of personal witness and responsibility in transmitting the faith. However, ecclesial ministry cannot be separated from the presence of the Holy Spirit within the Church, which holds a position of greater pre-eminence.

9. A basic principle of Catholic thought sees the relationships between God and His creatures, between nature and grace, history and salvation as defined neither by forms of equality or trends towards equality (which may be well-hidden!), nor through radical inequality. Only in this way – by rejecting an exclusive either/or – can there be similarity within a greater dissimilarity.

   In this sense, this analogy, properly understood, preserves both the absolute sovereignty of God and the freedom of His creatures. A positive distinction allows a genuine 'between' and an authentic 'and'. Only in this way can we avoid forced deductions and monisms.

10. Nowhere is it more apparent that, against all particularisms, rather than imposing limitations, any principle of catholicity removes barriers, allowing

us access to the unlimited expanse of the entire world and of an infinite God. Much the same applies to the definition of the relationship between introspection and historical manifestation, personhood and community, law and freedom, conscience and authority.

11. On account of this differentiated dialectic of life, to a great extent Catholicity conjoins freedom of conscience and the binding nature of norms and instructions, the general and the particular. Hence, Catholicism is freer than it generally appears from the outside. In this connection, the relationship between Gospel and law requires in-depth, nuanced examination, for which exegesis can provide indications that have been neglected so far. At issue here is not only the question of power and the exercise of authority, but above all the need to clarify the extent to which legal categories can express the nature of salvation: a new reality which is already present, but which is not yet fully realized and which, therefore, makes fundamental demands of the saved.[24]

12. One principle of Catholicity – and here I am formulating a hypothesis – might relate to *how* God's revelation arrives within the sphere of history and the human life-world, that is, how it is received and accepted: in light of the eschatological gravity of God's merciful affection for the world – God genuinely desires human salvation – the Catholic Church understands God's advent and the adoption of the faith, right up to the concrete, bodily dimension, as God's 'decided decision' (H. Schlier) for the world, one to which, of course, human beings must respond accordingly.[25]

Hence, Catholicism quite often seems 'naïve' in its characteristic loyalty not only to the spirit, but also to the 'letter' of the Gospel. This applies to the gravity of the Great Commission as understood literally, and to the lives of the saints, who live the Gospel 'sine glossa'. St Francis of Assisi is just one

---

[24]   See Erik Peterson, *Theologische Traktate* (Ausgewählte Schriften, vol. 1), Würzburg, Echter, 1994, p. 21, Fn. 21; idem, *Der Brief an die Römer* (Ausgewählte Schriften, vol. 6), pp. 194, 213; idem, *Johannesevangelium und Kanonstudien* (Ausgewählte Schriften, vol. 3), p. 174; idem, *Der erste Brief an die Korinther und Paulus-Studien* (Ausgewählte Schriften, vol. 7), p. 72. Ernst Käsemann, *Sätze heiligen Rechtes im Neuen Testament*, in idem, *Exegetische Versuche und Besinnungen*, vol. 2, Göttingen, Vandenhoeck & Ruprecht, 1964, pp. 69–82. Erich Dinkler, *Die Taufterminologie in 2 Kor 1,21f.*, in idem, *Signum crucis. Aufsätze zum Neuen Testament und zur Christlichen Archäologie*, Tübingen, Mohr, 1967, pp. 99–117; see also pp. 121ff. and 205ff.

[25]   For a more in-depth exploration of these issues that attempts to analyse the Church and its instrumental role in the history of salvation, see André Birmelé, *Le salut en Jésus Christ dans les dialogues oecuméniques*, Paris, Editions du Cerf, 1986.

impressive example of this. Such an understanding also has consequences for obedience with respect to the Word of God, but also for ways of life such as an existence in accordance with the evangelical counsels, irrevocable fidelity within marriage and priestly celibacy understood in connection with poverty and obedience.

In realizing this principle, we must ensure that it does not promote misunderstanding in the shape of superficiality, unspiritness, hypocrisy, 'objectification' and superstition, and letter worship. This is why we must never stop pointing to the veiled nature, brokenness and hidden character of salvation and grace in history. Even in salvation, we are only saved in hope. The 'eschatological reservation' renders everything fundamentally provisional. We are on the way, but have not yet reached our goal.

Thus, Catholicism includes a profound knowledge of human sinfulness and the imperative of repentance, of the necessity for constant renewal and for perseverance in patience and hope. Consequently, in the Catholic sphere too, deep spirituality very often comprises a profound theology of the Cross.

This is a modest first attempt to identify principles of Catholicism. So far, Catholic theology has done too little in this regard, though it is important even from a phenomenology of religion perspective. But this unsatisfactory state of affairs must not persist indefinitely. Such an endeavour helps us understand one another better. To sum up, as it were, we might say: the more perfectly a Catholic principle is realized, the more true ecumenicalism is promoted. If 'Catholic' does not refer to a specific denomination, then churches other than the Roman Catholic Church may share in this catholicity – if they wish. Then the converse applies: the more true ecumenicalism is cultivated and lived, the greater the prospects for a living catholicity. Rather than a convenient label, 'Catholic' is the centrepoint of numerous challenges with which all of us are faced.

VIII

As we near the end of our discussion, it is essential[26] to provide a brief account of the term 'Catholicism',[27] which at first glance seems narrower than the broad term 'Catholicity'. It is evident here that 'Catholicism' often seems to have a broader meaning in other modern languages than in its German variant.

---

[26]   Here, I use extracts from my article 'Katholizismus' in *Lexikon Theologie. Hundert Grundbegriffe*, ed. Alf Christophersen and Stefan Jordan, Stuttgart, Reclam, 2004, pp. 170–74; see also the counterpart article 'Protestantismus' (Friedrich Wilhelm Graf), pp. 246–50.

[27]   For a very brief account, see Henri de Lubac, *Catholicisme*, Paris, Editions du Cerf, 1938, English title: *Catholicism: A Study of Dogma in Relation to the Corporate Destiny of*

In any event, the term 'Catholicism' is unstable, ambiguous and rather problematic. We can distinguish between the following key meanings:

1. Catholicism refers to the socio-historical form in which the mission of the Roman Catholic Church unfolds and finds expression in the world, under the specific conditions pertaining in a given case.

2. Particularly in contrast to 'Protestantism', but also to socio-political forces such as liberalism, Catholicism describes the Roman Catholic Church as a denominationally specific, generally 'closed' system of religious, cultural, social and political ways of thinking, living and acting.

3. Catholicism is especially focused on those forces inspired by the Catholic faith yet acting and shaping reality on the basis of their own conscience in society, economy, culture and law.

4. A basic structure of this kind may lead to the typical expression of individual endeavours to accept the Christian responsibility for the world, endeavours which exhibit a special character and which are determined by particular historical circumstances, such as political, social and cultural Catholicism.

5. Often, Catholicism means the totality of Catholics in a country or region as a social group within a pluralistic state, such as French Catholicism. It is here in particular that we find laypeople and their groupings.

We must make a distinction between Catholicism and the 'Church'. This is important because otherwise many historical and social phenomena *within* the Catholic Church might be interpreted as unchanging expressions of the essence *of* the Catholic Church. Catholicism indicates the sphere of action in which Catholics as individuals or as a group fulfil their responsibility for the world on the basis of their expertise and their conscience, inspired by their faith. One problem remains, however: the distinction between Church and Catholicism might imply the erroneous idea that the Church's impact on society is a feature *of* the Church only in an unreal sense, and that, in a state of

---

Mankind, London, Burns & Oates, 1950; Karl Gabriel and Franz-Xaver Kaufmann (eds.), *Zur Soziologie des Katholizismus*, Mainz, M. Grünewald, 1980; Klaus Schatz, *Zwischen Säkularisation und Zweitem Vatikanum. Der Weg des deutschen Katholizismus im 19. und 20. Jahrhundert*, Frankfurt am Main, Knecht 1986; Erwin Gatz (ed.), *Kirche und Katholizismus seit 1945*, vol. 1ff., Paderborn, Schöningh, 1998ff.; Albert Franz (ed.), *Was ist heute noch katholisch? Zum Streit um die innere Einheit und Vielfalt der Kirche*, Freiburg, Herder, 2001; 'Katholizismus', in *Lexikon für Theologie und Kirche*, vol. 5, Freiburg, Herder, 3rd edn, 1996, col. 1367–70 (Hans Maier); *Religion in Geschichte und Gegenwart*, vol. 4, Tübingen, Mohr Siebeck, 4th edn, 2001, col. 888–902.

ahistorical abstractness, the Church is always superior to the realities prevailing at a given time, itself having virtually no direct relationship with the public sphere. With this in mind, and despite the emphasis on the distinction between the two, it is clear that the Church is realized in concrete form through various Catholicisms.

We can understand the term 'Catholicism' only by anchoring it in its historical context. Since the Investiture Controversy of the eleventh and twelfth centuries, church and state have tended to maintain their own spheres of power and influence. The Reformation brought a new element into the relationship between the two. The Catholic Church was now no longer the states' only opponent or partner. As a term, 'Catholicism' appears to have been coined during the Dutch Reformation (Philips van Marnix). As a result of the contrast with 'Protestantism', its meaning has from the outset been limited denominationally. As the churches of the Reformation remained committed to the 'catholicity' of the Church, a linguistic change was bound to ensue: on this view, the 'Church of the origins' became the 'false church' when it became the 'Roman church' (with a special focus on the papacy and traditions). While the antithesis of Catholicism versus Protestantism took apologetic and polemical form in the oldest variants of Lutheranism (the 'Magdeburg Centuries' being an example), attempts were eventually made to explain this opposition in a programmatic and systematic way: both were claimed to constitute an oppositional structure from the very beginnings of church history (see for example F. C. Baur). Catholicism appears as a necessary moment in the process of 'Christian consciousness', but now, in light of the Hegelian conception of history for example, it seems to have been overtaken by the higher form of Protestantism. To this day, Schleiermacher's understanding has remained influential as a comprehensive interpretation and critique of Catholicism: in Catholicism, one's relationship to the Saviour is 'dependent' on one's relationship to the Church. A profession of faith in Jesus Christ is possible only if one is affiliated with the community of the Church. This is the origin of references to the principles of Catholicism and Protestantism. These two outlooks and modes of faith continue to coexist and are evident in very different styles of conduct of a cultural and political nature, which, over a long period of time, together form something of a 'denominational culture' and which are only now undergoing deep-rooted change.

At the beginning of the twentieth century, however, we may speak of a kind of *rediscovery of original Catholicity*. The foundations for this had been laid by the Liturgical, Biblical and Patristic Movement, especially in France, Belgium and Germany. The lay movement was an additional factor. The crucial aspects here are as follows:

1. The original breadth of the Catholic encounter with reality is regained: 'to

absorb all that can possibly be assimilated while imposing nothing lying outside of the faith' (H. de Lubac).

2. With respect to its truly universal mission, the Catholic Church is – all appearances to the contrary – by no means a 'closed society', but rather the only reality which has no need to oppose others for the sake of its existence and thereby attain legitimacy. The firmness of principles, which helps prevent lapses into false dependencies, also ensures great flexibility.

3. At the same time, there is a growing *sense of mission*, a desire to ready oneself for new encounters with other religions and cultures, but also with groups and strata closer to home (workers, young people, women, etc.) almost lost to the Church.

4. There is an increasing tendency to *reflect upon the historical conditionality* of the Catholic Church, whose institutional form reflects a given society in a dual sense. Aspects of a society's fundamental order are reflected within the Church (in constitutional elements and administration for example), and in addition the social strata help create the ranks in the Church as well as the clergy. The theologians mentioned already, such as K. Adam, Y. Congar, E. Przywara, R. Guardini, representatives of the ecumenical movement and writers such as C. Péguy and P. Claudel, are among the pioneers of this rediscovery of 'Catholicity'. H. U. von Balthasar and K. Rahner later developed it further. It became both evident and effective in decisive fashion in H. de Lubac's *Catholicisme*. This book, which appeared in 1938, not only brings together many preceding initiatives, but is itself the locus of a reorientation away from a denominationally overdetermined, ambiguous concept of 'Catholicism' towards its 'original, unsullied freshness' (H. U. von Balthasar). The assimilation of ecumenical impulses fits effortlessly into this picture. This is a major step towards realizing the goals outlined in the central statements of the Second Vatican Council – and beyond. The broad opening of Catholicism to fundamental issues facing the whole of society, to a wide range of tasks and international challenges (see for example the establishment of the organizations *Misereor* and *Adveniat*, *Missio* and *Renovabis*) also occurred in the wake of this development.

Future developments cannot be foreseen in any detail. The dialogue on the principles of Catholicism and Protestantism, particularly in the fields of ethics, law and politics, must, however, be intensified in a radical way. Pragmatic cooperation in many fields is fundamentally important and is already occurring. In future, the priority for Catholicism will not so much be to borrow from, let alone adapt to, alien religious practices or the crumbling 'secularized' world, but rather, together with all Christians, to remember the common origin and central foundations of the faith, so that on this basis we may ensure without inhibition, resolutely and unequivocally, its presence within the society of today and tomorrow. In light of the Church's dwindling impact on society, we may draw comfort from the ceaselessly compelling hopefulness and creative power of authentic Catholicity: *comprehensive fullness and particular form*. Here, the churches of the 'Third World' and individual local churches are becoming ever more important.

I would like to draw to a close at this point. Much remains to be said. The key lacuna is the historical dimension, which could demonstrate the wealth of forms taken by Catholicism. This does not suggest a desire to take refuge in arbitrary diversity. This I attempted to show in the 'principles of Catholicism' presented above. The task would now be to set out with even greater precision how this unity and comprehensiveness characteristic of Catholicism is currently being realized in a wide variety of relationships, not least within the ecumenical discussion, in dialogue with the non-Christian religions and with atheism.[28] But these issues cannot be tackled within the framework of this chapter.[29]

---

[28] For a very brief account, see Karl Lehmann, *Katholische Weltanschauung. Integration und Unterscheidung*, Freiburg, Herder, 2006; see also idem, 'Ist unter den Religionen und Konfessionen eine Verständigung ohne Relativismus möglich?', lecture given on 14 March 2006 at the Catholic Academy, Berlin; on the broader context, from a comprehensive political perspective, see also Harald Müller, *Das Zusammenleben der Kulturen. Ein Gegenentwurf zu Huntington* (1998), Frankfurt am Main, Fischer, 4th edn, 2001.

[29] See for example Karl Lehmann, *Zuversicht aus dem Glauben. Die Grundsatzreferate des Vorsitzenden der Deutschen Bischofskonferenz und die Predigten der Eröffnungsgottesdienste*, Freiburg, Herder, 2006, pp. 397ff., pp. 499ff.

2

Protestantism

Friedrich Wilhelm Graf

Strictly speaking, the above title is incorrect. It is certainly possible to speak of 'Catholicism' to designate that form of Christianity which, alongside the Orthodox churches on the one hand and those decisively inspired by the sixteenth-century Reformation, together with religious revivalist movements and 'sects' on the other, represents the third strand of Christian tradition: the Roman Catholic 'world church' centred on the office of the Pope. But there is neither a Protestant 'world church' comparable to Roman Catholic centralism nor any other kind of globally organized institution that might be in a position to unite the factual diversity of Protestant churches and groups. Since its beginnings in the reformist movements of the sixteenth century, 'Protestantism' has been a highly plural, multi-layered, even contradictory phenomenon, and there are many good reasons, from both a sociology of religion and a theological perspective, for consistent use of the plural 'Protestantisms' rather than the overly abstract collective singular. For 'Protestantism' or the adjective 'Protestant' exist solely within an almost overwhelming profusion of thousands of churches, voluntary communities, charismatic movements and groups. Despite elementary differences in piety, liturgical tradition, theological doctrine and moral behaviour, however, these converge in the fact that their roots can be traced back to the reformist protest of the sixteenth century and that, as a result, they understand the Christian church not as a powerful institution of salvation in which the ordained bishops and priests take spiritual precedence over the laity, but as a community of blessed sinners living the 'priesthood of all the faithful' and constituted by the Holy Spirit. In this sense of drawing, in a range of ways, on the reformist protest movements of the sixteenth century, we may use the collective singular 'Protestantism'.[1]

---

[1] I have recently summed up my view of the third largest form of Christianity after Roman Catholicism and the Eastern Orthodox churches in all its extremely complex, multi-layered reality in an essay aimed at the general reader: Friedrich Wilhelm Graf,

Rather than presenting 'Catholicism' as a global Christian religious culture alongside others, Cardinal Karl Lehmann, inspired by the intense debates on the 'nature of the Catholic' carried on over the course of the twentieth century, has focused on explicating the inclusive character of the 'universal Catholic Church' as a 'community of the holy' ideally embracing all Christians. In contrast, the special character of Protestantism in both religio-cultural and theological terms is outlined here in contradistinction to the Roman Catholic global church and Orthodox Christianity. I take my lead from the four key questions set out by Hans Joas in his introduction, but have reformulated them in light of the heterogeneity of Protestant lifeworlds. This generates the following questions:

First: What is the spiritual core, the basic religious 'inspiration', of the reformers and, subsequently, of the many modern Protestantisms? In view of the tremendous scope of the Protestant sphere, we must also ask: Do the many different Protestantisms share one central idea in the first place?

Second: How did the reformers and subsequently the Protestant theologians turn any basic religious idea into concrete religious practice? Which ecclesiological models were developed over the course of the history of these Protestantisms, and how was the relationship between the individual believer and the religious community conceived?

Third: What 'ideal political orders' and which conceptions of society were developed by the reformers and, later, the old and new Protestantisms? Is it possible to identify specifically Protestant political ideals, in sharp contrast, for example, to Roman Catholic models and strategies? How is the relationship of Protestant Christians to Christians of other denominations and, beyond this, to those of other faiths or no faith at all conceived?

Fourth: Which theories have been developed on the 'significance of Protestantism to the rise of the modern world' (E. Troeltsch), theories which aim to grasp the impact of the 'Protestant ethic' or 'Protestant spirit' beyond the specifically religious cultural sphere? Conversely, how have Protestant religious cultures, styles of piety and ideals of political order been determined 'from outside' by hard social factors such as political power, (above all capitalist) economics and the triumphant progress of functionally specific instrumental rationality, the scientification of all fields of life, the rise of free public spheres and, not least, the growing significance of the mass media?

Der Protestantismus. Geschichte und Gegenwart, Munich, Beck, 2006. This essay also provides a brief outline of the fascinating history of the term 'Protestantism'.

Every well-meaning reader will be aware that in view of the great complexity of the many Protestantisms, these questions can be answered within the framework of a short essay only if we have the courage to refer to ideal types, with all the overstatement that this entails. Whatever may be said in what follows about 'Protestantism' or 'the Protestant' sphere, one may for the most part cite important examples showing the very opposite with respect to specific Protestant lifeworlds. I am painfully aware of the analytical limitations of my proposed interpretations. Yet in their distance from the 'societas perfecta' of the Roman Catholic church, Protestants have in fact developed a highly pronounced sense of the provisional; they readily cultivate a radical awareness of sin, emphasize the immutable fallibility of every human being, and yet they believe themselves to have been graciously saved by a benevolent paternal God irrespective of merit and good works. They see themselves in fact, with an ambiguity particular to their denomination, as 'simul iustus et peccator', justified sinners.

Before answering thetically the questions posed above, I must begin with some methodologically imperative notes on the internal variety of 'Protestantism'.

Protestant plurality

It is part and parcel of the great variety of Protestantisms that there are no generally valid answers to questions about religious core, ecclesiological models, notions of political order and external influences. For, since its beginnings in the reformist protest movements of the early sixteenth century, Protestantism has been divided into a number of different denominations. The Wittenberg Reformation, in which Martin Luther and Philipp Melanchthon played the key roles, the Upper German and Swiss reform movements centred in Zurich and strongly influenced by Ulrich Zwingli, the Geneva Reformation of Jean Calvin and the diverse groups of the so-called 'radical Reformation' – mystical spiritualists such as Andreas Bodenstein von Karlstadt, Thomas Müntzer, Hans Denck and Sebastian Franck, Baptists such as Balthasar Hubmaier, Hans Hut and Melchior Hoffmann, Mennonites, Antitrinitarians – all agreed in their fundamental criticisms of the corrupt Papal church of Rome, but each produced very different ideals of the true church.[2]

At a very early stage, the various reformist movements organized themselves into very different or antagonistic ecclesiastical structures: within German Lutheranism, through the establishment of a system of church government

---

[2]   On the conflict-ridden diversity of reformist protest movements in the sixteenth century, see the recent, succinct overview in Gottfried Seebaß, *Geschichte des Christentums III. Spätmittelalter – Reformation – Konfessionalisierung*, Stuttgart, Kohlhammer, 2006.

centred on the sovereign princes, regional churches intricately meshed with the polity's political structures emerged, while in the reformed Protestantisms the individual parish took on far greater importance. The 'Independent' and 'Baptist' groups, whose theological legitimacy was denied particularly by the Wittenberg Reformers, organized themselves as highly active sects, and protest against the externalization of faith was sometimes expressed in the form of personalized mysticism. Ernst Troeltsch's famous distinction between three social forms of the Christian idea, the ideal types of church, sect and mysticism,[3] is essential to every interpretation of Protestantism, because the energies of reformist protest have coalesced in a particular way in each of these social forms.

As is apparent in the great disputes over communion of the sixteenth century, conflicts over 'images' in the church or the very different ways of dealing with church discipline, right from the outset, Protestantism has developed very different worlds of piety. The various Protestantisms differ not only with respect to theological teachings or church creeds, but also in regard to devotional books, songs, prayers, liturgies or liturgical forms for services; in short, in their styles of piety.

In all its denominational forms, Protestantism is deeply determined by class- or milieu-specific distinctions, evident above all in the manifold tensions between church doctrine formulated by academic elites – theologians and lawyers – on the one hand and the broad, colourful spectrum of popular piety on the other. The social and cultural divisions between different estates, classes and social milieux were also reflected in fragmentation with regard to religious culture. Fine religious differences marked the boundaries between, for example, aristocratic Protestantisms with a keen sense of distinction, bourgeois cultural Protestantisms, anti-modern and modern moral Protestantisms and the Protestant lifeworlds of the 'little people', whose intensely lived faith often helped them cope with the diverse privations of a hard and impoverished existence.

From the very beginning of its self-globalization, as it spread from Europe, particularly the British Isles, to the North American colonies, Protestantism was quick to display an expansionary dynamism and capacity for mobilization, one which still applies today. Both European and North American Protestants engaged in intensive missionary work and founded many mission churches in Asia, Latin America and above all Africa; then, however, in the twentieth century, through processes of decolonization, they saw the formation of

---

[3]   Ernst Troeltsch, *The Social Teaching of the Christian Churches* (1912), Chicago, University of Chicago Press, 1981; on the genesis of Troeltsch's distinction between church, sect and mysticism, see Arie L. Molendijk, *Zwischen Theologie und Soziologie. Ernst Troeltschs Typen der christlichen Gemeinschaftsbildung: Kirche, Sekte, Mystik*, Gütersloh, Gütersloher Verlagshaus, 1996.

numerous autonomous churches, particularly in the southern hemisphere, and marvelled, with a good deal of irritation, at the fascinating and successful religious revolution brought about by the Pentecostal churches, which emerged from Protestant Methodism in 1906, its members profoundly moved by God's all-transforming spirit – a development of which Western intellectuals and media are as yet scarcely aware. It is true that European experiences rapidly inspire a mood of depression: the established Protestant churches are being eroded; their culture of preaching, which once exhibited such intellectual sophistication, has been superseded by maudlin appeals to 'be good', shallow prattle about morality and a dreadful decline in the skilled use of language; the educational level of a ministry of an increasingly petit bourgeois character has declined markedly even with respect to core competences; with a few exceptions, Christian theologians, and even church leaders, lack both leadership ability and a clearly Protestant profile. But outside Europe, not only in the USA, but particularly in Africa and Latin America, new Protestantisms, above all the Pentecostals and their most successful off-shoots, charismatic groups, exhibit astonishingly high rates of growth, and though some Pentecostal churches are now stagnating as they become bureaucratized, overall their tremendous expansionary dynamism continues unabated. What applied to the mission churches, then to the non-European autochthonous churches, now also characterizes the global spread of the new Pentecostal Christianity: the hundreds of Pentecostal churches are profoundly shaped by local or regional cultures, and these processes of indigenization also make the religious culture of 'Protestantism' increasingly diversified in form, and more colourful.

Since the sixteenth century, Protestantism has influenced (or generated) very different models of political order and has paved the way for heterogeneous political developments, which – as is apparent in the passionate *Sonderweg* or 'special way' debate among historians and political scientists in the old West Germany – are continuing to have an impact on the present, particularly with regard to their differences: on the one hand, the enduring strengthening of state authority by a Lutheran social paternalism geared towards the *bonum commune* and public welfare, on the other, the laying of foundations for republicanism, democratic self-government and the notion of human rights in the more strongly parish-centred, Western (reformed) Protestantism with its presbyterian-synodal structure.

It was only very late on – in the context of the *Kulturkämpfe* or state–church struggles of the late nineteenth and early twentieth centuries – that Protestantism attempted to develop something like a shared Protestant consciousness. But in view of the internal political and cultural fragmentation within and between the individual Protestantisms, this has done little to guide action or forge an identity. Though 'world Protestantism' was readily invoked in the early twentieth century as a transnational Protestant ecumenical movement was taking shape, in reality it was no more than a highly ideological construct, anchored in church politics, that lacked an institutional foundation.

Since the late eighteenth century, Protestantism has been repeatedly characterized by processes of division of a political, religious, cultural and social nature, which developed primarily around the issue of the Christian legitimacy of the modern bourgeois society that emerged through Enlightenment, political revolution and capitalist industrialization. Alongside the traditional denominational differences within Protestantism between Lutherans and the reformed churches, there now emerged new religious-cultural, ideological distinctions, which were closely bound up with the gradual establishment of a multi-party political system. Through Enlightenment and idealism, there arose an educated or cultural Protestantism relatively open to modernity and closely associated with political liberalism, whose key social carriers were educated middle-class professionals and members of the business bourgeoisie. At the same time, there emerged a neo-religious church Protestantism, decidedly critical of modernity and politically and theologically conservative, made up chiefly of nobility, broad sections of the clergy and the 'core congregations' recruited largely from the old middle classes, which wished to make the church the counterweight to a 'secular' modern culture suffered as anti-Christian. Hence, since the early nineteenth century, there have been permanent 'Kulturkämpfe within Protestantism' (G. Hübinger) between liberals and conservatives. Finally, in seeking to come to terms with the 'social question' or the deleterious consequences of capitalist industrialization, there also emerged a social Protestantism informed by generally conservative values, the Protestantism of the Home Mission and its 'homes', of deaconesses with their revivalist piety and associated training centres, the Bahnhofsmission which helped rail travellers in need of assistance and the Anstalten or institutions run by the diakonische Bruderschaften (welfare and social societies), a Protestantism deeply involved in social welfare, one dedicated to rescuing those in need, and one that developed networks of lived charity and solidarity for people with disabilities and marginalized people of all kinds. To the present day, this welfarist social Protestantism is generally organized independently of the 'church as institution', often in the form of autonomous societies or foundations. It thus reinforces traditional differences.

Up to the present, Protestantism has been unable to reach a consensus about where its external boundaries lie, and it is unclear to what extent the more or less half-Catholic Anglicans, for example, are part of the 'Protestant family' or which 'sects' and new religious currents developing on the margins of the Protestant churches may be considered genuinely Protestant; if they expressly trace their origins to the reformist movements of the sixteenth century and claim to be their successors, they generate their own Protestant legitimacy.

The basic religious idea: *libertas christiana*

More than other Christian denominational cultures, many Protestantisms have reflected a great deal on their own identity. Such self-reflexivity or permanent discursive self-examination is particularly characteristic of the various cultural Protestantisms of the modern era. A prime example of this is the most influential German-speaking Protestant theologian of the nineteenth century, Friedrich Daniel Ernst Schleiermacher. He interpreted Protestantism and Catholicism as two fundamentally independent forms of Christianity, each with its own principles, principles between which it is impossible to mediate. In 1821/1822, in *The Christian Faith*, Schleiermacher famously expressed the basic difference between Protestantism and Catholicism in the following terms: 'the antithesis [...] may provisionally be conceived thus: the former makes the individual's relation to the Church dependent on his relation to Christ, while the latter contrariwise makes the individual's relation to Christ dependent on his relation to the Church'.[4]

This distinction has an important consequence. It shows that attempts to capture the nature of the specifically Protestant solely with reference to the confessional writings of the sixteenth century, any kind of church-approved 'valid doctrine' or through accounts of the dogmatic statements made by Protestant theologians are from the outset insufficient. For to take one's lead primarily from the institution of the church, the so-called *Amtskirche* and its teachings, has always been to adhere to a specifically Roman Catholic understanding of the church and thus to miss the insight, fundamental to all Protestantisms, that faith and piety are much more than and very different from mere ecclesiasticism. In defining the nature of Protestantism, the key point is to take account of the critical relativization of the religious institution and the fundamental autonomy of faith enjoyed by the faithful. 'Protestantism' always represents far more than just the 'Protestant church'. The term also covers the 'Christianity outside of the church' shaped by the reformist tradition and the many and diverse forms of 'private Christianity' or 'distanced Christianity' lying on the blurred edges of the institution.[5]

---

[4]   Friedrich Daniel Ernst Schleiermacher, *The Christian Faith* (1821/1822), Edinburgh, T. & T. Clark, 1928, p. 103.

[5]   For a basic overview of the theory of modern Christianity, see Trutz Rendtorff, *Christentum außerhalb der Kirche. Konkretionen der Aufklärung*, Hamburg, Furche, 1969; idem, *Theorie des Christentums. Historisch-theologische Studien zu seiner neuzeitlichen Verfassung*, Gütersloh, Mohn, 1972; on the differentiation of modern Christianity into individual, ecclesiastical and social forms, see Dietrich Rössler, *Grundriß der Praktischen Theologie*, Berlin, de Gruyter, 2nd edn, 1994.

If we wish to identify that which is 'essential' and constitutive of its identity, we must attempt to reconstruct the normative origins of Protestantism. There can be no relevant theory of Protestantism without recalling Martin Luther's pious protest against a generally omnipotent institution of the church. The academic, university context is important. For it was only by studying the Holy Scriptures, through hard exegetical desk work to prepare for lectures, that the Wittenberg Professor Biblicus Dr Martinus Luther came to realize that the existing church was deeply corrupt, rotten to the core, and that its practices ran fundamentally counter to the Word of God as affirmed in both the Old and New Testament. Luther formulated his reformist protest by basing himself exclusively upon the Word of God, as the absolutely binding source he had understood it to be through his individual scriptural studies. Luther grants authority solely to the Gospel, rather than to the church, let alone to a specific office-bearer within the church, such as the Bishop of Rome and Pope; in Protestant discourse, this radical commitment to the Scriptures is summed up in the term *sola scriptura*. Individual religious insight as attained by 'listening to the Word of God' becomes the ultimate source of authority. This radical relationship to the Word of God has undoubtedly instilled in all forms of Protestant piety a decidedly critical view of institutions; for it is the 'Scriptures alone', the normative source, that are recognized as a guide to action, rather than that which happens to exist, which has developed over time; in Roman Catholic diction, the tradition of the Church. Hence, the legitimacy of every empirically given form of Christianity, of each of its institutional crystallizations, always depends on the extent to which it embodies the Scriptures, rather than on its status as an enduring concretion of Christianity. The systematic theologian Paul Tillich, who fled to the USA from his chair in Frankfurt in 1933, called this the 'Protestant principle': 'It should be regarded as the Protestant principle that, in relation to God, God alone can act and that no human claim, especially no religious claim, no intellectual or moral or devotional "work" can reunite us with him. [...] In this sense the doctrine of justification is the universal principle of Protestant theology.'[6] As such, the point of departure for this justification is 'beyond being and spirit. It places a question mark over existence as such and takes no account of the partial reconciliation achieved by false being with true being'.[7] The principle of Protestantism is thus one

> that stands beyond all its realizations. It is the critical and dynamic source
> of all Protestant realizations, but it is not identical with any of them. It

---

[6]   Paul Tillich, *Systematic Theology*, vol. III, London, SCM, 1978, p. 224.

[7]   Paul Tillich, 'Der Protestantismus als kritisches und gestaltendes Prinzip', in idem, *Der Protestantismus als Kritik und Gestaltung* (Gesammelte Werke, vol. 7.1), Stuttgart, Evangelisches Verlagswerk, 1962, pp. 29–53, here p. 33.

cannot be confined by a definition. It is not exhausted by any historical religion; it is not identical with the structure of the Reformation or of early Christianity or even with a religious form at all. It transcends them as it transcends any cultural form. On the other hand, it can appear in all of them; it is a living, moving, restless power in them; and this is what it is supposed to be in a special way in historical Protestantism. The Protestant principle, in name derived from the protest of the 'protestants' against decisions of the Catholic majority, contains the divine and human protest against any absolute claim made for a relative reality, even if this claim is made by a Protestant church. The Protestant principle is the judge of every religious and cultural reality, including the religion and culture which calls itself 'Protestant'.[8]

The *sola scriptura* is closely, indissolubly linked with the *sola fide* and *sola gratia*. In this triad, in the *solus Christus*, we find, condensed into a concise formula as it were, the basic religious idea characteristic of all Protestantisms. *Sola fide*, by faith alone, stood for that fundamental theological insight gained by Luther through his existential struggle over the correct exegesis of Romans 3, one which corresponded to the true sense of the Scriptures. St Paul wrote to the congregation in Rome, which had faced so many challenges, including persecution:

(21) But now the righteousness of God has been manifested apart from the law, although the Law and the Prophets bear witness to it – (22) the righteousness of God through faith in Jesus Christ for all who believe. For there is no distinction: (23) for all have sinned and fall short of the glory of God, (24) and are justified by his grace as a gift, through the redemption that is in Christ Jesus, (25) whom God put forward as a propitiation by his blood, to be received by faith. This was to show God's righteousness, because in his divine forbearance he had passed over former sins. (26) It was to show his righteousness at the present time, so that he might be just and the justifier of the one who has faith in Jesus. (27) Then what becomes of our boasting? It is excluded. By what kind of law? By a law of works? No, but by the law of faith. (28) For we hold that one is justified by faith apart from works of the law.

Luther read this key passage in the same way as the great majority of Roman Catholic exegetes now do as well: as a clear message that the sinner is justified

---

[8]   Paul Tillich, 'The Protestant Principle and the Proletarian Situation', in idem, *The Protestant Era*, Chicago, University of Chicago Press, 1957, pp. 237–59, here pp. 239f.

before God 'without any merit or worthiness', that is, he himself, no matter what he might do, can contribute nothing to his salvation; he has only his basic trust in the prevenient grace of the benevolent, redeeming Creator of heaven and earth, which always precedes his existence. Thus, the *sola fide* may also be explicated as *sola gratia*: by grace alone. The reformers battled against every form of 'justification by works', particularly the notion, fundamental to the church's practice of expiation at the time, that the sinner in need of redemption might purchase specific permits to alleviate the punishment he could expect to receive in purgatory and hell in the market of redemptive goods administered by the church. Such merely 'superficial' piety, to use genuinely Protestant language, took the form, for example, of the so-called 'selling of indulgences', of the purchase of parts of the treasures of grace of the saints and martyrs, as well as the fees for remarkably expensive memorial services, with whose aid surviving relatives sought to positively influence the fate of their loved ones in the hereafter. The reformers recognized neither any punishments of hell that might be alleviated through contributions to the church, nor any kind of holy services that enhanced the prospects that God might place one among the good or suitable for heaven in the *extremum iudicium*, the Last Judgement. In contrast to Rome, at least as it then was, in Wittenberg, Zurich or Geneva one could neither reserve or buy any seats in heaven nor acquire any shares in redemption. There was no need for Protestants (or other sinners, at least according to their Reformation-inspired understanding) to actively obtain or possess salvation, because it has always already been conferred upon them despite all their constitutive sinfulness. In its religious core, Protestantism is a religion – or better, form of piety – of the 'always already'. All that is truly fundamental is not acquired, made or earned by me, but is always already given to me by my merciful God. For Protestant cultures of piety, this tendency towards the individualization of the focus on God or ties to God is so elementary that they have gradually generated their own highly differentiated language expressing a pronounced individuality.

Protestant discourses focus on the devout individual (and then on the community of the devout) rather than on church power structures and instruments of power. Traditionally, as the 'institution of salvation', the church administered the so-called *depositum fidei*, the 'deposit of faith', and, with its seven sacraments, was the source of those helpful means of salvation, which the faithful often experienced as magical, with which it could save the sinful human being from eternal damnation. By defining everything religious – faith, good works, redemption, salvation, damnation, eternal life – exclusively with reference to the institution of the church, the medieval church made the faithful dependent on it and exercised, and by no means only in a symbolic sense, tremendous power over people's minds. This is well illustrated through a distinction specific to modernity: under modern conditions, 'public' and 'private' are separate, 'inner' and 'outer' are kept apart. It is precisely these distinctions which late medieval church theology lacks. It possesses only the weakest of conceptual means to conceive of a possible internal space of religious subjectivity, such as the mystical soul's proximity to God, its oneness with God or Christ. For the devout individual's relationship to God was consistently conceived as mediated by the church. This church wished to standardize the faith of the pious and, as it were, to domesticate the individual's innermost being, his 'soul', within a church context as well. To this end, it developed a subtly differentiated apparatus of instruments of clerically based social control.

In perfect contrast to the institutionalism of the Catholic papal church, to its tying of all religious energies back to the institution of the church, defined essentially by the Pope, bishops and priests, Luther's reformist protest is marked by its fundamental elevation of the pious individual over the church as an institution. In his famous tract *De libertate christiana* or *On Christian Liberty*, published in both Latin and German in 1520, Luther links the freedom characteristic of the Christian with elements of obligation: 'A Christian is a perfectly free lord of all, subject to none'. Yet equally: 'A Christian is a perfectly dutiful servant of all, subject to all'.[9] We may interpret this tension-filled dual thesis in terms of modern sociological role theory: every 'Christian' plays certain roles, behaving as 'a dutiful servant'. Yet he is not entirely absorbed by any of his roles and, as an individual, is far more than and different from that which he has made of himself and which others are capable of discerning. It is precisely because of this that he as an individual is free in a fundamental sense.

Hence, the believer and his individual piety can no longer be adequately defined solely on the basis of his relationship to the church as institution. Rather, it is God's Word alone, *solus Christus*, that now crucially defines the religious sphere. In all Protestantisms, external control by the church and the imposed authority of clergy, their charisma of office based on their ordination, is replaced by an internal form of guidance geared solely towards God's indispensable Word. In Protestantism, the believer is released from the guardianship of the church as institution; in religious terms, he is defined solely by an immediacy to God mediated exclusively by Christ. Thus, in the diverse Protestantisms, a new and different mode of establishing authority was cultivated. The external authority of the ecclesiastical office was replaced by inner certainty, religious self-certainty, a subjective sense of being deeply moved by God's Word, faith in the Holy Spirit's capacity to manifest itself, an exclusive commitment to the indispensable Word

---

[9]   Martin Luther, 'Von der Freiheit eines Christenmenschen' (1520), in *D. Martin Luthers Werke. Kritische Gesamtausgabe*, vol. 7, Weimar, Hermann Böhlaus Nachfolger, pp. 20–38, here p. 21.

of God, which cannot be domesticated even by the church. This was the key argument put forward by the estates of the empire which, at the imperial diet of Speyer in April 1529, lodged a *protestatio* against the annulment of the decree enacted by the imperial diet of 1526 (and were thus described as 'Protestants' by the legal scholars of the time): 'In matters of God's glory and concerning the blessedness of souls, each must stand before God on his own behalf and give an account of himself.'[10]

Reform theology throws the individual more strongly back upon himself, giving the notion that man was made in God's image (Gen. 1:26f.), as found in the Creation myths of the Hebrew Bible, or Old Testament, a decidedly individualist interpretation. In his *Institutio Christianae Religionis*, Calvin declared that every human being, each and every individual, 'is the noblest and most perfect example of his justice, wisdom and goodness'.[11] The fact that the individual faces God as an individual through faith is, so to speak, an acknowledgement of the greatest individuality in the form of a religious symbol. In this sense it was no more than logical that the influential theorists of modern notions of human rights, above all John Locke, referred repeatedly to reformist, particularly Calvinist definitions of the *imago Dei* in interpreting the concept of human dignity.

When Protestant theologians and scholars more generally tried to define the specific nature of Protestantism, they developed languages of religious individu-alization. Tendencies towards internalization, spiritualization and subjectification are best illustrated through the Protestant concept of 'faith'. In Protestant discourse, having 'faith' does not mean considering something to be true, such as the teachings of the church as a whole or a particular church doctrine. Rather, faith involves the believer interpreting himself in a radically new way, a different perspective on himself, his life, the world. Faith is, as it were, an internal conversation with God, a process of reflection in which the individual ascertains the foundations of his life, his self. It is certainly not the church that brings about faith, through the charismatic authority of its bishops and priests for example, but the Holy Spirit alone, which moves us deeply through the Word of the Scriptures. But the Holy Spirit works when and as He pleases; in any event, as He creates new life, He is not tied down to the church as organization. Hence, the Catholic theological opponents of the reformers accused the Protestants of talking of faith in overly abstract and subjectivist fashion. They felt that the Reformation had brought the evil spirit of modern subjectivism

---

[10] 'Protestation der evangelischen Reichsstände, 20. April 1529', in *Deutsche Reichstagsakten Jüngere Reihe*, vol. 7.2: *Deutsche Reichstagsakten unter Kaiser Karl V.*, ed. Johannes Kühn, Göttingen, Vandenhoeck & Ruprecht, 2nd edn, 1963, p. 1277.

[11] John Calvin, *The Institutes of Christian Religion*, vol. I, ed. Tony Lane and Hilary Osborne, London, Hodder & Stoughton, 1986, p. 15, par. 1.

and individualism into the world, and the objection that the acatholici simply lacked sensuality and concreteness was soon part of the standard repertoire of their polemical anti-Protestantism. In the eyes of these critics, Protestantism was a pallid, plain religion, which reduced people to a single organ, the ear, through its fixation on the Word. In fact, with regard to faith, Protestants aimed neither to assimilate any kind of objectively fixed instructive substance nor to achieve direct sensory contact with 'holy' objects; Protestants have no icons to kiss, nor any saintly relics preserved in altars and subject to prayerful worship. In Protestant discourse faith is localized, as it were, on a categorically different level, through a kind of theory of religiously constituted individual subjectivity, and the origins of faith lie solely in the always individual state of being 'grasped' spiritually by divine truth. Thus, through an element of that which is fundamentally indispensable (the 'Word of God' or Gospel) faith simultaneously represents an element of the greatest subjectivity. Faith is my faith, or it is no faith at all. It therefore always brings about a fundamental individualization of piety, in the sense that all the devout individual's domestic social relationships, his ties to his family, his life within a particular class, his profession, but also his various social relationships within the community, are subordinate to the immediacy with which he is addressed by God's Word. It was precisely here, in the representation of individuality, that the Reformation brought about a linguistic revolution in German. In Protestant discourse, terms such as *Gewissen* (conscience), *innerer Mensch* (inner being), *Innerlichkeit* (introspection), *Herzensfrömmigkeit* (piety of the heart) and – since the eighteenth century – *Denkglaube* (belief in thought), *Vernunftglaube* (belief in reason) and *Persönlichkeit* (personality or personhood) functioned as emotionally charged formulae used to differentiate the *libertas christiana*, the 'freedom of a Christian' programmatically declared by Luther in 1520, from 'Roman spiritual coercion' and the 'spiritual servitude of the clergy'. Fundamentally, the 'priesthood of all believers' emphasized by the reformers meant the emancipation of the individual from having his mind made up for him by the church and from clerical control. It is true that modern political freedom cannot be derived directly from the religious autonomy outlined in the reformist theologies. Since Ernst Troeltsch's famous Stuttgart lecture, which became *Protestantism and Progress: A Historical Study of the Relation of Protestantism to the Modern World* [12] (1906), at the latest, it has been apparent that the Reformation and early Protestantism remained profoundly indebted to medieval concepts of order and that their religious impulses towards freedom with their inherent critique of tradition contributed to the achievement of political and social freedom only in a multiply fractured

---

[12]   Ernst Troeltsch, *Protestantism and Progress: A Historical Study of the Relation of Protestantism to the Modern World*, London, Crown Theological Library, 1912.

way, through extremely complex processes of mediation. But even such an uncompromising critic of all rash attempts to link Protestantism and modernity as the Heidelberg-based systematic theologian Ernst Troeltsch did not deny that the reformist movements had a modernizing impact over the long term, simply as a consequence of the denominational pluralization of Christianity, which entailed a permanent dispute over the correct interpretation of Christianity and replaced all dogmatically fixed truth and validity claims by a process of ongoing reflection. It is also apparent, with respect to the diverse religious reform and renewal movements within the various Protestantisms – that is, in acknowledging the role of Pietism, Puritanism, Methodism, the revitalization movement and North American Awakenings – that the self-mobilization of the resolutely pious always followed a pattern of critique of existing realities within Protestant worlds of faith; it was the nature of the Protestant church or of particular Protestant denominations at a given time that came under attack, as critics fell back on the *norma normans*, the Holy Scriptures, relativizing 'given' realities in light of the ideal source, the undiluted Word of God. They thus had an emancipatory impact in the sense that every institutional crystallization was made subject to a Protestant proviso. In their modern–anti-modern discontent with the contradictions of bourgeois society and capitalist economy, even the many conservative Protestantisms of the nineteenth and twentieth centuries continued to feature strong elements of protest underpinned by a salvation-oriented anarchism.

Through sects, small religious groups and revivalist circles as well as a strict form of church discipline (especially in the case of Calvinism), Protestantism helped shape a wide variety of new forms of moral obligation and stronger social discipline. At the same time, however, it made a profound contribution to the release of the individual from traditional ties, created an emotionally charged language of the individual in an immediate relationship with God, and opened up discursive spaces for radical institutional critique. All modern trends towards individualization begin with that culture of religious subjectivity founded in Martin Luther's reformist protest.

The Protestant view of the world: sacred profanity

The Jewish philosopher and cultural sociologist Helmuth Plessner has characterized Protestant piety, using a term from the eighteenth century, as *Weltfrömmigkeit* or worldly piety. We lack studies of the term's history. It is clear, though, that it was used critically before it took hold as an analytical key to a specifically Protestant piety. According to the Grimms' German Dictionary, the first evidence of the term is found as early as the political controversies over Nikolaus Ludwig Graf von Zinzendorf's Moravian Brethren. The Swiss doctor Johann Jacob Ritter for example, a prominent supporter of Zinzendorf, used the term to criticize a merely superficial, convenient, outward form of piety, devoid of genuine religiosity.[13] In the work of Goethe at the latest, however, *Weltfrömmigkeit* then took on a significantly different, positive meaning. The term now referred to a type of religiosity which endows life and the earthly realm as a whole with an attitude of fundamental awe in the face of the divine. Goethe contrasts the Pietists' *Hausfrömmigkeit*, which is focused on small private circles, with an active piety broadly anchored in the human realm:

> *Hausfrömmigkeit* is a principle from which we do not wish to withhold the praise it deserves. It forms the basis of the individual's security, upon which ultimately rest the stability and the dignity of the whole. But it is no longer sufficient. We must form the concept of *Weltfrömmigkeit*, put our genuine humanitarian concerns into practice on a broad scale, and further the good not only of those close to us but of all mankind.[14]

Later, it was above all keen readers of Goethe, such as Thomas Mann and Eduard Spranger,[15] who took up the term as a way of capturing, succinctly, the essence of a specifically Protestant focus on the earthly realm.

This 'new style of religious life' is crucially bound up with the fact that Protestantism developed an understanding of the world significantly different from that of Catholicism. In Protestant Germany, 'world', 'the worldly', 'secularism' and 'secularization' attained a resonance and meaning quite different from those they held in Roman Catholic discourse. All Catholic conceptions of 'culture', 'world' and 'society' are marked by a strict focus on the church as exclusive institution of salvation and powerful ethical institution. There is no Catholic theory of the social in which the ideal order of the community is not developed by the church as the institution with access to concise and unparalleled knowledge of the internal structures of the created world, the *ordines creationis* or orders of Creation. It is true that in a wide variety of interpretations of the *lex divina*, the divine law, and natural law, the Roman Catholic teaching office has always emphasized that, thanks to reason, everyone has some knowledge of these orders. But in its hamartiology, its doctrine of

---

[13]   See Johann Jacob Ritter, *Gedancken ueber die viele, die Herrnhuthische, eigentlich aber zu reden die Evangelischen Brüder Mährischer Unität betreffende Streit-Schrifften*, Leipzig, 1749, p. 57.

[14]   Johann Wolfgang von Goethe, *Wilhelm Meister's Journeyman Years* appears in *Conversations of German Refugees*, Princeton, Princeton University Press, 1995, p. 266 (translation modified).

[15]   See Eduard Spranger, *Weltfrömmigkeit*, Leipzig, Klotz, 1941.

sin, the Roman Catholic church also marks out the boundaries of this human capacity for rational knowledge of the true order imposed by original sin: as a sinner, the created human being discerns the good, divinely willed order of the world only in a distorted, obscured, limited way. Hence, he is dependent on the power of the church to provide direction and orientation, a church which not only provides people, or society in modern terms, with authoritative instructions on what they must do or refrain from doing, but above all provides such instruction to the powers that be – in modern terms, the state. Time and again, up to and including the most recent announcements by the teaching office of the Holy See, it is possible to observe the unambiguous assertion of the church's ethical predominance over the state, and society as a whole, in Roman Catholic discourse. At the same time, Catholic conceptions of the world, culture and society are often marked by a mode of thought involving two concisely distinguished but constitutively related spheres. In the Roman Catholic symbol system, the distinction between 'religious' and 'worldly', 'sacred' and 'profane' marks sharp dividing lines between imaginative worlds and spheres of life. In the focus on imagery, one of its key identifying features, in its cult of demonstrative sensuousness and visibility, the Roman Catholic church generates self-contained worlds of the sacred; these may be experienced physically, and represent the sacred Other of the mere world. It is chiefly here, at the holy sites of the *sancta ecclesia Romana*, that religious life takes place. Such localized sacredness – of churches, chapels, places of pilgrimage, altars, Marian columns, crosses or wayside shrines that define public space in religious terms, etc. – is partly constituted and partly reinforced by its consecration. In contrast to Protestant denominational cultures, in which the consecration of churches is conceived as their opening, namely their taking into use by the congregation, and is liturgically organized, in Catholicism all kinds of objects are consecrated, with the help of holy water and holy words, which often create the impression that we are now dealing with an object sanctified by the church. Catholic cultures of piety feature extensive belief in the spiritual efficacy of such holy objects, such as an image of the Madonna or a shroud depicting the face of Jesus himself, surrounded by an aura of authenticity, and there are ordained priests who kiss the altar and, through the swinging of censers, make it clear even to the individual's sense of smell that he is now present at a sacred place in which holy acts are performed. Hence, Protestant critics are quick to ascribe to Catholics a more or less magical relationship to the world – thus implying, at times, associations with sorcery or shamanism. However this may be, here the 'world' is consistently conceived as merely the sphere of everyday life, which contrasts with and is inferior to the sacred.

Protestantism on the other hand has an inherent tendency towards the religious valorization of the world. The doctrine of the Christian's 'worldly vocation', developed by Luther in his various ethical texts, is fundamental to reformist theology; this concept of vocation was radicalized further by other reformers. Luther sees the pardoned sinner set down by his Saviour in his own particular place in the world. Here, in his particular abode, he is to fulfil his specific responsibilities, in awe of God, to the benefit of his neighbour, as lived service to God. Rather than special holy acts, such as participating in pilgrimages, donating candles, or purchasing memorial services to influence the fate of the departed in the hereafter, it is every activity carried out in the service of one's neighbour that constitutes one's service to God, if performed by the individual with a strong awareness of religious responsibility, with humility before the Creator.

In a structurally analogous way to the teaching of the priesthood of all believers, this concept of vocation is anti-hierarchical in nature. The professor fulfils his obligations by being a good academic teacher and curious researcher, the farmer by actively ensuring the wellbeing of his fields and livestock. The mother serves God when she takes care of her children and looks after her household. But in Protestant vocational discourse there is no standardized hierarchy of activities. The work of the professor or doctor is no more valuable, religiously worthy, or pleasing to God than the mother's cooking, cleaning and changing nappies. For in all cases, prayer takes the form of deeds, and everyday life is organized in the spirit of service to God. In this way, the reformist teaching of the Christian's worldly vocation promotes a pronounced ethos of service, duty and achievement as well as a religious charging of that practical habitus for which the term 'responsibility' later took hold.

In his famous collection of essays published as *The Protestant Ethic and the Spirit of Capitalism* (1904/05), Max Weber attempted to shed light on the major practical cultural consequences of Luther's understanding of vocation. In Protestant discourse, 'vocation', 'duty', 'class' and 'world' take on the religious resonance of the crucial sites in which faith, a *vita Christiana*, is truly lived. Particularly with reference to the heroic work ethic of the Puritans, Troeltsch and Weber spoke of 'innerworldly asceticism' – though the two Heidelberg-based scholars, who enjoyed a 'friendship of experts', would not have been able to agree on who held the copyright on this suggestive term[16] – thus pointing to a crucial practical cultural consequence of the reformist doctrine of vocation: precisely because Protestantism, with its doctrine of justification, rejected all notion of meritorious works of faith or, in the language of the old polemical Protestant anti-Catholicism, all 'justification by works', it produced,

---

[16]   See Friedrich Wilhelm Graf, 'Friendship between Experts: Notes on Weber and Troeltsch', in Wolfgang J. Mommsen and Jürgen Osterhammel (eds.), *Max Weber and his Contemporaries*, London, Allen & Unwin, 1987, pp. 215–33.

paradoxically enough, a religiously founded, worldly attitude privileging the active pursuit of achievements, a habitus of divinely willed, unrelenting doing, creating and planning. At any rate, the religious energies of the ideal Protestant were directed towards changing the world for the better; tireless and industrious, he willingly embraced renunciation and was ready to make sacrifices. The term *Weltbemächtigung*, which implies taking power over the world, was coined in Protestant Germany. It is precisely the unspectacular, seemingly purely profane that takes on the character of a religious obligation. In this way, the world is on the one hand de-clericalized, and on the other religiously valorized. The divine is no longer marked off within specific realms of the holy, but rather shines through the worldliness of our profane life. However, these entirely everyday processes of active sanctification also entail the potential for escalation: a fair number of Protestants tend towards hyperactivity for its own sake, and they leave little time for themselves and others. It is, not least, temporal concepts and orders that lay bare specific features of Protestantism in contrast to Roman Catholicism: by abolishing the saints' days and other festivals, Protestants gained a far greater number of working days, a surplus of working hours. On top of this (though many Protestant church functionaries now seem unaware of this fact), the reformers allowed the faithful to work on Sunday because work is itself service to God.[17] In this sense, 'the Devil finds work for idle hands' may be regarded as a genuinely Protestant saying.

Protestants' tendency towards consistent, religiously inspired rationalization of their way of life is particularly apparent in the Protestant approach to time. The ideal Protestant divides up his time with great precision; no layabout, he cultivates an attitude of rational self-discipline. In contrast to 'Catholic zest for life', 'baroque joie de vivre' and the economically unproductive 'idleness of pilgrims', as the most common stereotypes would have it, Protestantism, particularly its reformed variants and the diverse 'sects', also means obeying the law, strict morality, rigorously applied, and compulsive standardization. This mania for order is one of the key reasons for the moral terrorism which Calvin and Zwingli encouraged in Switzerland in the name of 'church discipline'. Particularly within the English-speaking Protestantisms, there also developed a kind of 'Golden Rule Christianity':[18] the transformation of lived faith into a moral code for both individuals and groups of the devout.

But over the long term, the reformers themselves and their successors were concerned less with the imposition of external or 'social discipline' on the part

---

[17]   See Michael Maurer, 'Der Sonntag in der frühen Neuzeit', *Archiv für Kulturgeschichte*, 88 (2006), pp. 75–100.

[18]   See Nancy Ammerman, *Pillars of Faith*, Berkeley, University of California Press, 2005.

of church or political authorities than with a dramatically increased, religiously induced willingness to discipline oneself. An internal sense of obligation always achieves more than external coercion (however strong and perfect it may be); but this assertion already reflects the attitude of a Protestant. 'To overcome oneself', to resist the many sensual temptations, refrain from taking the easier path, to diligently do one's duty, to cope with the (Kantian) opposition between duty and inclination, to follow the unconditional demands of conscience, and to accept the isolation which may result from the moral decision – this is the semantics that characterizes this form of religious readiness. On the one hand, the tendency towards strict moral self-discipline may be associated with compulsiveness, harshness (towards oneself and others) and a strict morality, thin lips and arrogant belittlement of sinners. Yet on the other hand, it also fosters the 'cultural surplus value' of a strict, rationalized way of life: more time, increased efficiency, an emotionally charged view of objectivity.

Since the classical debates on the 'cultural significance' of Protestantism, the question of the extent to which Protestantism or particular Protestantisms have helped shape the modern world has been posed time and again. In view of the great internal diversity of Protestantisms, generalizing statements are too abstract to be of much use. It is nonetheless possible to state that, in its many and diverse shades and refractions, Protestant *Weltfrömmigkeit* encouraged the formation of a specifically bourgeois elite culture, especially in Western Europe and the USA. As a rule, devout Protestants have been far more willing to adopt a way of life that eschewed hedonism than Catholics, and when they enjoy, they often do so with a 'bad conscience'. Conscious of sin, they cultivate ascetic struggle and the renunciation of pleasure, while the suppression of urges may also be a sign of particular fidelity to God. Because the ideal typical Protestant cannot and has no wish to 'let himself go', he must 'restrain' himself, 'do his duty' and 'work on himself'. Prussian virtues gained a Protestant patina, as did intellectual diligence and pleasure in progress. This makes many Protestants seem strangely compulsive and tends not to make them the most cheerful of individuals. Quite the opposite: with their moral fervour and their earnestness with respect to fulfilment of duty, abiding by the law and self-discipline, they can be very hard work. But their pronounced embrace of religiously grounded self-discipline has also increasingly enabled them to accumulate both cultural and financial capital, and by no means only within the bourgeois Protestantisms of the economic and educational elite. The economic success stories of the Pietists, as well as the high growth rates of the new Pentecostal churches in competitive religious markets today, show that a moral economy marked by Protestant stringency, a willingness to practise innerworldly asceticism and the rational-ization of one's way of life already provides profits of redemption in the midst of the earthly realm. As they are more diligent and industrious, Protestants can put more 'aside', save, build capital. The intensely lived faith of the diverse revitalization movements of the late eighteenth and nineteenth centuries already helped the 'little people' to attain a degree of prosperity through abstention. Protestant *Weltfrömmigkeit* often functioned as a motive for, and aid to, social advancement as well: the dense networks of solidarity that developed in the small circles and prayer groups of the especially pious reinforced a work ethic that created surplus value through hard work. We may, for good social historical reasons, dispute Max Weber's thesis that the innerworldly asceticism of the Puritans in seventeenth-century England fostered the development of a 'spirit of capitalism'. But the categories through which Weber sought to reconstruct the genesis of a habitus compatible with capitalism, imparted partly through religion, are analytically helpful at least to the extent that they sensitize us to possible non-religious consequences of Protestant piety. This applies particularly with respect to the present: in his classic work *Tongues of Fire: The Explosion of Protestantism in Latin America*,[19] British sociologist of religion David Martin has shown that in Latin America the conversion of women, their rejection of the Roman Catholic church and embrace of the Pentecostal communities, is partly bound up with the expectation of being better able to cope with their difficult lives and escaping the poverty trap. All the studies of the revivalist revolutions engineered by the Pentecostalists in Latin America, Africa and Asia show, with very different methodological tools, that this ecstatic neo-Protestantism, whose origins lie in the pious worlds of US Methodists and Evangelicals, owes its fascinatingly rapid missionary successes in part to a *kerygma* of well-being: because they have experienced their individual dignity through the Holy Spirit, the Pentecostals feel better, and thanks to their very Protestant ethos of hard work, cleanliness, focus on the nuclear family, faithfulness in marriage and investment in their children's education, they are soon living much better as well – by the next generation at the latest. As a result, the English-speaking literature often characterizes the faith of the Pentecostals as the 'prosperity gospel' or the 'health and wealth gospel'.[20]

One of the consequences of the boom in an economic- and business-oriented ethic observable over the past twenty years or so is that old questions about the affinity of modern Protestantism with capitalism have been reformulated in a number of ways. From a German perspective, we must relativize the notion,

---

[19]   David Martin, *Tongues of Fire: The Explosion of Protestantism in Latin America*, Oxford, Blackwell, 1990; see also his chapter in the present volume.

[20]   See Stephen Hunt, 'Winning Ways: Globalisation and the Impact of the Health and Wealth Gospel', *Journal of Contemporary Religion*, 15 (2000), pp. 331–47. With particular reference to Africa, see David Maxwell, 'Delivered from the Spirit of Poverty', *Journal of Religion in Africa*, 28 (1998), pp. 350–73.

consistently promulgated in the USA in particular, that in its high regard for the free, active, entrepreneurial individual, Protestantism is the religion of the free market. Protestantism as such, in all its various forms, neither promotes capitalism nor is it even well-disposed towards it. Many believers in Protestant churches reacted to the dramatic social crises associated with the rise of modern bourgeois society, and especially capitalist industrial production, by throwing themselves, in a quite fascinating way, into welfarist activities in aid of the newly marginalized. In Germany, ministers influenced by Pietism and revivalism, but also aristocrats and members of the educated middle classes distinguished by their 'piety of the heart', took the initiative to found societies of the 'Home Mission', which wished to provide a 'buffer' for those uprooted by the radical changes taking place at the time, which were experienced as catastrophic. This included institutes for people with disabilities, sanatoriums for the mentally ill and insane, homes for unemployed youths, institutions for the care of orphans, elite schools for the especially pious, *Bahnhofsmissionen* for those stranded within the new rail system and a wide variety of other aids to integration for economic migrants, immigrants and those who had, in one way or another, gone astray. The religious message bound up with this, that only one's bond with the Saviour gives one's life an aim, meaning and stability, may be thought socio-politically naive or aimed at restoring the old order – but it would be very hard to deny that this social Protestantism, with its strong paternalistic tenor, offered concrete, valuable support to a very large number of people in dire straits and, in terms of political ideas, provided powerful impulses for the debate on the welfare state in the German empire and especially Bismarck's statist social corporatism. Hence, time and again within the debates on the 'cultural significance' of the diverse Protestantisms, the thesis has been put forward that the reformed, Calvinist Protestantisms primarily strengthened human rights, participatory democracy and republicanism, whereas, thanks to their traditional orientation towards the *bonum commune* and doctrine of the three estates, the Lutherans had their main political impact in the direction of social ethics and ideals of the social or welfare state. Alongside developments in Germany, which saw Lutheran neo-corporative social paternalism and the Roman Catholic code of social ethics play a formative role as 'ideal orders', that is, both as models of institutional architecture and as resources of legitimacy, evidence of this is also to be found among the Lutheran *Volkskirchen* of Scandinavia; here, in the predominantly, almost exclusively Protestant north of Europe, welfare state and *Volkskirche* are so closely intertwined, so fused together, that Lutheran thought and ethical *theologoumena* continue to influence the social democrats' concepts of the welfare state.

Another example of this statist social Protestantism, which is more or less critical of capitalism, was the *Bund der Evangelischen Kirchen in der DDR* (BEK), the federation of Protestant churches in the GDR. While the guiding theological figures of the church Protestantism of the GDR saw themselves as prophets of a very different, better German Protestantism, in a number of ways they continued the traditions of an anti-capitalism anchored in a romantic view of society that dominated the ethical discourses within German Lutheranism from the early nineteenth century on.[21] In their debates on the aims of the state and the order of society (which they imagined primarily as a morally binding community), leading Lutheran ethicists consistently displayed a profound anguish at the rise of modern bourgeois society. Conservative anti-capitalism and moral abhorrence towards the competitive economy; a habitus marked by reserve towards parliamentary democracy and a qualitative understanding of freedom that contrasted with liberal 'formalism', an understanding that enables one to conceive of freedom in terms of an ethical bond with the community, in terms of responsibility and morality; traumas brought about by the experience of that permanent temporal acceleration specific to modernity and a profound scepticism towards the modern belief in happiness, the idea that the novel, the modern is also the better – all are key elements of a mentality of scepticism towards modernity still characteristic of some milieux within German church Protestantism.

Even clearer traces of this mentality were to be found within the church Protestantism of the GDR, and the phrase 'church through socialism' in particular, promoted by leading representatives of the GDR federation of churches, shows that, regardless of the massive persecution of many Christians by the East German state and its *Stasi* secret police, prominent church functionaries were of one mind with the country's rulers in their critique of Western economic liberalism. If we are to grasp the multiply fractured 'elective affinities' between Protestantism and modernity with the necessary degree of historical subtlety, we must also take account of these firmly anti-liberal currents of Protestantism. Time and again, to be sure, many Protestants have described themselves as specifically well-suited to modernity, quite often with the emotional charge of progressive liberality. Yet already from the late eighteenth century, particularly in Germany, when Protestantism split into at least two competing milieux, moral Protestants with an awareness of social crisis also developed a great ability to diagnose the whole range of social upheavals, costs, damage to society and psychological disasters associated with this dramatic 'modernization'. Protestants were both emphatic modernizers and utterly distraught by modernity.

---

[21]   See Friedrich Wilhelm Graf, 'Eine Ordnungsmacht eigener Art. Theologie und Kirchenpolitik im DDR-Protestantismus', in Hartmut Kaelble, Jürgen Kocka and Hartmut Zwahr (eds.), *Sozialgeschichte der DDR*, Stuttgart, Klett-Cotta, 1994, pp. 295–321.

Enjoying the boom: the holy *Zeitgeist*

Notions of the continuation or completion of the Reformation, of a 'second Reformation', the legitimation of programmes of social and political reform by harking back to the Reformation of the sixteenth century and, ultimately, the interpretation of the Reformation as *the* cultural 'Revolution', have moulded the self-interpretations of Protestant elites since Pietism and the early Enlightenment at the latest. Fundamentally, 'history' and the conflictual plurality of historical processes are interpreted in a dynamic way, as a break with an erroneous past, as critique of tradition, departure from ossified forms and new beginning, as permanent reform on the basis of principles legitimized in light of the normative source, the Holy Scriptures. Liberal Protestants in particular wished to be prime movers, marching in the vanguard of social progress; while associating Catholicism with 'traditionalism', 'inertia', 'fixation on authority', 'backwardness' and the 'Dark Ages', they eagerly linked Protestantism, not least on account of the principle of the *ecclesia semper reformanda*, with 'dynamism', 'movement', 'mobility', 'adaptability', 'flexibility', an ever new 'modernity' and openness to the *Zeitgeist*. Rather than taking their lead from that which is supposedly eternally unchanging and timeless, as symbolized with unparalleled perfection in a trans-generational institution which asserts its legitimacy in terms of the apostolic succession, Protestants, at least liberal ones, were – the expression comes from Catholic polemics on Protestantism – 'christened with eau de Cologne', that is, trendy.

Protestant self-attribution of marked sensitivity to the present and openness to modernity points to a highly ambivalent and ambiguous aspect of religious culture. On the one hand, Protestant elites kicked off and contributed to processes of cultural modernization to a far greater extent than leading Catholic groups, and they were the leading innovators, the avant-garde, in the most varied of cultural spheres. On the other hand, this also exposed them more to the temptations of the *Zeitgeist* and thanks to their strong focus on their own religious subjectivity, they were less resistant to all kinds of modern ideologies of integration and attempts to establish new religious doctrines. With their susceptibility to 'movement', the various new Protestantisms arising from the eighteenth century on were prone to fusion with a diverse array of political ideologies of mobilization to a far greater degree than the various Catholicisms. It was above all the most important modern ideology of integration, nationalism, that the leading Protestant thinkers credited with a positive impact in terms of social morality. In all the dominant Protestant countries in Europe as well as in God's own country across the Atlantic, models of the nation were drawn up to a striking degree with specifically Protestant theologoumena, such as notions of the God-given holy land or the metaphor, rooted in the theology of predestination, of the chosen people.[22] When the Protestant Prussian empire without Austria was created through the war of 1870–1871, Prussian historians, along with Protestant philosophers, theologians and cultural interpreters of every stripe celebrated the foundation of the Reich as the political 'completion of the Reformation'. The Protestant transfer of religious energies to the 'cultural nation' and its 'cultural state', the sacralization of one's own nation, which became a worldly source of salvation, inevitably entailed the stigmatization of non-Protestants as second-class citizens. In Germany, this by no means applied solely to the Jews, who many Protestant scholars and intellectuals expected to convert reasonably rapidly to Protestantism for the sake of the nation's internal unity, but just as much to the Roman Catholic minority, who were accused of all those things for which 'Muslims' are now being attacked within the depressing debate on religious policy unfolding in Germany: lack of commitment to the nation, dependence on foreign powers, unwillingness (or inability) to integrate, educational deficiency and cultural inferiority, worshipping in a foreign language. In the harsh state–church struggles which occurred in many denominationally mixed European societies in the nineteenth century, and which became particularly virulent in its second half,[23] the various Protestantisms demonstrated explosive mental fusions of cultural arrogance, fantasies of omnipotence, intolerance and contempt. Through the linkage of a cultural nation integrated through Protestant cultural values with anti-pluralist models fixated on homogeneity, the proud valorization of the 'freedom of a Christian', for which Luther had once fought, could rapidly be replaced by discrimination against and exclusion of the Other. Tremendous ambivalence is not a specifically Protestant phenomenon; it is constitutive of all symbolic religious languages. For religious semantics, such as the notion of God, may sensitize the individual to his finite nature, encourage him to impose restrictions upon himself in a considered way and thus strengthen the potential for humble respect for the other. Yet to precisely the extent to which the *homo religiosus* equates himself with God and feels himself to be in a state of harmony with God through direct mystical union, religious symbolism may also lead to the drawing of exclusionary boundaries, absolutization of the self and megalomaniac fantasies. All religions, and by no means only the three monotheistic religious families of Judaism, Islam and Christianity, have exhibited and continue to exhibit something of this tendency. But it may be that, as a

---

[22]   Some case studies of sacralized Protestant models of the nation can be found in Heinz-Gerhard Haupt and Dieter Langewiesche (eds.), *Nation und Religion in der deutschen Geschichte*, Frankfurt, Campus, 2001.

[23]   See James Hunter, *Culture Wars*, New York, Basic Books, 1991; Christopher Clark and Wolfram Kaiser (eds.), *Culture Wars: Secular–Catholic Conflict in Nineteenth Century Europe*, Cambridge, Cambridge University Press, 2003.

result of the programmatic pre-eminence of the devout individual over the institution of the church, Protestants are at particular risk here. At any rate, the tremendous scope of 'political Protestantism' supports this conclusion. The spectrum ranges from radical socialist left-wing Protestantisms to profoundly authoritarian Protestant thinkers on the political right focused on social order. A history of ideas concerned specifically with Protestant political concepts would include eco-Pietist crackpots and religious members of undogmatic leftist groups alongside radical nationalist, anti-Semitic 'German Christians'. Through the representative example of greater Berlin, recent research in social history has shown the unbridled intensity with which the great majority of the Protestants and especially ministers living there allowed themselves to be mobilized, on a huge scale, for the Nazis' 'German Revolution' – or, to be more precise, through their faith in the inner unity of Protestantism and nation, joined the new movement of their own accord.[24]

In the USA, the 'rainbow coalition' is also legitimized with reference to the spirit of the nation's Protestant origins, as is an evangelical Biblicism which abhors the open, liberal society as sinful secularism and thus, in a cultural struggle against evil couched in dramatic eschatological terms, seeks out ever new opponents or, in line with its self-image, enemies of God, which it wishes either to exclude from the national community or even to eliminate. The aggressive intolerance of these evangelical 'fundamentalisms' is notorious, as is their tendency towards crusading rhetoric and their battle to replace the theory of evolution with creationism in state schools (or at least to achieve equal status for it). The question of why these hard-core evangelical Protestantisms have continually managed to attract so many new followers and have markedly increased their political power over the last thirty years is surely of greater analytical interest than the sermonizing so common within the German discourse. Severe religion demands a great deal, but offers a great deal as well: a crisis-resistant, and thus identity-strengthening worldview featuring clear distinctions between in-group and out-group, between 'us and the evil others'; clear moral norms and a system of 'values' that is unconditionally binding because it is rooted in divine law itself, a system which offers reliability and secure guidance in times of 'repressive tolerance' (H. Marcuse), 'new lack of clarity' (J. Habermas) or the 'dictatorship of relativism' (Benedict XVI); thorough socialization into stable communities, networks of lived charity characterized by the homogeneity of their political ideas; a religious practice marked by the experience of rebirth, certainty about one's status as chosen, the presence of the Holy Spirit and prayerful fidelity, a practice which makes it possible to develop

---

[24]   See Manfred Gailus, *Protestantismus und Nationalsozialismus. Studien zur nationalsozialistischen Durchdringung des protestantischen Sozialmilieus in Berlin*, Cologne, Böhlau, 2001.

a very strong identity; and the humble proud awareness of oneself as a unique individual being before God and for God.

As much as Lutherans in particular wished to concretize 'God's law' in stable worldly institutions, in 'good worldly orders' in which people who simply are sinful would live together in the most peaceful and secure way possible, Protestant introspective anarchism, observable among Lutherans as well as among Calvinists, also made its presence felt in an extraordinarily unstable political mentality. Twentieth-century German Protestantism featured examples, both irritating and repulsive, of a political habitus which may be described in terms of the over-moralization of the political; a hunger for 'holistic' evidence; professions of faith to political ends; and the giving of prophetic witness. Markedly less often than Catholics, at least in the German 'century of extremes' (E. Hobsbawm), Protestants committed themselves once and for all to just one political milieu, from the cradle to the grave as it were. Many Protestants readily act on conviction, moral heroes of the unity of the inner and outer world, and as a result tend to have little time for pragmatism and compromise. In terms of political mentality and habitus, it is often possible to observe a specifically Protestant pattern: having successfully devalued the institution of the church, Protestants invest a great deal of mental energy in the political sphere, which is over-legitimated in religious and moral terms; the flipside of de-clericalization is the tendency to endow the political realm with a religious charge, to over-moralize political conflicts and hold pragmatic arrangements in low regard. Prominent 'church leaders' and theologians are particularly well known for moving right across the political spectrum during times of historic upheaval, but with the proud certainty that they have merely remained true to themselves and have always been right (and still are). Theologians who distinguished themselves as bitter opponents of the Weimar Republic and campaigned for the *Deutschnationale Volkspartei* could in 1933 celebrate the National Socialists' 'German revolution' as a divinely ordained *kairos* for a comprehensive re-Christianization of the *Volksgemeinschaft* or People's Community perverted by 'secularism', yet following the Allied victory and the foundation of the two German states along national Protestant lines, reject 'Adenauer's Western state' as a project of Catholic clerics and, opposing integration into the West, rearmament and NATO membership, now involve themselves partly in Gustav Heinemann's *Gesamtdeutscher Volkspartei* or All-German People's Party and partly in the pacifist *Deutschen Friedensunion* or German Peace Union, before switching, in view of the GVP's ongoing lack of success, to the SPD in 1957. There are good social historical reasons to doubt that such a polarizing figure as Martin Niemöller represented the patterns of mentality, perception of the world and habitus of German Protestantism as a whole. Yet his political routes, sometimes circuitous, 'from the U-Boot to the pulpit', which led a Nazi party voter to concentration camps as Hitler's 'personal prisoner', and later brought the world war hero to the podia of the peace movement as Hessian regional church leader, may be considered significant, at least to a particular milieu of church Protestantism. A self-perception unhindered even by flagrant mistakes and an understanding of one's role, often enough resistant to reality, as a political preceptor with special moral competence are at any rate still characteristic of the public statements of some Protestant church leaders.

Ecclesiological minimalism: tolerance of ambiguity

Complexes of theological ideas, such as the notion of the omnipotence of God, of His sovereignty, of the indispensability of His Word; or the notions of His two kingdoms, modes of ruling and governance; or the notion of a permanent struggle between God and the Devil; or the structuring of time in line with models of a *Heilsgeschichte* which places responsibility on the Christian to gradually bring about the Kingdom of God, etc. – always have a more or less implicit political content as well. Even those who consider Carl Schmitt's famous thesis that all significant concepts of the modern theory of the state are merely secularized theological concepts [25] overdone or false will not dispute that scholarly discussions of God *sub specie Dei*, with a view to the absolute, inevitably sketch out certain ideal orders of Creation, of the world as whole, of the good life. In theological doctrines, the basic structures of created reality, for example, are inferred (or set out), so-called 'orders of Creation', which are granted a binding normative force for human beings, God's noblest creation. In addition, since the original laying down of God's laws in Sinai, all three great monotheistic religious families have been guided by the notion that all human law-making must be logically grounded in the *lex divina*, *lex aeterna*, God's eternal law; thus, 'positive' law, laid down by human beings, must correspond to the law of God in terms of its inner content. [26]

When, in the language games of old European metaphysics, theologians refer to God's omnipotence and endow the Christian 'observer God' (N. Luhmann) with attributes such as omniscience and perfect wisdom, they must also necessarily explain the abilities and powers attributed to God with regard to His impact on the world, His active preservation of that which He has created. Is worldly power strengthened or limited by God's omnipotence? When pious

---

[25]   See Carl Schmitt, *Political Theology: Four Chapters on the Concept of Sovereignty* (1922), Cambridge, MA, MIT Press, 1985, p. 36.

[26]   On the history of the notion of God's law and the associated present-day legal conflicts, see Friedrich Wilhelm Graf, *Moses Vermächtnis. Über göttliche und menschliche Gesetze*, Munich, Beck, 2006.

individuals live their faith actively and attempt to have their religious and moral convictions accepted beyond their own religious community, their faith becomes politically significant. With the centuries of ever new conflicts between pope and emperor, church and state, faith and politics at the latest, it becomes apparent that, in metaphorically coded form, symbolic religious languages always sketch out ideal orders of social co-existence and communicate claims to a role in shaping (or helping to shape) the political sphere. The theological discourses of the reform Christianities have had a particularly powerful political impact. On account of Protestants' great importance within political elites, reformist theologoumena have become particularly important to both the legitimation and limitation of political power and construction of political institutions. In all these processes, however, the theological traditions of the various Protestantisms proved to be politically ambiguous. Images and concepts found in the doctrine of Creation could be used both to draw up theories legitimating a strong early absolutist state and as models justifying the limitation of the monarch's powers by self-confident estates. Far more than the medieval church (and, later, Roman Catholic doctrine), the reformers underlined the essential sinfulness of human beings, their enslavement to the destructive power of the Evil One. The more critical, the more negative the view of the human being, the greater the need to create powerful institutions which act as countervailing powers to keep a tight rein on evil and evil people; this is the political point of Lutheran hamartiology, the doctrine of the constitutive sinfulness even of the saved. But the religious languages of Creation and the dogmatic *locus de creatione* also open up the possibility of formulating very different political perspectives on the human being as citizen. The human being is created *in imago Dei*, in the image of God, and thus every woman and every man possesses a dignity as God's highest creation that precedes the state, with which each is endowed by her or his personal Creator; human dignity and the human rights derived from it are the most momentous political transformation of the assurance provided in Genesis 1:27: 'So God created man in his own image, in the image of God he created him'.[27] Hence, in his famous study *The Declaration of the Rights of Man and of Citizens*, with a certain amount of cultural Protestant pride, the Heidelberg-based scholar of constitutional law Georg Jellinek, son of a liberal Viennese rabbi and close friend of Ernst Troeltsch and Max Weber, demolished the thesis that modern human rights were first codified in the French Revolution,

---

[27]   Of the wealth of political texts relevant in this context, I will mention just the American Declaration of Independence of 4 July 1776: 'We hold these truths to be self-evident, that all men are created equal, that they are endowed by their Creator with certain unalienable Rights, that among these are Life, Liberty and the pursuit of Happiness.'

constructing a genuinely Protestant, Calvinist-Puritan genealogy of modern notions of human rights.[28]

No social or cultural science possesses a theory sophisticated enough to capture the ways in which ideas, let alone the conceptual contents of religious consciousness, mould and impact upon society. The one certainty is that ideas always have an impact. As hopeful images of a better future, they may mobilize people and instil fanaticism, or as models of contempt and prejudicial stereotypes they may help produce tremendous hatred, legitimizing exclusion, violence and even annihilation. Current trends, which entail the return en masse of religious actors to public spaces, illustrate perfectly the fundamental ambivalence of all religious phenomena, which may sacralize subjective certainties in such a way that they take on the aura of ultimate truth, beyond discursive interrogation, and trigger strong emotions. Of course, ideas not only have an impact, but are also brought about, shaped and partly determined by social realities, cultural institutions, political conflicts, the specific interests of particular groups such as estates and corporations, classes or new social movements. This may explain why the political theories of the various Protestantisms turned out so differently; depending on the context, the basic religious ideas of the Reformation could assume concrete form in very different models of political order and institutions.

The differences in ethical doctrine between Lutherans and the reformed churches have been a key topic of Protestant theology and cultural theory since the eighteenth century. In the *Vormärz*, the period of German history from 1815 to the revolution in March 1848, under the influence of new religious movements in all churches, Carl Bernhard Hundeshagen and Matthias Schneckenburger in particular sought to grasp the basic differences between the Lutheran and reformed ethos and to explore the political consequences of their theological models of order. They had no hesitation in working with a basic distinction between active and passive, activist and quiescent. Lutheranism was ascribed a more passive political mentality, a tendency to accept given circumstances, Calvinism a clamorously progressive political activism. In their studies of Protestantism, Weber and Troeltsch also took their lead from this overdrawn contrast between the political and economic consequences of the two Protestant denominations. For them, the reformed, Calvinist, western Protestantism was the more modern,

---

[28]   Georg Jellinek, *The Declaration of the Rights of Man and of Citizens: A Contribution to Modern Constitutional History* (1895), Westport, CT, Hyperion, 1979; on the discursive milieu of cultural Protestantism, a milieu which had a formative influence on constitutional and international legal scholars, see Friedrich Wilhelm Graf, 'Puritanische Sektenfreiheit versus lutherische Volkskirche. Zum Einfluß Georg Jellineks auf religionsdiagnostische Deutungsmuster Max Webers und Ernst Troeltschs', *Zeitschrift für Neuere Theologiegeschichte/ Journal for the History of Modern Theology*, 9 (2002), pp. 42–69.

impactful form, while Lutheranism was associated with a cult of authority and an acceptance of given circumstances involving a willingness to suffer. As recently as the debates on a German *Sonderweg* or special path to modernity, in the historians' dispute over the question of whether the political disaster of the Nazi dictatorship must be traced back to elementary, long-term flaws in German political culture, this critical view of a submissive dependence on the powers that be, allegedly specific to Lutheranism, played a key role. However, recent research in the history of Christianity, and above all the debate on conversion to denominational status carried on by historians studying the early modern period, have radically revised this picture. Time and again, Lutheran ministers protested against authorities which, in their theological view, were failing to take their lead from God's law, and within Lutheran denominational cultures the message was always conveyed, as a knowledge of difference, that the world as it is at present is far from the status of paradise.[29]

In Calvinism and Lutheranism, it proved possible to combine the genuinely Protestant principle of the priesthood of all the faithful with very different models of political order. Developments in the Lutheran territories of the old Reich were chiefly determined by so-called 'church government by the sovereign princes', the transferral of Episcopal functions to these rulers. In many Lutheran lifeworlds, this encouraged tendencies towards the blending of the political and the religious, worldly and church institutions, with the result that loyalty to the rulers was sacralized to the point of 'state piety'. Knowledge of the provisional nature and fragility of all worldly orders, formulated above all in theories of the church, was crucial to the great internal diversity of Protestantism and the constant branching off of new Protestant denominational cultures. In the *Confessio Augustana*, the Protestant estates of the empire settled on a minimalist understanding of the church. Article VII '*De Ecclesia*/Of the Church' states: '[1] Also they teach that one holy Church is to continue forever. But the Church is the assembly of all believers, in which the Gospel is purely preached and the Sacraments rightly administered according to the Gospel. [2] And unto the true unity of the Church, it is sufficient to agree concerning the doctrine of the Gospel and the administration of the Sacraments. [3] Nor is it necessary that human traditions, rites, or ceremonies instituted by men should be alike every where.'[30]

This theological insight that the 'nature' of the church must be defined in solely functional terms, with reference to the preaching of the Word and administering of the sacraments, opened up to the various Protestantisms a tremendous adaptability and elasticity with respect to all issues of organization.

---

[29]   See Thomas Kaufmann, *Konfession und Kultur. Lutherischer Protestantismus in der zweiten Hälfte des Reformationsjahrhunderts*, Tübingen, Mohr Siebeck, 2006.

[30]   Adapted from http://www.ccel.org/ccel/schaff/creeds3.iii.ii.html.

At the same time, it relieved them of the burden of conceiving of the workings of the Holy Spirit in fixed institutional terms, and opened up the prospect of greater tolerance of ambiguity. US-based theologian Mark Noll has identified 'the gift of ambiguity' as a characteristic of Lutheranism in particular. The Protestant individual lives in the midst of the world while being aware that he is different from it. He remains bound to its many ambiguities while finding distinct self-certainty in the knowledge that he is saved by his merciful God. Aware of the provisional nature of this world, he also knows that it is safe in God's hands – an understanding which daily strengthens his readiness to shape the world in a responsible way.

3

The Departure and Return of God: Secularization and Theologization in Judaism

Eckart Otto

Our experience of religions is ambivalent. In Central Europe, particularly Germany, the public importance of religious communities, especially the Christian churches, seems to be declining; this appears to be the continuation of a long-term trend that is constantly invoked or regretted. In other parts of the world, we are seeing a truly astonishing revitalization of religious communities within Islam, Hinduism and Buddhism, but also Christianity, in North and South America for example. Taking one of the world religions, Judaism, as a paradigm, this chapter investigates the causes of each process, the secularization and theologization of public life, but above all the question of whether there are connections between these developments, which appear to run counter to one another. We will see that the dialectic of secularization and theologization merely involves shifts within one and the same system, which, already discernible in antiquity, are by no means a characteristic only of modernity, but which constitute a universal of religious history: processes of secularization trigger processes of theologization and vice versa. In this sense, it makes no difference whether one believes oneself a member of the descending or ascending branch of religious history, as the philosopher of religion and Protestant theologian Ernst Troeltsch put it as early as the 1920s.[1] The questions raised here can be answered only if we correlate religion as a system of ideas with its forms of social organization in a given case.

---

[1]   See Ernst Troeltsch, *Der Historismus und seine Probleme I. Das logische Problem der Geschichtsphilosophie*, Gesammelte Schriften III, Tübingen, J. C. B. Mohr (Paul Siebeck), 1922, p. ix.

In 1912, Ernst Troeltsch presented his substantial study *The Social Teachings of the Christian Churches* as the first volume of his collected works.[2] In these studies, he brings out the interaction between religious phenomena and their organizational forms of churches, sects and mysticism. In his economic ethics of the world religions, Max Weber planned to take up this approach and extend it to the world religions, including Judaism. In the text itself, however, which remained uncompleted, he concentrated not primarily on the interaction between religious ideas and forms of social organization described by Troeltsch, but on the issue raised by his Protestantism–capitalism thesis of 1904/1905 on the origins of modern capitalism, which was expanded to include the issue of the origin of Western rationalism only from 1910/1911 on. This was bound up with a shift away from the question as posed by Troeltsch. The aim in what follows is to take up once again Troeltsch's approach and, with more than a sidelong glance at Weber, evaluate it in light of a body of research on ancient Judaism that has developed considerably over the last hundred years since the time of these thinkers. But let us hear first from Max Weber.

Max Weber's view of state, economy and Jewish religion

In the years between 1913 and 1919, Weber engaged in fairly intense dialogues with his Jewish friend Ernst Josef Lesser on the future prospects of the Zionist project in Palestine. While the latter conceded to Weber that it is hard to separate religion from the national dimension, the real basis on which all the Zionist parties came together, those indifferent to the Jewish religion and those espousing Torah Judaism, 'is not religion, but the national idea, whose symbol is the revitalized Hebrew language'.[3] According to Lesser, Weber countered by stating that while it was certainly entirely possible to establish a few 'colonies' in Palestine, this would not achieve the goal of the rebirth of the Jewish people. 'Ezra went to Jerusalem clutching the Torah – what do you have?' Probably further to a conversation with Lesser in 1913, Weber sent a letter to his friend dated 18 August 1913 because the conversation had been broken off at precisely the point 'where the true *internal*

[2]   See Ernst Troeltsch, *The Social Teachings of the Christian Churches*, London, Allen & Unwin, 1931.

[3]   As stated by Ernst Josef Lesser in a letter to Marianne Weber of 12 June 1922 with reference to a conversation in 1919; see Max Weber, *Briefe 1913–1914*, ed. M. Rainer Lepsius and Wolfgang J. Mommsen, Max-Weber-Gesamtausgabe (MWG) II/8, Tübingen, Mohr, 2003, pp. 312f. The letter can be found in the Geheimes Staatsarchiv Berlin, unpublished works by Max Weber, no. 29, pp. 6–9.

problems of Zionism begin'.[4] According to Weber, the Zionist idea of founding a Jewish national state in Palestine was scarcely compatible with the utopian ideas of the Jewish religion. Certainly, one could establish a small state with functioning hospitals and even a university, but could this 'ever function as the "fulfilment" of those magnificent "promises" or would it in fact constitute their critique? [...] What is the key ingredient missing here? *It is the temple and the high priests. If these* were to be found in Jerusalem, all else would be of minor importance'. Max Weber expresses here very perceptively a basic opposition between the organization of the Jewish religion, which, in analogy to the Catholic papacy, had in the high priest, as the hierarch of world Judaism, the guarantor of the dignity of every Jew, believer or unbeliever, and a Jewish national state,[5] an opposition which to this day can be moderated only through compromise within the state of Israel and in its relationship to world Judaism.

When Weber engaged in these dialogues on Zionism with Lesser, he had already subjected ancient Judaism to intense study.[6] As early as the section on 'ancient Israel' in the article 'Agrarverhältnisse im Altertum', appearing in the third edition of the *Handwörterbuch der Staatswissenschaften* (dictionary of political sciences) and later published in English as *The Agrarian Sociology of Ancient Civilizations*, Weber dealt in disproportionate detail with the biblical law of the Sabbath year, already mentioned in the oldest legal code in the Hebrew Bible, in Exodus 23:10–11: 'For six years you shall sow your land and gather in its yield, but the seventh year you shall let it rest and lie fallow, that the poor of your people may eat; and what they leave the beasts of the field may eat. You shall do likewise with your vineyard, and with your olive orchard.'

The Old Testament scholarship of the time held that this was a very old law, possibly dating back to nomadic origins, reflecting the remnants of a 'social economy', a view that was still being advocated by Julius Wellhausen. Against

---

[4]   Weber, *Briefe 1913–1914*, pp. 313f. The letter is in the Jewish National and University Library, Autograph Collection/Max Weber.

[5]   If, in his conversations with Lesser before and after the First World War, Weber argues in favour of a purely religious organization of world Judaism as appropriate to the Jewish religion, and that this alone could form the basis of Jews' sense of dignity, he is expressing a view still common within reform Judaism between the world wars; see Michael A. Meyer, *Response to Modernity: A History of the Reform Movement in Judaism*, Oxford, Oxford University Press, 1988, pp. 326ff.

[6]   On Weber's study of Judaism, see Eckart Otto, *Max Webers Studien des Antiken Judentums. Historische Grundlegung einer Theorie der Moderne*, Tübingen, Mohr, 2002, pp. 1–245; idem, 'Einleitung', in Max Weber, *Die Wirtschaftsethik der Weltreligionen. Das antike Judentum. Schriften und Reden 1911–1920*, ed. Eckart Otto, Max-Weber-Gesamtausgabe I/21.1–2, vol. I, Tübingen, Mohr, 2005, pp. 1–157.

this, in his article on agrarian relations in antiquity[7] and then repeatedly up to his great study on ancient Judaism, part of his economic ethics of the world religions,[8] Weber viewed this law as a latecomer in the Old Testament in literary and legal terms; in his view, it is hopeless to attempt to strip the regulation, as it exists for us today, of its utopian character and explain it rationally, whether in terms of agricultural imperatives or socio-political factors. Rather, we are dealing here with 'those prescriptions which [...] derive from religious exhortation', with 'a moral prescription, not a legal regulation'.[9] Only in late Judaism, according to Weber, did the law have not only theoretical validity, but practical consequences, as is apparent in the numerous responses of the rabbis relating to conduct towards illegally grown crops – Weber refers here to the Mishna tractate Demai ('doubtful produce') and its development in the two Talmudim.[10] The law of the Sabbath year played a role even in Zionist attempts at settlement in Palestine in the nineteenth and early twentieth centuries, such that Weber adds the following explanatory note to his remarks on this law: 'The rabbis of Jerusalem had spoken for the commandment. If I remember correctly, German Jewish authorities had done likewise. The Eastern Jewish rabbis, however, declared allegedly the settlement of the land to be such God-pleasing work that one might dispense with the old prescription.'[11] As the biblical Sabbath year law requiring the cessation of agricultural activity in the seventh year refers only to the land of Israel, but not to the Jewish Diaspora, this law became a practical problem only with the Jewish settlement of Palestine in the wake of the Zionist settlers' movement, and it continues to be a problem in modern-day Israel. Prior to the fallow year of 1889, rabbis began to discuss whether it was acceptable to lease or sell land used for agriculture to non-Jews for this year. While the Russian rabbi Isaac Elhanan Spektor from Kovno permitted its sale for two years, the Ashkenazi community of Jerusalem, led by the rabbis Moses Joshua Judah Leib Diskin and Samuel Salant, opposed this dispensation. In the fallow year of 1910, the debate began again. At this time, Weber interpreted the fallow year law in his study on the 'Religious Groups' as a 'product of post-exilic urban scholars learned in the law', which had taken on force within their sphere of influence despite the fact

---

[7]   See Max Weber, *The Agrarian Sociology of Ancient Civilizations* (1909), London, New Left Books, 1976, pp. 137–38.

[8]   See Max Weber, *Ancient Judaism*, Glencoe, IL, Free Press, 1952.

[9]   Weber, *Ancient Judaism*, p. 48.

[10]   See Lazarus Goldschmidt, *Der Babylonische Talmud*, vol. I, Berlin, Jüdischer Verlag, 1930, pp. 309–22. The treatise is concerned with questions and rules relating to the use or destruction of crops in cases where it is uncertain whether they were correctly tithed or properly grown and acquired.

[11]   Weber, *Ancient Judaism*, p. 437, fn. 24.

that, initially intended as a purely theoretical-religious statement, it hampered efficient, intensive agriculture.[12] For Weber, this is one of the many examples of the worldly consequences, including those for the economy, of a Jewish religion originally oriented towards otherworldly goals, a religion whose most prominent exponents had been the Hebrew prophets.

Both in his dialogues on the future prospects of the Zionist project and in his detailed discussion of the Sabbath year law, which shares a common context with his study of the prohibition on receiving interest in Deuteronomy (Deut. 23:20–21),[13] Weber wished to bring out the incompatibility of the otherworldly-utopian aims of Jewish religion with the political goals of a nation state or a rationally organized economy. However, Weber by no means wished to claim that all religions are from the outset fundamentally incompatible with state and economy. In the ancient context, Egyptian religion was for him a prime example of a successful synthesis of the religious, state and economic systems.[14] Neither did Weber wish to assert that the Jewish religion was distinguished by such incompatibility from its very beginnings; rather, he grasped the features which stood in the way of a synthesis as something which had developed over time, such as monotheism, which encouraged a distinction between religion and social reality and which had been the result rather than the origin of Jewish religious history in biblical times.[15] In Weber's view, the Sabbath year law had been formulated among urban intellectuals of the Persian era, who no longer had any connection to agriculture, as an expression of religious theory. Beyond these biblical impulses, the incompatibility of the promises of Jewish religion with the Zionist idea of a Jewish national state was for Weber partly a consequence of the stateless existence of post-exile Jewry as a community under the foreign rule of the Babylonians, the Persians and the Hellenes and of a two-thousand-year history in the Diaspora.

It is now time to leave Max Weber's interpretation of Judaism for the time being and to ask how, around one hundred years later, we may best describe the state of research on the development of the religious identity of Judaism in biblical times and, on this basis, the development of the interrelationship of religion, state and society. Here, I use the term 'Judaism' in Weber's comprehensive sense, with the inclusion of biblical Israel and Judah; I thus reject the distinction between biblical Hebraism and the Judaism of the post-exile or post-Hadrian era common

---

[12]   See Max Weber, *Economy and Society*, vol. 2, ed. Guenther Roth and Claus Wittich, New York, Bedminster, 1968, p. 618.

[13]   See Weber, *Ancient Judaism*, p. 63f., 343. See what follows for more on this.

[14]   For Weber's interpretation of the Egyptian economic ethic, see his *Ancient Judaism*, pp. 252–58.

[15]   See Weber, *Ancient Judaism*, pp. 153f., 204f., 309, 370 and passim.

in the Protestant theology of the day, a distinction which aims to remove from Judaism the Hebrew Bible, and above all prophecy.[16]

'We must obey God rather than men': the emancipation of the Jewish religion from the function of legitimizing the state

The literary history of the Hebrew Bible begins in the Assyrian crisis affecting Israel and Judah in the eighth and seventh centuries BC, in which both states became vassals of the Neo-Assyrian empire as the hegemonic power. Subjugation to the Assyrian state, sworn to the gods of the Assyrian pantheon, inevitably roused resistance in Judah, in part with respect to religious politics, especially following the destruction of Israel between 722 and 720 BC. As the Assyrian state ideology[17] was disseminated in royal inscriptions, Jewish intellectuals who resisted this ideology in the name of the Jewish god JHWH also had to do so in written form.

In the coronation hymn of the Assyrian king Ashurbanipal (669–c. 630 BC) preserved on a tablet in the Museum of the Middle East in Berlin[18] the gods of the Assyrian empire ascribe to him the tasks of ensuring economic prosperity and a balanced society and endow him with the ability to carry them out:

> May Ashurbanipal, King of Assyria, be favoured by the gods of this land!
> May he be gifted with the talents of eloquence, understanding, law and justice!

---

[16]   See Eckart Otto, *Max Weber*, Tübingen, Mohr, 2002, p. 99. On Ernst Troeltsch, see Otto, *Max Weber*, pp. 246–71.

[17]   See Stefan Maul, 'Der assyrische König – Hüter der Weltordnung', in Jan Assmann et al. (eds.), *Gerechtigkeit. Richten und Retten in der abendländischen Tradition und ihren altorientalischen Ursprüngen*, Munich, Wilhelm Fink, 1998, pp. 65–77.

[18]   On the text and its translation, see Eckart Otto, *Krieg und Frieden in der Hebräischen Bibel und im Alten Orient. Aspekte für eine Friedensordnung in der Moderne*, Stuttgart, Kohlhammer, 1999, pp. 43–46. Alasdair Livingstone (*Court Poetry and Literary Miscellanea*, State Archives of Assyria 3, Helsinki, Helsiniki University Press, 1989, pp. xx iiif.) has rightly underlined that this text is a coronation hymn. This coronation hymn was absorbed into the Hebrew Bible and reinterpreted with pacifying intent in Psalm 72; see Martin Arneth, *'Sonne der Gerechtigkeit'. Studien zur Solarisierung der Jahwe-Religion im Lichte von Psalm 72*, Beihefte zur Zeitschrift für Altorientalische und Biblische Rechtsgeschichte 1, Wiesbaden, Harrassowitz, 2000, pp. 18–170.

> May the citizens of Assur buy 30 kor of grain for one shekel
> [around 8 g] of silver!
> May the citizens of Assur buy 3 seah of oil for one shekel of
> silver!
> May the citizens of Assur buy 30 minas of wool for a shekel of
> silver!
> May the lowlier speak and the mightier listen!
> May the mightier speak and the lowlier listen!
> May harmony and peace be established in Assyria!
> [The god] Assur is King – truly Assur is King,
> Ashurbanipal is the image of [the god] Assur.

The king was not only entrusted with ensuring the internal welfare of the state, as expressed in low prices and a balanced society, but also, as a tool of the god of the empire made in his image, with the task of securing this god's domination over the peoples of the world. May the gods, so goes the hymn, give Ashurbanipal a mighty sceptre to extend his dominion over land and peoples. In a prayer that follows the hymn, the five leading gods of the Assyrian pantheon confer their powers on the king. The gods Anu and Enlil, as the most ancient gods, provide him with crown and throne and thus the insignia of world domination, while the god Ninurta gives him his weapons: in the Assyrian myth Bin Sar Dadme,[19] the god Anzu steals the Tablets of Destinies of the creator god, disturbing the order of the divine and earthly realms. Ninurta goes into battle against Anzu, restoring order by bringing under control the mythical chaos represented by Anzu. Equipped with Ninurta's weapons, King Ashurbanipal is to be the battler against chaos of the human world, spreading war over the land of those peoples who refuse to submit willingly to the imperial god Assur and thus to Assyrian rule, just as, within the Assyrian empire, every rebellion is nipped in the bud as an expression of the chaotic disruption of the order of creation.[20] The prayer that follows the coronation hymn thus ends with the words:

> Put the weapons of battles and wars in his hand,
> Deliver to him the black-headed ones [humankind],
> So that he reigns over them as their shepherd!

Though the Assyrians did not launch religious wars in order to spread their

---

[19] See Otto, *Krieg und Frieden*, pp. 47f.

[20] See Eckart Otto, 'Die besiegten Sieger. Von der Macht und Ohnmacht der Ideen in der Geschichte am Beispiel der neuassyrischen Großreichspolitik', *Biblische Zeitschrift* (New Series), 43 (1999), pp. 180–203.

religion, their wars, which the Assyrian king had to wage annually, did in fact have a religious foundation, one which represented a challenge to the Judaean intellectuals in the priestly circles of Jerusalem. The oath of loyalty (Akkadian *adê*) to the king Esarhaddon (681–669 BC), Ashurbanipal's predecessor, which the grandees of the Assyrian empire, among them the Judaean king Manasses (696–642 BC), as a vassal of the Assyrians, had to swear in 672 BC in order to secure the line of succession to the throne, was sworn to the Assyrian imperial gods.[21] Hence, the question of Judaean identity was not only a political but also a religious one. The Assyrian oath of loyalty of 672 BC demanded absolute loyalty to the king and his designated successor. Section 10 of this *adê* thus states:

> Should you hear a wicked, bad, inappropriate word, that is not fitting, not good, for Ashurbanipal, the crown prince of the royal house, son of Esarhaddon, the king of Assyria, your master, whether from the mouth of his enemy or from the mouth of his friends, or from the mouth of his brothers, his uncles, his cousins, or his family, the descendants of his father's house, or from the mouth of your brothers, your sons, your daughters or from the mouth of a prophet, an ecstatic, one who questions the word of God, or from the mouth of any person, as many as there are, you should not keep quiet about it but come to Ashurbanipal, the crown prince of the royal house, son of Esarhaddon, King of Assyria and report it.

The obligation to report all forms of criticism of the king and crown prince is expanded in Section 12 into the obligation to immediately lynch the traitor:

> Should someone tell you of an uprising, rebellion with the aim of killing, murdering, eliminating Ashurbanipal, crown prince of the royal house, son of Esarhaddon, King of Assyria, your master, who in his favour has subjected you to the oath of loyalty, and you hear it from the mouth of any person, you should seize the instigators of rebellion and bring them to Ashurbanipal, crown prince of the royal house. If you are in a position to seize them, to kill them, then you should seize them, kill them, eliminate their names and their descendants from the land. If you are not in a position to seize them, to kill them, you should report it to Ashurbanipal, crown prince of the royal house, assist him in seizing, in

---

[21]   On the following Akkadian and Hebraic texts and their interpretation in terms of legal history, see Eckart Otto, *Das Deuteronomium. Politische Theologie und Rechtsreform in Juda und Assyrien*, Beihefte zur Zeitschrift für die alttestamentliche Wissenschaft 284, Berlin, Walter de Gruyter, 1999, pp. 15–90.

killing, the instigators of uprisings, in eliminating their names and their descendants from the land.

As the incarnation of the divine task of combating and limiting chaos in the world, it was vital to protect the king at any price against rebellion, an expression of chaos that went against creation. The idea that the individual might suffer at the hands of the king or his organs of state was alien to this way of thinking, as the order they represented was the only possible framework for successful life.

In the second half of the seventh century BC, in the basic literary layer of Deuteronomy 13:2–10, Section 10 of the oath of loyalty to Esarhaddon was expanded, by motifs found in Section 12 for example, and received subversively, in that it was sweepingly reinterpreted in such a way that the Judaean god JHWH replaced the Assyrian king and his crown prince as the object of demands for absolute loyalty. The oath of fealty was now *opposed* to the Assyrian state ideology:

> If a prophet or a dreamer of dreams arises among you [...] and if he says, 'Let us go after other gods and let us serve them', you shall not listen to the words of that prophet or that dreamer of dreams. [...] But that prophet or that dreamer of dreams shall be put to death, because he has taught rebellion against the LORD your God. [...] If your brother, the son of your mother, or your son or your daughter or the wife you embrace or your friend who is as your own soul entices you secretly, saying, 'Let us go and serve other gods', [...] you shall not yield to him or listen to him, nor shall your eye pity him, nor shall you spare him, nor shall you conceal him. But you shall kill him. (Deut. 13:1–9*)

This literal reception of the Assyrian oath of loyalty has a subversive character: by transferring the demand for loyalty to the Judaean god JHWH, it de-legitimizes the rule of the Assyrian king and thus of the hegemonic power. As is apparent in the curses found in the Assyrian oath of loyalty received in Deuteronomy 28*, the demand for loyalty to God in Deuteronomy 13* is also confirmed by oath. If the demand for absolute loyalty to the god of the Judaeans is redirected in that the objects of the demand for loyalty are swapped and the Assyrian king is replaced by the Judaean god, this subversive reception can nonetheless pick up the thread of Neo-Assyrian motifs, such that an Assyrian method of the religious legitimation of power is revolutionized by means of Assyrian motifs: in the recently published Neo-Assyrian oracles,[22] which were

---

[22]   See Simo Parpola, *Assyrian Prophecies*, State Archives of Assyria 4, Helsinki, Helsinki University Press, 1997, pp. 22–27.

recited when King Esarhaddon acceded to the throne, the sworn pledge of a 'covenant' (Akkadian *adê*) between the king and the imperial god Assur takes centre stage. Thus, the 'covenant' between divinity and human being is not, as Weber thought, a specific feature of Jewish religion in contrast to the religions of the ancient Middle East, whose gods supposedly functioned only as witnesses to contracts and the making of alliances.[23] The specifically Jewish feature with respect to the idea of a covenant is rather the creation of an alliance between the deity and the people while disregarding the king, who functions in the Assyrian context as sole covenant partner, thus becoming the conduit of divine blessing for the people. This is a rejection of the claim, characteristic of the legitimation of the Assyrian ruler, that the people have no access to the world of the divine pantheon other than through the king, that is, the organs of the state.

The subversive reception of the legitimation of the Assyrian ruler in Deuteronomy set in motion a development of importance to the Jewish religion. In coming to terms with the political theology of Assyria, which, by binding the Assyrian king to the imperial and creator god Assur as one made in his image, links all prospect of a successful life to obedience to the state organs represented by the king, Deuteronomy puts the state in its place: absolute loyalty is due not to the state, but only to God. This is the birth of a paradigm distinguished by the notion that it is more important to obey God than to obey human beings; in terms of its Christian reception, this found its classical expression in Luke's Acts of the Apostles 5:19, while its Greek counterpart is Sophocles' *Antigone* (lines 471–473) with its reference to the 'unwritten laws of God' as a critical authority vis-à-vis the positive law of the state. As a result, stripped of all his political power, in Deuteronomy the king becomes the leading devotee of the Torah among his people (Deut. 17:14–20), whose cohesion is no longer to be ensured by the organs of the state, but rather, according to Deuteronomy, is to be constituted as a community of worship around the one central shrine, common to all, in Jerusalem.

Beginning with Deuteronomy, the Hebrew Bible counters the intermeshing of state and religion (which is even tighter in Egypt than in Mesopotamia, with the conception of the king as the son of god and brother of the goddess Ma'at, who maintains the order of the natural and social world [24]) – with the idea of the religious community, to which state functions are subordinated if necessary (in order to preserve the community). This idea was realized with the destruction of the Judaean state in 586 BC by the Babylonians and, with the exception of the brief interim of the Hasmonaic and Herodian state, remained characteristic

---

[23]   See Weber, *Ancient Judaism*, p. 79 and passim.

[24]   See Jan Assmann, *Ma'at. Gerechtigkeit und Unsterblichkeit im Alten Ägypten*, Munich, Beck, 1990, pp. 201–36.

of Judaism up to the founding of the state of Israel in 1948. In the Pentateuch, Moses is portrayed as a counter-type to the ancient Middle Eastern king, and this is linked with the secularization of state legitimation through the separation of state and religion introduced in Deuteronomy; it is true that as the Pentateuch was developed further, Moses takes on the characteristics first of the Assyrian, and later of the Babylonian and Persian king, but he finally emerges in the Persian era, in Deuteronomy, as scriptural teacher, one consistently on the side of the people.[25] Moses certainly imparts the revelation of the law, up to and including the Decalogue, to the people, but they are God's immediate covenant partners, such that in Deuteronomy Moses, as scriptural teacher, has the function of serving the people and, in contrast to the ancient Middle Eastern state religion, there is no sign of the idea that the people have access to God only through him. This became bound up with a characteristic of Jewish religion important in terms of legal history. If, as is detectable not least in the prologue and epilogue of the 'codex' of King Hammurabi, the king is considered a source of law in both Mesopotamia and Egypt, the Hebrew Bible is distinguished by the fact that it attributes this function of king directly to JHWH. This places a key function of the state, as the source of legal order, in the hands of the community of worship and of the priestly scriptural scholarship found within it (Ex. 4:15; Deut. 1:5).[26]

Secularization and theologization of ethics in Jewish community theology

The secularization of the legitimation of state power leads to a new form of organization in the shape of a community[27] – a process which can be observed

---

[25]   See Eckart Otto, *Mose. Geschichte und Legende*, Beck'sche Reihe 2400, Munich, Beck, 2006, pp. 27–75.

[26]   On the different forms of legal legitimation in Mesopotamia, Egypt, Iran and the Hebrew Bible, see Eckart Otto, 'Die Rechtshermeneutik des Pentateuch und die achämenidische Rechtsideologie in ihren altorientalischen Kontexten', in Markus Witte and Marie Theres Fögen (eds.), *Kodifizierung und Legitimierung des Rechts in der Antike und im Alten Orient*, Beihefte zur Zeitschrift für altorientalische und biblische Rechtsgeschichte 5, Wiesbaden, Harrassowitz, 2005, pp. 71–116, featuring further references to relevant texts. On the legal history of the Hebrew Bible, see idem, 'Recht im antiken Israel', in Ulrich Manthe (ed.), *Die Rechtskulturen der Antike. Vom Alten Orient bis zum Römischen Reich*, Munich, Beck, 2003, pp. 151–90.

[27]   The term 'community' is used here in the Weberian sense to refer to a type of *Vergemeinschaftung* or *Vergesellschaftung*, the former indicating the emergence of 'communal', the latter 'associative' relations, which differs from that found in kin groups and that proper to the political association in that the community religion is neither linked with

in pre-exilic Deuteronomy initially on a theoretical level, and which took on concrete form with the destruction of the state in 586 BC by the Babylonians. Already in the late pre-exilic era, towards the end of the seventh century BC, when the Davidian state still existed, the theological programme of Deuteronomy aims to achieve the integration of the religious community, not through the king as divine instrument and embodiment of the state, but through shared worship, with the inclusion of the poorest members of society (Deut. 16), at the one shrine common to all in Jerusalem (Deut. 12). Without this separation of state and community, already carried out in the theory found in late pre-exilic Deuteronomy, Judaism would not have survived the destruction of the Davidian state by the Babylonians. A further momentous development in terms of religious history is bound up with the secularization of the state in Deuteronomy and the separation of state and religious community. In Deuteronomy, the demand that God alone be worshipped was formulated for the first time prior to the formulation of the First Commandment of the Decalogue, in the shape of the Shema Yisrael ('Hear, O Israel'), the profession of faith in the oneness and uniqueness of God in Deut. 6:4–5, the main component of worship in the synagogue to this day:

> Hear, O Israel!
> JHWH is our God
> JHWH is One.

Just as in Deuteronomy, state and religious community move apart, in a process which must be described as secularization, so too God and the world move further apart in Jerusalem as a result of the demand that only JHWH be worshipped, as Judaean polytheism is eliminated. If mythic religion mediates the complexity of conflicting experiences such as life and death, success and failure, etc. through the gods, acting in human ways, as representatives of these experiences, and if this meta-empirical mode of mediation characteristic of myth collapses, the means of mediating contradictory experiences must be sought anew in the empirical realm. In the exilic era, as further developments result in the theory of monotheism, which denies the existence of other gods, the commandment to worship one God becomes stricter, to the extent that now the world becomes disenchanted, a world stripped of the divine forces; it becomes the counterpart of the sole God. This phase in the religious history of Judah towards the end of the seventh and during the sixth century BC may be understood as a process of the secularization of how the world is understood

---

ancestor worship nor serves the sacral legitimation of domination through the *Verbandsgott* or God of the social group; see Weber, *Economy and Society*, vol. 2, pp. 452–57.

in the sense of its disenchantment as described by Weber.[28] In connection with this, profound shifts now occurred in the field of ethics as well, which may be described as the vanquishing of magical practices in favour of action oriented towards internalized ethical norms.

Again, Deuteronomy itself and subsequently, as it was developed further, the Pentateuchal Torah in its entirety, reflect this profound shift: the community is now obligated to comply with the Commandments and legal provisions which 'shall be on your heart' (Deut. 6:6) 'with all your heart and with all your soul' (Deut. 26:16). It is inadequate to subsume this cluster of developments in Deuteronomy – the breaking away of the religious community from the state, linked with the rise of sole worship of the Judaean God within the community and the elimination of genealogically based ethics of a 'magical' character (in the sense that it was not geared towards the ability to make ethical decisions) in favour of a decision-based internalization of norms of action – under the term 'secularization', as the tendency expressed in this process of the conceptual separation of empirical knowledge and meta-empirical divine world demands the reverse process: the conceptual mediation of that which has been separated, of 'God' and 'world'. And this trend towards the theologization of ethics, which runs counter to the tendency towards secularization, is also reflected in Deuteronomy, and on this basis in the theory of revelation found in the Pentateuch, which is linked with Mount Sinai and the land of Moab. The secularized, that is, desacralized world, the 'disenchanted' world in Weber's sense, is subjugated to the divine will to create (which binds the 'hearts' of the members of the community in their actions through the revelation of the Commandments) in order to sanctify the disenchanted world as a whole.

We now require an outline of the social-historical point of departure for this dialectical process of disenchantment and concurrent sanctification. Up to the Assyrian crisis in the eighth and seventh centuries BC, Hebrew ethics was structured by family genealogy in the sense that the degree of mutual solidarity owed was determined by the degree of genealogical proximity.[29] This form of genealogical-familial ethics, the original location of the core precepts of the Decalogue,[30] was religiously founded through a familial religion in the shape of ancestral worship, with the ancestors being considered members of the family who supported its living members and were provided for by them in the realm of the dead in return. In the Assyrian crisis, in anticipation of an attack by the

---

[28] See Max Weber, *General Economic History*, Mineola, NY, Dover Publications, 2003, pp. 361–62. See also what follows.

[29] On the history of Hebrew and Jewish ethics in antiquity, see Eckart Otto, *Theologische Ethik des Alten Testaments*, Stuttgart, Kohlhammer, 1994.

[30] See Otto, *Theologische Ethik des Alten Testaments*, pp. 32–47, 208–19.

Assyrian army, the Judaean king Hiskia (725–697 BC) had a large proportion of the rural population resettled in fortified towns. This resulted not only in the loss of the graves and with them ancestral worship, but also in the dissolution of extended peasant families. This development was further intensified by the Assyrian conquest of Judah, which spared only Jerusalem, and the deportation of a far from negligible portion of the population, such that decades later the land of Judah had to be repopulated by settlers from Jerusalem.[31] But the land was desacralized in that after the destruction of the local shrines in villages and towns by the Assyrians, the temple of Jerusalem attained the status of the *sole* legitimate central shrine (Deut. 12). The authors of Deuteronomy sought to cushion the impact of the ethical vacuum concomitant with the desacralization of the land and the destruction of family-based ethics through a sibling-based ethics that declared each and every Judaean to be brother and sister and demanded conduct appropriate hitherto only within the family, but not beyond its genealogically defined boundaries. This sibling ethics took on programmatic force particularly in the field of the economy, with the prohibition on receiving interest (Deut. 23:20–21) or demanding back credit beyond the year of provision (Deut. 15:1–11).[32] The desacralization of the land was cushioned by a consistent theologization of ethics, in which conduct was no longer guided by genealogy and the magic of ancestral worship but was instead subordinated to the ethical will of JHWH, the one God. The Deuteronomic demands for credit without interest, on whose repayment one must refrain from insisting in certain circumstances, were presaged by the social law of the 'covenant book', which preceded Deuteronomy by some decades in terms of literary history, in Exodus 21–23, including the commandment regarding the fallow year in Ex. 23:10–11.[33]

In contrast to Weber's view, we are by no means dealing here with the late insertion, in terms of literary history and ethics, of the 'theological quest

---

[31]   See Otto, *Theologische Ethik des Alten Testaments*, p. 180, which provides further suggestions on relevant literature.

[32]   On the ethics of Deuteronomy, see also Eckart Otto, *Gottes Recht als Menschenrecht. Rechts- und literaturhistorische Studien zum Deuteronomium*, Beihefte zur Zeitschrift für Altorientalische und biblische Rechtsgeschichte 2, Wiesbaden, Harrassowitz, 2002, pp. 92–275.

[33]   On the literary and legal history of the oldest legal code in the Hebrew Bible, the so-called Book of the Covenant from the eighth–seventh centuries BC, which was incorporated, together with the Decalogue, into the Sinai pericope in Exodus 20 in the post-exilic era (fifth century BC), see Weber, *Ancient Judaism*, pp. 48–68, 126–38, and Eckart Otto, *Wandel der Rechtsbegründungen in der Gesellschaftsgeschichte des antiken Israel. Eine Rechtsgeschichte des 'Bundesbuches' Ex XX 22 – XXIII 13*, Studia Biblica 3, Leiden, E. J. Brill, 1988.

for consistent conclusions' into the Book of the Covenant,[34] but rather with a religiously motivated regrouping of partial fallows to make a full fallow, whose encroachment on the economy is as negligible as the social consequences of aid for the poor, who are supposed to receive the naturally growing produce. But in fact even this law, formulated by priests, was realized only half a millennium later, with the first fallow year documented only for the year 164/163 BC. The laws on freedom from interest and forgoing repayment in Deuteronomy, which revolutionized the entire lending business as one of the pillars of the ancient economy, were intended to intervene far more profoundly in economic behaviour. These demands were no longer compatible with the logic of the economy of Judaea, with its rent-capitalist structure, and were likewise ignored until the canonization of the Pentateuch, only to be annulled at the beginning of the Common Era through the introduction of the institution of the Prozbul in the form of a certificate of safekeeping deposited at a court, to which the waiving of debts did not apply.[35] If Deuteronomy conceived of the Jewish people as a religious community integrated not by a religiously legitimized state but by worship at the central shrine, this was linked with an ethics of charity which, borrowed from the kin group and applied to the community of the Jews, 'God's people', inevitably came into conflict with the logic of the economy of ancient rent capitalism, which was geared towards the pursuit of profit, an ethics which thus remained on the agenda in biblical times.[36]

With the aid of Deuteronomy, we can shed much light on the process

---

[34]   Weber, *Ancient Judaism*, p. 49.

[35]   In the second millennium BC, the same fate befell the ancient Babylonian institution of the 'act of justice', carried out by the king, of waiving debts, found in the first millennium BC (see Fritz Rudolf Kraus, *Königliche Verfügungen in altbabylonischer Zeit*, Leiden, E. J. Brill, 1984), as it was possible to include in Neo-Assyrian loan contracts the stipulation that an act of justice by the king was not applicable to the contract in question; see Eckart Otto, 'Soziale Restitution und Vertragsrecht', *Revue d'Assyriologie*, 92 (1998), pp. 125–60.

[36]   On rabbinical responses to the prohibition on receiving interest, see Eberhard Klingenberg, *Das israelitische Zinsverbot in Torah, Mišnah und Talmud*, Wiesbaden, Franz Steiner, 1977. On the Christian reception, which had a hard time answering the question posed by Deut. 23:20–21 of who is a brother and who a foreigner for the Christian, see Benjamin N. Nelson, *The Idea of Usury: From Tribal Brotherhood to Universal Otherhood*, Princeton, Princeton University Press, 2 edn, 1969, and Eckart Otto, 'Gerechtigkeit und Erbarmen im Recht des Alten Testaments und seiner christlichen Rezeption', in idem, *Kontinuum und Proprium. Studien zur Sozial- und Rechtsgeschichte im Alten Orient und im Alten Testament*, Orientalia Biblica et Christiana 8, Wiesbaden, Harrassowitz, 1996, pp. 342–57 (reprinted in Jan Assmann et al [eds.], *Gerechtigkeit*, Munich, Fink, 1998, pp. 79–95).

of community formation as part of a dialectical process of secularization and theologization. In the formation of the religious community, Weber sees a 'result of [the] routinization [*Veralltäglichung*]' of prophetic charisma, 'of a process whereby either the prophet himself or his disciples secure the permanence of his preaching and the congregation's distribution of grace, hence ensuring also the economic existence of the enterprise and those who man it, and thereby monopolizing as well the privileges reserved for those charged with religious functions'.[37] The emergence of the post-exilic community of the Jews as a transformed product of pre-exilic prophecy serves as a paradigm for Weber.[38] Nearly a century later, the formation of a community emerges not as a process of the quotidianization of charisma through the institutionalization of religious functions within the circle of worshippers of the charismatic prophets, but as the result of a process of transformation in which religion is liberated from the function of legitimizing rule and the religious community confronts the state as a community. This process was inaugurated on a programmatic level fairly late on within the pre-exilic period in Deuteronomy and subsequently put into action with the destruction of the Judaean state by the Babylonians.

This process of the separation of religion from the symbiotic relationship with the state characteristic of the ancient Middle East, which must be described as secularization, was accompanied by the desacralization of the land through the abolition of the many local shrines in favour of a central shrine in Jerusalem, which was to function as the integrative centre of the community. The counterpart of these processes of secularization was a countervailing process of the theologization

---

[37]   Weber, *Economy and Society*, vol. 2, p. 452.

[38]   See Weber, *Ancient Judaism*, pp. 320–82, and the introduction to and commentary on this text of Weber's in *Das antike Judentum* (MWG I/21–22); with this thesis on post-exilic community formation, Weber was dependent on the Protestant Old Testament scholarship of the time, particularly that of Julius Wellhausen (*Prolegomena to the History of Israel*, Atlanta, Scholars Press, 1994, pp. 402–406). In the post-exilic development of the community as hierocracy on the basis of the Torah, which was raised to the status of law, Wellhausen saw a retrograde step vis-à-vis the universal ethical religion of the prophets: 'The concept had been raised to the level of morality by the prophets. Now it was re-materialized; while the moral dimension is not cast off, but is fused entirely with the liturgical dimension' (*Israelitische und jüdische Geschichte*, Berlin, Georg Reimer, 7th edn, 1914, p. 168). Weber always kept his distance from such value judgements of Old Testament scholarship, which were at the same time value judgements about contemporary Judaism. Finally, Rudolph Sohm's thesis of the routinization or quotidi-anization of Christian charisma in the early Catholic church also influenced Weber's interpretation of Jewish community formation; see Rudolph Sohm, *Wesen und Ursprung des Katholizismus*, Berlin, Teubner, 2nd edn, 1912, p. 55 and passim.

of ethics, a process which placed the desacralized land under the power of this one God, as conveyed pragmatically by the commandments, which were traced back to the Judaean god JHWH. But there was a tension between the ethics valid within the community and the economic logic that applied within society, in that the former demanded that those in the lending business forgo any interest in profit within the community. For Weber, the distinction bound up with this between internal and external morality, which featured no religious requirements regarding economic conduct towards the Other,[39] was evidence of the traditionalism of a Jewish pariah capitalism from which, Weber argued (against the views of Werner Sombart[40]), it was not possible to trace a path to the rationalization of Western capitalism. However, in the course of his study of ancient Judaism, Weber did come to realize that the rationality of the prophets and of the priestly-levitical legal corpora, especially Deuteronomy, came into force in the Christian West through its Christian reception in the form of the Greek translation, that is, in the Septuagint:

> Thus, in considering the conditions of Jewry's evolution, we stand at a turning point of the whole cultural development of the West and the Middle East. Quite apart from the significance of the Jewish pariah people in the economy of the European Middle Ages and the modern period, Jewish religion has world-historical consequences. Only the following phenomena can equal those of Jewry in historical significance: the development of Hellenic intellectual culture; for western Europe, the development of Roman law and of the Roman Catholic church resting on the Roman concept of office; the medieval order of estates; and finally, in the field of religion, Protestantism. Its influence shatters this order but develops its institutions.[41]

---

[39]   The numerous rabbinical responses to the prohibition on receiving interest show that the distinction between internal and external morality in Deut. 23:20–21 did not mean carte blanche to engage in the irresponsible exploitation of the Other. In distinguishing between internal and external morality, Weber was concerned not with value judgements, but with the issue of the religious 'priming' of economic success.

[40]   See Werner Sombart, *Jews and Modern Capitalism* (1911), London, Transaction, 1997. Weber's harsh criticism of this monograph is apparent in the notes in the margins of his personal copy, sent to him by Sombart (see Otto, *Max Weber*, pp. 20–24), and in Weber's letter to Sombart of 2 December 1913, in which Weber assured him that he considered 'almost every word' of the 'book on the Jews' to be wrong as far as religious aspects were concerned; see Weber, *Briefe 1913–1914*, p. 414.

[41]   Weber, *Ancient Judaism*, p. 5. In the manuscript on ancient Judaism 'Ethik und Mythik/Rituelle Absonderung' ('Ethics and Myth/Ritual Separation') from the Deponat

This is according to the author of the thesis on Protestantism and capitalism. The significance of Hebrew prophecy for the history of Western rationalism can in fact scarcely be overstated, so that we have still to examine the question of the importance of prophecy within the dialectic of the secularization of political theology and the theologization of ethics.

Weber locates the rationality of Hebrew prophecy in the necessity to render communicable charismatic-ecstatic experiences by interpreting them ethically.[42] Modern-day prophetic research has largely refrained from seeking out the ecstatic experiences of historical prophets as the point of departure for the prophetic sayings in the prophetic books of the Hebrew Bible, as scholars have come to understand that not even the *ipsissima verba* of the prophets are accessible, but at best merely literary reminiscences of the prophets' followers, which formed the point of departure for centuries of further literary development into the Hellenistic period. The transcribed words of the prophets were interpreted anew in every new historical situation and could in turn give rise to new prophetic words in the course of literary reinterpretation. Increasingly, the prophetic writings became the work of scribes who adopted the mantle of the prophets by updating the prophetic books: the words of the prophets no longer obtain their meaning from an original situation, in which they are said to have been spoken, but from the literary context with which they are bound up. Thus, the rational

---

Max Weber of the Bavarian state library in Munich, written in 1912 and published as part of the Max-Weber-Gesamtausgabe, Weber applies the term 'pariah' to Judaism for the first time; see *Das antike Judentum*, pp. 205–206 with critical commentary in i–i. With his cultural history-based interpretation of Judaism, Weber consistently rejected a racial interpretation as advocated by, among others, Houston Stewart Chamberlain (*Foundations of the Nineteenth Century*, London, Allen Lane, 1910, pp. 299–444). On Weber's application of the term 'pariah' to ancient Judaism and the contemporary context of the use of this term, see Otto, 'Einleitung', pp. 66–70, and *Max Weber*, pp. 43–53, 74–78, 264–69 and passim.

[42]   Above all, Weber is here upholding the neo-Romantic spirit of Hermann Gunkel's interpretation of the prophets ('Die geheimen Erfahrungen der Propheten Israels. Eine religionspsychologische Studie', in Friedrich Daab and Hans Wegener [eds.], *Das Suchen der Zeit. Blätter deutscher Zukunft*, vol. I, Gießen, Alfred Oskar Töpelmann, 1903, pp. 112–53) and the interpretation by Gustav Hölscher, conceived in terms of psychology of religion and influenced by Wilhelm Wundt's physiological psychology and *Völkerpsychologie* or ethno-psychology (*Die Profeten. Untersuchungen zur Religionsgeschichte Israels*, Leipzig, J. C. Hinrichs'sche Buchhandlung, 1914). On Weber's interpretation of the prophets, see Eckart Otto, 'Die hebräische Prophetie bei Max Weber, Ernst Troeltsch und Hermann Cohen. Ein Diskurs im Weltkrieg zur christlich-jüdischen Kultursynthese', in Wolfgang Schluchter and Friedrich Wilhelm Graf (eds.), *Asketischer Protestantismus und der 'Geist' des modernen Kapitalismus. Max Weber und Ernst Troeltsch*, Tübingen, Mohr, 2005, pp. 201–53.

character of the Hebrew prophetic literature is not the result of the secondary rationalization of ecstatically experienced charisma, but of a correspondence, already characteristic of the beginnings of the literary history of the prophetic books in the form of individual prophetic sayings (proclamations of disaster), between the critique of the religious and social conduct of the people, in light of the Hebrew concept of justice (*ṣ^edaqā*), and the conclusion regarding the disaster which will befall the people, reached on the basis of analysis of the intellectual structure of a synthetic philosophy of life characterized by the unity of deed and personal outcome.[43] Hebrew prophecy differs fundamentally from its Hellenistic counterpart, which, as Plato puts it in the *Timaeus*, is deployed to 'pass judgement on divinely inspired prophecies' and is thus the 'interpreter, but not the author, of a divine vision or saying'. In Greek thought, the obscurity of the oracular utterance is itself evidence of its origins in a meta-empirical, unknown world; the ambiguity – as Giorgio Colli states – is 'an allusion to the metaphysical breach' between a divine wisdom open to interpretation by human beings and its rationalization in the words that embody human understanding.[44]

If the prophetic utterances of the Hebrew Bible draw conclusions on the basis of empirical experience regarding the potential for the future inherent in it, for Hellenic thought, the reason why the future is foreseeable is not that 'there exists a consistent link between the present and the future and someone is, in some mysterious way, in a position to grasp this necessary connection in advance: it is foreseeable because it is the reflection, expression and manifestation

---

[43]   When the editors of the prophetic sayings preface these with the formula 'thus says Yahweh', they are highlighting this reality as guaranteed by God: the destiny presaged by the prophets corresponds to the will of God as stipulated by this order. Old Testament scholarship has recognized that some of the biographical data in the prophetic books are theological constructions by later scribes, who continued the prophetic traditions found in the prophetic books. I wish merely to point out here that historical and critical non-Muslim research on the Koran acts in line with this very insight when, in contrast to traditional Koranic exegesis, it seeks to explain the suras of the Koran not on the basis of the Prophet's life situations but according to literary and religious historical criteria independent of the Prophet's life.

[44]   See Giorgio Colli, *Die Geburt der Philosophie*, Frankfurt, Europäische Verlagsanstalt, 1981, p. 41. A spectacular example of the obscurity of the oracles, rooted in their ambiguity, is the Delphic oracle to Croesus, reported by Herodotus (*Histories* I, 87), that he will destroy a great empire if he crosses the Halys to battle Cyrus. While Croesus took this oracle to refer to his victory over the Persians, he in fact ended up destroying his own empire; see Veit Rosenberger, *Griechische Orakel. Eine Kulturgeschichte*, Darmstadt, Wissenschaftliche Buchgesellschaft, 2001, pp. 160–65. On the overall context, see also Eric Robertson Dodds, *The Greeks and the Irrational*, Berkeley, University of California Press, 1951, pp. 102–104.

of a divine reality'[45] which enters the world in ecstatic-irrational fashion.[46] In the prophetic literature of the Hebrew Bible the dialectically interrelated tendencies are far more clearly discernible than in Deuteronomy, namely secularization, which no longer left the world to the mythic powers and with them the religiously legitimated state (the prophets' sharp criticisms of the king are a clear expression of this difference), but at the same time theologization, which saw the establishment of an ethics which was geared towards standards of justice set by God, but which also made it possible to grasp human action as divinely decreed order in light of the connection between ethics and the success or failure of the life of both the individual and the collectivity.

One may ask what drove the authors of the prophetic books to produce a rational theology of this kind, and the answer can only be that for them, in view of the reality of injustice, God's justice had become a key issue. As is discernible in Hosea, when these authors took the proclamation of destruction to the extreme (Hos. 12) they turned the empirical point of departure for their theology upside down in favour of a speculative starting point in the mercy of a God that suffers in sympathy with human beings and overcomes His wrath (Hos. 11:1–9).[47] The only way for the Jewish community to exist happily was through JHWH's merciful embrace. This shift away from a theological approach centred on the empirical world to one oriented towards a speculative concept of God is also apparent in parallel form in the wisdom saying, as the point of departure shifts from the experiential saying in Proverbs 10–30 to a speculative approach featuring a pre-existing saying prior to all Creation in Proverbs 1–9, centred on Proverbs 8.[48]

---

[45]   According to Colli, *Die Geburt der Philosophie*, p. 43.

[46]   Just how much Weber, along with the Old Testament scholars of his time, interpreted Hebrew prophecy within a Hellenistic framework is apparent in his intensive reception of the study by the authority on ancient Greece, Erwin Rohde (*Psyche: The Cult of Souls and Belief in Immortality among the Greeks*, London, Kegan Paul, 1925).

[47]   See Otto, *Theologische Ethik des Alten Testaments*, pp. 104–11, and idem, 'Die Geburt des moralischen Bewußtseins. Die Ethik der Hebräischen Bibel', in Eckart Otto and Siegbert Uhlig, *Bibel und Christentum im Orient*, Orientalia Biblica et Christiana 1, Glückstadt, J. J. Augustin/Wiesbaden, Harrassowitz, 1991, pp. 9–28.

[48]   On the history of the Hebrew saying in relation to that of Egypt and Mesopotamia, see Otto, *Theologische Ethik des Alten Testaments*, pp. 117–75. The Hebrew wisdom saying, which first appeared in the eighth century BC with the reception of parts of the Egyptian doctrine of Amenemope from the ninth century BC, received this doctrine conservatively, replacing the classical Egyptian theory of life with that referred to as 'personal piety' – reflecting the worldview found in the Egyptian teachings of the second millennium BC. Ultimately, the Hebrew wisdom saying arrived at the point at which the Egyptian saying characteristic of Amenemope had stood in the Hellenistic era.

The agents of this dialectic of secularization and theologization through Torah, prophecy and saying are intellectuals who first emerged in the Neo-Assyrian crisis of the eighth and seventh centuries BC, but who advanced the formation of the Hebrew Bible into the Hellenistic era. Particularly with respect to prophecy, the dialectic of secularization and theologization is undoubtedly comparable to the process of the extraction of philosophy from myth and subsequent speculative theologization in Greek philosophy.[49] Yet there is a crucial difference: in Judaism, the dialectically interrelated processes of secularization and theologization occurred within traditional Jewish religion, rather than emigrating from religion as did Hellenic philosophy. In contrast to its Jewish counterpart, Hellenic religion lacked an intellectual class of religious specialists functioning as agents of the ethical rationalization of religion. As a religion of sacrifice, Greek religion merely expected each individual to carry out his sacrificial obligations and did not facilitate the emergence of a priestly class of autonomous intellectuals alongside the ruling political classes, who obtained their role models from an aristocratic warrior ethos. In ancient Judaism, all secularization and enlightenment took place within the bounds of traditional religion, which still applied, as is discernible in Moses Mendelssohn,[50] to the Jewish 'Berliner Haskala',[51] which thus retained features of the German Enlightenment even within the boundaries of Protestant Christianity in the sense of a 'shared history'.

---

[49]   See Eckart Otto, 'Recht und Ethos in der ost- und westmediterranen Antike. Entwurf eines Gesamtbildes', in Markus Witte (ed.), *Gott und Mensch im Dialog. Festschrift für Otto Kaiser zum 80. Geburtstag*, vol. I, Beihefte zur Zeitschrift für die Alttestamentliche Wissenschaft 345/1, Berlin, Walter de Gruyter, 2004, pp. 91–109; idem, 'Law and Ethics', in Sarah Iles Johnston (ed.), *Religions of the Ancient World*, Harvard University Press Reference Library, Cambridge, MA, Harvard University Press, 2004, pp. 84–97.

[50]   See Moses Mendelssohn, *Jerusalem, Or, On Religious Power and Judaism*, Hanover, NH, University Press of New England, 1983. (See also *Jerusalem oder über religiöse Macht und Judentum. Mit dem Vorwort zu Manasse ben Israels Rettung der Juden und dem Entwurf zu Jerusalem*, Philosophische Bibliothek 565, Hamburg, Felix Meiner, 2005, and the introduction by Michael Albrecht, pp. vii–xlii).

[51]   See David Sorkin, *Moses Mendelssohn and the Religious Enlightenment*, London, Peter Halban, 1996, and Shmuel Feiner, 'Eine traumatische Begegnung. Das jüdische Volk in der europäischen Moderne', in Michael Brenner and David N. Meyers (eds.), *Jüdische Geschichtsschreibung heute. Themen – Positionen – Kontroversen*, Munich, Beck, 2002, pp. 105–22.

'Textualized existence' and the yearning for redemption: sect formation in post-biblical Judaism

The Jewish priest Flavius Josephus, who became a writer in Rome after being taken prisoner by the Romans and who wished to enhance the credibility of the Jewish cause in Rome among non-Jews, sees Judaism in Palestine in the second and first pre-Christian centuries divided into three 'sects' (Greek *haireseis*) 'which held different opinions concerning human affairs; the first being that of the Pharisees, the second that of the Sadducees, and the third that of the Essenes'.[52] For the Roman period, we must add a fourth grouping, that of the Zealots and the Baptist sects of John and the early Christian community.[53] To inquire into the

---

[52]   See Josephus, *Jewish Antiquities*, xii–xiii, Cambridge, MA, Harvard University Press, 1998, xiii 5.9. (p. 311). The term 'sect' is used here in Troeltsch's sense (*Social Teachings*, pp. 331–32). The contemporary pejorative use of the term is absent in both cases. The term should not be used, moreover, in the sense of the deviation of a minority from a pre-given norm characteristic of a majority. The use of the term 'sect' in the work of Troeltsch and Weber is very different from its colloquial usage. At the first German sociology conference in Frankfurt am Main, in his lecture 'Stoic-Christian Natural Law and Modern Profane Natural Law', Troeltsch presented for discussion his typology of church, sect and mysticism as found in *Social Teachings*; see *Verhandlungen des Ersten Deutschen Soziologentages vom 19.–22. Oktober 1910 in Frankfurt a. M. Reden und Vorträge […] und Debatten*, Tübingen, Mohr, 1911, pp. 166–92. Three different principles, regulating the relationship of the faithful to the demands of natural and social life, were claimed to be associated with these three sociological types. The church, on this view, is characterized by the compromise of living with the laws of the world without giving up one's faith in the kingdom of God, while sects are distinguished by a rigorism which rejects all compromise between heavenly kingdom and world. In the ensuing discussion, Ferdinand Tönnies (pp. 192–96) derived the sect as type from the cities' resistance to the power of the church. Weber (pp. 199–200) objected that this was too monocausally materialistic. In antiquity, he asserted, sects were to be found in the countryside, and also in the city in the medieval period, yet the idea of the church had developed on this foundation. In his study of *Ancient Judaism* (pp. 380–82), Weber assumes a social opposition between the urban and rural population which fostered the development of urban sects because, as he puts it in the pre-war manuscript 'Ethik und Mythik/Rituelle Absonderung' and in the study 'The Pharisees' (*Das antike Judentum* [MWG I/21.1], pp. 385–424), it was more difficult to comply strictly with the rules on purity in the rural context.

[53]   See Gerd Theissen, 'Der jüdische Jesus', in idem, *Jesus als historische Gestalt. Beiträge zur Jesusforschung*, Forschungen zu Religion und Literatur des Alten und Neuen Testaments 202, Göttingen, Vandenhoeck & Ruprecht, 2003, pp. 33–131. The flows of Diaspora Jewry, particularly in Alexandria, where Jews made up a third of the population, must once again be set apart from these inner-Jewish groupings in Palestine.

reasons for the development of these Jewish sects in the Hellenistic and Roman periods, which also gave rise to Christianity, is a far from simple endeavour, though the scrolls found since 1947, hidden from the Romans in the caves around the scriptorium of the Essenes at Qumran on the Dead Sea, have shed somewhat more light on the matter.[54] The process of Jewish sect formation has a part in the contemporary move towards conventicle formation, also observable in the non-Jewish context, in the entire Hellenistic-Roman world first of the Middle East, but then also of the western Mediterranean, as a religious movement running counter to a tendency towards political and cultural universalization.[55] Yet the contemporary trends engulfing the entire Hellenistic-Roman world do not sufficiently explain Jewish sect formation, as it contradicts the idea, central to the religion of ancient Judaism, of God's covenant with his people as a single covenant community. The idea of a covenant itself would have been a sufficient motive for uncoupling the Jewish community, as an indivisible community, from the contemporary trend towards sect formation. Weber identified two developments as responsible for the process of Jewish sect formation. First, he asserted, the 'priestly [...] power' succeeded in pushing prophetic charisma to the margins of Judaism, such that the 'activities of these seers', in the form of apocalyptic thought for example, became the affair of sects and mystery cults, while, second, the social opposition between the urban demos of farmers, craftsmen and merchants on the one hand and worldly and priestly families in the countryside on the other led to a situation in which members of the urban petit bourgeoisie considered themselves the Chosen People, the pious and poor in contrast to their opponents.[56]

This necessary recourse to the constellation of power interests which make use of religion and also create it remains unsatisfactory in two respects and, around one hundred years later, must be modified – on the basis above all of the discovery of the Qumran scrolls. As recent research on the literary interaction between Pentateuch and prophetic writings shows, it is true that the priestly scribes responsible for the literary history of the Pentateuch in the Persian era brought to an end the prophetic tradition of authors who opposed them, as in the Book of Jeremiah, by adopting a prophetic mantle, such that writing that traced its origins to prophetic figures was relegated to apocalyptic circles and

---

[54]   See Hartmut Stegemann, *The Library of Qumran: On the Essenes, Qumran, John the Baptist and Jesus*, Grand Rapids, MI, Eerdmans, 1998.

[55]   Demotic papyri provide a good insight into this process of religious community formation in the late Egyptian period; see Françoise de Cenival, *Les associations religieuses en Egypte d'après les documents demotiques*, Cairo, Institut français d'archéologie orientale du Caire, 1972, pp. 139–213.

[56]   See Weber, *Ancient Judaism*, pp. 380–82.

found canonical recognition only with the Book of Daniel. Yet this does not yet explain how, as now documented by the Qumran scrolls, sect formation could occur within the priesthood. The apparent reason for the founding of the sects of the Essenes was the expulsion of the legitimate high priest of Jerusalem by the Hasmonian Jonathan in 152 BC. As the 'teacher of justice', in exile he gathered around him a group of followers which attracted many new members in Palestine and grew into a powerful movement; it broke with the temple in Jerusalem and claimed to be the only authority maintaining the purity demanded by the Torah. The Essene Torah Midrash 4QMMT[57] published in 1994 confirms that these were priestly disputes within Jewish scholarship,[58] but that, up to the middle of the second century BC, tendencies towards priestly divisions resonated far beyond the immediate conflicts over the office of high priest and the question of purity, such that the Essene movement was able to develop further as a distinct sect, incorporating an apocalyptic-eschatological self-understanding as the true community of God in the imminent divine judgement[59] into the Roman era. Exclusivity as a community of the perfect, which demands compliance with the laws on ritual purity (which originally applied only to the priests, but were now extended to the entire community) and belief in the impending kingdom of God, which would mean the annihilation of those not belonging to the community of the chosen, were closely interrelated in the Essene sect.

The sects of the Essenes, Pharisees and Sadducees interpreted one and the same Torah of the Pentateuch with different methods, which were bound up with different lifestyles. But what unites them is the attempt to fulfil the Scriptures by living a 'textualized existence' (Thomas Mann).[60] The greater the eschatological-apocalyptic expectation of imminent salvation in the sects, the greater their indifference to the world. This connection is well illustrated in the sect of John

---

[57]   See Elisha Qimron and John Strugnell (eds.), *Qumran Cave 4, vol. V: Miqsat Ma'a'se ha-Torah*, Discoveries in the Judean Desert 10, Oxford, Clarendon Press, 1994, pp. 109ff. On the topic of purity in the Qumran texts, cf. Hannah K. Harrington, *The Purity Texts*, London, T. & T. Clark, 2004.

[58]   On the priestly context of Jewish scriptural scholarship, see Eckart Otto, 'Vom biblischen Hebraismus der persischen Zeit zum rabbinischen Judaismus in römischer Zeit. Zur Geschichte der spätbiblischen und frühjüdischen Schriftgelehrsamkeit', *Zeitschrift für altorientalische und biblische Rechtsgeschichte*, 10 (2004), pp. 1–49.

[59]   See Troeltsch, *Social Teachings*, p. 331.

[60]   See Michael Fishbane, 'Canonical Text, Covenant Communities, and the Patterns of Exegetical Culture', in A. D. H. Mayes and R. B. Salters (eds.), *Covenant as Context: Essays in Honour of Ernest W. Nicholson*, Oxford, Oxford University Press, 2003, pp. 135–61. On scriptural exegesis in the Qumran texts, see Jonathan G. Campbell, *The Exegetical Texts*, London, T. & T. Clark, 2004.

the Baptist, which was originally independent of the early Christian community. By withdrawing into the desert, the Baptist sects increased their distance from the traditional Temple Judaism of Jerusalem, and further dramatized the expectation of imminent punishment by God through the assumption that it would apply also to those devout individuals who were not baptized. One final possible means of escaping God's judgement was the baptism of repentance which entailed the forgiving of sins (Mk 1:4) combined with penitence as a fundamental renunciation of a world subject to divine judgement (Mk 1:1–8; Mt. 3:1–12; Lk. 3:1–8).[61] The tendency towards intra-Jewish delineation was further intensified by the fact that the Jewish religion as a whole, even in Palestine, came under cultural pressure from Hellenism,[62] which confronted the Jews as a force of cultural modernization that accelerated processes of secularization and triggered corresponding responses – namely a greater need for theology in order to preserve Jewish identity. But this dialectic played itself out in highly dissonant fashion, as the Jewish responses to Hellenism ranged from a critical interpretation of Hellenistic thought in the *Qohelet*, a book of wise sayings, to brusque rejection by the Essenes.

What was the result of this process of the fragmentation of Judaism into sects in the Hellenistic and Roman period, combined with an increasing indifference towards the extant world in favour of the expectation of the world to come? All the historical and social historical reasons mentioned above played a part, but they do not constitute an adequate explanation. Here, the dialectic of the secularization of world view and the theologization of ethics, which characterized Jewish religious history over the course of centuries, made its presence felt and revealed its aporias. The monotheism which made its breakthrough in the sixth century BC acted as a powerful stimulus to the process of disenchantment and desacralization of the external lifeworld, already set in motion from the seventh century BC, which endured from the fifth century BC into the Roman era. The response to the disenchantment of the lifeworld was an ethical theologization which saw the secularized external lifeworld as a field to be shaped pragmatically in line with God's laws.

The prerequisite for this form of ethics was the idea that the acting individual, as well as his external lifeworld, as fields of action, were subject to the order-creating rule of the God JHWH as the Creator of heaven and earth (Gen. 1–3), and thus that deed and personal outcome ought to form a unity, such that good action in conformity with the rules laid down by this God would result in a successful life. But because people's actual experience of life could not confirm this expectation, prophetic circles projected it into the future, in which God as

---

[61]   See the concise summary in Jürgen Roloff, *Jesus*, Beck'sche Reihe 2142, Munich, Beck, 3rd edn, 2004, pp. 60–104.

[62]   See Martin Hengel, *Judaism and Hellenism*, London, SCM, 1974, pp. 58–106.

Creator would intervene anew, stirring hopes of liberation from this world.[63] But the greater the gulf between the religious idea of lifeworlds ordered by God and experience, particularly in the second century BC as the Jewish people and their religion struggled to survive in the Maccabean wars, the greater the hopes of God's redemptive intervention and, along with it, the more popular an increasing indifference, even hostility, towards extant lifeworlds. This stimulated processes of distancing from the traditional activity of religion as well; these were associated with redefinitions of true piety and fidelity to the laws that produced rules of scriptural interpretation, and thus of correlated lifestyles, distinct from those of others.[64] If the traditional religious system was no longer capable of integrating distressing experiences, such as the Maccabean wars, that appeared to contradict its claims, this system was radicalized through the tension between idea and empirical experience in favour of the hope of redemption. At the same time, it demolished its social form and frayed into conflicting sects, whose only common feature was now their commitment to the one – though hermeneutically differentiated – Torah, the Pentateuch; in view of conflicting modes of interpretation, however, it could no longer provide a bond uniting the

---

[63]   In contrast to Egyptian religion, which in the second millennium BC sought to mediate the tension between religious theory and de facto experience of life by extending the theory of the link between deed and experience to the realm of the dead in the hereafter, the Hebrew Bible received the idea of the resurrection only on its canonical edges, in Daniel 12, in the second century BC, amid the dire circumstances of the Maccabean wars. This represented a significant burden on ancient Jewish religion, as it prevented innerworldly mediation between idea and experience. Post-biblical Judaism managed to diminish this rupture: while the expectation that the Apocalypse would occur in the near future was suppressed, hopes of resurrection gained currency.

[64]   The overall picture of Jewish lifestyles, based on differing styles and techniques of scriptural exegesis, emerges as yet more diverse if we include the Diaspora Jewry in Syria, Mesopotamia, Asia Minor, Greece, Italy and above all Egypt, centred in Alexandria. In view of the surge of modernization and rationalization stimulated by Hellenistic philosophy, authors within the Hellenistic Jewish world were confronted in a special sense with the task of helping demarcate and preserve identity and at the same time aiding assimilation into a culturally unfamiliar environment. Hellenistic-Jewish authors proceeded *defensively* by securing, interpreting, defending and updating the biblical traditions and at the same time *offensively* by pointing to the moral, religious and cultural superiority of their tradition over that of Hellenism and Hellenistic philosophy, which were traced back to Jewish precedents: the entire Hellenistic Paideia was attributed to Moses as a teacher of Hellenic philosophers and his Torah. See Reinhard Weber, *Das Gesetz im hellenistischen Judentum. Studien zum Verständnis und zur Funktion der Thora von Demetrios bis Pseudo-Phoklides*, Arbeiten zur Religion und Geschichte des Urchristentums 10, Frankfurt am Main, Peter Lang, 2000.

Covenant People. This was provided only by the disasters of the Jewish wars of the first and second centuries AD, which triggered a return to, and focus on, the originally priestly Torah exegesis in the Halacha[65] and hence the weeding out of the apocalyptic sects.[66]

An overview of modern Judaism in the state of Israel

Since 1948, in the recent history of Judaism in the state of Israel, numerous motifs of a many-layered Jewish religious history, which must be traced back into antiquity, have been present subcutaneously in secularized garb. The Israeli historian Amnon Raz-Krakotzkin[67] has pointed out that modern national Jewish historiography in Israel fosters a narrative of the 'negation of exile', that is, of Diaspora Judaism, of a consciousness 'which, in the contemporary Jewish settlement of Palestine and sovereignty over Palestine, sees the "return" of the Jews to a land that is regarded as their home and which is supposed to have been uninhabited before their return. The "negation" of exile seemed to be the highpoint of Jewish history and the realization of long-held expectations of redemption'.[68]

The historian of ancient Judaism sees the parallels with the Jewish processing of the 'exile' of 586–539 BC. Though only a small part of the Jewish upper class was exiled, while the rest of the population remained, in the prophetic literature and chronicles of the post-exilic era the exiles, who included the priestly-intellectual literati, managed to enforce the view that during the exile the land had been empty, and thus that the history of 'Israel' after the exile had been that of resettlement by the exiles. The difference between the historiography of the

---

[65] See Eckart Otto, 'Vom biblischen Hebraismus der persischen Zeit zum rabbinischen Judaismus in römischer Zeit', pp. 39ff. with suggestions on further reading.

[66] In early Christianity, meanwhile, apocalyptic theology, already led by Jesus (Lk. 10:18), lived on and was finally overcome only with the integration of natural law.

[67] See Amnon Raz-Krakotzkin, 'Geschichte, Nationalismus, Eingedenken', in Michael Brenner and David N. Meyers (eds.), *Jüdische Geschichtsschreibung heute. Themen, Positionen, Kontroversen*, Munich, Beck, 2002, pp. 181–206.

[68] See Raz-Krakotzkin, 'Geschichte, Nationalismus, Eingedenken', p. 186. It is certainly a paradox that 150 years earlier, Heinrich Graetz felt compelled to accuse Christian historians of burying 1200 years of Jewish Diaspora history, which had, he asserted, featured a great deal of theoretical, scientific and philosophical creativity (see Heinrich Graetz, *Geschichte der Juden von der ältesten Zeit bis auf die Gegenwart*, vol. IV, Leipzig, Oskar Leiner, 4th edn, 1908, pp. 4–5), and of writing the death certificate of Jewish history; see Heinrich Graetz, *The Structure of Jewish History* (1864), translated and edited by Ismar Schorsch, New York, Jewish Theological Seminary of America, 1975, p. 94.

time and that of today is merely that in modern Jewish historical interpretations, against the backdrop of Zionism, the motif of the 'empty land' is divested of the explicitly religious argument that JHWH, the God of Israel, ensured that His People were led out of the country and brought back again. In Zionism, the divine promises of land made to the Patriarchs in the Pentateuch, as well as the promises of return in Deutero-Isaiah (40–55), which proclaim the triumphant return of the Jewish people from exile to the once promised land, have been stripped of their divine origin and nationalized after being cast in secular form:[69] 'God had been excluded from the discourse, but his Word, the divine promise, continued to set the course for political activity and served as a source of legitimation for the process of colonization, which is understood as the fulfilment of the biblical promise and the prayers of Jews throughout the ages.'[70]

Since the early modern period, traditional Jewish religion, like Christianity, has become incapable of defending and shielding its promises of salvation against the disappointment resulting from the concrete life experiences that contradict them.[71] As a consequence, both religions were submerged within a 'shared history' of the Enlightenment, which went hand in hand with a phase of intense secularization in both religions;[72] this found expression in the Jewish case primarily in assimilation to Western European modernity.[73] This approach was called into question by the fate of European Jewry in the nineteenth and above all in the twentieth century. Regardless of the disputes between socialist-secular and national-religious Zionists, which characterized the Zionist movement from the outset and continue to determine Israeli politics to this day, the Zionist idea as a whole entailed the secularization of religious hopes of a Jewish rebirth, which, as traditional Judaism sees it, should be the work of God. Secularization was bound to produce conflict between the religious and the national idea or a loss of substance in the religious idea. Max Weber, as we have seen, expressed

---

[69]   See Michael Wolffsohn, *Wem gehört das Heilige Land? Die Wurzeln des Streits zwischen Juden und Arabern*, Munich, Piper, 2002.

[70]   See Raz-Krakotzkin, 'Geschichte, Nationalismus, Eingedenken', p. 187.

[71]   See Hans Blumenberg, *The Legitimacy of the Modern Age*, Cambridge, MA, MIT Press, 1983.

[72]   On the increasing number of Jewish studies in recent times that understand Judaism and Christianity as religions within a common discursive framework, see Feiner, 'Traumatische Begegnung', pp. 105–12.

[73]   For a paradigmatic study, see Michael Brenner, 'Warum München nicht zur Hauptstadt des Zionismus wurde – Jüdische Religion und Politik um die Jahrhundertwende', in Michael Brenner and Yfaat Weiss (eds.), *Zionistische Utopie – israelische Realität. Religion und Nation in Israel*, Beck'sche Reihe 1339, Munich, Beck, 1999, pp. 39–52.

this perceptively as early as 1913.[74] Yet, predictably, as was the case in antiquity, a trend towards theologization is again bound up with that of secularization.

'I said to myself: if He [God] wishes it, I will avenge Him, [...] if the Torah instructs you to do something you are reluctant to do, you still do it. [...] I see the situation in Israel as a cultural struggle between two parties: the atheist, extreme left, which promises the people bread and games, and the religious right.'[75] This is how fundamentalist assassin Yigal Amir justified the murder of the Israeli prime minister Yitzhak Rabin. Despite secularization, centuries-old religious conflicts resurface in disputes over the city of Jerusalem as the holy city of three world religions.[76] The boundary between religion and the state in Israel remains blurred and a source of conflict. The separation of religion from the state, which first began in the seventh century BC, is the many-layered historical background to these conflicts. And just as we might expect given the events of antiquity, with the counter-movement of theologization, the formation of sects also increases. The groupings led by the rabbis Schach and Hirsch, the latter extremely anti-Zionist, but the former a 'helpful activist' in the camp of the fundamentalists who wish to hasten God's intervention, are representative of this development. If we seek to grasp what links processes of secularization in antiquity with those of modernity, it is the disappointments triggered by the deficits of the different religious systems. In view of its subjugation to the religiously legitimized power of the Neo-Assyrian empire, the Judaean state ideology – which the Davidian rulers, as is apparent in the royal psalms, such as Psalm 2, also legitimized through religion – was also subjected to criticism, and religion was separated from the function of legitimizing rulers. The pressure of external events, to which the religious system could provide no adequate answer, led, as may be reconstructed into the Roman era, to the renovation of the religious system, which filled the gap created by secularization. This is most strikingly evident in the universalization of a brotherly ethos following the collapse of familial ethics and in the universalization of hopes of salvation in apocalyptic thought. As a response to processes of secularization, those of theologization must be described

---

[74]   Yet as apparent in the revitalization of the Hebrew language, which was already ousted by Aramaic as the language of everyday life in Persian times and became a purely holy language, even the sacred was merely given a profane patina within Zionism. For traditional Judaism, the resurgence of Hebrew was linked with the messianic era as the end of history.

[75]   Quoted in Feiner, 'Traumatische Begegnung', p. 105.

[76]   See Eckart Otto, *Jerusalem. Die Geschichte der Heiligen Stadt bis zur Kreuzfahrerzeit*, Urban-Reihe 308, Stuttgart, Kohlhammer, 1980, and Gershom Shaked, 'Jerusalem in der hebräischen Literatur. Himmlische und irdische Stadt', in Brenner and Weiss (eds.), *Zionistische Utopie*, pp. 102–22.

as processes of the transcendence of the concept of God, which was increasingly contrasted with empirical experience,[77] along with the resulting universalization and internalization of ethics.

The ethics of the Hebrew Bible shows very concisely how a theologically founded social ethics emphasizing responsibility for the weak in society responds to the social differentiation of society into poor and rich classes, in order, ideally, to ensure the cohesion of a society drifting apart. But theologization may also take a regressive form, as is evident in recent fundamentalisms worldwide. It may entail a refusal to renovate the religious system (on the basis of a view of secularization as a positive challenge to the modernization of religion), falling back on models long since outgrown in religious historical terms, until, isolated with regard to cultural history and lapsing into sectarianism, it finally leaves the secularized world to itself or seeks to dominate it through terrorism. Only when the dialectic of secularization and theologization is brought to an end will secularization become a one-sided process of religious decline within society.

Yet – and here I would like to sum up this chapter – it is not to be expected that this dialectic will ever cease. To discover it both in the sources of ancient Judaism and in modernity, even when modernity follows the special path of Western rationalism characteristic of the core European countries – which constitutes a blueprint neither for the North American continent nor for its African and Asian counterparts – reveals its universal significance throughout history. Processes of secularization, in the sense used here of the legitimation of domination, law and ethics, are accompanied by those of theologization in other spheres. What we observe in both antiquity and modernity are merely shifts within one and the same religious system. Hence, we are dealing here with a law that applies universally throughout religious history, which in this sense features no progress. It thus makes no difference whether one believes that one is living through an ascending or descending branch of religious history.[78]

But it is also true that not all religions are the same in terms of how they elaborate the dialectic of secularization and theologization. You will permit me to refer to an important difference between Christianity and Judaism, which renders the latter particularly resistant, in the best sense of the word, to processes of

---

[77]   Already in antiquity, the avoidance of the Jewish name for God shows the tendency towards transcendence of the concept of God. When Moses Maimonides (1135–1204) tried to derive the Mosaic law from reason, this idea of a secularization of theonomic ethics, which pre-empted the idea of the moral autonomy of reason in the Enlightenment, served to uphold the transcendence of the Jewish God.

[78]   See Troeltsch, *Historismus*, p. ix; see also Ferdinand S. Tönnies, 'Troeltsch und die Philosophie der Geschichte', in idem, *Soziologische Studien und Kritiken*, Zweite Sammlung, Jena, Gustav Fischer, 1926, pp. 381–429, here p. 429.

secularization and thus also to exaggerated processes of theologization. More than in Christianity, there is in Judaism a core of messianic non-conformity to the everyday lifeworld, which will be resistant to every compromise between transcendent God and the world.[79] The reasons for this are, first of all, of a historical nature. In contrast to Christianity, Judaism has completed no Constantinian turn, not only because of the Diaspora situation in the Roman empire, but above all, as we have seen with the help of Deuteronomy (Deut. 13), because it would be a 'sin against the spirit' of the Hebrew Bible. Unlike Christianity, for this very reason Judaism has not received ancient natural law in its various forms.[80] Finally, Judaism preserves a structural difference from the world, but this does not take the form of indifference to the world, but of the active organization of the world in line with the will of God. From the outset, Christianity mediates God and the world Christologically through the idea that in Jesus Christ God has come into the world as its saviour. We would have to go far beyond the framework laid down in this chapter in order to ask, let alone answer, the question of whether Christianity, in contrast to Judaism, contains within its structure the seed of secularization, ultimately even its own self-abolition.[81] Yet in the case of Christianity as well, the dialectic of secularization and theologization will persist.

---

[79] In an extremely secularized form, this core of utopian-messianic non-conformity shows through even in the philosophy of the Jewish thinker Ernst Bloch; see Ulrich Sieg, *Jüdische Intellektuelle im Ersten Weltkrieg. Kriegserfahrungen, weltanschauliche Debatten und kulturelle Neuentwürfe*, Berlin, Akademie Verlag, 2001, pp. 274ff. on 'Geschichtsverzweiflung und jüdischer Messianismus'.

[80] The Sophoclean prioritizing of the 'immutable unwritten laws of Heaven [which were] not born today or yesterday' (*Antigone*, ll. 471–73; see *Sophocles*, vol. I, translated by F. Storr, London, Heinemann, 1916) over positive law, on the other hand, results in the theory of a natural law which was hindered in Deuteronomy through its integration into a theory of revelation tied to Moses as a prophet.

[81] Friedrich Gogarten's distinction between secularism and secularization continues to be helpful because it distinguishes the theologically positive aspects of the 'disenchantment' of traditional ways of understanding the world from misguided attempts to destroy religion. See Friedrich Gogarten, *Verhängnis und Hoffnung der Neuzeit. Die Säkularisierung als theologisches Problem*, Stuttgart, Friedrich Vorwerk, 2nd edn, 1958, pp. 85ff.

4

Islam and Secularization

Gudrun Krämer

For a number of years, public debate has distinguished more clearly between Islam and Islamism than was formerly the case, and quite rightly so: Islam is a world religion with well over a billion followers, who live and experience their religion in a wide variety of ways. Sunnis differ in certain respects from Shiites, traditionalist Muslims from liberal ones; some seek a spiritual path to God, others want nothing to do with mysticism; some lead an ascetic lifestyle, others enjoy life to the full; many see politics as an important aspect of their religion, while others reject politics in the name of Islam. Different ways of understanding and living Islam stretch far back into history; in the present era, they have taken on distinctive, specifically modern aspects. Overall, Islam is certainly as plural and diversified as Christianity, and it has been so from the very beginning, particularly with respect to how Muslims have imagined community and society, the good life and good government. Islamism, which receives so much attention today, is therefore just one possible way among several of applying Islamic teachings to individual conduct and the social order. The boundary between Islam and Islamism is, however, not always easy to draw. In many fields, Islamists now dominate to such an extent that one might think that they are in fact the only legitimate representatives of Islam (and this is, of course, how they view themselves). This applies especially to the issues, under consideration here, of society, law, politics and culture, with respect to which Islamists literally 'set the tone'. There is thus no question of a 'failure of political Islam', which a few years ago some observers thought they had discerned.[1] The topic of secularization makes this abundantly clear.

It is Islamist claims that determine general perceptions in this regard

---

[1]   The French political scientists Roy and Kepel have attracted most attention; see Olivier Roy, *The Failure of Political Islam*, Cambridge, MA, Harvard University Press, 1996; Gilles Kepel, *Jihad: The Trail of Political Islam*, London, I. B. Tauris, 2002. The events of 11 September 2001 have prompted a re-evaluation of political Islam.

(particularly in the West), above all the Islamist notion of the 'unity of religion and state', which makes secularization appear illegitimate from the outset, if not impossible. From an Islamist point of view, religion and state cannot and must not be separated. According to this view, any separation is an offence against Islam as well as a violation of Muslim identity – both individually and collectively.[2] In this connection, the linkage of religion, identity and authenticity is of fundamental importance. Islam, so the Islamists postulate, is a self-contained, all-embracing, holistic system of norms and values that must shape individual conduct and the social order, economy, law and politics. This system of norms and values, generally known as Sharia, is based on divine statute and is revealed in the Qur'an, the unadulterated word of God, and in the prophetic traditions (Sunna), which inform us about the conduct of the Prophet Muhammad, who implemented God's commandments in exemplary and binding fashion. Decreed by God and embodied by the Prophet, the Sharia is fundamentally unchanging and beyond all human intervention, an argument clearly directed at authoritarian claims to power and thus attractive to many Muslims who otherwise have no Islamist leanings.

For many Muslims, Islam implies first and foremost belonging to the community of Muslims, or *Umma* in Arabic. For them, being a Muslim means being a part of a worldwide community of believers that transcends the boundaries of local society without necessarily being in conflict with it. Faith creates belonging; each must be displayed through pious deeds. Here the Islamists go one step further: according to them, Islam can be realized only within the framework of an 'Islamic order' in which the divine commandments are made binding for all – both believers and non-believers. Thus non-practising Muslims, agnostics and non-Muslims are also in principle subject to the Sharia, though the latter are granted some leeway in certain fields, such as personal status and family law. Islam, so the Islamists insist, demands the 'application of the Sharia' as the system of law and values laid down by God for all times and places. The 'application of the Sharia' in turn presupposes an Islamic state authority. Hence, Islam is not only, as assumed by many devout Muslims past and present, 'religion and world' (*al-islam din wa-dunya*). It is also 'religion and state' (*al-islam din wa-daula*).

What appears here as a *statement* about Islam, as a norm confirmed by history, is in fact an *argument* within a political contest, if not a full-blown clash of cultures, in which Islamists are opposed not only to the West but also to other

---

[2]   There exists an extensive literature on this subject. For an introduction, see my chapter 'The Contest of Values: Notes on Contemporary Islamic Discourse', in Hans Joas and Klaus Wiegandt (eds.), *The Cultural Values of Europe*, Liverpool, Liverpool University Press, 2008, pp. 338–56, and my monograph *Gottes Staat als Republik. Reflexionen zeitgenös-sischer Muslime zu Islam, Menschenrechten und Demokratie*, Baden-Baden, Nomos, 1999.

Muslims with their own understandings of Islam. The enemy of the Islamists is on the one hand an external one: it is the West, which they believe suppressed Islamic norms, values and institutions in the colonial period[3] and which now, in the name of a struggle for human rights and the principles of 'good governance', demands of Muslims an enlightenment, a reformation and, as a prerequisite for their entry into modernity, a process of secularization, based on the affirmation of the secular principle. The other enemy is to be found within the Muslim community in the shape of 'secularists', an ill-defined category, whom Islamists have fought in a dogged and polemical struggle: apart from individual intellectuals and writers, the key figures here are politicians such as Kemal Atatürk in Turkey and Habib Bourguiba in Tunisia, who did in fact attempt to secularize politics, law and society by authoritarian means, and to some extent succeeded in doing so. But individuals and groups that merely reject demands for the 'integral' application of the Sharia are also counted among the enemy. The charges have a familiar ring: secularism is said to be tantamount to godlessness, devoid of values and without respect for the bounds of custom and decency.[4] At the same time – and this is a feature specific to the debate in non-European countries, especially those with a colonial past – secularist ideas and aspirations are said to be induced from outside, or at the very least inspired by the West, if not controlled remotely by it, and realizable in Muslim societies only by authoritarian means. Thus, the domestic enemy is associated not only with his external counterpart, but also with the enemies of democracy.[5]

---

[3]   This is not the place to investigate the religious policies pursued by European colonial powers, which generally amounted to non-intervention in religious affairs in order to prevent conflict in this sensitive field. In India, however, with the introduction of the so-called Anglo-Muhammadan Law, the British interfered profoundly with the existing legal order. In the Ottoman Empire, meanwhile, which was never directly colonized, the reforms of law, constitution and administration in the era of the Tanzimat (1839–78), reforms that advanced secularization both individually and in their entirety, emanated from the Ottoman elites, who were merely *inspired* by European models.

[4]   This is clearly apparent in the term *la-diniyya*, for a long time the term for secularism in Arabic: it refers to the 'absence' or 'denial' of religion. Today, *'almaniyya* is more common in Arabic, a word which is often associated with *'ilm*, 'knowledge', though this is not entirely convincing linguistically.

[5]   There is an extensive, often polemical literature critical of secularism; for a representative example, see Yusuf al-Qaradawi, *Al-tatarruf al-'almani fi muwajahat al-islam (namuzaj turkiya wa-tunis)* (Secularist Extremism in Confrontation with Islam: The Example of Turkey and Tunisia), Cairo, Dar al-Shuruq, 2001; for Qaradawi (b. 1926), one of the most influential Muslim scholar-activists of the early twenty-first century, see my 'Drawing Boundaries: Yusuf al-Qaradawi on Apostasy', in Gudrun Krämer and Sabine Schmidtke (eds.), *Speaking for Islam: Religious Authorities in Muslim Societies*, Leiden,

Secularization and secularism (the two are seldom distinguished within the political debate, and the distinction is made even more rarely with respect to secularism and laicism) thus carry a heavy burden, with which their advocates struggle to cope.[6] Critics attack secularization as the core of a project of modernization imposed from outside, which damages, if not destroys, the 'identity' of Muslim societies, to the benefit of their enemies. The political argument – secularization and secularism as tools of colonization and alienation, secularists as supporters and lackeys of authoritarian regimes – counts for much in this context, particularly in the age of globalization. If we overlook the political dimension, we fail to understand the intensity of a debate in which all parties show little inclination to make these important distinctions. This is most apparent in the Arab world and Iran. The situation is quite different in Turkey, the Central Asian successor states of the Soviet Union and Muslim societies of South Asia and Southeast Asia.[7]

A brief conceptual clarification

I would like to follow, although in a slightly modified form, the distinctions proposed by José Casanova to elucidate different aspects of secularization.[8] Casanova identifies three dimensions of secularization:

Brill, 2006, pp. 181–217. See further Ibrahim Abu-Rabi', *Contemporary Arab Thought: Studies in Post-1967 Arab Intellectual History*, London, Pluto Press, 2004, and Kate Zebiri, 'Muslim Anti-Secularist Discourse in the Context of Muslim–Christian Relations', *Islam and Christian–Muslim Relations*, 9.1 (1998), pp. 47–64.

[6]   Many Arab secularists have published in French; see Fouad Zakariya (Egypt), *Laïcité ou islamisme. Les Arabes à l'heure du choix*, Paris, La Découverte, 1991; Mohamed-Chérif Ferjani (Tunisia), *Islamisme, laïcité et droits de l'homme. Un siècle de débat sans cesse reporté au sein de la pensée arabe contemporaine*, Paris, L'Harmattan, 1991; and Abdou Filali-Ansary (Morocco), *L'islam est-il hostile à la laïcité?*, Paris, Actes Sud, 2002. Among the best-known champions of secular thought is Aziz al-Azmeh, a prominent scholar of Islam originally from Syria; see his *Al-asala aw siyasat al-hurub min al-waqi'* (Authenticity or the Politics of Flight from Reality), London, Dar al-Saqi, 1992, and *Die Islamisierung des Islam. Imaginäre Welten einer politischen Theologie*, Frankfurt am Main, Campus, 1996. For a different perspective, see also the Europe-based Islamic activist and intellectual Tariq Ramadan, *Les musulmans dans la laïcité. Responsabilités et droits des musulmans dans les sociétés occidentales*, Lyons, Tawhid, 1994.

[7]   Among the scholarly publications, see especially Rajeev Bhargava (ed.), *Secularism and its Critics*, New Delhi, Oxford University Press, 1999; Azzam Tamimi and John Esposito (eds.), *Islam and Secularism in the Middle East*, London, Hurst, 2000; Talal Asad, *Formations of the Secular: Christianity, Islam, Modernity*, Stanford, Stanford University Press, 2003.

[8]   José Casanova, 'Chancen und Gefahren öffentlicher Religion. Ost- und Westeuropa

First, secularization as *religion's declining relevance* with respect to how individuals interpret the world and live their lives, a process which may lead to professed agnosticism and ultimately to atheism. To this extent it corresponds to Islamist fears. (The concept of religion that undergirds this definition cannot be generalized. However, the concept seems appropriate for monotheistic religions based on the notion of a personal God, which would include Islam.) Here, secularization is synonymous with the declining relevance and binding power of norms and values based on religion and religious law vis-à-vis daily conduct, political orientation and public order.

Second, secularization as the *relegation* or *withdrawal* of religion to the private sphere. There is an obvious difference between relegation and withdrawal. In any case, it remains to be clarified how the spheres of 'public' and 'private' were and are defined and, if applicable, demarcated in specific cultures and societies at different times.

Third, secularization as the *institutional and constitutional separation of church and state*. Here the models of Europe and the United States, with their Christian heritage, are especially conspicuous, making transcultural comparison all the more imperative.

The separation of church and state

We could make things easy for ourselves and declare the institutional dimension irrelevant with respect to Islam: there is no church in Islam in the form of a hierarchically structured institution with established doctrinal authority and thus no 'institution of salvation' offering, or possibly even monopolizing, services relevant to redemption.[9] Islam has never developed such a church and shows no sign of doing so now. The contrast with the Catholic church is obvious, and is frequently discussed by Muslims. Differences with the Protestant churches are

im Vergleich', in Otto Kallscheuer (ed.), *Das Europa der Religionen*, Frankfurt am Main, Fischer, 1996, pp. 181–210, and *Public Religions in the Modern World*, Chicago, University of Chicago Press, 1994. Particularly influential is Charles Taylor, 'Drei Formen des Säkularismus', in Kallscheuer (ed.), *Das Europa der Religionen*, pp. 217–46, and 'Modes of Secularism', in Bhargava (ed.), *Secularism and its Critics*, pp. 31–53. See also Danièle Hervieu-Léger, *Le pèlerin et le converti. La religion en mouvement*, Paris, Flammarion, 1999, and, much discussed in the German context, Jürgen Habermas and Joseph Ratzinger, *Dialectics of Secularization: On Reason and Religion*, San Francisco, Ignatius, 2006.

[9]   See Friedrich Wilhelm Graf, *Die Wiederkehr der Götter*, Munich, Beck, 2004, and his chapter in the present volume.

less pronounced, while the parallels to Judaism are clearly evident.[10] However, already in early Islam, religious and legal scholars (*ulama* and *fuqaha*) emerged, aspiring to record and systematize the religious and legal teachings of Islam and impart them to the community of Muslims.[11] The vast majority of these were men, though women too were to be found in specific fields, such as the collection of prophetic traditions (*hadiths*, Sunna). Their activities were largely focused on interpretation of normative texts and of the canon of authoritative writings based on these texts, rather than mediation of salvation. This applies to the majority of Sunni Muslims. The situation is different with regard to Shia doctrines of the imamate as well as to mystical notions of a spiritual path to God, neither of which was based primarily on book learning.

Interpretation of the texts and transmission of religious knowledge, both of which require a mastery of classical Arabic, were successively regulated and professionalized. Only in the eleventh and twelfth centuries of the Christian era, several hundred years after the death of the Prophet, did the first religious colleges (*madrasas*) develop as institutions for the production and transmission of knowledge relevant to religion.[12] In cases of advanced professionalization, education and habitus suggest that we should speak of the *ulama* as a social group in its own right, one which differentiated itself from other social groups. In certain cases, we may even speak of a clergy, which not only held religious knowledge, but also carried out religious tasks (Friday sermons, religious instruction and legal services, as well as the administration of religious foundations) and controlled the corresponding institutions and finances. This applies to the Shia *ulama* in Iran from the sixteenth century, and, in a different way, also to their counterparts in the period since the Islamic Revolution of 1979. But even in Iran no hierarchically structured church developed. The hierarchy of scholars in the Ottoman Empire (*ilmiyye*) was a bureaucratic apparatus made up of those scholars who served the sultan; it did not allow for the emergence of an independent church. To this day,

---

[10]   Non-monotheistic cults and religions are rarely considered in the Muslim debate or in the scholarly literature.

[11]   See Dominique Iogna-Prat and Gilles Veinstein (eds.), *Histoires des hommes de Dieu dans l'islam et le christianisme*, Paris, Flammarion, 2003; Marc Gaborieau and Malika Zeghal (eds.), 'Autorités religieuses en Islam', special issue of *Archives de Sciences Sociales des Religions*, 49/125 (2004); Gudrun Krämer and Sabine Schmidtke (eds.), *Speaking for Islam: Religious Authorities in Muslim Societies*, Leiden, Brill, 2006, particularly the introduction. A brief overview is provided in my *Geschichte des Islam*, Munich, Beck, 2005.

[12]   See Hasan Elboudrari (ed.), *Modes de transmission de la culture religieuse en islam*, Cairo, Institut français d'archéologie orientale du Caire, 1993; Nicole Grandin and Marc Gaborieau (eds.), *Madrasa. La transmission du savoir dans le monde musulman*, Paris, Editions Arguments, 1997.

there are institutions of higher Islamic learning with far-reaching influence within the Sunni world, such as al-Azhar University in Cairo, yet there is no equivalent of the church institution.[13]

If we turn to the other side of the equation – the state or the authorities – the contrast between pre-modern Islamic and pre-modern European societies is less pronounced: until the nineteenth century, religion and government were no more closely associated in Islamic societies than in European ones. In the former too, as is well known, religion and state could be linked in a variety of ways. As prophet and charismatic leader of his community, Muhammad is and remains an exception. But the prophetic era is de facto limited to the decade after his departure from Mecca (the *hijra*), during which Muhammad was the supreme leader of the community in Medina (622–632 CE). It is an open question whether in his lifetime religion, law and politics were really so indissolubly interwoven as is commonly assumed by both devout Muslims and most non-Muslims.

Under the early caliphs religion, law and politics were certainly linked, but they were not completely fused. (As above, I am referring here to the majority Sunni, rather than Shia, doctrines of the imamate, which would require separate consideration.) The caliph certainly saw himself as 'God's shadow on earth'; the principle of divine right featured in Sunni Islam, too.[14] But according to Sunni teachings, he had no part in the prophetic mission, which ended with Muhammad as 'the seal of the prophets'.[15] The caliph had to protect the religion by defending the external borders of Islam or, rather, by continuously expanding them (hence the great importance of *jihad*, in the sense of armed struggle for 'God's cause', in the early Islamic period). Domestically, the caliph was responsible for the

---

[13]   See especially Malika Zeghal, *Gardiens de l'islam. Les oulémas d'Al Azhar dans l'Egypte contemporaine*, Paris, Presses de Sciences Po, 1996; Jakob Skovgaard-Petersen, *Defining Islam for the Egyptian State: Muftis and Fatwas of the Dar al-Ifta*, Leiden, Brill, 1997.

[14]   See Patricia Crone and Martin Hinds, *God's Caliph: Religious Authority in the First Centuries of Islam*, Cambridge, Cambridge University Press, 1986, and, from a broader perspective, Patricia Crone, *God's Rule: Government and Islam*, New York, Columbia University Press, 2004.

[15]   Charismatic figures have in fact appeared repeatedly throughout Islamic history who, sometimes drawing on cyclical notions of history, claimed prophetic status or were ascribed this status by their followers. Most emerged from Shia milieus. In the fourteenth, fifteenth and nineteenth centuries, new communities were founded which in some cases even broke away from the Islamic Umma (above all the Babis and Baha'is, while the Alevis and Ahmadis still consider themselves Muslims, and the Druze may or may not see themselves as part of the Muslim community depending on their situation and interests).

maintenance of law and order, enforcing compliance with Sharia (which was, however, chiefly developed by the religious and legal scholars rather than the caliphs). The caliph exercised a certain influence on the legal and educational system, with patronage playing a crucial role. At least in the major centres of the empire, the caliph appointed the judges, intervened in the assignment of teaching posts within major *madrasas*, and founded institutions for religious and legal scholars and for mystics (Sufis). Hence, directly or indirectly, he also controlled the spread or marginalization of theological and legal schools. As 'guardian of the faith' he was also charged with the suppression of heresy, apostasy, freethinking and all other ideas and practices condemned as un-Islamic or anti-Islamic. It was perhaps inevitable that his relationship with religious and legal scholars would be ambivalent and often tense, since such scholars, resisting the caliph's claims to religious authority, firmly and self-confidently declared themselves the 'heirs to the prophets' (in the plural).[16]

On balance, the term 'state religion', when applied in an Islamic context, emerges as problematic. The ruler, at least within the territory of Islamic dominion (*dar al-islam*), was a Muslim; the Sharia was considered the foundation of morality and law; and it was chiefly Islamic institutions – from mosques to shrines to institutions of Islamic learning – that were patronized by the ruler. But those ruled often deviated from the religious belief of the ruler, either in that they were not even Muslims or that they followed another branch of Islam. The early Islamic, the Ottoman and the Mughal empires serve as examples of the first scenario, with the majority of the population being non-Muslim. In India, moreover, Hindus made up the majority of the population, a religious group which according to classical Islamic doctrine was not counted among the monotheistic 'people of the book', who were granted the status of protection (*dhimma*). Thus, Muslim community, Muslim society and Muslim state were not congruent. A classic example of the latter (an Islamic creed divergent from that of the ruler held by the majority of the population) can be found in the Maghreb and Egypt under the rule of the Ismaili Fatimids in the period from the ninth to the twelfth century, where the rulers were Ismaili, while the majority of the ruled were Sunni (or Sunni and Christian in the case of Egypt).

The principle *cuius regio eius religio*, established by the Peace of Augsburg of 1555, according to which subjects had to follow the confession of their sovereign, was *not* a guiding principle in Islam. The enforcement of Twelver Shiism in Safavid Iran in the sixteenth and seventeenth centuries, which was accompanied

---

[16]   See Muhammad Qasim Zaman, *Religion and Politics under the Early 'Abbasids: The Emergence of the Proto-Sunni Elite*, Leiden, Brill, 1997; Michael Cooperson, *Classical Arabic Biography: The Heirs of the Prophet in the Age of al-Ma'mun*, Cambridge, Cambridge University Press, 2000.

by the persecution of Muslims of different persuasions, is still the nearest thing to a state religion that the Islamic world has seen, at least in the pre-modern period.[17] However, the Safavid experiment is no more characteristic of pre-modern Islamic states and polities than was caesaropapism in Christianity. The Ottoman sultan, for example, even when he made more systematic use of the title of caliph in the sixteenth century, was no more 'Muslim' than French or Spanish kings were 'Christian' (they were, after all, 'most Christian majesties'). Precisely because there was no clerical institution, the sultan-caliph lacked an important means to exercise religious control over his subjects. The abolition of the caliphate in the new Turkish Republic in 1924 brought a formal end to an institution that had lost its erstwhile status hundreds of years before. Worthy of note, however, is the claim to religious authority asserted by the Moroccan king, which he derives from his (alleged) descent from the Prophet and his own powers of blessing (*baraka*), and which he brings to bear particularly in the field of Islamic law (not least in order to enforce legal reforms in favour of women) – a highly unusual phenomenon in Sunni Islam and currently claimed by no other Muslim monarch.[18]

The significance of religious norms, or: the application of the Sharia

If we look at Islam past and present, it is not the institutions of church and state whose linkage or separation indicates the degree of secularization. Rather, the key factor is the validity of the Sharia as the foundation and framework of individual conduct, social order and political action. The majority of Muslims do not question the fundamental validity of the Sharia. However, Sharia can mean different things to different Muslims (from decency, morality and justice very generally, to an economy based on fairness and equity, to strict law-and-order policies), and by no means do all Muslims desire its integral 'application' as

---

[17]   See Said Amir Arjomand, *The Shadow of God and the Hidden Imam: Religion, Political Order, and Societal Change in Shi'ite Iran from the Beginning to 1890*, Chicago and London, University of Chicago Press, 1984; Rula J. Abisaab, *Converting Persia: Religion and Power in the Safavid Empire*, London and New York, I. B. Tauris, 2004; on countervailing tendencies, see Kathryn Babayan, *Mystics, Monarchs, and Messiahs: Cultural Landscapes of Early Modern Iran*, Cambridge, MA, and London, Harvard University Press, 2002.

[18]   See Abdellah Hammoudi, *Master and Disciple*, Chicago, University of Chicago Press, 1997; Mohamed Tozy, *Monarchie et islam politique au Maroc*, Paris, Presses de Sciences Po, 2nd edn, 1999; for broader comparison, see my 'Good Counsel to the King: The Islamist Opposition in Saudi Arabia, Jordan and Morocco', in Joseph Kostiner (ed.), *Middle East Monarchies: The Challenge of Modernity*, Boulder, Lynne Rienner, 2000, pp. 257–87.

demanded by contemporary Islamists (whose forebears may be found in earlier centuries). As a rule, those advocating 'application of the Sharia' refer to the norms and values it contains, not to the modes of its interpretation and de facto implementation. Nor do they refer to the 'personnel' entitled to implement it. We might speak here of the 'fiction of self-evidence', the assumption that the Qur'an and Sunna are unambiguous, immediately intelligible to their readers (or at least to the Muslim believer) and applicable to practice without further ado. In view of the linguistic and methodological prerequisites for a plausible understanding of the text, this assumption is highly problematic. Particularly among Sunnis, critics focus on this Islamist assumption, warning of the dangers of human control of 'divine' norms and insisting that there is no clerical rule resembling the papacy within Islam. Incidentally, similar arguments are made by Shia critics of the Islamic Republic of Iran.[19]

This critique gives fresh urgency to the question of religious authority in Islam – particularly nowadays, after the Sunni caliphate has long since been abolished and, according to Twelver Shiism, the Imam 'went into occultation' more than a thousand years ago to return at the end of time as saviour (*mahdi*). In this situation, who has legitimate authority over the interpretation of religious and legal norms that are frequently described as 'divine'? This is a hard question to answer, considering what we have just said about clergy, church and state. There is also debate over whether, in various Muslim milieus and societies, we do in fact witness processes of increasing individualization of religious views and practices.[20] Many scholars have spoken of a *fragmentation* of religious authority in the modern age. I consider the term *pluralization* more appropriate, not least in order to counter the impression that religious authority was unquestioned, uniform and thus not 'fragmented' in earlier times. This was not the case. As a rule, though, only a small number of people had access to alternative views of Islam or competing authorities; few had opportunities to acquire information and form opinions independently. Such opportunities have expanded significantly in the wake of increased mass education, greater mobility,

[19] See Krämer, *Gottes Staat als Republik*, pp. 80–86; Katajun Amirpur, 'A Doctrine in the Making? Velayat-e faqih in Post-Revolutionary Iran', in Krämer and Schmidtke (eds.), *Speaking for Islam*, pp. 218–40; and Katajun Amirpur and Ludwig Ammann (eds.), *Der Islam am Wendepunkt. Liberale und konservative Reformer einer Weltreligion*, Freiburg, Herder, 2006.

[20] See Armando Salvatore and Schirin Amir-Moazami, 'Religiöse Diskurstraditionen. Zur Transformation des Islam in kolonialen, postkolonialen und europäischen Öffentlichkeiten', *Berliner Journal für Soziologie*, 12.3 (2002), pp. 309–30; Levent Tezcan, 'Das Islamische in den Studien zu Muslimen in Deutschland. Literaturbericht', *Zeitschrift für Soziologie*, 32.3 (2003), pp. 237–61.

and global communication – and concomitant claims to religious autonomy and authority.[21]

However loudly the Islamists may call for the Sharia to be enforced, it is not in fact applied 'integrally' and 'exclusively' in most Muslim countries, not even in the Islamic Republic of Iran or the Kingdom of Saudi Arabia.[22] In many states, however, rules and norms derived from the Qur'an and Sunna and identified with Sharia inform personal status and family law. They are less relevant to the fields of economy (including the prohibition on charging interest and on insurance), social security (alms tax), and politics. Only a few states apply the rules of criminal law found in the Sharia in one form or another. (The distinction between these fields, incidentally, reflects modern, Western perspectives rather than the structure of classical Islamic law.) With few exceptions, we observe neither an integral application of the Sharia (whatever this may mean) nor a total break with the rules and norms of Islamic law (*fiqh*). Rather, most governments pursue strategies of evasion and avoidance that fence in traditional legal norms substantially or procedurally; the formal suspension or abrogation of the rules of inherited *fiqh* is rare, especially if they are based on an explicit textual reference in the Qur'an or the Sunna.[23] Only in a small number of states, such as Turkey and the former Soviet republics of Central Asia, has the Sharia been formally abolished.

The wide spectrum of what may be subsumed under the term 'public morality' is of crucial importance to the so-called application of the Sharia. It covers not

---

[21]   For more detail, see Krämer and Schmidtke (eds.), *Speaking for Islam*; also Dale F. Eickelman, 'Print, Islam, and the Prospects for Civic Pluralism: New Religious Writings and their Audiences', *Journal of Islamic Studies*, 8 (1997), pp. 43–62; Dale F. Eickelman and Jon W. Anderson, *New Media in the Muslim World: The Emerging Public Sphere*, Bloomington and Indianapolis, Indiana University Press, 1999; Gary R. Bunt, *Islam in the Digital Age: E-Jihad, Online Fatwas and Cyber Islamic Environments*, London, Pluto Press, 2003.

[22]   See for example Talal Asad, *Thinking about Secularism and Law in Egypt*, ISIM Papers 2, Leiden, Brill, 2001, and John R. Bowen, *Shari'a, State, and Social Norms in France and Indonesia*, ISIM Papers 3, Leiden, Brill, 2001. For excellent overviews, see Abdullahi A. Na'im (ed.), *Islamic Family Law in a Changing World: A Global Resource Book*, London, Zed, 2002, and Rudolph Peters, *Crime and Punishment in Islamic Law: Theory and Practice from the Sixteenth to the Twenty-First Century*, Cambridge, Cambridge University Press, 2005.

[23]   Classic examples are the modifications made to personal status and divorce law that restrict the ability of the Muslim male to marry up to four women (which he is entitled to do according to a common interpretation of the Qur'an) or to divorce his wife at any time and without giving reasons. Other modifications extend wives' opportunities to file for divorce themselves and enhance their legal claim to maintenance and the custody of shared children.

only topics such as drugs, alcohol and prostitution, along with alternative lifestyles and unconventional patterns of behaviour more generally, but also the freedom of expression, science and art. Religious freedom is of key importance here, or more specifically, the freedom of Muslims to change their religion – not because this happens frequently, but because it illustrates the binding power of religious norms. 'Moral politics' also provide a link to the third aspect of secularization as outlined by Casanova.

The significance of religion for private life

The vast majority of Muslims hold firmly to their faith, even if they do not continuously contemplate it. Public criticism of basic religious assumptions is strongly disapproved of. (Conservative) notions of custom and decency that, rightly or wrongly, are traced back to Islam, are generally considered binding. This is by no means to say that they are consistently complied with, but it does make it easier to censor unwanted forms of expression and behaviour. This shows above all in the context of alternative lifestyles and sexual preferences, and artistic and academic freedom. Islamic belonging is often expressed in a demonstrative compliance with religious duties (the so-called pillars of Islam: profession of faith, ritual prayer, almsgiving, fasting during the month of Ramadan, pilgrimage to Mecca) and the observance of certain dietary rules and dress codes as well as specific practices, which, contrary to the convictions of many of those concerned, are not necessarily grounded in the Qur'an or Sunna. They apply, incidentally, to both men and women. The central issues here are abstention from alcohol; separation of the sexes in public; and 'modest clothing', particularly the veil in its various forms, from the headscarf to the *burka* and *chador*. The turn to Islam, closely observed, albeit by no means comprehensively documented, is manifested in the spread of Islamic media and an 'Islamic' consumer and mass culture, which extend significantly beyond the realm of what is commonly perceived as political Islam.[24]

Islam is a public religion par excellence. According to classical legal notions, the minaret must be taller than all other buildings. It has been a long time since this applied, with modern high-rise buildings overshadowing all minarets, even in the Saudi Arabian capital of Riyadh, but it is still a subject for discussion in the immediate vicinity of mosque and church, temple or synagogue. In most

---

[24]   The journal *ISIM Report* reported regularly on these topics, covering a considerable geographical area. For case studies, see Günter Seufert, *Politischer Islam in der Türkei*, Istanbul and Stuttgart, Steiner, 1997, and Gregory Starrett, *Putting Islam to Work: Education, Politics, and Religious Transformation in Egypt*, Berkeley, University of California Press, 1998.

Muslim-majority societies, the call to prayer is a public proclamation of the truth of Islam. Similar practices of other religious communities are heavily restricted, if they are admitted at all. At the same time, non-Muslim places of worship and identifying markers (clothing, hairstyle, head coverings) are a normal part of everyday life in most Muslim societies.

The Islamic claim to dominance in 'Islamic lands' is clearly felt in two areas: the prohibition of non-Muslim mission and of unrestricted conversion to another religion, which apply de facto almost everywhere, even in those places where they are undefined in terms of criminal law. It is true that a large number of Muslim majority states have signed the 1948 UN Declaration of Human Rights and subsequent human rights conventions. A fair number of states, however, have qualified the right to freely change religion, a right which also allows Muslims to give up their faith (so-called apostasy). Many constitutions guarantee the religious freedom of their citizens, but impose restrictions on it in other places, and these restrictions are not always immediately apparent (the annulment of marriage in cases of apostasy being an example). Here, the boundary between public and private is blurred or defined in such a way that the (essentially private) act of changing religion appears as a (public and political) act of treason, through which the apostate betrays his or her homeland and the Muslim community: 'Islam', as one often hears in this context, 'is the Muslim's fatherland'.[25]

This is not solely a matter of state restrictions. In many countries, the majority of the population have a fairly illiberal attitude. The right to free speech, which includes public criticism of religious dogma, if not of Islam at large, is rarely granted at present. The cartoon controversy of 2005/6 offered an insight into the emotions that are released (or that may be deliberately stirred by interested parties), if it is felt that core religious values of Islam are being offended – here in the form of the denigration of the Prophet. (According to classical legal doctrine, 'blaspheming the Prophet' [sabb an-nabi] ranks with the offence of apostasy and triggers the corresponding sanctions with respect to civil and criminal law.) Thus, unlike in Europe and the United States, in Muslim majority societies there is no free market in religions open to non-Muslim religions and cults. A free market of this kind is not regarded as desirable by the majority of Muslims. Competition exists only *within* the 'framework of Islam' – and the framework of course requires specification.

---

[25]   See Krämer, 'Drawing Boundaries'; Abdullah Saeed and Hassan Saeed, *Freedom of Religion, Apostasy and Islam*, Aldershot, Ashgate, 2004; and Heiner Bielefeldt, *Philosophie der Menschenrechte. Grundlagen eines weltweiten Freiheitsethos*, Darmstadt, Primus, 1998.

Conclusion

None of this arises necessarily or, as it were, naturally from Islam – or to be more precise, from the normative textual foundations of the Qur'an and Sunna. Rather, it reflects contemporary interpretations, which in many ways express political experiences and expectations. As a glance, however cursory, at history shows (with the possible exception of the Prophet's charismatic leadership of the community), religion and state 'in Islam' were no more closely linked than in Europe in the Middle Ages, the early modern period and in some cases even the modern era. Rather, the feature specific to Islamic societies is the importance of Islamic law and ethics, the Sharia, which is also at the centre of current debates. Hence, the crucial issue is not the separation of church and state but the relationship between Sharia and public order.

An equally cursory glance at present realities shows that Muslims (devout, practising Muslims) can certainly live in secular states. They do so not only in the non-Muslim diaspora (in Western Europe, the USA, Canada and Australia), in which, according to classical *fiqh*, other rules apply than in the territories of Islamic dominion, the *dar al-islam*. They do so and have done so in India, which was under Muslim rule for centuries. They do so in Muslim majority societies such as Turkey, the Central Asian republics or Tunisia, which were (at least to some extent) secularized 'from above' in authoritarian fashion. They even do so in Indonesia, where, in the name of the state ideology of Pancasila, Islam represents just one of several recognized religions. Some Muslims are in favour of a far-reaching, openly declared secularization of constitution, law and politics, not least in the hope that such secularization might limit the widespread political use of religion and curb violence when it is practised in the name of religion. The majority has reservations about the principle of secularism because they view it as politically loaded and contaminated. The conflict thus remains unresolved.

5

Hinduism

Heinrich von Stietencron

Statistics have taught us to regard Hinduism as the third largest contemporary religion in terms of number of adherents, after Christianity and Islam.[1] Hindus make up 89 per cent of the population in Nepal, 82 per cent in India, 52 per cent on Mauritius, 38 per cent and 37 per cent in the South Pacific and the Caribbean; and they also live, as extremely large and, for some years, rapidly growing minorities, in the USA and Canada, Australia, Southeast Asia, the Arab countries, Africa and Europe. Hindus number around 900 million in total. If, as has been argued for many years with reference to the Indian constitution by the 'World Hindu Council', the highly active *Vishva Hindu Parishad* (VHP),[2] we add all religions originating in India, in other words Buddhism, Jainism and the indigenous tribal religions, Hinduism even appears, statistically, to be the second largest of all religions. On this point, the authors of the constitution have followed the views of Vināyak Dāmodar Sāvarkar, who describes as Hindus the followers of all religions originating in India.[3] Such religions fulfil all the fundamentals of Hinduism: common land, common culture and common origins (*jāti*). The gods invoked within them inhabit the holy land of India.

But is Hinduism *one* religion in the first place? Some years ago, I pointed out that so-called Hinduism comprises a whole number of different religions, which, however, coexist so peacefully and are blended together to such an extent

---

[1] Christianity: 2.1 billion, Islam: 1.3 billion, (agnostics/atheists: 1.1 billion), Hinduism: 900 million (www.adherents.com: 'Major Religions of the World, Ranked by Number of Adherents', 2005).

[2] The Constitution of India, Art. 25, 2b, Explanation II: 'In sub-clause (b) of clause (2) the reference to Hindus shall be construed as including a reference to persons professing the Sikh, Jaina or Buddhist religion, and the reference to Hindu religious institutions shall be construed accordingly'.

[3] V. D. Savarkar, *Hindutva: Who is a Hindu?*, Nagpur, V. V. Kelkar, 1923, repr. 1989 (Essentials of Hindutva).

on the Indian subcontinent that Europeans, used to bloody religious conflicts, inevitably come away with the impression that we must be dealing with just *one* religion.[4]

In fact, though, Hinduismus, as it has become differentiated over the course of 3500 years and as it is now officially presented in the VHP, contains several different types of religion:

1. The more than 3500-year-old *polytheistic* religion of the Veda, whose holy texts, the four *Vedas* (second to early first century BC), are still considered a source of religious inspiration and ultimate authority;

2. two originally *atheistic* religions (Jainism and Buddhism),[5] which took shape in the fourth century BC and strongly influenced India's tradition of spirituality, renunciation of the world, refraining from harming living beings and non-violence;

3. two important *monotheistic* religions (Vishnuism and Shivaism), which appeared between the fourth and second centuries BC, rapidly developing into India's most influential religions, a status they have retained up to the present;

4. the *Advaita Vedānta*, a highly successful monistic religion and philosophy, which postulates as its highest principle not a personal deity but an abstract primordial consciousness, the *brahman*, which is also present in all beings as *ātman* and which thus pervades the entire world;

5. a *pantheism*, which to some extent represents the flipside of the above-mentioned monism. If absolutely nothing exists in this world that is not pervaded with *Brahman*, then such monism may turn into pantheism at any time: *Brahman* is present everywhere, in every stone, in every plant, in all that exists.

Each of the religions within Hinduism mentioned so far has its own, extremely rich literature, featuring various holy writings and countless scholarly

---

[4]   See H. von Stietencron, 'Hinduism: On the Proper Use of a Deceptive Term', in G. D. Sontheimer and H. Kulke (eds.), *Hinduism Reconsidered*, Delhi, Manohar, 1989, pp. 11–27. For a more detailed account deploying medieval sources, see idem, 'Religious Configurations in Pre-Muslim India and the Modern Concept of Hinduism', in V. Dalmia and H. von Stietencron (eds.), *Representing Hinduism: The Construction of Religious Traditions and National Identity*, New Delhi, Sage Publications, 1995, pp. 51–81.

[5]   Representatives of both these religions resist their incorporation into the *Vishva Hindu Parishad*. They see their religion as a conscious break with the Vedic-Hindu tradition.

theological treatises that fill great libraries. One would have to compare each of them individually with Islam or Christianity.

But these are by no means all the types of religion included in the statistics of modern-day Hinduism. In addition, there are a large number of different tribal religions, in which it is primarily earth and mountain deities that are worshipped. Religious specialists, chosen as mediums by ancestors or deities, serve as intermediaries between this world and the worlds beyond. They enter into contact with the world of the ancestors in order, if necessary, to pacify their anger or ask for their help in resolving conflicts within a family or tribe. Above all, they characteristically serve the gods and ancestors as a medium, making themselves available as their mouthpiece.

Around all these forms of religion – chiefly in rural areas, but also among the urban underclasses – there extends a broad sphere of less contemplative but very lively and tradition-steeped *popular religion*. This takes up conspicuous elements, rituals, festivals and conceptions of the beyond from adjacent religions, simplifies them, refashions them in some cases and preserves certain elements far longer than is the case in the rapidly changing cities. In popular religion as well, worship of the gods Shiva and Vishnu, the local goddesses and a number of regionally powerful spirits (Bhūt, Nāg) is associated with animism and with possession phenomena, whose role in coping with social conflicts in the family and local community should not be underestimated.

Finally, and this brings our listing of the Hindus' key religions to a close for the time being, we must also mention so-called *neo-Hinduism*. This arose in the nineteenth century as a reaction to the harsh critique of religion produced by the colonial powers, above all Christian missionaries. In response, north Indian intellectuals attempted to bring about a radical reformation from 1828 on. Efforts were made to rationalize, to de-mythologize, to bring about a significant reduction of the multitude of religious practices and to outlaw all particularly offensive practices such as human sacrifice, widow-burning and child marriage, to mention only the key emotive issues for Christian missionaries and colonial officials. The result was a rigorous, almost Protestant self-cleansing of the indigenous religious tradition. This occurred above all in Bengal, where the *Brāhmo-Samāj*, a religion of intellectuals under the leadership of Rām Mohan Roy, gained influence, and in Punjab, where Dāyānanda Sarasvatī founded the *Ārya Samāj*, which drew on the Vedic tradition and which spread chiefly across northwest India. Both movements served the modernization and self-assertion of the Hindu tradition in view of the political, social and economic change entailed in foreign rule under the colonial powers. This also applies to the Rāmakrishna mission founded by Swāmī Vivekānanda. In 1898, at the World Congress of Religions in Chicago, he enjoyed breathtaking success with his account of the teachings of the *Advaita Vedānta*, which he portrayed as overarching and completing all religions. To this day, the Rāmakrishna mission is among the most important bearers of a new religious self-consciousness in urban Indian society.

Considering the large number of religions and types of religion, Hinduism as a whole can scarcely be termed a 'religion'. It is more of a 'civilization' – and indeed an extraordinarily tolerant civilization, in which it was possible for a number of religions to coexist in peace for hundreds of years. In many places this still applies.

Is Hinduism, then, not to be considered among the world religions? Strictly speaking, no. But at least four of the dominant religions which arose within Hinduism and which still constitute elements within it are unquestionably among the world religions: Vishnuism, Shivaism, Shāktism and Vedānta. These four religions differ fundamentally with respect to the identity and nature of the highest deity and also with regard to the path to salvation. However, in their philosophical analysis of the human being and of the most important preconditions for self-purification and attaining salvation, they work on the same basic assumptions. Hence, as far as human beings, their values, their responsibility and the prerequisites for attaining salvation are concerned, I can place these four religions under a single heading. Buddhism differs fundamentally from them because it denies the existence of a transmigrating soul. It does without a soul, but with respect to values and a salutary lifestyle it is very similar to the high religions of the Hindus.

Fundamental insights from the Vedic period

The notions of world and human being, which are still of fundamental importance today, are already laid down in the Indians' oldest holy texts, the *Vedas* (second millennium BC):

1. There is a meaningful and eternal cosmic order (*ṛta*), which is closely bound up with the concept of truth (*satya*) and which comprises the natural laws as well as the specific character of all forms of life and the moral principles. Maintaining this order is the gods' central task.

2. But there is also a dynamic principle which entails change, restlessness and even occasional catastrophes and which thus poses a serious threat to order from time to time, but which at the same time prevents stagnation, releases unrestrained forces and thus enables destruction and renewal. This element of unbridled dynamism is embodied by the demons. They are in a state of perpetual conflict with the gods.

3. Thus, in contrast to the sphere of eternal and absolute being, the order of this world is under constant threat. It falls to the human being to

strengthen the gods, comply with pre-established functions and moral order (the *dharma*)[6] and thereby to play his part in protecting the world order.

For their part, the gods help those who bring them fortifying offerings while singing elaborate songs of praise. They support their friends in wars and other difficult situations, they bless people with children, with the spoils of war, health and a long life.

Key changes in the late Vedic period

In the period of the older *Upanishads* (eighth to sixth centuries BC), an observation made at an earlier stage became the subject of philosophical reflection: it is *cyclical movements* that are inherent to the world order. This is evident in the movements of the sun, moon and planets; it is apparent in the cycle of the seasons and months, it can be seen in the vegetational cycle of plants, which sprout at the start of the rainy season, then flower, bear fruit and die away again before repeating the same sequence the following year. It is also visible in the cycle of water, which falls to the ground as rain, sets the vegetational cycle in motion, is finally evaporated by the sun and collected in the sky before once again fertilizing the parched earth as rain. Coming into being, passing away and then arising anew – this constitutes a principle that prevails throughout the whole of the natural world.

Such cyclicality offers an explanatory model for many previously unexplained phenomena. It assigns the human being a clear task within the cycle of food. This cycle begins and ends with the gods. The gods send rain, the rain causes the plants to sprout, the plants offer nourishment for animals and people and the animals also provide food for each other and for people. But it falls to human beings to provide the gods with food through their sacrifices. This completes the life-sustaining cycle of nourishment.

However, as one of the principles of worldly existence, cyclicality leads to another momentous realization. If all living creatures have a soul, what then is

---

[6]   The *dharma*, often wrongly translated as 'religion', is the behavioural norm which is assigned to every created being – in accordance with their particular stage of life, situation or purpose. In the case of human beings, it determines social conduct in every stage of life down to the fine details. It may include religious, moral, social or economic components. It is the *dharma* of the thief, for example, that he practises his profession of stealing with the greatest possible skill. *Dharma* is by no means limited to the human sphere. It is part of the *dharma* of the beast of prey that it kills other animals, the *dharma* of the fire that it burns, and that it devours everything in its path, but also that it bears up to the gods in its smoke the offerings made by human beings. Clearly, 'religion' is a very poor translation for *dharma*.

the origin of the myriad souls they contain, souls which manifest themselves anew every year even in mosquito swarms, mayflies, worms, cockroaches and vermin of all kinds?[7] The answer is plain to see: it is always the same souls. They cast off an old body and assume a new one, some after a brief pause, others straight away, just as the snake casts off its old skin and forms a new one. While the bodies change, the souls remain the same. In the case of vermin, rebirth immediately follows death, so that the prospects of breaking out of the cycle of life are extremely dim. Applied to humans, this gave rise to the doctrine of rebirth, which came to characterize a number of Indian religions.

The doctrine of rebirth works on the assumption of an unlimited number of originally equal souls, whose source is absolute consciousness or the highest divinity, to which they return when released from the cycle of births. They may incarnate anywhere within the realm of the living, from mosses to all plants, animals, human beings, demons, ghosts, snake spirits and heavenly beings, including the gods. Only the highest divinity and his wife remain beyond this worldly realm, unless the God deliberately incarnates on the earth in order to intervene helpfully in crisis situations, as applies for example to the two currently prominent incarnations of the god Vishnu: Krishna and Rāma. Every soul has the potential to sully and purify itself; desire, cruelty, lies and selfishness bind it to matter as well as clouding the soul's power of understanding, while selflessness, truthfulness, empathy for all beings and asceticism purify the soul and increase its powers of understanding.

Karma – a word with which everyone will be familiar nowadays – refers to the positive or negative impact brought about in the soul by every good or bad, every self-seeking or selfless act: good *karma* leads to a better rebirth, while bad *karma* has the opposite effect. It is thus the actor himself who shapes his future destiny through his own acts and thoughts. Selfless acts produce no *karma*.

Release from the cycle of births occurs when no more *karma*, good or bad, is present. Such diminution of *karma* comes about a) through experiencing the consequences of deeds, b) as the fruit of self-purification through yoga or asceticism, c) through the purifying effect of good deeds, d) through the fulfilment of ritual obligations, and above all e) through the grace of God, who is obliging to those who worship with care and attention, enabling the redeeming encounter between believer and divinity.

The idea of rebirth emerges as extremely helpful in interpreting physical and mental differences: it makes happiness and unhappiness appear as the consequences of a self-created psychological disposition from previous lives; it legitimizes inequality; and it feeds the hope of achieving a better form of existence in future by paying off in the present those debts accrued earlier. There is no longer any

---

[7]   *Chāndogya Upanishad* 5.10.8, taking account of commentaries.

need for a punitive God or Prince of Darkness. This notion sometimes still serves as a deterrent, but has generally been superseded by the doctrine of rebirth.

The positive or negative consequences of actions (*karma*) are stored as information that is impressed automatically in the psychological organ, information which, depending on its quality, reduces or increases the receptivity of this organ as well as control over the body and its organs. The less *karma* one accumulates, the closer one comes to release. When it has been removed entirely, release from the cycle of births can occur.

The doctrine of rebirth had the advantage of providing incentives for a way of life bound by the ideal of truthfulness, charity and hospitality in deeds, words and thoughts, which guaranteed the making of sacrifices to the gods and ancestors, which could protect the community from the selfishness of the rulers and from thieves and enemies, and which was capable, above all, of passing on the religious and ritual tradition to the children. Present adversities (illnesses, physical or mental defects, poverty, low social status and the obligation to provide impure services) could be made more bearable through hopes of a better life.

It soon emerged, however, that the prospect of a new life also entailed new problems, as every future life ended once again with death. It was clearly impossible to escape transience in this way and thus rebirth was an unsatisfactory perspective over the long term. The desire to leave this cycle led to renunciation of the world, to meditation and asceticism and to the formation of monastic communities in the case of Jainism and Buddhism. The pursuit of salvation was given priority over the pursuit of power and wealth. The state and economy lost their sharpest minds to monastic orders and hermitages.

This situation posed a threat to the community. But from the fourth century BC a counter-movement set in. Its exponents were made up of princes on the one hand and urban materialists on the other. The demand now was for the selfless fulfilment of one's duties within society rather than renunciation of the world. The most famous literary embodiment of this doctrine is found in the *Bhagavadgītā*, a section of the great epic *Mahābhārata*, which continues to make a profound impression on readers to this day. It is the god Krishna (later seen as the earthly incarnation of the god Vishnu) who proclaims this message: the human being is responsible for himself and for society. He has certain duties already laid down through birth into a particular caste. To do these conscientiously is his most pressing task and generates no *karma* if they are carried out without selfishness.

From this point forward and up to the present day, freeing oneself from the cycle of births became the true goal of the religious person, and this meant: always acting selflessly, only doing one's (carefully considered) duty,[8] and keeping

---

[8]   Much of the *Mahābhārata* epic, one of the outstanding early works of world literature, is devoted to the dilemma of conflicting duties.

one's actions free of self-interest. Those who act selflessly attract no *karma*, either good or bad. When all *karma* has been used up, the cycle of births ends and salvation is within reach. The individual soul returns to its source, the highest divinity.

But the doctrine of rebirth has another important consequence confirmed by ancient Vedic knowledge: in reality, the dead live on. They are invisible, for their bodies now take on a subtle form; yet they remain capable of acting in certain respects. If they die as heroes in battle, so it was long believed, they enjoy the delights of hunting, dancing, music and heavenly nymphs in the paradise of Indra.

In the era of the older *Upanishads*, when the doctrine of the migration of souls emerged, it was assumed that only a small number of the dead are pure enough to take the path that leads via the sun to salvation. Most of the dead remain at the very beginning of this path, on the moon. There they await their rebirth – and are, like all living things, hungry, and thus dependent on the edible offerings made by their descendants. To provide sufficient nourishment for the ancestors during the period between death and rebirth, through sacrificial offerings, is consequently one of their descendants' indispensable ritual obligations to this day.

High gods

Towards the end of the Vedic period in the sixth or early fifth century BC, the situation in the Punjab and upper Mesopotamia changed significantly. Sixteen tribal areas (Janapada) had developed in which the Aryan tribes, who had formerly migrated with their herds of cattle, had settled. Fortified settlements had developed, the hereditary kingdom had replaced the election of a temporary leader for military campaigns, and trade had taken on considerable importance. With the concentration of power in the kingdom, the conception of the gods changed too. In place of a flexible group of divinities with various spheres of control, who hasten to the place of sacrifice or crisis areas as fast as the wind on war chariots drawn by a team of horses, a powerful but very distant figure now came onto the scene as king of heaven. The new high gods are rulers of the world. They may delegate tasks to underlings, but share with no one their unlimited and eternal power.

Among the divinities who rose to prominence in this period are four already known from the *Veda*, but who were not centre stage there: the gods Vishnu, Rudra, Sūrya and Prajāpati-Brahmā. With the exception of Prajāpati-Brahmā, who is integrated into Vishnu's acts of creation, each of them subsequently formed the centre of a new, monotheistic religion. That of the sun god Sūrya, who was credited with the healing of skin diseases, was a thousand-year success story and was maintained even longer, especially in noble circles and among astrologers. But because sun worship was integrated into both Vishnuism and Shivaism in the last quarter of the first millennium BC, it gradually lost its independence.

Vishnu is a helpful god with a friendly attitude towards the world. Laksmī, the goddess of luck, is his wife. Māyā, illusion, is the means by which he creates a peopled world seemingly separate from him. A lotus rises from his navel and from it the four-headed god Brahmā who, as the basis of all creation, holds the *Veda* and instruments of sacrifice in his hands, overlooks the entire world, north, south, east and west, and sets in motion the ongoing creation of the world. Transience is inherent to this world of Māyā from the outset, but the variety is divine and beautiful, and a return to the source can be achieved by understanding the original identity of individual and absolute consciousness.

Vishnu intervenes in the salvation history of the world through several incarnations; of these, it is Krishna and Rāma more than Vishnu himself who now constitute the focus of their followers' religious attention, in much the same way as it is not so much God the Father as His son Jesus Christ and his mother who form the fulcrum of worship within Christianity.

By contrast, the god Rudra is a wild, dangerous god in the *Veda*. Through the new name of Shiva, the friendly one, he is urged to be more approachable to his worshippers. Distinguished by the phallus as the symbol of fertility and ashes as symbol of the destruction of the world, this god creates and moves the world through dance, enriches it through music and the arts and overcomes it through yoga and meditation.

Both major gods, Vishnu and Shiva, are at once male and female in nature, the male part representing an imaginative and intellectual element, the female part a dynamic and realizing one. As with Vishnu and Māyā, Shiva and Shakti also form an androgynous unity, and here again the production of ideas and invention are ascribed to the male part, while their realization in worldly reality is down to the Great Goddess, who proceeds in active fashion. It is also the Goddess who is capable of warding off the demonic dangers threatening the world she has realized and which she protects. Over the course of time, numerous regional and local fertility cults and goddesses of war merged with the Goddess. The one who gives birth to all, but also the one who ultimately devours all, the Great Goddess, often compared with Mother Earth, breaks with her partner Shiva towards the end of the first century AD and, as the 'Great Mother', becomes the centrepiece of the Shakti cult in India.

The three great monotheistic religions mentioned above – Vishnuism, Shivaism and Shāktism – dominate the religious life of India to this day. Each of them has generated a vast theological literature, and each has exercised a decisive influence on the arts and society.

History and secularization

Now that we have endowed the near-boundless field of Hinduism with a clearer structure, subdividing it into various religions, we can turn to the phenomenon of secularization. Yet here again, we find ourselves immediately confronted with major problems. Secularization implies two presuppositions: first, the existence of a church or collective priesthood which can influence the state leadership, providing guidance and evaluation and setting its own interpretation of the law as a standard; second, as a response to this and under changing political and economic conditions, the emancipation of state law and state administrative structures from traditional role models which arose under religious control, and the taking on of what were originally church functions by the state. Both of these presuppositions hold true in India only for the periods of foreign rule, the Islamic from the thirteenth to the eighteenth century and the British in the nineteenth and twentieth centuries.[9] This also affects modern-day India as a legacy of colonial rule.

In the millennium before this foreign rule, the traditional India of the Hindus was certainly profoundly shaped by religion, but – in contrast to Christianity – there was no central authority that might have exercised religious control and impressed its values and demands upon the state. There was no holy book (such as the Qur'an or the Bible) valid for all believers, no equivalent of the binding tradition detailing the conduct of the Prophet (*Hadith*) and nothing like the decisions of the Christian councils and the Apostolic See. Guidelines of this kind, determined by the church and universally binding, did not exist in India. There were, however, a number of textbooks on correct behaviour written from a Brahmanic perspective and commissioned by the state – called the *Dharmashāstra* or 'textbook of the *dharma*' – which described the normative guidelines covering law and custom and the duties applying to the four stages of life, from childhood to old age. These have exercised a decisive influence on the social fabric of society, still being felt today.

In India, deeply internalized social and religious values are the foundation of public morality. Their origins lie in a tradition which assumes a hierarchically structured society in which specific traditional rules apply to each social stratum.

---

[9]   In the case of Islam, this applied during the time of the Mughal ruler Akbar in the second half of the seventeenth century, when he abolished the special taxes for unbelievers and even provided a Hindu temple with financial support – both in the face of fierce opposition from the Sunni priesthood; and later, under British rule in the eighteenth century, when the East India Company, against the will of the church, took on the traditional role of the indigenous princes and thus the protection and administration of the Hindu temples. Both phases of secularization were of short duration only. Both may reflect credit on the foreign rulers, but cannot be assigned to Hinduism.

The higher the stratum, the greater the responsibility for society as a whole and the more conscientious the transmission of traditional values and norms. Respect for one's parents, teachers and those who strive to attain understanding (*sādhus*, *gurus*) underlines the key importance of knowledge and of the transmission of knowledge in the society's hierarchy of values. A high value is traditionally placed on asceticism, self-control, meditation and yoga. Vegetarianism is common among Brahmans and Vaisyas (the bourgeoisie), but not among the nobility, the armed forces or the urban and rural lower castes. Those who practise self-discipline and meditation are respected. Originally developed as rules of conduct for ascetics and monks, the periodic withdrawal of older people into solitude and a frugal existence in preparation for death is also greatly respected. Jainas and Buddhists possessed clear rules of conduct for monks and laypeople and a coherent view of the human being aimed at the diminution of desires and liberation of the self. They sought release from the world, and hence distance from the state as well, but at the same time they also required from the rulers protection and economic support for the community of the faithful. They were open to their material contributions and, for their part, stood ready to provide political advice.

The Hindu religions on the other hand were embedded in a vast torrent of learned and ritual tradition, a torrent which, from the time of the *Vedas* in the second century BC up to the present, has included a large number of teachings and holy books but no comprehensive organization. These traditions resembled a sea, one which certainly has borders and into which numerous rivers flow, but within whose waters no stable forms take shape. They too featured normative legal texts, numerous holy writings, and distinguished theologians. Anyone in search of knowledge can find it all here; he may also test everything and develop it further. There is no censorship. An assembly of scholars may, however, feature differences of opinion aired in public. Such an assembly may be summoned by the ruler for purposes of clarification. A famous example from the nineteenth century is the conference convened in Rajasthan, in which Dāyānanda Sarasvatī had to defend his theses.

The ancient sources of religious tradition offer yardsticks for one's own thinking: the *Veda*; the sacred knowledge of prehistory; and tradition, handed down in two epics[10] and numerous *purāṇas*, *āgamas* and *tantras*. There has never been a single authority which, through selection and exegesis, was in a position to derive a universally binding canon from the wealth of post-Vedic holy writings.

---

[10]   Particularly in the *Mahābhārata*, which has become an important witness to ancient Indian legal history in light of its extensive passages on the *dharma* of the warrior castes.

Several major philosophical schools developed, whose concerns included epistemology, the nature of God and the relationship of the human soul to the divinity. Believers' approach to the divinity began to be characterized by a strong emotional charge and an emphasis on loving service, captured by the term *bhakti*; this changed religious practice, which formerly emphasized ritual, and prompted the emergence of new religious communities within the three great religions, whose founders – in much the same way as Luther in northern Europe – continue to this day to exercise a formative influence. Philosophers explored the question of the nature of the human soul: Is it identical with absolute consciousness (or with the highest divinity) when, in striving to return to its source, it has overcome the barrier of the *māyā*? Is it different?

Such reflections by no means amounted to the mere splitting of hairs. They were a serious business. If the origins of the highest state of bliss lie in beholding God, praising God and service to God, then fusion with the divinity (this was the highest goal of the *Advaita Vedānta*, which dominated the philosophical discussion) may be felt as an emotional loss. It is only through separation that longing and love arise; fusion means the loss of the Other and along with it the greatest human happiness. The theologian Madhva, an exponent of the doctrine of the enduring difference between human soul and divinity, cogently illustrated his rejection of the doctrine of *Advaita*[11] by reference to an everyday phenomenon: if you love sugar, you want to taste it, not to be it! In his view, the same goes for the relationship between human being and God.

It is the advantage of a religious community not led (or dominated) by any church organization that it is permitted to formulate every conceivable idea. If opposition arises, this triggers a dispute and the more convincing arguments prevail. Within this constellation, myths, philosophers and ritual tradition play an important role: myths, because they convey an image of the nature and doings of the gods, because they embed light and darkness, success and failure, good and evil within a holistic view of the structure and forces of this world; philosophers, because they try to describe the nature of human beings, identify the causes of fortune and misfortune and to show the paths to overcoming suffering and death; and rites, because the basic values of the society are revealed within them. Time and again, on this basis, and taking meditative experiences into account, new systems of thought emerged. Their oral transmission from teacher to students and students-of-students led to additions, commentaries, changes, innovations. Religious and philosophical knowledge was also subject to a process of growth

---

[11]   *Advaita* = non-duality, identity. The doctrine dates from the time of the older *Upanishads*, and was taken up again and renewed very convincingly by the philosopher Shankara (eighth century), whose teaching continues to exercise a significant influence on Indian philosophy.

in which some impulses might peter out if they were not viable, but in which others thrived, producing new blooms.

The Hindu religions share three key foundations:

1. consciousness of a hierarchical structure characteristic of all living beings;

2. the doctrine of rebirth; and

3. a recognition that each individual has a responsibility for the cohesion of the world.

The astonishing extent to which Hindus are prepared to allow each person his individual belief in this or that divinity shows that it is not so much the individual's faith as the continuity of his ritual and social obligations that is of key importance to the Hindu identity. Almost every day of the Hindu calendar is filled with ritual practices, most of which contribute to the wellbeing of family members, the ancestors and the gods and which are carried out in the private sphere of the home. Ritual action of this kind has its roots in the family and its obligations to relatives, the ancestors and the gods. Only those who are prepared to serve and to make a donation can expect these three groups to provide protection and promote their wellbeing: it is the sacrificial offering which ties human beings, ancestors and gods together to form a single great community of interest.

Consequently, offering sacrifices is the human being's most important, life-sustaining task. By strengthening the gods, he also contributes indirectly to the preservation of the world order. All taking demands giving – not necessarily a direct counter-gift, but at the very least a gift to a third party. Not only the cosmos, but also human society, is founded on this principle.

As far as the family and its ancestors is concerned, there are seven generations for which the sacrificing paterfamilias must provide: grandfather, father, son and grandson plus at least three generations of ancestors on the father's and mother's side; or, if only three or even just two generations are living, proportionately more generations of ancestors.

Within a framework in which people firmly expect to be reborn, the ancestors are very lively and active. Often, particularly if the grandparents' marriage was a happy one, it is assumed that the deceased grandfather is re-embodied in the grandson or great-grandson. The deceased grandmother, it is hoped, returns to earth in the shape of the girl who will eventually marry the grandson. Ideally, then, the marriage continues across generations. The value placed on marriage is extraordinarily high because it is not only the prerequisite for the continuity of the family, but also for the performance of household ritual: only with marriage does one attain the authority to engage in ritual contact with the gods and ancestors, and this represents a central aim in life, one that links heaven and earth.

In line with this, the descendants produced by the marriage not only help ensure the parents' wellbeing in old age, but also the continuity of the family's ritual obligations. The ancestors remain linked with their families and may, particularly as far as healthy descendants are concerned, be a major source of welcome help. But should they feel neglected, their fury may bring disaster.

Much the same goes for the gods. It is true that each person has the right to devote himself to a particular favourite divinity in a personal way, and this will be the main addressee of his ritual practice. But he also inherits the divinities of his forefathers, both those worshipped in the male line and those which the various wives brought with them from their family traditions and whose small bronze figures have been placed in the household shrine since their arrival. Hence, polytheistic elements are to be found both in the landscape, inhabited by numerous gods, as well as in the family tradition, which is characterized by marriage alliances. Domestic ritual does in fact continue to play an important role and it is often the women who contribute most to the ritual safeguarding of the family.

Such polytheism, also practised daily through visits to various temples, should not obscure the fact that behind or above this multitude of gods there always exists a highest divinity or a highest principle (Brahman), which is at once the source of all multiplicity and the goal of every desire for salvation.[12] Whether one imagines this divinity as an abstract, formless presence and calls it *Brahman* (a neuter noun), or whether one imagines the divinity in a personified way as Lord of the World or as the Great Mother, depends on the theological tradition into which one was born or to which one devotes oneself consciously of one's own accord. But in all cases, this divinity determines the path and the goal of one's pursuit of salvation.

Today, the religious devotion of the Vishnuites is directed primarily towards Vishnu's incarnations as Rāma and Krishna; Shiva, who integrates stark differences within himself, who stands for procreative power and asceticism, for creative dance and world-extinguishing meditation, continues to be worshipped through the symbol of the phallus; and among the numerous manifestations of the Great Mother, it is the bloodthirsty ones such as Kālī and Chāmundā or the victorious such as Durgā who stand centre stage. The worship of destructive

---

[12] By way of comparison, this is for example reminiscent of the vast number of frequently invoked saints within Catholic Christianity who, as mediators and helpers in times of need, draw their strength from their relationship to God the Father or to Christ.

power is intended, on the one hand, to ensure the sparing of one's own sphere of life, but it also takes account of the fact that destruction plays a necessary role in the process of the world and that it creates space for the emergence of the new.

The community is strongly marked by traditional values. At its core is the welfare of the family, which entails four key components: physical wellbeing; preservation of the inherited culture; tending to the needs of the gods, ancestors and needy relatives; and self-control through yoga and the acquisition of religious knowledge. The latter three components relate to three successive stages of life: education; marriage, family and career; and old age. Responsibility for the greater community of the village, the party, etc. falls in the middle stage of marriage and career.

The community's most important function is to create living conditions which help the individual carry out his two main tasks: first, to ensure the continuity of families and thus also the care of the old, the ancestors and the gods through good education, healthy children and material improvement; and secondly, to support people's pursuit of salvation and their focus on self-purification by ensuring that social peace prevails within society, thus engendering freedom from fear and creating a suitably calm environment for meditation and contemplation. The ideal as portrayed in classical Indian texts is a hermitage, whose inhabitants live in the inner and outer purity of contemplation, see to their sacred tasks and are vegetarians, living solely on roots and leaves. Such peace reigns around them that the lion and the deer mingle without fear or violence with the hermits and their domestic animals, and the virtues of purity, peaceableness, non-violence and justice blossom throughout the realm.

The state, however, has only limited means to ensure such ideal conditions. Its primary responsibility is to fill the key posts with individuals of integrity and wisdom and to protect the people from external military threats and from thieves within the country itself. Further, with respect to educating the young, the task – one shared by parents and schools – is not only to provide useful knowledge, but also to transmit the basic, time-honoured rules of ethical behaviour to the next generation. There exists a famous ancient legal code, the Code of Manu; according to P. V. Kane,[13] it was composed between the second century BC and the second century AD, though it was probably revised in the golden age of the Gupta empire around AD 400 from the perspective of the Brahmans. It still has an important place within the Indian legal tradition, though there are a great many later (that is, more modern) legal texts. After nine detailed chapters on the moral and legal foundations of an ideally conceived

---

[13]   The issue of dating is dealt with in depth in P. V. Kane, *History of Dharmashastra*, vol. 1, Poona, Bhandarkar Oriental Institute, 1930, pp. 306–49.

society, particularly the two influential and responsibility-laden strata of the nobility and the Brahmans, the guiding moral principles are again summed up concisely in the middle of the tenth chapter as follows:

> Injure no living being, speak the truth, do not steal, pay attention to cleanliness, rein in the sense organs: this is what Manu referred to as a right way of life (dharma), common to the four social classes.[14]

In addition, there are of course professional and status-related rules specific to each caste.

It is clear that the validity of these virtues is not restricted to one religion. But the stressing of non-aggression towards all living creatures, holding first place among the virtues – as opposed to sixth in the Judaeo-Christian tradition – clearly shows that human beings are not regarded as the summit of creation in and of themselves. Rather, they are viewed within the context of all living beings, a point about which the doctrine of rebirth leaves us in little doubt: every form of life, from the mosses to the gods, is seen here as a potential site of incarnation and experience for individual souls. At the same time, however, the heavy emphasis on non-violence points indirectly to the fact that latent rivalry and a propensity for violence may be fairly prominent features of caste society, requiring defusing by ethical norms.

If we turn our attention to later historical developments and secularization, we are again led back to political history. With the establishment of Islamic rule in India – first bases in the Indus Valley from AD 712, control of much of northern India from AD 1206, formation of a number of Islamic principalities in the southern half of India from AD 1296 – Islam became the dominant religion of India's ruling class, not only in the north but also in much of the south. India's history and culture was shaped by a number of major dynasties, the last and most splendid being that of the Mughal emperors from the sixteenth to the eighteenth century. Only the Hindu regional kingdoms of Vijayanagar in the south and Orissa in the east maintained their independence until the mid-sixteenth century. The Marathas, who re-established Hindu rule in the eighteenth century in Mahārāshtra, proved little more than marauding robbers who spared neither Muslim- nor Hindu-ruled areas. Their raids did, however, erode Mughal rule across large swathes of the country, thus paving the way for the period of British rule in India.

The subsequent Anglicization of Indian public life and education marked the

---

[14]   *ahiṃsā satyam asteyam śaucam indriyanigrahaḥ | etaṃ samāsikam dharmaṃ cāturvarṇye 'bravin manuḥ ||* Manusmṛti 10, 63.

entire nineteenth century and continued until independence in 1947. It began in earnest after Lord Bentinck's 1835 decision to switch from Sanskrit, Urdu and Persian to English in the fields of education and administration. Otherwise, as colonial masters, the British simply tried to take over the role of the previous rulers and, as they had done, present themselves as the guardians of the indigenous religions and cults.

This attempt failed for two reasons. First, the British found themselves confronted with customs among the indigenous tribes and Rajputs entirely at variance with their norms of human conduct. The key emotive terms are well-known and already mentioned above: widow-burning, human sacrifice, child marriage (which meant that the girl became a widow as a child if the boy died prematurely). The acceptance of regional traditions reached its limits here, above all because the British public, not yet knowledgeable about far-off India, became highly agitated. In addition, missionaries of several Christian denominations poured into the country, defamed Hindu rituals with their representations of gods as idolatry, and launched intensive efforts to Christianize the hitherto marginalized tribal peoples of India. In the diversity of holy writings and traditions of the Hindus the Christians saw only the discrepancies, not the historical developments, and in the cults they saw only the barbaric aspects, not the religious intensity. All social injustices, largely the consequence of foreign rule and exploitation, were blamed on the Hindus' religion.

The Brahmanic intelligentsia, who had to defend themselves against such accusations, particularly in centres of British rule such as Calcutta, Delhi, Bombay and Madras as well as the holy city of Benares, began a process of reform intended to endow the religious multiplicity with a clear structure, which was possible only by radically excluding large parts of tradition and religious practice. There emerged a purified version of Hindu practice of an almost Protestant tenor, what we now refer to as neo-Hinduism.

As we might expect, this reformation took shape in a number of regional cells. Two of them attained outstanding importance and still exist to this day: the *Brāhmo Samāj*, established in 1828 in Bengal under the leadership of Rām Mohan Roy, and the *Ārya Samāj*, founded in 1875 by Svāmī Dayānanda Sarasvatī, which spread chiefly in the northwest of India. Both linked the political goal of opposing the Christians, Muslims and Sikhs with a Hindu alternative capable of attracting a majority with a drastic reduction in religious diversity and the reorganization of ritual. The *Ārya Samāj*, which, drawing on the *Veda*, the *Upanishads* and the ancient Indian law codes, propagated a Hinduism cleansed of all medieval developments, even launched a counter-mission. The lesson was quickly learned that in the political system established by the British, majorities were required in order to achieve political goals. Hence, alongside the need to protect religious practice against criticism, there soon emerged the political rationality that demands strong religious groupings. This became the driving force of a new Hindu mission: attempts were made to court tribal peoples, to win back Buddhists for the community of Hindus and even peasant castes which had converted to Islam under Muslim rule. The threat to religious tradition posed by criticism and mission led to surprisingly extensive secularization.[15]

Towards the end of the nineteenth century, religion began to be unambiguously politicized; in the twentieth century, in the wake of the national liberation movement directed against the colonial power, this process was further intensified. Muslims and Hindus took part in the revolts against British rule. But when success seemed to be in the offing, partnership turned to rivalry. It was the demands of Muslims and Hindus that now came to the fore. The former ruled India (including the modern-day Pakistan and Bangladesh) for hundreds of years, leading it to splendour and glory. The latter have far older claims to the subcontinent and are the inheritors of its ancient culture, though they had divided it up into small warring states. Something like the Pax Britannica existed only during the time of Ashoka in the third century BC.

Against Gandhi's will, the impending participation in power became a bone of contention. Nehru and his comrades-in-arms in the Congress Party were unable to reach agreement with Mohammed Ali Jinnah, spokesman for the Muslim League. What the British had feared came to pass: with power, the old religious conflicts emerged. Religious majorities now determined the territorial division of British India and prompted the resettlement of around 17 million people and the worst bloodshed in Indian history.[16] 59 years have passed since then, but India and Pakistan have been unable to come to terms with the regional and emotional losses imposed on them by the partition of 1947.

Not long after achieving independence, conservative Hindu politicians, particularly of the extreme right wing, began to feel the need for a strong religion uniting all Hindus. They strove to create a politically influential religious force on the model of Islam and Christianity, something achievable only through the organizational fusion of the many different religious groups. This programme has been pushed for years by the *Vishva Hindu Parishad* (VHP),[17] partly through

---

[15] 'Secularization' here refers to the acceptance of criticisms, emanating from the state under foreign rule, of religion as traditionally practised, and corresponding reorganization of the criticized aspects.

[16] There are no reliable statistics on expulsions. Estimates of the number of those killed in the course of resettlement are approximations only. Generally, the figure is put at around 100,000 deaths. The horror of Partition has poisoned relations between India and Pakistan for more than half a century.

[17] The *Vishva Hindu Parishad* (VHP) or World Hindu Council is a political offshoot of the *Rāshtrīya Svayamsevak Sangh*. It represents the interests of all Hindus worldwide, receives

argument, partly through financial incentives, and carried out by the *Rāshtrīya Svayamsevak Sangh* (RSS)[18] at the village level through the deployment of young priests trained in special training centres. The objectives of the RSS and its political wing, the VHP, are secular and nationalist rather than religious. The attempt to fuse together the many religious forces of India[19] is meant to help homogenize state and society. Religion is subordinated to national politics and severely manipulated. In contrast to communism, we are not dealing here with the eradication of religion but with a process of rendering it subservient to the state. This will be possible only by bringing to an end the diversity of its manifestations. Religious plurality and cultural history are being subordinated to the political desideratum of the ideological unity of the Indian people.

------

financial support from Hindus all over the world and uses these resources for religious festivals and programmes, the building of temples, restoration and such like.

[18]   The *Rāshtrīya Svayamsevak Sangh*, roughly the 'National Self-Help Federation', was founded as early as 1925 by the Maratha Keshav Baliram Hedgewar as a rigidly organized paramilitary youth organization intended to correct the image of the meek Indian and play an active role in building a strong India capable of shaking off all foreign rule. Today, the RSS is a force present throughout the country. It trains youths in villages and cities throughout India in martial arts and discipline, maintains its own schools and colleges for boys and girls, and its members hold posts in local and district administrations, universities and state governments. It produced both the last prime minister of India, Atal Bihari Bajpeyi, as well as the longstanding leader of the Bharatīya Janata Party, L. K. Adhvani, and his successor Rājnāth Singh. The RSS has an aggressive attitude towards foreign religions, attempts to put a stop to Christian missions in Indian tribal areas by force, and has also come into conflict with Muslims on a number of occasions.

[19]   I consciously avoid using the term 'fascism' here.

6

Secularization:
Confucianism and Buddhism

Rudolf G. Wagner

'Secularization' is a Latinism used in European languages referring to the helplessness of the individual whose world-regulating God has died on him.[1] All that is left to him is to cope, at his own risk and taking full responsibility, with the finite and fragile nature of his individual and social existence in this time and in this world.

The word claims to describe a historical state of global dimensions. It is difficult to conceive of the existence of God as a regional or local phenomenon and just as difficult to imagine that His absence applies only as far as the Bosphorus. Yet, however much the notion of secularization may make sense in Europe, it fails to do so in the USA of the 'moral majority', the revivalist gatherings of the Pentecostal movement in Latin America or in large parts of the Islamic world. With his finger on this contemporary pulse and one eye on the newspaper headlines, Jürgen Habermas, in conversation with Cardinal Ratzinger, believes we have already entered a 'post-secular age'.[2] While in this reading we have now wound up with the opposite of secularization, we are not out of the woods yet. Our horizon is still dominated by monotheism, and that means we have remained within a geographically and culturally delimited part of the world, for the notion of secularization or that of the post-secular age makes sense solely within this horizon.

We are in fact quite familiar with the general process from religious history. A deity loses its power, seems no longer willing or able to offer rain, sunshine, prosperity, health or victory in return for prayers, sacrifices and good behaviour.

---

[1]   See Hermann Zabel, Werner Conze and Hans-Wolfgang Strätz, 'Säkularisierung, Säkularisation', in Otto Brunner, Werner Conze and Reinhart Koselleck (eds.), *Geschichtliche Grundbegriffe*, Stuttgart, Klett-Cotta, 1984, pp. 789–829.

[2]   See Jürgen Habermas and Joseph Ratzinger, *Dialectics of Secularization: On Reason and Religion*, San Francisco, Ignatius, 2006.

Rather than a crisis of secularization, the result is the fall of this particular house of God, cult or place of pilgrimage and a search for other deities that have proved more satisfactory in this particular place or indeed in places far distant from it, but definitely at this particular time.

It is possible to argue that the upsurge in Christian or Islamic fundamentalism is not simply the perpetuation of established religious practice, but amounts to a crisis-triggered reorientation of this kind, even though the name of the deity remains the same. This would make fundamentalism the dialectical twin of secularization. This is surely correct. Yet there remains the fundamental distinction that so far only the belief in a single God, monotheism, leads to fundamentalist radicalism at times of crisis. The alarming prospect of the loss of the one and only God seems to justify desperate steps. These are everywhere in evidence in our history books as well as in the daily newspapers.[3]

How do things stand with respect to secularization in East Asia? The East Asian world, moulded by Buddhist and Confucian traditions, has a long history, is geographically extensive and of growing contemporary importance, but it is just as inherently historical – and that means multiform – as its essentialized counterpart, 'the West'.

Buddhism is a doctrine of salvation which arose around 2400 years ago in northern India. It spread to Southeast, Central and East Asia and in recent times to Europe and the USA as well, taking on various, internally diverse forms up to the present day. In the Indian subcontinent itself on the other hand, with the exception of Sri Lanka, the Buddhist tradition came to an end around 1200 years ago.

When the first Buddhist monks arrived via the Silk Road in what is now known as China around 2000 years ago, they encountered the highly developed state of the Han dynasty (206 BCE–220 CE). The chief concern of the political class of this dynasty was to secure state order. Philosophy and social teachings, the management of the state and religious thought – all were pervaded by this concern. This educated class was called the Ru, actually a job title for civil servants educated in the canon of classical knowledge and classical skills. The

---

[3]   In light of the form they sometimes take, some of the religious conflicts between Hindus and Muslims in India can also be classed as fundamentalism. On the part of the Hindus, these conflicts are nourished by an attempt to make the 'Hindu' identity the centrepiece of the identity of citizens of the Indian nation state, though India has the most Muslims of any country in the world. Most sociologists see this clash in the context of a long tradition of 'communal violence' in India, which may be sparked off by the most varied of social conflicts. The most common element of fundamentalist movements, the belief in the task set by a single omnipotent God to stop and reverse the ruination of the world, conveyed unambiguously and without room for interpretation through vision or text, is not found among the Hindu groupings.

'Ru School' was the common umbrella term for the many and diverse individual currents within this general orientation and professional identity.

In the West, since Jesuits such as Matteo Ricci changed the name of Kong Qiu or Kong fuzi (Master Kong), held in high regard by the Ru as spiritual forebear, into the pleasingly Latinate 'Confucius' towards the end of the sixteenth century, 'Confucianism' has been the translation of the Chinese Rujia (Ru School), while the Ru all became 'Confucianists'. As a result of their close involvement in the centralized state of the Han dynasty, this class lost much of its intellectual liveliness and attraction. A non-state private and personal sphere thus began to take shape in which were discussed issues of human mortality, the connection between behavioural morality and individual fate, the human costs of integration into the state civil service and a spiritual or drug-enabled route out of the narrow constraints of the human condition in general.[4]

The newly arriving Buddhist monks were able to provide answers to these questions on many levels: the institution of the monastery with its frugal and ascetic lifestyle far removed from the state and the family; a radical philosophical analysis of consciousness as the creator of a world which in itself is empty and devoid of all essence; and on top of all this and most importantly, a meditational route to enlightenment as the end of attachment to this empty world.

The success of Buddhism – and in its wake older Chinese currents with a similar orientation – was so sweeping that for almost a thousand years the Ru School lost all significance. Around 800 years ago, in the Song era, a revival now referred to as 'neo-Confucian' enriched this doctrine, generally focused on state order, with many Buddhist elements of personal life such as meditation and with philosophical reflection and categorization. As a result of its radicalization of the demand for the absolute subordination of subjects to their ruler, of women to men, etc., it gained protection as a new state doctrine. It was granted this status first by emperors, for whom this doctrine of subordination came in very handy, namely the descendants of Kublai Khan in the Mongolian Yuan dynasty, but retained it until the end of the Chinese empire and beyond.[5]

---

[4]   The newly emerging popular Daoist religion, which referred to Laozi (Lao-tse) as the highest authority and which received patronage even from the imperial court, developed rituals of repentance in order to prevent past transgressions from becoming future blows of fate. Under the Ru it became socially acceptable to withdraw from the civil service and construct an existence as a highly regarded private citizen, jushi, with a public voice. On the culture of psychedelic and immortality-inducing drugs, see Rudolf Wagner, 'Lebensstil und Drogen im chinesischen Mittelalter', T'oung Pao, 59 (1973), pp. 79–178.

[5]   James T. C. Liu, 'How did a Neo-Confucian School Become the State Orthodoxy?', Philosophy East and West, 23.4 (1973), pp. 483–505.

Both currents reached Korea and Japan, the Buddhist from around 1600 to 1300 years ago, and the neo-Confucian shortly after its revival. Through interaction with the cultures and institutions of Korea and Japan indigenous currents developed, yet East Asia remained a common market of ideas, writings and individuals. This was facilitated above all by the 'Latin' of East Asia, the Chinese characters and written language used in China, Korea and Japan.

What about secularization in this vast East Asian world? Here, such developments generally did not come with a heightened sense of existential menace and crisis. This is not to say that the people of East Asia did not find other reasons for killing each other. The two East Asian traditions mentioned above of Buddhism and Confucianism are, moreover, well aware of their own historicity – and that means the instability of their own existence.

The Ru School had to cope with an interruption of the 'correct tradition' of more than a thousand years; after the end of the empire in 1912, until the end of the century, it fell into disrepute as the 'Confucian Shop' which it was thought best to close, and suddenly, over the last few years and months, its remaining stock has been rehabilitated by its keenest opponents, the Chinese Communists, as a means of maintaining state order. While neither history nor the newspapers tell us about collective or individual acts of violence born out of the desperation of followers of the Ru School at the key moments in its decline, they do tell us about a great deal of patient work to demonstrate the contemporary relevance of their own teachings.

The idea of the historical religious crisis is to be found in Buddhism as well. The Buddha is said to have stated that people's willingness to follow his teaching would decline and even die away completely within seven hundred years after his nirvana. Hence, bound up with the ancient Indian notion of world ages, each of which ends in a great world fire, we find as a recurrent theme the fear of the 'end of the *dharma*', that is, of Buddhist teachings and thus of their path to salvation. But it is not heretics deserving of eradication who are to blame for this, but solely the overwhelming pressure of the world and the fact that the route out of this world is gradually becoming overgrown as the temporal distance from a living Buddha increases. Here again, the response was not to launch Buddhist crusades from China, Korea or Japan to India, to liberate Buddha's birthplace from the followers of Shiva or Krishna for example. What we see instead are attempts to develop forms of religious practice which were open to even the simplest souls, such as Amida Buddhism, or alternatively which promised the sharpest of minds a short-cut to 'sudden enlightenment', such as Chan or Zen Buddhism – if, indeed, whole villages did not set about engraving Buddhist texts onto thousands of great stone tablets which, stowed away in a mountain, could survive the world fire.[6]

---

[6]   See Lothar Ledderose, 'Carving Sutras into Stone before the Catastrophe: The

This difference in temperature – if I may be permitted to use this climatic metaphor – in the ways in which the monotheistic and the East Asian doctrines deal with a spiritual-religious crisis points to a very different interpretation of world, state, society and religion. Within Buddhist doctrine, in all its different historical and regional forms, gods and spirits generally play a modest role. Wherever Buddhist teachings spread, they accepted the local religions in so far as they could be seen as the first steps towards encouraging behaviour in accordance with basic Buddhist values. These religions were looked upon as phenomena characteristic of a simple, mostly rural population; of women in the households of the educated; but also of soldiers unwilling to dispense with miracles as they went about their risky business.

To this day, countless Buddhist monks regard it as one of their duties to take part in popular religious rites, in order to help those who begin at this simple level of understanding to attain greater insight. Within Mahayana Buddhism, the branch of the religion most common in East Asia, this is part of *upaya*, of a teaching that is adapted to the listener's level of understanding. Through this gradual increase in the level of understanding, so the argument goes, the fictitious and 'empty' nature of the gods and spirits will become apparent of its own accord, with no need for the violent destruction of 'idols'. From this perspective, insight into the emptiness of the divinity or divinities which one formerly worshipped does not mark a crisis of faith to which one must respond with redoubled religious fervour, but welcome progress on the path to understanding.

At the same time, the relationship between the various levels of religious insight is different here than in the monotheistic religions. In both camps, attempts are made to establish a critical continuum between the simplest and the highest forms of religious understanding and religious practice. However, within the monotheistic religions, the core elements of personal worship and faith in the Scriptures are retained and sublimated. In Mahayana Buddhism, as one's knowledge deepens, one gains ever greater awareness of the emptiness of the objects of knowledge and of knowledge itself. This insight eliminates the root of the reproduction of suffering in and from the world, namely attachment to the world, which in this sense includes religious faith in gods just as much as the craving for sex, money and power. From this point of view, at the highest level of Buddhism, there is little more left than a sense of unease at the turgid enslavement of one's individual self and the germ of death in every undertaking, which might have prompted novices to seek divine help from a higher realm. In

Inscription of 1118 at Cloud Dwelling Monastery near Beijing', *Proceedings of the British Academy*, 125 (2004), pp. 381–454; idem, 'Felsinschriften für die Ewigkeit', *Ruperto Carola: Forschungsmagazin der Universität Heidelberg*, 1 (2005), pp. 4–8.

this process, the specific elements of faith, of religious practice and the canonical texts are not sublimated but understood in their intrinsic emptiness. Thus, in Mahayana Buddhism, we find neither buddhological sublimations of popular religious practices nor any elevation of the Buddhist doctrine itself to some higher stature. All are merely stepping-stones on a path that loses all meaning once the goal has been attained.

Hence, as a religion, Buddhism really begins where the crisis of monotheism sets in. Here, the human being is above all the victim of his own worldliness and sensuality. His 'secularity', his abandonment to the world, is his existential *conditio humana*, rather than a tragic historical moment in his history as conceived in the notion of secularization as crisis. Through the attachment entailed in this abandonment to the world, living beings reproduce themselves in an endless moral cycle whose prime mover is *karma* and which operates with the charming rigour of a calculator.

In its place of origin in India, this notion of the cycle of karmic retribution was widely held rather than being a specific feature of Buddhism. Around 2000 years ago in East Asia, before the arrival of Buddhism, in the Eastern Han period, the notion of a personal fate formed through the moral quality of one's own actions was beginning to emerge. Here, the doctrine of karma, now seen in China as the core of Buddhism, not only offered a detailed picture of the human world as veritable product of attachment to the world; as religion and way of life, Buddhism also offered a route out of this wholly 'secular' iron cage with its equally iron internal laws of motion.

As a distant goal, this path aims to achieve 'enlightenment', the realization of the emptiness of all elements of being and the associated freedom from all attachment to them. This realization brings the karmic cycle to an end for the individual. Hence, in the radical formulations of Mahayana Buddhism, the distinction between the secular world of *Samsara* and its negation in *Nirvana*, between the holiness of a Buddha and the bare existence of a stone, between the many volumes of the Buddha's teachings and a 'silence like a lion's roar' as the answer to a question as to the content of enlightenment, also disappears.

It is at this high level that the social teachings of Mahayana Buddhism begin. Mahayana means Great Vehicle. It marks itself off with irony from the Hinayana, the lesser vehicle, which it accuses of making space for only a few religious specialists to overcome the suffering of this world, specialists who, however ascetic they may be, are after nothing other than their own enlightenment and make it clear by this very fact that they have failed to free themselves of all attachment. There is room for everyone in the Great Vehicle. It takes up the challenge posed by living beings' collective enslavement to the world through a Buddhology whose aim is their complete liberation.

The ideal of the Great Vehicle is the *bodhisattva*. A *bodhisattva* is one who, in his pursuit of highest enlightenment, has reached a stage of insight into the emptiness of all entities that frees him from all attachment. Mindful of the enormous task of freeing all living beings down to the last worm, rather than attempting to extinguish his existence and all attachments in Nirvana, he volunteers to participate in the cycle of existence as a 'guest', until such time as all living beings have been freed, through his efforts and those of other *bodhisattvas*, from this eternally secular world.

He can and will do everything that furthers this aim. As he himself is liberated from all attachment, he can wade knee-deep in the sludge of the world without getting dirty. Hence, depictions of the Buddha or of *bodhisattvas* often show them sitting on the blossom of the lotus, a flower whose pure white blooms can be seen emerging from the thickest of bogs. The help provided by the *bodhisattva* is not focused on alleviating general human suffering such as hunger, illness, violence or injustice. It relates, first of all, not just to humans but to all living creatures. Among them, the human individual, in most schools the male in particular, has arrived at that point on the long path towards salvation through the cycle of rebirth at which there is some prospect of real liberation. The possibility of consciously shaping how one deals with the world arises only at the existential stage of the human being, whether through caring for other living beings, abstinence, meritorious works, or liberating one's own consciousness by means of meditation. Here, then, human life is above all the opportunity to rid oneself of attachment to the world. The work of the *bodhisattva* consists in encouraging people to recognize and seize this opportunity while offering them guidance.

In line with this religious principle, the proof of *bodhisattva* status is the lived freedom from attachments rather than ordination as a monk. To my mind, one of the most beautiful of Buddhist texts, and rightly one of the most famous, is the *Vimalakirtinirdesa*, composed around 1900 years ago. To all appearances, Vimalakirti is a rich lay Buddhist. In order to advance the understanding of the Buddha's leading disciples, he embroils them in complex conversations. Through these conversations, it is the layman Vimalakirti who shows the Buddha's most famous followers the way rather than vice versa.[7]

The diverse institutionalized forms of the Buddhist religion such as the monastery, ordination as a monk, the rules of discipline or the canon of teachings function as tools with which to pursue the ultimate goal and in this

---

[7]   English translation: *The Vimalakirti Sutra*, translated by Burton Watson from the Chinese version of the *Kumarajiva*, New York, Columbia University Press, 1997. French translation: *L'enseignement de Vimalakirti (Vimalakirtinirdesa)*, translated by Etienne Lamotte, Louvain, Publications Universitaires, 1962.

sense they are important and helpful crutches along the way, but they are of no value in themselves beyond this instrumental role. Consistently enough, Buddhist institutions are rather underdeveloped in comparison with those of some other religions. There is no institutionalized human or textual authority on the correctness of the teachings, no access to understanding privileged institutionally vis-à-vis the laity, no fixed way of dealing with texts, and no other way of dissociating oneself from those who take a different view than the opinion, occasionally expressed in debates, that their way does not lead to the goal. Even the Buddhist monks, sometimes referred to as missionaries, who came to East Asia and who achieved, according to the unfortunate title of an otherwise excellent book, a 'Buddhist conquest' of China,[8] were sent by no one and wrote no reports on conversion to any central institution. Buddhism sees itself as offering a way out of imprisonment in the world. There is no mandate to convert others which can be evaded only at risk of divine punishment.

In this sense, the Buddhist community is only loosely structured, but in the reality of people's lives it is of considerable importance. It consists of two parts, the monks in the monasteries and the laity. The monks have a long tradition of wandering the land in search of a master, so that their ties to a particular monastery tend to remain weak. The obligation, which is not always complied with, to live from the gifts of the laity, means that monks depend upon the acceptance and respect of the laity; householders might withhold donations from a degenerate monastic community. The term 'layman' is far from having a fixed content. Many laymen may have spent years as monks; others, while remaining laymen, follow a lifestyle generally geared towards the monastic rules, while still others fall back on Buddhism and the community of Buddhist monks in particular circumstances. For most of them, their relationship to Buddhism is inclusive rather than exclusive. In its living reality, Buddhism does not cover every sphere of life. What it offers relates to liminal realms of existence, that is, death with its endless karmic cycle and enlightenment as the route out of it. Other spheres are covered by others.

Regardless of this relative institutional softness of the Buddhist community, the *sangha*, the community of monks, is one of the 'three treasures', *triratna* in Sanskrit or *san bao* in Chinese. These three are Buddha, *dharma*, in other words the Buddhist teachings, and *sangha*, the community. They are the definitional core of that which we refer to as Buddhist, but they provide no definition of what the Buddha, the teachings or the community are. This core allows the free flow of individuals, texts and ideas across the boundaries of schools, monasteries, languages and countries and makes Buddhism a truly transnational, transcultural

---

[8]   See Erik Zürcher, *The Buddhist Conquest of China*, Leiden, Brill, 1959.

and multilingual religion. This idea lives on today. Since the end of the nineteenth century, it has made it possible for Japanese, Chinese, Ceylonese, Tibetan, Thai, etc. Buddhist monks to come together regardless of borders to secure and make accessible the legacy of Buddhist writings. Anyone today who goes on a meditation retreat in a Buddhist monastery in the Black Forest, in Texas or Taiwan, which espouses Zen or Chan Buddhism (itself internally diverse), will be able to visualize this easygoing as well as serious contact that pays little heed to possible boundaries.

In one respect, the *sangha* in China takes on a new quality. The Buddhist monk who *chujia*, 'leaves his family' in order to enter the monastery, breaks in a quite radical way with one of the most deeply anchored Chinese traditions: he leaves his parents, does not take care of them when they are old and provides them with no descendants to look after the family graves and worship the ancestors. Countless polemics against Buddhism have underlined this point. Yet at the same time, the Buddhist doctrine of karma altered the fate of human beings after death in a quite radical way. While people had formerly thought in terms of a shadow kingdom of 'yellow springs' after death, structured more or less analogously to our world, Buddhism introduced the doctrine of retribution as one of its didactic centrepieces. According to this conception, depending on the moral quality of their lives, people pass through a graded series of purgatories after death. These are administered not by the anti-Buddha, but by a *bodhisattva* called Ksitigharbha. For all their shocking concreteness, these hells constitute a beneficial educational institution, and pamphlets providing detailed descriptions are on display in Buddhist temples, their authors having been taken from this life too early as a result of a mix-up over names and permitted to return to life as eyewitnesses after a guided tour. This purgatory is said to cure people of any notion of wanting to continue engaging in sinful, karma-producing behaviour, before a new being, condensed out of the moral substance of the previous life, comes into being and sets off again on the arduous path leading away from attachment to the world. This moralization of the cycle of births was accepted within every strand of Chinese religion, and even the Confucian statesman was suddenly quite unclear about what happened to his own parents after their death.

One story, which appears for the first time in the early Tang era around 1300 years ago, tells of a monk named Mulian who sets about saving his dead mother from these torments. In a certain sense, he is thus assuming the old burden of tending the grave and worshipping the ancestors. However, he is not himself strong enough to wrench open the gates of hell. He returns and asks Buddha for help. The latter tells him that only the combined strength of the *sangha*, the community, is capable of saving his mother, who, as it happens, had worked as a butcher, from the torments. This combined strength of the *sangha* assumes the form of a ritual, in which the monastic community prays together for a deceased individual in order to shorten his passage through purgatory. The development of a notion of the transferral of merit, according to which the living could transfer their moral services to the dead and thus alleviate their fate, was bound up with this.[9] The practical guidance developed on this basis, which is characteristic of popular Buddhism, had a decisive impact on life in China. On almost half of all the days in the year, the descendants are expected to ease the existence of the dead through vegetarian meals, sexual abstinence, sacrifices and prayers.[10] The *upaya*, teaching adapted to one's understanding, is developed in a comprehensive and tangible form on every level.

The lay Buddhist turns to the wide range of advice provided by the Ru School when it comes to administration of the state as a civil servant, and the management of the family. If the problem is the ongoing lack of a son, the Daoist priests are welcome, and the newly created Shintoism lends itself to the celebration of the eternal Japanese nation. This sense of accord between the different religions, schools or currents, featuring a division of labour, was, at least in historical China, a quite explicitly formulated notion; ultimately, from the foundation of the Ming dynasty around 650 years ago, it even became government doctrine: *san jiao wei yi*, 'the three teachings [Ru School, Buddhism and Daoism] form a unity'. After the Second World War, the American occupation government experienced this for itself in Japan. It organized a census which required respondents to put a cross next to their religion, in order to determine the size of the individual religious communities. The total number of crosses was three times the population of Japan.

Buddhism has little interest in the management of this world. It has nonetheless produced a conception of the ideal ruler: that of 'the king who sets the wheel – the wheel of the *dharma* – in motion', the *cakravartinraja* in Sanskrit. This is a ruler who is himself on a personal quest to attain understanding and who, in addition, leads his state in such a way that he promotes Buddhism and creates favourable conditions for a religious life. This he does by providing a living example of a lay Buddhist life, and perhaps even taking part in meditation exercises in a monastery from time to time as a regular monk, honouring and promoting Buddhism as a teaching, donating generously to the community, supporting projects such as the dissemination of Buddhist writings and allowing his subjects to become monks or nuns and to make their property over to Buddhist monasteries. This is far from simple.

---

[9]   See Stephen Teiser, *The Ghost Festival in Medieval China*, Princeton, Princeton University Press, 1988.
[10]   See Henri Maspero, 'Chine', in *Mythologie Asiatique Illustrée*, Paris, La Librarie du France, 1928.

In terms of the interests of the state, in light of its peacefulness and tendency to protect life, Buddhism poses no threat, yet at the same time it is an economic and military burden. The monks have no income, produce no surplus value, pay no taxes and live from begging, that is, from others' donations. They have vowed not to kill, and are therefore ill-suited to military service. They practise celibacy and produce no children who then go on to produce goods, pay taxes, do their military service and bring more people into the world. They leave their families, even give up their family names and are not around to look after their ageing parents. And, as these things tend to go, believers then transfer their land to the monastery, making it tax-exempt; savvy peasants pretend to do so, sharing the saved taxes with the monastery, and so on. Finally, the often enormous donated monastic Buddhas are of bronze. Bronze is essentially copper, and copper is the metal from which coins were made. When cash was in short supply, there was a strong motivation for the court to close a couple of monasteries, melt down the Buddhas and thus stimulate the market. In brief, a ruler who wished to be a patron of Buddhism had to be quite serious about it, because it clashed with too many obvious state interests.

By the end of the nineteenth century, Buddhism was faced with a new, and new type, of challenge. In China, since the neo-Confucian revival, the appeal of the Buddhist monastic orders to the best and brightest had long been in decline, and the patronage of the Manchurian rulers of the last dynasty (the Qing) was directed above all at the intellectually less attractive lamaist Buddhism of Tibet and Mongolia. In the middle of the nineteenth century, the first major radically modernist Chinese grouping, the Taiping movement (1851–64), saw itself as part of the Second Great (Christian) Awakening of these decades, with its leader 'God's second son' Hong Xiuquan; it assailed Confucianism and Buddhism with fundamentalist radicalism and pillage. Both were accused of having led China astray, away from its original belief in a single God, and were blamed for its decline.[11] Its dream of a New Jerusalem in Nanjing combined theocratic power structures with an emphatic modernizing agenda fuelled by the understanding that the Western Christian nations had been blessed with order and prosperity because of their direct contact with God. The Taiping movement was eventually crushed through an alliance of Han Chinese reformers with indirect support from the West. In the next generation, along with the 'modernization package' inherent to the concept of the nation state, the new Chinese educated classes, increasingly influenced by the West, also adopted the secular worldview inscribed in this concept. In the

---

[11]   See Rudolf Wagner, *Reenacting the Heavenly Vision: The Role of Religion in the Taiping Rebellion*, China Research Monograph 25, Center for Chinese Studies, Berkeley, University of California Press, 1984.

social Darwinist struggle in which all nations were engaged, all that counted was the 'survival of the fittest'. These classes – very much like the Taipings, but without the religious superstructure – now called on the Chinese people to take up arms against the real ideological, religious and institutional structures holding China back within this race. These included both the neo-Confucianist system of examinations and popular religion, which had incorporated a good deal of Buddhist thought.

But as a religion, Buddhism had fewer problems with this secularism inherent in modernity than with the worldly craving for wealth and power that often went hand in hand with it. It was not Buddhist monks, but laypeople such as Yang Wenhui in Nanjing who took up the challenge of modernity, who constituted the most important intellectual core and formed transnational linkages. A number of the most important reformers of the late nineteenth century entered into a dialogue with Yang. They fell back on the ideal of the *bodhisattva* as one who has a duty to enlighten people, in order to grasp and overlay conceptually their own role as enlighteners of the masses mired in the darkness of feudalism. Borrowing from the Christian example of charitable institutions, the Buddhist concept of empathy became the foundation of a social doctrine of mass welfare as a responsibility of the state. The instrumental, non-essentialist character of the Buddhist texts made it possible to deal with them, rapidly and very successfully, in a scientific way. Up to the present day, many of the most important and knowledgeable buddhological authors in Japan and now in Taiwan are Buddhist abbots, and Buddhist universities distinguished by high scholarly standards are to be found in many places outside the PR China. With their emphasis on the emptiness and non-reality of existence and their non-separation of knowledge and object of knowledge, the philosophical approaches of East Asian Buddhism have resonated so profoundly with modern physicists that allusions to Buddhist and above all Zen Buddhist concepts or narratives can be found even in scientific lectures.[12] Buddhism, for which the world has never been anything other than secular, has sparked a great deal of interest as religious teaching and meditational practice within a secularized Western world.[13]

The Ru doctrine or Confucianism could hardly form a sharper contrast. Many Chinese traditions relating to culture, social conduct and state orientation, which reach back long before the time of Kong Qiu or Confucius, are now

---

[12]   An example is the popular introduction to quantum mechanics by Gary Zukav, *The Dancing Wu Li Masters*, New York, Morrow, 1979.

[13]   A number of institutions and online networks have developed that provide information on Buddhist literature, meditation centres and so on. Examples include the Buddhist Network (http://www.buddhistnetwork.org) and the Kuroda Institute in Los Angeles (http://www.zencenter.org/bookstore/kuroda/htm).

identified with this Confucianism because it absorbed them, provided them with names and intellectual respectability and thus integrated them into a doctrine of the state, morality and social life. Here, the problem facing the world is not the uncertain presence or even non-presence of God or human attachment to the world, but rather the constant, natural and fatal tendency of human society to depart from the general cosmic order and descend into chaos. Order is the happiness and salvation of the world, chaos its crisis. This principle alone reveals how much even the grave-diggers of Confucianism, the Chinese Communists, remained faithful to their arch-enemy. 'Order and union' and now 'harmonious society' constitute the guiding principles of the very long period of return to what they call the 'socialist market economy'.

The Ru present themselves as those who shoulder the difficult burden of opposing this perpetual onslaught of chaos. The roots of this chaos lie not in the rebellious people, so that the only response must be a draconian machinery of state; rather, the source of order and chaos is one and the same: it is the ruler. If he, standing at the summit of the state structure, openly displays extravagance, excess and laziness, this will trigger the people's natural tendency to pursue mammon. Hence, everyone will compete to imitate him; no one will want to sweat away in the fields for a few extra copper coins a year; the economy will go off the rails, society will come apart at the seams and the struggle of all against all will begin. The Ru are able to establish order because, for years and decades, they have studied the writings of the sages of Chinese antiquity, the classical authors, and have passed state exams which show that they have understood them in line with the officially valid reading. This study, along with a practice of meditation and self-control borrowed from Buddhism, has turned them into figures who, as shining examples of controlled behaviour, are able to exude an aura that creates order, even without taking any specific measures. Their efforts are primarily directed towards preventing the ruler from conducting himself in a way that creates chaos and encouraging him to take his lead from their own behavioural ideal. In a statement that has turned into a proverb, Confucius says *junzi zhi jiao dan ru shui*, 'the conduct of the nobleman is bland like water' (while that of the petty careerist is of course 'sweet and sticky like liqueur').[14] The proverb's intention is not to mock the boring, but to describe the ideal state official. Only through this pronounced blandness will a Ru be in a position to

---

[14]   *Liji*, 34.23 (*Li Gi, das Buch der Sitte des älteren und jüngeren Dai: Aufzeichnungen über Kultur und Religion im Alten China*, translation from the Chinese and commentary by Richard Wilhelm, Jena, Diederichs, 1930, p. 159); see also *Zhuangzi*, chapter: 'Shanmu' (R. Wilhelm, *Das wahre Buch vom Südlichen Blütenland*, Düsseldorf, Diederichs, 1969, p. 151), featuring a slightly different version in which this statement is not attributed to Confucius.

keep in check the ruler's tendency to show off and the rapacity of the people triggered thereby.[15]

Many decades ago, Max Weber developed a famous and extremely influential analysis of the relationship between the Protestant ethic and the spirit of capitalism by contrasting this ethic with Confucianism. Confucianism came off badly in this comparative analysis. According to Weber, the Confucianists lacked the inner tension resulting from the need to prove oneself before an incalculable God. Weber had in mind China around 1900, which, as the 'sick man of East Asia', seemed helpless, weak and foolishly arrogant in the face of the challenges posed by modernity. He sought to identify the spiritual roots of China's weakness in contrast to the spiritual roots of Europe's strength.[16]

History sometimes has its own form of quiet irony and has now set its sights on Weber. If a present-day Max Weber set about explaining the spiritual roots of the economic dynamism of various countries and cultures, he would presumably begin with inverted premises, seeking out the spiritual basis of the dynamic developments in Japan, Taiwan, South Korea, Singapore and the PR China and reasons for the lack of such dynamism in Europe. And he would show us that Confucianism is the reason for this East Asian miracle because here industriousness, asceticism with a view to capital accumulation, flexibility and a keen focus on education are combined not with radical individualism, but with solidarity within the family and other social networks. There is no need to invent this variant; it already appears nicely printed in governmental publications and bookshops in Singapore, Taipei or Canton. I confess that I find both explanatory variants equally suspect, because they only explain what presently exists and have never faced the test of predicting future developments.

The Ru do not constitute a community in any institutional sense. From

---

[15]   For a stimulating study on blandness as a Chinese ideal, see François Jullien, *In Praise of Blandness: Proceeding from Chinese Thought and Aesthetics*, New York, Zone, 2004. See also Rudolf Wagner, 'Biographie als Lebensprogramm. Zur normativen Funktion der chinesischen Biographik', in Walter Berschin and Wolfgang Schamoni (eds.), *Biographie — 'So der Westen wie der Osten'? Zwölf Studien*, Heidelberg, Mattes Verlag, 2003, pp. 133–42.
[16]   See Max Weber, *The Protestant Ethic and the Spirit of Capitalism*, London, Unwin, 1965; idem, *The Religion of China: Confucianism and Daoism*, London, Macmillan, 1964. Weber had nothing but the available Western literature to go on and proceeded with his usual brilliance. Nonetheless, he was unable to see through the preconceived ideas and prejudices uniformly and emphatically presented as science in these texts. The first challenge to Weber's preconceptions about Confucianism, which were also highly influential among Sinologists, can be found in Thomas A. Metzger, *Escape from Predicament: Neo-Confucianism and China's Evolving Political Culture*, New York, Columbia University Press, 1977.

time immemorial, schools and academies for the aspiring Ru created networks of connection; in addition, there were loyalties to the teacher and thus to schools as well, or rather traditions of textual transmission. The neo-Confucian renaissance in the Song era around 900 years ago was accompanied by a dramatic rearrangement of the machinery of state. To select officials, this machinery increasingly fell back on state exams which chiefly tested knowledge of the classics and the ability to interpret them. As a result of access to privileged positions within the state administration through education which this opened up, there was an explosion in the number of those who attempted to make their way along this prestigious career path. But at the same time, this class became increasingly tied to and oriented towards the state, especially because, regardless of whether they found a position within the machinery of state or not, this state granted all those who passed the state examination social, tax and legal privileges. In this sense, these Ru were a school of political science, but at the same time the classics became a canonical core common to the educated class, a core which permitted broad scope for interpretation and for the practice derived from it. We would be hard put to find a case of tighter fusion, akin to a religious community and anchored in religious practice.

As addressed earlier, given the complementarity of intellectual and religious currents in East Asia, a great number of these Ru would put a cross in two or three different boxes if they were asked about their religion or spiritual orientation. After his retirement or simply even when off-duty, the same individual who, in his official function, radiates Ru principles right down to the grammatical structure of his sentences and the gestures of his hands, is transformed into a being with a very different interior landscape and external attire, one characterized by a very different mode of human relationships and a very different set of canonical texts, whose values overlap only slightly with the so-called Confucian canon, if they do not in fact protest openly against it.

The Confucian and neo-Confucian tradition develops its notions of an ideal state and an ideal society not primarily on the basis of experience and thought, but on the basis of the reading and interpretation of classical texts in light of one's own experiences and thoughts. The basis of the legitimacy of the Ru's status, which was never safeguarded by laws, is the claim that all their ideas and suggestions have been developed solely in light of the legacy of the ancient sages. The most important of these texts to the development of the state is the *Zhouli*, the rites of Zhou.[17] It is attributed to the Duke of Zhou, one of the founders of the Zhou dynasty more than 3000 years ago. He is said to have written it for his

---

[17]   This text has so far been translated only once into a Western language, and that a long time ago. See Edouard Biot, *Le Tcheou-li: ou, Rites des Tcheou*, Paris, Imprimerie Nationale, 1851, 3 vols.

young nephew and future generations as a guide to the construction of the state. The text was unknown until a prince of the Han dynasty extended his palace, demolishing the house of Confucius in the process. Texts 'in old characters', so the story goes, were found in a wall. This of course sounds highly suspicious and did so even at the time, above all because the librarian, to whom the text was eventually given, teamed up with Wang Mang. Wang Mang was a high-ranking official who took it upon himself to replace the Han dynasty with a new one, which was named, accordingly, the New Dynasty or Dynasty of Renewal. This Wang Mang made the *Zhouli* the foundational text of his new dynasty. Though a whole series of failed dynastic founders consulted it, the *Zhouli* retained its status as a classic which, as it were, described the imaginary ideal Chinese state. The doubts about the extent of its authenticity have now diminished, as it emerged that the information it provides on, for instance, the design and layout of the graves of people of differing status corresponds so closely with recent grave finds from the early Zhou era that it is now routine to have a look at the *Zhouli* in order to determine the status of a tomb's inmate.

It is a very curious book. Without appealing to any kind of divine authority, it begins each chapter with 'A king who establishes a state ...' and then immediately launches into an exceedingly detailed description of the officials whom he appoints, the powers they possess and the number of officials under his command. It describes in a similar way the ruler's communication with his officials. One will search in vain for a theoretical exposition of the state and its goals anywhere in this long book. Religion appears only on the margins as a formalized act of state in the shape of regular sacrifices and ceremonies. The book is wholly concerned with a secular state order that has taken on institutional form. The state emerges here as a kind of collective performance of ritualized order. Actual order-creating interventions are a rarity. Essentially, the system rests upon the laying of the key foundations for order in the families and villages below and beyond the state machine. This order consists above all of a clear hierarchization that includes both subordination and responsibility. The minister must submit to the prince and the wife to the husband, but the prince must listen to the advice and criticisms of his ministers and the husband must show that he cares for the wife. With the ideal of ritualized order modelled by the state, this self-regulating society requires state intervention only in extreme cases – but then with great severity. The corporal punishment provided for by the *Zhouli*, which immediately calls to mind the liberal use of the death penalty in the PR China today, is intended, like the death penalty, to act as a deterrent, but also, through the severity of the punishment, to highlight the great value of social order and stability, which have been put at risk by wrongful acts.

The *Zhouli* describes a state which is indispensable as a guarantee of order, which is also the cause of chaos in the absence of correct leadership, but one in which no divine authority appears as a source of order or ruination. No institutions of election, acclamation or other forms of consent are introduced in order to prevent chaos; instead we find numerous institutions of bureaucratic self-regulation. The most important is remonstrance, the right and the obligation to criticize the ruler when he behaves inappropriately. This right is spelt out in cascading form from the top officials all the way down to the crimson remonstrance stone in the village, on which one may stand to protest against an official's abuse of authority. If, within a fixed period, the competent officials have failed to respond, they are themselves guilty of an offence. This institution of remonstrance within the state machine, but also anchored beyond it, is one of the key Chinese political concepts, and has done a good deal to ensure that the Chinese state apparatus has remained vigorous and flexible over such long periods of time.

The state of the *Zhouli* is distinguished by a dense web of communication between state and society. This communication revolves around information, through which the regions and the ruler keep one another up to date; it entails the selection of personnel and supervision, with local officials being proposed by their localities and serving there, so that they have precise knowledge of the situation, while at the same time their work is subject to regular state evaluation and supervision; and it involves wide consultation all the way down to the village elders at times of crisis such as war, famine, moving the capital or when there is no successor to the throne. The *Zhouli* describes a state characterized by ritual performance, whose legitimacy rests solely upon achieving the state goal of order, a state which intervenes rarely and only when all other preventative, chaos-inhibiting measures have failed. This state, one of 'great peace', has never existed in this form in reality, but its key features became the Chinese state's imaginary ideal, in light of which every concrete reality could be critically evaluated, as has repeatedly occurred.[18]

When the Ru, representing the state, were confronted with the Western challenge towards the end of the nineteenth century, the question arose as to the compatibility of Western institutions with Chinese ideals of the state. Where else to look but the *Zhouli*? The first Chinese ambassador to London for example, Guo Songtao, read the newspapers every day: the first important Chinese-language newspaper from Shanghai, the *Shenbao*, the government newspaper from Bejing and the London papers. In his diary, he notes that the function of newspapers is to ensure communication between the high and the low, between Court and society. He then cites passages from the *Zhouli*, according to which the ruler discusses his plans with the envoys from the regions and receives regional reports. This

---

[18]   On the role of such imaginary institutions, see Cornelius Castoriadis, *The Imaginary Institution of Society*, Cambridge, Polity, 1987.

demonstrates to him that while the medium of the newspaper does not appear in the *Zhouli*, the ideal realized by the newspaper does. He is not alone. A large number of those who concerned themselves with Western institutions towards the end of the century came to the conclusion that these went so well together with the old Chinese ideals that one even wondered whether these Western institutions were not derived from the *Zhouli*; after all, the Europeans were still living in the trees when the *Zhouli* was composed. But while they now existed in China only in the rarefied sphere of the ideal, they had survived in the West. This way of reading West and East transformed the appropriation of the menacing Other into a return to the best of oneself. We have the author of the last great commentary on the *Zhouli*, Sun Yirang (1848–1908), to thank for a comparison, now systematic rather than anecdotal, between Western institutions and the ideal of the *Zhouli*. This comparison was intended – and worked – to encourage the reforms, geared towards the Western model, of the 'new policy', *xin zheng*, adopted by the Chinese Court in 1901.[19]

As a whole and compared, for example, with the Islamic world, the Buddhist and Confucianist cultures of East Asia had no difficulties in assimilating the secular agenda of the modern nation state, including its nationalistic and socialist variants. One key reason for this probably lies in the radically secular outlook of both these spiritual currents and the basically rational worldview established on this basis. There was no need here for the death of an all-powerful God; no holy book of His words had to be dismantled with philological industriousness and declared the historical result of centuries of very human writing.

This reading of the essential compatibility of the imaginary Chinese ideal state with the modern Western nation state did not, however, last long and following the end of the empire in 1912 the entire culture of the empire, now denounced as Confucianist, feudal and autocratic, was damned as a primitive 'cannibalistic society' with a philanthropic 'Confucian' veneer.[20] Yet the Confucian concept of the state influenced even its bitterest opponents. The Communist Party is or is intended to be meritocratic, features a strict hierarchy with no legal protection for subordinates, is a self-appointed elite with no democratic legitimation, but attaches great importance to the acceptance of the quality of its governance by the

---

[19]   See Sun Yirang, *Zhouli zhengyao*, Rui'an, Putong xuetang, 1902.

[20]   This oft-cited image was first evoked by Lu Xun in 1917 in his 'A Madman's Diary' (in Lu Xun, *Selected Stories of Lu Hsun*, London, Norton, 2003). It picks up on the association of cannibalism with a primitive developmental stage of society, a notion being disseminated in China and Japan at the time through translations of Western works. For a popular example of this, see Edward Jenks, *A History of Politics*, London, Richard Clay and Sons, 1900, Chinese translation by Yan Fu, 1901. Here, cannibalism is associated with the stage of 'savage society'.

population. It has an intricate system of internal self-control designed to avoid the abuse of power and loss of legitimacy. All of these are elements of the Confucian state, re-legitimized above all by Lenin's doctrine of the party. If today the Communist Party leadership is rehabilitating aspects of Confucianism such as its heavy emphasis on hierarchical subordination as well as probity, industriousness and thrift among the people, then this is happening because at a profound level they share an orientation towards social order as the highest good and radical secularism as the religious Gospel of modernity and economic advance.

7

From Hostility through Recognition to Identification: State–Church Models and their Relationship to Freedom of Religion

Winfried Brugger

To a significant degree, the origins of the modern Western state as a form of political organization lie in its departure from the medieval unity of state and Christian church. This occurred because the state no longer had to deal only with one Christian church, but rather with Protestantism and Catholicism. The competition between these religions, which was carried on within the various political camps, along with struggles for dominance between religious and political power, made peace impossible. This resulted in the chaos of civil war, and terrible wars between states. The secularization of worldly power thus seemed inevitable over the long term.[1] The idea was that politics should focus on worldly concerns

---

[1]   See Ernst-Wolfgang Böckenförde, 'The Rise of the State as a Process of Secularization', in idem, *State, Society and Liberty*, New York and Oxford, Berg, 1991, pp. 26ff.; Christian Walter, *Religionsverfassungsrecht in vergleichender und internationaler Perspektive*, Tübingen, Mohr Siebeck, 2006, pp. 23ff.; Heinhard Steiger, 'Religion und die historische Entwicklung des Völkerrechts', in Andreas Zimmermann (ed.), *Religion und Internationales Recht*, Berlin, Duncker & Humblot, 2006, pp. 11ff.; *County of Allegheny v. A.C.L.U.*, 492 U.S. 573, 610 (1989): 'The government does not discriminate against any citizen on the basis of the citizen's religious faith if the government is secular in its functions and operations. On the contrary, the Constitution mandates that the government remain secular, rather than affiliate itself with religious beliefs or institutions, precisely in order to avoid discriminating among citizens on the basis of their religious faith. A secular state, it must be remembered, is not the same as an atheistic or antireligious state. A secular state establishes neither atheism nor religion as its official creed.'

– on worldly welfare. With respect to religious matters, the attainment of salvation in the hereafter, the sword of state power should no longer function as a means of sanction for ensuring the dominance of whichever religion was preferred by the government, though Christian thought long continued to make itself felt.[2] In most European states and in the USA, this development ultimately led to a structural differentiation of the spheres of state and religion or state and church. Areas of responsibility were also divided: the state would take care of worldly welfare, while the churches would attend to salvation in the hereafter.[3] The pursuit of salvation itself was to adhere to the principle of freedom: within the context of freedom of religion, it was to be the responsibility of the individual and his conscience.[4]

It is therefore no surprise that modern liberal constitutions mostly separate the spheres of control of the state and of religious organizations ('church') by means of a structural norm, and anchor freedom of religion in the section on basic rights. The classic example is the First Amendment to the Constitution of the United States of 1787/1791: 'Congress shall make no law respecting an establishment of religion, or prohibiting the free exercise thereof ...'. In the first part of the sentence we find the structural non-establishment clause, in the second the basic right to religious freedom. Art. 137, par. 1 of the Weimar constitution (WRV), incorporated into the current German constitution (GG) through art. 140, makes similar provisions: 'There is no state church'. Freedom

---

[2]   See Joseph Story, *Commentaries on the Constitution* (1933), reprint edited and introduced by Ronald D. Rotunda and John E. Nowak, Durham, NC, Carolina Academic Press, 1987, p. 701 (§ 990): 'religion [...] can be dictated only by reason and conviction, not by force or violence'.

[3]   See Böckenförde, 'The Rise of the State', pp. 27ff.; with regard to the school system, see also the remarks by Justice Jackson, dissenting in *Everson v. Board of Education*, 330 U.S. 1, 22ff. (1947): religious schools, in this case Catholic schools, teach the 'mission', 'the faith and order of the Church' (p. 23), while state schools, detached from such messages, 'inculcate all needed temporal knowledge [...] [and] worldly wisdom' (p. 24). See also the majority opinion, p. 15: 'The structure of our government has, for the preservation of civil liberty, rescued the temporal institutions from religious interference. On the other hand, it has secured religious liberty from the invasions of civil authority.' See also the 'Memorial and Remonstrance Against Religious Assessments' by James Madison, pp. 63ff. on the 'light of revelation' (p. 70) in contrast to the 'liberties, the prosperity, and the Happiness of the Commonwealth' (p. 72) quoted in the appendix to this ruling.

[4]   On the history of religious freedom, see Rainer Grote, 'Die Religionsfreiheit im Spiegel völkervertraglicher Vereinbarungen zur politischen und territorialen Neuordnung', in Rainer Grote and Thilo Marauhn (eds.), *Religionsfreiheit zwischen individueller Selbstbestimmung, Minderheitenschutz und Staatskirchenrecht. Völker- und verfassungsrechtliche Perspektiven*, Berlin, Springer, 2001, pp. 3ff.; Steiger, 'Religion und die historische Entwicklung des Völkerrechts'.

of religion is protected through art. 4, pars. 1 and 2 of the GG: 'The freedom of belief and conscience and the freedom to profess a particular religion or ideology [*Weltanschauung*] are inviolable. Freedom of worship is guaranteed'.

As exemplified in this citation from the German constitution, formulations of religious freedom are generally more specific and comprehensive in more recent constitutions than in older, shorter ones. Art. 9 of the European Convention on Human Rights (ECHR) makes even finer distinctions. The protection of religious freedom[5] entails the following elements: freedom of thought, conscience and religion, the right to change religion or belief, and the freedom to carry out these activities individually or collectively, which includes religious worship, teaching and observance.

In sum, the modern Western constitutional state is characterized by religious freedom as an antidote to state coercion in religious matters and by a structural division of the spheres of control of state and church. Although this statement is legally correct and generally reflects public attitudes in most Western states, a more nuanced picture is called for. For within the basic dual legal model of structural division and individual and collective religious freedom, certain variants have taken shape within the community of states that demand recognition. It is also imperative to clarify which state–church relations are eliminated as a result of this core feature of modern Western developments. In what follows, I propose to distinguish six models of the relationship between state and church (see Table 1).[6]

---

[5]   The ECHR includes no structural norm on the relationship between state and church because, like other human rights agreements, it is not a 'constitution' but rather a treaty under international law; but regulation of the state–church relationship is an aspect of the internal organization of a state. This does not rule out the possibility that internationally anchored religious freedoms may have indirect effects on the state–church relationship. See Jochen A. Frowein, 'Religionsfreiheit und internationaler Menschenrechtsschutz', in Grote and Marauhn (eds.), *Religionsfreiheit*, pp. 73, 78ff.; Walter, *Religionsverfassungsrecht*, pp. 201, 332ff.; Christoph Grabenwarter, 'Religion und Europäische Menschenrechtskonvention'; Eckart Klein and Bernhard Schäfer, 'Religionsfreiheit und Internationaler Pakt über bürgerliche und politische Rechte'; Rainer Hofmann, 'Religion und Minderheitenschutz', all in Zimmermann (ed.), *Religion und Internationales Recht*, pp. 97ff., 127ff., 157ff.

[6]   On this typology, alongside nn. 20 and 23 below, see also Krystina Daniel and W. Cole Durham, 'Religious Identity as a Component of National Identity: Implications for Emerging Church–State Relations in the Former Socialist Bloc', in Andràs Sajó and Shlomo Avineri (eds.), *The Law of Religious Identity: Models for Post-Communism*, The Hague, Kluwer Law International, 1999, pp. 117, 118ff.; W. Cole Durham, 'Perspectives on Religious Liberty: A Comparative Framework', in Johan D. van der Vyver and John Witte (eds.), *Religious Human Rights in Global Perspective: Legal Perspectives*, The Hague, Kluwer Law International, 1996, also in Vicki C. Jackson and Mark Tushnet (eds.),

These extend from hostility through recognition to identification and are to be found, in approximate form, in specific countries.

Six models of the relationship between state and church

Table 1.   *Six classificatory models of the relationship between state and church*

1. Hostility between state and church	2. Strict separation in theory and practice	3. Separation and consideration	4. Division and partial cooperation	5. Formal unity of church and state	6. Material unity of church and state

1. Rivalry or hostility between state and church

The political regime of a country may have an anti-religious stance and thus suppress religions and churches, restricting them to the private sphere or making them illegal, or even eliminating them with respect to the official ideology, constitution and political practice. Communist Albania was aggressively anti-religious. Art. 37 of the 1976 constitution of Albania stated: 'The state recognizes no religion and supports and propagates atheist propaganda in order to inculcate in the people the scientific materialist worldview'. Before their collapse towards the end of the 1980s, all communist regimes tended to oppose religions and churches. This comes as no surprise in light of Karl Marx's reference to religion, in his 1844 critique of Hegelian philosophy of law, as the opium of the people.[7]

But hostility towards or at least disapproval of religions is not limited to Marxism-Leninism. Quite apart from this, there have been repeated political and intellectual endeavours of an anti-clerical character opposed to the interference of religious representatives in political and state affairs in general and church

---

Comparative Constitutional Law, New York, Foundation Press, 1999, pp. 1157ff. We are dealing here with ideal types, to which of course the legal systems and concrete realities in particular states correspond only more or less; this includes rather than excludes transitional forms straddling particular models.

[7]   See Karl Marx, 'A Contribution to the Critique of Hegel's "Philosophy of Right"', in idem, *Critique of Hegel's 'Philosophy of Right'*, ed. Joseph O'Malley, Cambridge, Cambridge University Press, 1970, p. 131: 'The wretchedness of religion is at once an expression of and a protest against real wretchedness. Religion is the sigh of the oppressed creature [...] It is the opium of the people' (Marx's emphases deleted). Further passages on the Marxist critique of religion are collected in Iring Fetscher (ed.), *Der Marxismus. Seine Geschichte in Dokumenten*, Munich, Piper, 2nd edn, 1973, pp. 56ff.

aspirations to dominance in particular.[8] France is often mentioned in this context.[9] Anti-clericalism is not automatically anti-religious, either in its objectives or in the means by which it pursues them. This is plainly apparent in the fact that in many (though not all)[10] of its forms, French laicism is more concerned to preserve the state's powers in the face of prevailing religious, and in this case Catholic, influences than with combating religion in general. Hence, within anti-clericalism, we may distinguish between two ideal-typical variants. Inasmuch as resistance to such church aspirations occurs in a hostile way, anti-clericalism must be classed as a relatively moderate variant of the first model. To the extent that only a strict separation is required in the (alleged) best interests of church and state and in order to preserve their characteristic structures, this constitutes an endorsement of the second model.

2. Strict separation in theory and practice

This model (see Table 2) is a variant of the US doctrine of a 'wall of separation' between state and church, to use Thomas Jefferson's term.[11] Insofar as a wall of separation of this kind is demanded, it is first of all intended to oppose the spatial

---

[8]   See J. Salwyn Schapiro, *Anticlericalism: Conflict between Church and State in France, Italy and Spain*, Princeton, NJ, Van Nostrand, 1967, p. 3: 'The conflict between church and state has been one of the outstanding problems in the history of modern Europe. It took different forms in different countries and in different periods, yet the fundamental issue was always and everywhere the same, namely which was supreme over the other.' See also René Rémond, *L'Anticléricalisme en France de 1815 à nos jours*, Brussels, Fayard, 2nd edn, 1999, pp. 23ff.; on the motives for anti-clericalism, which has primarily targeted Catholicism: 'L'Eglise menace l'Etat, la nation, les individus, la famille'.

[9]   See Schapiro, *Anticlericalism*, p. 112: 'France, the classic land of anticlericalism'; see also Rémond, *L'anticléricalism en France*; on p. 357, however, Rémond also mentions Belgium, Italy, Spain, Portugal and South American states, in fact all countries which always were or still are profoundly shaped by Catholicism, in which waves of anticlericalism have occurred and in some cases have been a dominant feature.

[10]   The term *laïcité*, often mentioned in this context, has connotations (at least sometimes) of religious critique. See Thomas Giegerich, 'Religionsfreiheit als Gleichheitsanspruch und Gleichheitsproblem', in Grote and Marauhn (eds.), *Religionsfreiheit*, pp. 241, 291ff., and Hans-Michael Heinig, *Öffentlich-rechtliche Religionsgesellschaften*, Berlin, Duncker & Humblot, 2003, pp. 43ff. See also Michel Troper, 'The Problem of the Islamic Veil and the Principle of School Neutrality in France', in Sajó and Avineri (eds.), *The Law of Religious Identity*, pp. 89, 91: 'In the minds of some of its advocates, laïcité carries strong antireligious overtones'.

[11]   Thomas Jefferson, 'Letter to a Committee of the Danbury Baptist Association' from 1 January 1802, quoted in Michael McConnell, John Garvey and Thomas Berg, *Religion and the Constitution*, New York, Aspen, 2002, pp. 54ff.

coincidence of state and church, such as religious education in state schools. The wall of separation is also meant to prevent the organizational involvement of churches in the spheres proper to the state and the fusion of religious and state ideologies.

Table 2.   *Elements of the strict separation model*

Strict separation applies to	1. The content of state ideology (welfare as opposed to salvation) 2. Physical locations (state versus religious buildings) 3. Organization (no cooperation)
Unconstitutional	Direct and indirect, strong and weak rapprochements and support
Result for the private sphere	Strong positive and negative religious freedom
Result for the public sphere	Strong positive and negative religious freedom
Result for the state sphere	Maximum degree of negative religious freedom from state paternalism; beneficial to 'radical' and/or disapproved-of religions

A famous example is the US case *Everson v. Board of Education*.[12] In 1941, the state of New Jersey enacted a law which provided for state subsidies for the transportation by bus of pupils from their homes to school. These subsidies also benefited pupils in private Catholic schools. The minority judges of the Supreme Court saw this as a violation of the non-establishment clause in the First Amendment to the Constitution. They expressed sympathy for the parents of the Christian pupils, who had to pay taxes to fund the state schools, but who should not in their view be allowed to enjoy their buses. This, they stated, undoubtedly represented a financial burden on, in fact almost a form of punishment of, the religious pupils and parents. Yet it was necessary to accept this. Were the state to take a single step in the direction of providing churches with financial aid, then more far-reaching provisions could not be ruled out. The financial disadvantage must be seen in light of the de facto advantage: strict separation guarantees the maximum degree of freedom for minority religions vis-à-vis hostile mainstream religions or other majority preferences. In this sense, the total separation of state and church, which includes spatial, organizational and content-related aspects and also rules out indirect subsidies or rapprochements, is 'best for the state and best for religion'.[13] 'It is only by observing [the separation rule] rigidly that the state can maintain its neutrality and avoid partisanship in the dissensions inevitable

---

[12]   330 U.S. 1 (1947). 'U.S.' stands for the official casebook of the US Supreme Court.

[13]   *Everson*, p. 59.

when sect opposes sect over demands for public moneys to further religious education, teaching or training in any form or degree, directly or indirectly.'[14]

3. Strict separation in theory, consideration in practice

The majority of the judges in the Everson case saw this differently, despite taking the wall of separation as their point of departure as did the minority. They argued as follows: it is true that the non-establishment clause in the First Amendment prohibits the raising of taxes specifically for religious purposes. But different rules must apply if the taxes are raised neutrally. If a subsidy is provided which benefits not only state but also church schools and which, in addition, applies to classical state responsibilities such as police protection, refuse collection, the fire brigade or, as in this case, road safety, then this is legally tenable. Here, freedom of religion requires that the religious schools and their pupils are not excepted.[15]

---

[14]   *Everson*, p. 59. See also p. 19 on 'complete and uncompromising separation', p. 26 on rapprochements that occur 'directly or indirectly' and on the language of the non-establishment clause expressed 'in absolute terms' and its 'rigidity', and p. 60 on 'complete separation'. In *Zorach v. Clauson*, 343 U.S. 306, 319 (1952), Justice Black states in his dissent: 'it is only by wholly isolating the state from the religious sphere and compelling it to be completely neutral, that the freedom of each and every denomination and of all nonbelievers can be maintained'. See also *Lynch v. Donnelly*, 465 U.S. 668, 710 (1984) (Justice Brennan, dissenting) against a 'blur[ring of] the distinction' between secular and religious elements; the state must be 'scrupulously neutral' (p. 714) towards religions; even a 'small step' (p. 725) towards preferential treatment is out of the question. Cultivation of the religious heritage is 'the exclusive prerogative of our Nation's churches, religious institutions, and spiritual leaders' (p. 725). Brennan, in *Allegheny v. A.C.L.U.*, 492 U.S. 573, 639 (1989) is equally strict. The very term '*Christmas* tree' makes this object a religious symbol that must not be displayed by the state: '[The] attempt to take the "Christmas" out of the Christmas tree is unconvincing'. One opponent of strict separation refers to the 'relentless extirpation of all contact between government and religion': Justice Kennedy, dissenting in *Allegheny*, p. 657.

[15]   This majority opinion is also to be found in recent rulings on financial aid for schools. See the summary in Philip J. Prygoski, *Constitutional Law*, St Paul, MN, Thomson West, 9th edn, 2003, ch. XIX B 2, pp. 294ff.: *Board of Education v. Allen*, 392 U.S. 236 (1968) (neutral funding for schoolbooks in state, private, as well as religious schools); *Witters v. Washington Department of Services for the Blind*, 474 U.S. 481 (1986) (permissibility of financial support for disabled pupils at private and religious schools); *Zobrest v. Catalina Foothills School District*, 509 U.S. 1 (1993) (same ruling with respect to sign language interpreters); *Zelman v. Simmons-Harris*, 536 U.S. 639 (2002) (permissibility of a programme of school vouchers which parents could use to send their child to a state, private or religious school as they saw fit). For a counter-example, see *Lemon v. Kurtzman*, 403 U.S. 602 (1971) (impermissibility of financial support for teachers in religious schools).

All other solutions infringe positive religious freedom and may be understood as a hostile attitude towards religious parents and children. The state must indeed be neutral towards religions and churches, but this must not turn into hostility. Rather, the state should neither impede nor aid religions.[16]

This moderate, 'accommodating'[17] view of the wall of separation makes it clear that the wall is lower and thinner than according to the narrower, stricter version. Beyond this specific case, Everson does not clarify where exactly the limits of the state's taking account of religion lie. However, in 1971 the Supreme Court developed the so-called Lemon Test (see Table 3), which identifies three elements to help specify the requirements of the non-establishment clause: 'First, the statute must have a secular legislative purpose; second, its principal or primary effect must be one that neither advances nor inhibits religion; finally, the statute must not foster an excessive government entanglement with religion.'[18] If even one of the criteria is unfulfilled, this amounts to a breach of the constitution.[19]

Table 3.   *Elements of the 'Lemon Test'*

I Unconstitutional provision	II Constitutional provision
1. Exclusive or primary goal is the promotion of (a) religion	1. Goal of promoting (a) religion is secondary or marginal
2. Exclusive or primary effect is the promotion of (a) religion	2. Effect of promoting (a) religion is secondary, marginal or non-existent
3. Excessive or strong organizational entanglement of state and church/religion	3. Only weak or marginal organizational contact

---

[16]   See *Everson*, p. 18. This idea is accepted even in France, despite the separation of state and church. See Claus Dieter Classen, *Religionsfreiheit und Staatskirchenrecht in der Grundrechtsordnung*, Tübingen, Mohr Siebeck, 2003, pp. 14ff.: 'today, "laïcité" must be understood to mean tolerance and equal treatment, even positive neutrality [...] since 1959, private Catholic schools in particular have therefore received financial support from the state' alongside state and other private schools. This would, however, be impossible in the USA.

[17]   In the USA, advocates of this approach are called 'accommodationists', in contrast to the advocates of strict separation in theory and practice mentioned earlier, the 'separationists'.

[18]   *Wallace v. Jaffree*, 472 U.S. 38, 55 f. (1985) (Moment of Silence Law), citing *Lemon v. Kurtzman*, 403 U.S. 602, 612–613 (1971). The test is named after this case.

[19]   See *Wallace v. Jaffree*, p. 56.

4. Division and cooperation

There is no wall of separation between state and church if, on the basis of fundamental separation, the state not only takes account of religion, but the two cooperate in certain fields. This is the situation in Germany,[20] where the state–church system is often classified as a 'limping separation system'.[21] In Germany, the fundamental separation between state and church follows from the individual and collective level of freedom of religion and ideology (*Weltanschauung*) in art. 4, pars. 1 and 2 GG. This norm leaves us in no doubt that we are dealing here with an opposition between powers: on one side stand religion and church as bearers of fundamental rights, on the other side stands the state, bound to uphold basic rights. Art. 140 GG in conjunction with art. 137, par. 1 WRV makes it clear that state churches are impermissible. Religious societies must be formed from below by believers and supporters rather than decreed from above by organs of the state. Even so, this distinction leads not to total separation but to partial cooperation and mutual coordination. This is apparent in art. 7, par. 3 GG, which permits religious education as a regular subject at state schools, and art. 140 GG in conjunction with arts. 137, 138 and 141 WRV, which, among other things, provide for organizational assistance in raising taxes and in addition refer to many and diverse modes of cooperation and support provided for by *Land* constitutions, laws and treaties. Art. 140 GG in conjunction with art. 137, pars. 5 and 6 WRV, which provide for or facilitate conferment of the status of public corporation on particular religious societies, must also be seen within this context.[22]

---

[20]   See Gerhard Robbers, *State and Church in the European Union*, Baden-Baden, Nomos, 2nd edn, 2005, pp. 77ff., 577ff., and Norman Dorsen, Michael Rosenfeld, Andras Sajó and Susanne Baer (eds.), *Comparative Constitutionalism*, St Paul, MN, Thomson West, 2003, p. 977: 'The German approach to church–state relations is often considered as "cooperationist". Regardless of the relevant constitutional provisions, Spain, Italy, Poland, Hungary, as well as some Latin American countries cooperate with an increasing number of (major) churches, through agreements and concordats with the Vatican.'

[21]   See Bernd Jeand'Heur and Stefan Korioth, *Grundzüge des Staatskirchenrechts*, Stuttgart, Boorberg, 2000, marginal note 161.

[22]   Conferment of the status of public corporation might be understood as abandonment of separation, but this would be a misunderstanding: what we are seeing here is merely a formal incorporation into state structures, but in fact the organization remains a religious one. It will receive certain benefits such as the collection of the church tax by state organs (art. 137, par. 6 WRV); in addition, it enjoys certain advantages with respect, for example, to taxation and planning regulations. In return, it has to make certain concessions with respect to loyalty to the constitution; see BVerfGE 102, 370. As a result, it is not as free and is unable to advocate such radical ideas as would apply

5. Formal unity of church and state alongside differences in terms of content

State and church may be more closely linked organizationally. This is the case if the polity formally establishes a state church or palpably identifies itself with a particular church as the national church in other ways. We must distinguish between two types of arrangement: a primarily formal unity of, or identification between, the two powers and a unity or identification that is also material in nature.[23] We are dealing with merely formal identification and thus with the fifth model, if, despite a state profession of loyalty to the state or national church, there exist five material factors of separation: (1) Both essentially constitute separate organizations. (2) They pursue differing goals (welfare versus salvation). (3) They make their own decisions. (4) The church is not a state power in the narrow sense, that is, it cannot apply external force. (5) The freedom of religion and belief of all believers and non-believers is in the main respected.

This is for example[24] the situation in the UK, Greece and Israel. Why do countries such as Britain and Greece choose a formal model of unity of this kind? The answer, it seems, is: in order to maintain a powerful religious tradition of importance to the polity. The majority tradition in question is to be publically recognized and certainly supported as well in a weak sense, without this turning

---

with the notion of strict separation – there are thus both advantages and disadvantages for religious communities. But apart from this, the influence of the state is still reduced: no religious society is forced to become a public corporation; it has the right to regulate its internal affairs independently, without interference from the state (art. 137, par. 3 WRV). It may also cite the defensive rights detailed in art. 4 GG.

[23]   On the differences among the fourth to sixth models, see Dorsen, Rosenfeld, Sajó and Baer (eds.), *Comparative Constitutionalism*, p. 980: 'At one extreme, the state may identify strongly with a particular religious tradition. In the extreme case [sixth model], this may lead to a virtual theocracy such as in Iran, or it may lead to official establishment of religion (with varying degrees of toleration or non-toleration for other religions) [fifth model]. A milder version of state identification involves endorsement of a particular religious tradition and the special role it has played in a country's history and culture, without necessarily making it the official established church in a country [fourth and perhaps third model].'

[24]   See the relevant chapters in Ernest Caparros and Louis-Leon Christians (eds.), *Religion in Comparative Law at the Dawn of the 21st Century*, Brussels, Bruylant, 2000; European Consortium for Church–State Research (ed.), *Religions in European Union Law*, Milan and Baden-Baden, Nomos, 1998; Robbers, *State and Church*. On Israel, see the relevant contributions in Winfried Brugger and Michael Karayanni (eds.), *Religion in the Public Sphere: A Comparative Analysis of German, Israeli, American and International Law*, Berlin, Springer, 2007.

into serious coercion or significant discrimination.[25] In the case of Israel, the gathering together of Jews scattered across the world and their territorial safeguarding within their own state was in fact a motive for founding the state and is a criterion of the polity's legitimacy. As far as discrimination between state or national church and other religious communities is concerned, much depends on the constitutional set-up in question and the relationship between the right to organize and the relevant basic rights to freedom and equality. The spectrum may extend from (1) more or less equal treatment of dominant and minority religion or non-religion in all respects other than symbolic and formal distinction, through (2) a small amount of discrimination to substantial inequality, at least in the 'soft' sense of, for instance, providing only the state church with direct or indirect financial support. At the other end of the spectrum are measures (3) in the 'hard' sphere of, for example, legal discrimination in important areas such as access to public office. This last step brings us closer to my sixth and last model.

6. Formal and material unity of church and state

Here, the state church or national religion is not merely represented symbolically and formally and linked with the state in a small number of fields, mostly in a 'soft' fashion; it is also deeply interlinked with the state with respect to practical policies and organizational forms. This comes close to being a theocracy, in which the division or separation model is lost: here, a legal requirement is often a religious one; the infringement of the law tends to be defined as a sin as well. External and internal coercion may be fused, increasing its overall intensity. In terms of basic rights, the theocratic system devalues negative religious freedom and sets limits to worldly power – when push comes to shove, it must not contradict the religious law. The degree to which people are suppressed and told what to think will increase, partly and primarily because binding and sanction-attracting guidelines are produced on people's ultimate, innermost beliefs about the meaning of the world and the highest moral authorities. The obligation to belong to the one correct religion and/or church and to demonstrate true belief fits into this union of church and state, as does the prohibition present in some Islamic states on leaving the one true religion.[26] An extreme example of this

---

25   Advocates of the model of strict separation often regard this line as having been crossed here.

26   See Dorsen, Rosenfeld, Sajó and Baer (eds.), *Comparative Constitutionalism*, p. 977: 'Apostasy (leaving one's religion) is a crime punishable by death in certain Islamic republics, in accordance with the Koran'. For further general evidence, see pp. 1002ff.; and Natan Lerner, *Religion, Beliefs, and International Human Rights*, Maryknoll, NY, Orbis, 2000, ch. 4: 'Proselytism and Change of Religion', pp. 8off. See here also the Islamic Charter presented by the Central Council of Muslims in Germany in 2002,

type is the Taliban regime in Afghanistan prior to intervention by America and NATO in 2002.[27]

Another example of a Muslim theocracy can be found in a summary by the Supreme Court of Pakistan, which described the following hallmarks of the Islamic law prevailing in Pakistan in *Zaheeruddin v. State*:[28] '(i) Islamic law or Shari'ah is the supreme law of the land, and all legislation, including the Constitution, must yield to it; (ii) Islamic law is a self-evident and fixed normative code, one that can be deployed without any revision or development to seek answers to all problems confronting a state in modern times, including issues of constitutional governance and fundamental individual rights [...] (v) in a Muslim-majority state, no protection needs to be provided to religious beliefs and practices which are out of step with, and offend, the majority; and (vi) the dictates of international human rights law must yield to the pronouncements of Islamic law and are thus irrelevant in a Muslim state.'[29]

More moderate forms of theocracy exist in other Muslim countries.[30]

---

which mentions the freedom to choose one's religion and to change religions in art. 11, discussed in Heiner Bielefeldt, *Muslime im säkularen Rechtsstaat. Integrationschancen durch Religionsfreiheit*, Bielefeld, Transcript, 2003, pp. 68ff.

[27] See Larry P. Goodson, *Afghanistan's Endless War: State Failure, Regional Politics, and the Rise of the Taliban*, Seattle, University of Washington Press, 2001, pp. 18ff., 116ff.; Neamatollah Nojumi, *The Rise of the Taliban: Mass Mobilization, Civil War, and the Future of the Region*, New York, Palgrave, 2002, pp. 152ff. Even after the intervention of the West and the 'liberalization' of the country, the old ideas continue to dominate. In March 2006, Abdul Rahman, a convert from Islam to Christianity, was to face charges and probably be sentenced to death in Afghanistan for changing religion. Only after considerable political pressure was applied by the West was it possible for Rahman to flee the country; he was granted asylum in Italy.

[28] *Zaheeruddin v. State*, 26. S.C.M.R. (S. Ct.) (1993) (Pakistan), quoted in Tayyab Mahmud, 'Freedom of Religion and Religious Minorities in Pakistan: A Study of Judicial Practice', *Fordham International Law Journal*, 19 (1995–96), pp. 40, 44.

[29] *Zaheeruddin v. State*, quoted in Mahmud, 'Freedom of Religion', p. 51.

[30] The same applies to Islam as to Christianity: both have a long history and have taken various forms; diversity must be factored in. We would, for example, have to distinguish between orthodox or even fundamentalist interpretations and systems and more moderate and liberal ones within Islamic states. Political and religious leadership are often closely bound up, while on the other hand authorities on Islam also refer to 'the Islamic legacy of resisting governmental efforts to impose religious doctrine': L. Carl Brown, *Religion and State: The Muslim Approach to Politics*, New York, Columbia University Press, 2000, p. 178. See also the collection of fundamentalist Muslim perspectives on the one hand and those incorporating secular concerns on the other in Bielefeldt, *Muslime im säkularen Rechtsstaat*, pp. 59ff. There are even distance systems, as in Turkey.

Substantive moderation exists if, to a greater or lesser extent, those of other faiths are 'tolerated', but there is no real safeguarding of basic rights and no institutional differentiation.[31] Organizational moderation exists if, to a greater or lesser degree, the organs of the state and the religious leaders are different people, but in such cases the key point is how extensive the mutual influences are. More moderate systems in which there is a greater distance between church and state bring us closer to the fifth model.

The new constitution for Iraq must also be placed in this context.[32] In the preamble and in arts. 1 and 2, it describes Iraq as a republican, federal, democratic and pluralist state. Art. 2 contains two statements on state–church relations. First, Islam is identified as the official state religion and as a fundamental source of authority for making laws. Second, the same article guarantees the Islamic identity of the majority of the state, but at the same time the full religious freedoms of all individuals are also to be guaranteed, with special mention of Christians among others. This is a clear case of a compromise formula between the fifth and sixth models. It remains to be seen which route Iraq will in fact go down.

On the exclusion of models 1 and 6 in modern law

Taking an overall look at these six models of the state–church or state–religion relationship, we may state the following with respect to their legal acceptance. Within the framework of liberal constitutions and in light of human rights agreements, models 1 and 6 are unconstitutional and in breach of international law. Hostility towards religions and churches, enforced with state instruments, violates the right to religious freedom to which everyone is entitled. Each person must have the opportunity to decide for or against a belief as such or a particular religion; this choice must not be denied. Religions must be given space to develop. If a state does not permit this and champions an aggressive atheism, this state becomes totalitarian in nature: it not only claims responsibility for worldly tasks such as security and prosperity, but also implicitly for otherworldly, transcendent tasks relating to ultimate or comprehensive frameworks of meaning. It occupies and, as it were, fuses the immanence and transcendence of life, permitting no other organizations of a genuinely religious character.

Though located at the other end of the spectrum, the sixth model is not so far removed from the first. In the model of the material unity of state and

---

[31]   On this point, see Martin Kriele, 'Habeas Corpus als Urgrundrecht', in idem, *Recht, Vernunft, Wirklichkeit*, Berlin, Duncker & Humblot, 1990, pp. 71, 78ff.: 'Rechte und Toleranzen'; Bielefeldt, *Muslime im säkularen Rechtsstaat*, pp. 24ff., see also Dorsen, Rosenfeld, Sajó and Baer (eds.), *Comparative Constitutionalism*, pp. 975ff.

[32]   Quoted in www.washingtonpost.com, site accessed 12 October 2005.

church, aggressive atheism, as a quasi-religion, is replaced by the union of an explicit religion and the state, along with its instruments of threat and coercion. Religious freedom is formally guaranteed, but only for one religion, the state church – if people are not in fact forced to confess to a particular faith. Other religions are not tolerated; they do not enjoy equal rights, though in practice there may be de facto spaces of toleration here or there or even in a number of respects. Thus, a coercive and discriminatory attitude towards those of other faiths generally prevails, or at least in case of conflict. This too is incompatible with a liberal conception of the constitution and contemporary notions of the safeguarding of human rights.

The assessment of systems of formal unity in the fifth model

Formal systems of union as found in the fifth model are more difficult to categorize legally; these profess their faith in a national church or national religion but combine this structural religious bias with individual and collective religious freedom. To the extent that, within the framework of the fifth model, this is not only propagated politically but also practised in reality and legally controlled, we are dealing with a hotch-potch of bias and neutrality, freedom and mild coercion to the advantage of the preferred religion and church. The fact that such systems have long existed and continue to exist is due to the fact that no state in the world developed as a religious *tabula rasa*. Many states were and are moulded by a religion; in some cases, religion is the leading influence. If such states continue to profess their faith in a national church, essentially in a formal sense and only to a marginal degree in a material one, rather than switching to a division or separation system like other states, then legitimate or at least understandable reasons relating to the safeguarding of tradition and identity may be put forward for this.

International law and human rights agreements do not from the outset rule out these systems of formal unity; the key limitation is that religious freedom is guaranteed as a human right for believers and non-believers of every shade and colour, at least fundamentally, and preferably in comprehensive fashion.[33] Formal systems of unity as in Greece and the United Kingdom do in fact provide for this. It goes without saying that tensions arise here, and this is most clearly illustrated in the rulings of the human rights courts with responsibility for applying the law to relevant conflicts. The fifth model is in fact in decline in Western states, as apparent, for example, in Sweden's 2000 break with the previous state–church system in which the Lutheran church had the status of national church. But for

---

[33]   See n. 5 above.

states which have thus far featured a strict system of the material unity of state and church/religion, the model of basically formal unity may be an attractive means of gradually effecting at least a certain liberalization and pluralization of religious life in times of external coercion or internal pressure. From a political or constitutional perspective, the Muslim world is for example unlikely to see a transformation directly from the system of material unity to a Western model of division and separation, as in the second to fourth models. Within the context of the new constitution of Iraq, for example, it is more likely, though not certain, that such gradual liberalization and pluralization of religious life will prevail.

The structure of striking a balance within separation and division models: a number of examples

How is the issue of achieving a balance dealt with in the second to fourth models of separation and division dominant in the West? The legal criteria essential to answering this question have been clarified by the preceding remarks. The structural separation of state and churches or religions corresponds with the criteria of independence, neutrality, equal treatment and non-identification. In terms of basic rights, the model of separation leads to religious freedom as a basic freedom by excluding the possibility of forcing people to embrace a religion; it leads to religious equality by requiring that there be no discrimination. Further, two of the American tests on the operationalization of these criteria were presented: the 'strict test' and the 'Lemon Test'.

Table 4. *The relationship between structural norm and basic right in the separation and division model*

I State–church relationship	1. Independence
	2. Neutrality
	3. Equal treatment
	4. Non-identification
II Religious freedom as basic right	1. Basic freedom: no compulsion
	2. Right to equality: no discrimination

Although the validity of these legal criteria is uncontested in the second to fourth models, their concrete application is highly contentious. This is bound up with the fact that each of these criteria may be applied strictly and rigidly, as it were absolutely. Each criterion may, however, be understood by the courts in a more open way, with greater willingness to compromise, in a more relativizing, accommodating fashion. There are two reasons for this. The first reason for compromise is a case of conflict between the structural separation of state and church and the taking account of individual religious freedom, if both norms are applied to the same case. The second reason for compromise lies in the taking account of the de facto and legal moulding of a polity by a religion/church. Whether the courts tend to take the approach of strict separation and equality, as provided for in the second model, or whether they tend, in the spirit of the third and fourth models, to permit state and churches to move closer together and take account of majority religions, depends on a multitude of often scarcely separable factors: the text of the constitution, the historical point of departure, the political atmosphere, various understandings of integration, the legal test for interpreting state–church norms, and whether the constitutional courts see themselves as having a passive or active role. As a science, jurisprudence can bring out and analyse these conflicts, but in reality its ability to resolve them is limited: it can clarify the preconditions for and consequences of the selection of particular state–church models, point to their differences, ascertain the acceptance of the models within the framework of modern law and outline room for interpretation. In this light, I conclude by sketching out a number of well-known conflicts and possible answers. Typically, conflicts arise in situations in which state and church/religion are moving closer together, whether as a result of the objective of providing support, organizational closeness or the effects of support.

1. From the point of view of the strict separation of state and church, religious education should not, for example, be provided in state schools, as 'spatial separation' is an aspect of the wall of separation between state and church.[34] This principle is upheld in the USA. But endeavours to take account of religion are possible within the framework of the second model and probable within that of the third model. In the USA, it is for example permissible, within the framework of a state programme of support for state and private (religious) schools, for employees in both types of school to provide lessons in strictly secular subjects.[35] There is no danger of any discrimination here. Further, the context makes it clear that the aim of the support is a secular rather than a religious one; as a result, the state may also finance school books in secular subjects for state and religious schools.[36]

2. From the standpoint of strict separation it is also unacceptable in principle for an official to take a religious oath on being sworn in, as this constitutes to all appearances a fusion of office and religion. Prohibiting religious oaths would,

---

[34]   See *McCollum v. Board of Education*, 333 U.S. 203 (1948) and n. 15 above.

[35]   See *Agostini v. Felton*, 521 U.S. 203 (1997).

[36]   See *Board of Education v. Allen*, 392 U.S. 236 (1968).

however, impair the religious freedom of the individual taking up the post, which is why the strict structural rule of separation is relativized here for reasons of basic rights: the person taking up the new post may take an oath but has no obligation to do so.[37]

3. From the point of view of the model of strict separation, all kinds of state financial support are in fact also prohibited, even if they consist solely of a subsidy for the transport of pupils from their homes to the state and religious schools, in line with the views of the minority in the Everson case.[38] If one wishes to relativize this stance within the framework of the American model, one may anchor one's position, as did the majority in the Everson case, in arguments of equality (between state and religious schools, religious and non-religious pupils), the possible infringement of the religious pupils' freedom of religion (financial disadvantages) as well as the prohibition on hostility towards religions. Much the same would apply to a state programme of school vouchers, which pupils' parents could use to send their child to either a state school or a private, religious school: from the perspective of a strict view of separation, this would already be too close a relationship, but by deploying the arguments mentioned above, it would be defensible from an accommodating perspective.[39]

4. As far as the use of religious symbols or messages by holders of state offices is concerned, a longstanding and profound dispute between the supporters of the strict and accommodating models of separation runs through American jurisprudence.[40] According to the model of strict separation, it is for example impermissible for local and city governments to erect Christmas trees in public parks, on public streets or in state buildings such as courts or seats of government during the Christmas period. The very element 'Christ' in 'Christmas tree' represents support not only for religion as such, but for a particular religion, and thus fails to maintain the necessary distance, and in this model that means clear and considerable distance.[41] The religious message contained in a nativity scene would be all the more unconstitutional. From the standpoint of the model of strict separation, it would be no different if this were accompanied by the symbol of another religion, such as

---

[37]   This is the practice in the USA, and is also provided for by the German legal system. See arts. 56 and 64, par. 2 GG.

[38]   See nn. 12ff. above.

[39]   See *Zelman v. Simmons-Harris*, 536 U.S. 639 (2002).

[40]   See especially *Lynch v. Donnelly*, 465 U.S. 668 (1984) and *County of Allegheny v. A.C.L.U.*, 492 U.S. 573 (1989) on representations of Christmas in public spaces.

[41]   On this perspective, see the quotation from Justice Brennan, n. 14 above. Brennan was an advocate of strict separation.

Judaism, or secular symbols of a more commercial character. This would certainly go some way to countering the accusation of bias and help maintain neutrality; also, it would generally avoid offending against individual religious freedom; but the criterion of structural separation may be stricter or more severe, such that a clear distance must be maintained from religion as such and from every particular religion as something required by the state.

Advocates of the accommodating separation perspective relativize this strict position: to the extent that the context of representations of Christmas makes it clear that there is no clear preference for one religion, that other religions or secular symbols are also shown and inasmuch as there is no conspicuous locational linkage of a religious symbol with state power (as represented for example by a courtroom), this is still regarded as in accordance with the constitution. Advocates of the accommodating perspective on separation regard such representations as a secularized 'ceremonial deism' which can be clearly distinguished from genuinely religious events. According to the third model, this also applies for example if religious messages such as the Ten Commandments have long been presented together with other formative ethical and legal maxims on state sites, without any conflicts arising between the religions or between believers and non-believers.[42] This indicates, as it were, the step from the genuinely religious to the civil religious or partially secularized symbol. The situation may be considered to be different – and this is contested ground in the USA – if the Ten Commandments are shown on posters in state schools.[43]

5. If we take the fourth model, as applies in Germany, as our starting point, that of a 'limping separation' between state and church, then it is conceivable for state and religion/church as such as well as state and majority religions to move somewhat closer together, though this is contested as well, for some members of the German judiciary wish to move the model of separation and cooperation

---

[42]   See the recent case *Van Orden v. Perry*, 125 S. Ct. 2854 (2005) on a stone monument featuring an engraving of the Ten Commandments within the grounds of the Texan state government, which was surrounded by numerous other secular representations of historical importance; by contrast, a majority of the US Supreme Court considered a representation of the Ten Commandments in court buildings to be unconstitutional: *McCreary v. A.C.L.U.*, 125 S. Ct. 2722 (2005). The argument was that legislative history reveals the undoubted goal of promoting Christianity; this 'illegitimate goal' is not rendered acceptable by displaying other, secular symbols and documents (such as the Declaration of Independence).

[43]   According to *Stone v. Graham*, 449 U.S. 39 (1980) this is unconstitutional; from the accommodating standpoint, constitutionality would be judged by context (use of the message as religious or partially secular; are other secular messages present?).

further in the direction of strict separation as found in the USA. The German Federal Constitutional Court has for example permitted a Christian prayer in class led by a teacher in state schools, as long as this occurs voluntarily, those of other faiths and of no faith are able to opt out and there is no question of discrimination against non-Christians.[44] According to the strict American view of separation, such an arrangement is ruled out for several reasons: structurally, the mandatory locational separation between religious and school events is abolished; in terms of basic rights, one religion, namely the dominant Christian religion, is singled out and clearly given a positive evaluation – this exerts subliminal pressure on those of other faiths and discriminates implicitly or explicitly against those of other faiths. Thus, the constitution is violated in a number of ways.[45] The fact that coercion and discrimination are marginal or subliminal is irrelevant from the strict separation perspective: any kind of rapprochement is forbidden.

6. With respect to the USA, one might take a different view of a case in which, before the lesson begins, pupils have the option of saying a prayer or meditating within the context of a minute's silence. In this case, there is no particular pressure to engage in religious prayer. The equality between religious and other beliefs is preserved. Because everyone participates, it is not even clear who is a believer and who a non-believer – there is no danger of discrimination and insider/outsider effects. Within the framework of the accommodating view of separation, and perhaps even the strict view, everything seems to suggest that such a minute's silence should be permitted. If a majority of the Supreme Court nonetheless regarded a corresponding provision as unconstitutional, this is because in the view of the majority the objective of the provision was specifically to promote prayer – though factually and according to the legal text other types of meditation (or non-meditation) were possible.[46]

7. What is the position with regard to the establishment of 'Christian community schools' in separation and division models? According to the two US positions, such titles are structurally impossible, as they signal a closeness to, indeed identification with, a particular religion. With respect to basic rights, that is, religious freedom and religious equality, such schools would also be highly suspect, because as compulsory state schools, they would force non-Christians into Christian schools. With respect to basic rights, much, perhaps everything, depends on what the word 'Christian' in this title means. In two judgements

---

[44]   See BVerfGE 52, 223.

[45]   See *Engel v. Vitale*, 370 U.S. 421 (1962).

[46]   See *Wallace v. Jaffree*, 472 U.S. 38 (1985).

from 1975,[47] Germany's Federal Constitutional Court carried out a legal rescue operation on this front, for it is also clear within the German 'limping separation model' that significant pressure or discrimination are unacceptable and that the state must keep its distance, structurally, from genuinely religious organizations. The Court regarded this form of German school as in keeping with the constitution. However, it is so only under the conditions, characteristic of separation models, that genuinely religious elements are absent from the sphere of the state. In this spirit, the word 'Christian' in the context of 'Christian community schools' must stand for the cultural significance and secularized content of the Christian faith in Germany. There must be no attempt to convert pupils to Christianity and discrimination must be eliminated.

8. What is the position with regard to crosses on walls in state schools? One would think that in Germany, within the framework of the 'limping separation system', such symbols would be permissible if they comply with the above-mentioned secularizing or neutralizing conditions, if, that is, the cross in the school is (or can be) understood merely as an allusion to the profound significance of history to a country's identity, if it is not actively brought into play during general teaching, if it expresses at most weak, general support for the 'values' of Christianity such as respect for the dignity of every individual or solidarity with the poor and weak. An accommodating interpretation of this kind would have been perfectly possible, but was not chosen by the majority of the Federal Constitutional Court in 1995.[48] The Court believes that the cross primarily expresses the genuinely Christian message of redemption through Christ and ascribes to the hanging cross a missionary effect with respect to the pupils as well, which distinguishes between Christians and non-Christians, advantaging the former and seeking to target the latter.

As we have seen, the consensus on the fundamental division or separation of state and church and on the elimination of coercion and elimination quickly vanishes, giving way to vehement disputes, when concrete issues come into play. Scholars and citizens need not be discouraged by this. For scholars, such disputes are an expression of the ambivalence and complexity of the relevant legal regulations, which provide for the taking into account of a number of criteria – between which tension often prevails. Further, the norms in question and their interpretations have developed in historical situations seldom characterized by a religious *tabula rasa* or the unproblematic equality of a number of religions; more often, particular religious orientations dominated, and were sooner or later confronted with

---

[47]   BVerfGE 41, 28 and 41, 88.

[48]   See BVerfGE 93, 1.

competing religions or secular worldviews. As with the principle of democracy, which throws up similar problems, it would be foolish to see from the outset only risk or only opportunity, solely negative or solely positive aspects in majority situations. The key issue is always mutual consideration for majority and minority within contexts shaped by specific forces, primarily Christian in Europe and primarily Muslim in the Middle East and parts of Asia.

To renounce such identities entirely is politically and legally difficult, sometimes impossible and not, perhaps, always advisable. As scholars and citizens, who often have 'two souls' and thus competing values dwelling in our breasts, we must, for the sake of peace and successful coexistence, find convincing or at least somehow acceptable criteria for striking a balance between majority and minority positions, whether political or religious. All those countries which comply with the division and separation model, and in fact also the model of formal unity, have already taken important steps in this direction, because in all these models individuals are largely free to make their own decisions with respect to both religion and belief. Though disputes about religion are often intense, in Germany they generally occur within the framework of universally acknowledged principles. And if this foundation of consensus is transgressed, as with the fundamentalist critique by some Muslims for example, then this should prompt us to reflect upon, strengthen and perhaps also partially readjust our approach to the relationship between state and church or religion, rather than to regard it from the outset as a clash of civilizations.

8

'Science Doesn't Tremble': The Secular Natural Sciences and the Modern Feeling for Life

Ernst Peter Fischer

Anyone attempting to comment on the fate of religion and the religious in the face of the rise of the modern world immediately finds himself confronted with a term used by countless authors as a skeleton key to all the rooms in the shared house of modern Euro-American humanity: secularization. What was initially no more than a legal term referring to the more or less violent acquisition of church property by the organs of the modern nation state following the French Revolution developed over the course of the nineteenth century into one that seemed to address the overall trend characteristic of the competition between church and state – a positive one in the eyes of progressives and laicists, a negative one in the opinion of Catholic modernism. In Catholic milieux, secularization was referred to like an epochal crime committed by a narcissistic and humanistic modern world rebelling against its God-given origins. For progressives, the notion of secularization entailed the promise that humanity could break away from its unworthy, religiously dictated history through work and self-determination.

So begins Peter Sloterdijk's 'Note on the Changing Form of the Religious in the Modern World'.[1] Here the author does not distinguish between two meanings that are usually kept apart in German: the concrete use of church property by

————

[1] Foreword to William James, *Die Vielfalt religiöser Erfahrung*, Frankfurt am Main, Insel Verlag, 1997, p. 11.

secular authorities – *Säkularisation* – and the spiritual process 'which, over the course of modern European history, has endowed individuals with ever greater autonomy over their own lives and with respect to church and religious systems of order' – *Säkularisierung*, as the entry on secularization in the German encyclopedia Brockhaus (vol. 19, 1992) puts it. 'Modern European history' – for a historian of science, this begins in the early seventeenth century, roughly during the era of the Thirty Years' War, a time when *The Birth of Modern Science* in Europe was taking place – to quote the title of a book by Florentine scholar Paolo Rossi. This occurred through the efforts of those individuals referred to in the opening quotation as the 'progressives', because the idea of progress accompanied the rise of the then pioneers of natural science. Many people no longer believed in a golden age of the past, but turned in the opposite direction, towards the future. With a new astronomy in particular (Johannes Kepler) and a new science in general (Galileo Galilei), they hoped to build a new Atlantis (Francis Bacon) in which it would be possible, with new methods (René Descartes), 'to ease the conditions of human existence' and to make a better life on the basis of individuals' inherent powers of rationality rather than divine grace.

Explanations under unfavourable conditions

These and many other men of science helped create an 'imaginary reality without borders [...] a Republic of Science that worked itself, against the odds, into difficult, often dramatic, and sometimes even tragic social and political contexts'.[2] The idea of experimentation is one of the concepts developed during this period in the early seventeenth century. Anyone in the twenty-first century who wishes to state as concisely as possible what the practitioner of natural science actually does will fall back on this notion. The answer might be: she attempts to explain the world – or nature – without recourse to higher powers or miracles under the less favourable conditions of the experiment. This applies to the motion of the stars as well as to the way horses run; for a long time, it was not known whether there is a moment when a horse has all four legs in the air and is no longer in contact with the ground.

This is, no doubt, an enormous task that scientists have set themselves, but no one would seriously dispute that they have, in some cases at least, risen to the challenge (and even capitalized on their answers). If, for example, a hurricane forms, then natural science analyses the surface temperature of the oceans, examines the air currents, the rotation of the earth and other measurable parameters and finally, on the basis of atmospheric and meteorological laws, provides an explanation of the natural phenomenon, of whose potentially

---

2   Paolo Rossi, *The Birth of Modern Science*, Oxford, Blackwell, 2001, p. 1.

disastrous consequences we are only too well aware. We want to protect ourselves against such phenomena, and this we do not through invocations or hopes of help from beyond, but by deploying technological-scientific means to which we ourselves have access. These are not always effective – and this may have consequences, and not only secular ones.

As is well known, New Orleans was ravaged by a tropical cyclone (as we tend to say, though to be accurate, or neutral, we ought to say that the city lay in its path) in late 2005. Much of New Orleans was simply swept away, as was evident in many TV images. However, when the media reported the disaster, reference was not only made to explicable natural forces and politically induced technical failings (maintenance of levees). Other voices could also be heard in the newspapers (such as the *Frankfurter Allgemeine Zeitung* of 18 January 2006). The ruined city's mayor, for example, explained what had happened as the result of the wrath of God, who was, he suggested, partly responsible for his region's misfortune. 'God is mad at America. He sent us hurricane after hurricane after hurricane.'[3] Conservative preachers came to the aid of the despairing politician by portraying New Orleans as a 'hotbed of vice' and expressing their regret that these divine floods were insufficient to wipe out this impression, along with the unsavoury goings-on.

The return of God

As far as scientifically accessible phenomena are concerned, God is once again involving Himself actively in the affairs of society. This is apparent in tropical cyclones and epidemics – and here again, there is no lack of 'hotbeds of vice' deserving of divine punishment. But even among researchers, God has become very modern, as professed atheists endeavour first to understand Him scientifically as a product of evolution and then to locate Him, in the form of stimulation (to be precise, a small-scale epileptic fit), in the temporal lobes.[4]

Things were very different when I was growing up and developing an interest in the natural sciences. About half a century ago, it was figures such as Francis Crick, the British co-discoverer of the double helix in 1953, who impressed me. In the wake of his insight, he stated that this achievement of structural chemistry and molecular biology had solved the puzzle of life; there were no more mysteries. With a complete lack of irony, Crick recommended converting all the churches into swimming pools.

---

[3]   http://www.breitbart.com/article.php?id=D8F65JUG5&show_article=1.

[4]   Daniel C. Dennett, *Breaking the Spell – Religion as a Natural Phenomenon*, New York, Viking, 2006; Andrew Newberg et al., *Why God Won't Go Away – Brain Science and the Biology of Belief*, New York, Ballantine Books, 2002.

I can still hear Yuri Gagarin's words when he returned from space in the early 1960s. Gagarin informed us that the heavens were empty and uninhabited; he had, in any event, encountered no deity there.

Towards the end of the 1960s, the exponents of a new science called futurology announced that in the future – the present, from our perspective – society would be almost entirely devoid of religiously motivated forces; above all, no violence would emanate from the religious sphere.

I liked that, and it made sense to me. Here, it seemed, a triumphant science was forcing God into rearguard action, curbing His room for manoeuvre to an ever greater extent. Soon – so I thought – science would leave no space at all for the 'God of Gaps', providing explanations of the world entirely devoid of His presence. Yet when Stephen Hawking did exactly that in his worldwide bestseller *A Brief History of Time* from 1988, proclaiming that in his universe a Creator has nothing to do and has thus lost nothing at all (Hawking's arguments were couched in the language of mathematics, which forms equations, whose solution depends on so-called boundary conditions, and these did not include God; he was thus absent even from the margins of reality), such claims seemed to me both forlorn and irrelevant. I was, and am still, in no doubt about 'the extraordinary value, for explanation and prevision, of those mathematical and mechanical modes of conception which science uses'; they continue to inspire my admiration. But 'what thin, pallid, uninteresting ideas' science deploys here: 'weight, movement, velocity, direction, position', whose meagreness is never more apparent than when confronted with descriptions of those dramatic aspects of reality in which 'religion delights to dwell'. 'It is the terror and beauty of phenomena, the "promise" of the dawn and of the rainbow, the "voice" of the thunder, the "gentleness" of the summer rain, the "sublimity" of the stars, and not the physical laws which these things follow, by which the religious mind still continues to be most impressed.'[5]

The varieties of religious experience

These quotations are from the year 1902. They appear in the lectures on the 'varieties of religious experience' given by the American philosopher and psychologist William James in the early years of the twentieth century. The quotation that opens this chapter appears in the preface to the new (1997) German edition of James' book, published by Insel Verlag; to discover how much this book can still teach us to this day, one need only read the first lecture. Here, James discusses the relationship between 'religion and neurology' – a

---

[5]   William James, *The Varieties of Religious Experience*, New York, Simon & Schuster, 1997, pp. 385–86.

topic which is being rediscovered in our time by brain researchers with their imaging techniques, which uncover God in various convolutions of the brain and then wish to limit Him to these. James presents his contemporaries' medical and materialist efforts to trace religious feelings back to organic processes with potentially pathological side-effects (such as epileptic fits) in order to make it clear that this is completely missing the point, and that we must instead be prepared 'to judge the religious life by its results exclusively'. Of course, people may have a 'neurotic temperament' underpinning their receptiveness to 'inspiration from a higher realm', but there, according to James, we should let the subject of religion and neurology 'drop'.[6] He at least is unwilling to be troubled further by it, and if I had three wishes, one would be to follow his example.

The fact that modern neurology has failed to heed James' well-meaning advice (or, very likely, is quite unaware of it), points to a curious interplay – a kind of *yin–yang* complementarity. It is true that science allows God less space within society and its decision-making processes, which are increasingly rationalized and left to acknowledged experts with their laptops and Internet access. Yet at the same time, God and religious notions are huge topics among the ranks of scientific researchers. As James stated more than 100 years ago, our grandfathers imagined a God 'who conformed the largest things of nature to the paltriest of our private wants'.[7] Meanwhile, 'the God whom science recognizes must be a God of universal laws exclusively, a God who does a wholesale, not a retail business'.

This applies precisely, for instance, to Albert Einstein, who explicitly professed his faith in a God evident in the harmony of the universe, a harmony revealed to us through physical laws. Einstein talked of being 'cosmically religious'; he could not imagine a God who interferes in the private sphere or makes His presence felt in our personal lives.

We should note here that the great physicist's tremendous popularity is due more to his discourses on God than to his insights into the nature of space and time. This also applies to Hawking, whom we met above, who became a star not because he can operate a universe mathematically, but because he has developed opinions on God while attempting to do so.

The presence of God in the science of a secularized world – His return – is also unmistakably evident in evolutionary biology, which is ceaselessly urged to entrust the emergence of humankind to an intelligent designer, rather than seeking to identify natural processes which could lead to this result and bring forth our species. It was just a few years ago that the German science magazine *Spektrum der Wissenschaft* (November 1999) carried an article analysing

---

6   James, *Varieties of Religious Experience*, p. 35 and p. 38.
7   James, *Varieties of Religious Experience*, pp. 382–84.

the veracity of a headline appearing in *Newsweek* the year before: 'Science Finds God'. While it is unclear what precisely this means (have scientists discovered Him within themselves or in the cosmos?) it is clear that, according to one survey, religious belief among scientists has remained static over the course of the twentieth century. Such studies always appear against the backdrop of the assessment made by Nobel Prize-winning British physicist George Thomson, who once wrote, 'Probably every physicist would believe in a creation if the Bible had not unfortunately said something about it many years ago and made it seem old-fashioned'.[8]

As it happens, *Newsweek*'s question was prompted by a conference on 'Science and the Spiritual Quest', organized in 1998 by the John Templeton Foundation, which supports projects aimed at reconciling faith and the natural sciences by means of generous financial aid and prizes. Its founder, financial expert John Templeton, calls his programme, which holds much appeal for many scientists, 'humility theology'; his hope is that representatives of both camps – believers and 'knowers' – recognize their own limitations.

The rationality of the world and the hypothesis of God

Let us look again at the opening quotation on secularization and the origin of this idea. It alludes to the historical fact that while the diminishing importance of religious systems of order and the increasing willingness to create one's own life and worldview, which we attempt to capture through the concepts of *Säkularisation* and *Säkularisierung*, began long before the nineteenth century, it was only during it that these processes made their presence felt in a particularly tangible way. During this period, 'humanity', to which Sloterdijk refers in the opening quotation, wished to rid itself of the constraints entailed in a powerful Christian faith, as can be seen most clearly by examining individuals such as the French mathematician Pierre Simon Laplace (1749–1827). By 1800, Laplace, briefly minister of the interior under Napoleon Bonaparte, had drawn on his specialist knowledge to brilliantly develop the infinitesimal calculus introduced by Newton and Leibniz (still part, in unchanged form, of the modern school syllabus) in both practical and theoretical terms; thanks not least to the arithmetical (rational) assistance provided by the infinitesimal calculus, he went on to complete a 'celestial mechanics' (*Mécanique céleste*), ultimately enabling him to present a world system, his *exposition du système du monde*. This is not merely the expression of a scholar's whimsy, but is an endeavour with far-reaching aims. He was attempting to cope with fear. The astronomers of the day had observed

---

[8]   Quoted in Simon Singh, *Big Bang: The Most Important Scientific Discovery of All Time and Why You Need to Know About It*, London, Fourth Estate, 2004, pp. 361–62.

irregularity (acceleration) in the motion of the moon, and some of Laplace's contemporaries feared that a global catastrophe on a cosmic scale might be in the offing. Fortunately, Laplace was able to dispel these concerns – in literally rational fashion – with his celestial mechanics, by solving the problem of how the position of each planet could be determined at any given moment – even if he took into account disturbances of the celestial bodies resulting from mutual gravitational pull. With his system of calculation he was able to demonstrate that the observed irregularities occur periodically and thus entail no risks to our existence at these moments. Even the large planets Jupiter and Saturn should give us no cause for concern, as Laplace calculated in a second step, despite the fact that their orbiting speeds change appreciably. As the celestial mathematician was able to infer from his figures, the diameter and basic structure of their orbits remain the same.

In other words, Laplace and his calculations, and thus his rationality, guaranteed the stability of the solar system (and consequently the entire cosmic realm), in which, moreover, the laws of nature held absolute sway. There was no longer any need to appeal to higher powers to obtain a guarantee of the continued existence of the world and the survival of humankind. It was thus no surprise that Laplace cut such a self-confident figure, answering Napoleon's famous question as to where God was to be found within his world system by stating that he had no need of such a hypothesis in carrying out his calculations.

Incidentally, Laplace had of course not yet understood the heavens and the bodies moving within them with complete accuracy or in any definitive way. There were still gaps in his knowledge of the celestial sphere and its laws. Subsequently, both the measuring data and the fundamental insights into physical connections (principles of conservation) increased, uncovering a surprise. At the beginning of the twentieth century, when Laplace's compatriot Henri Poincaré produced his three-volume work *New Methods of Celestial Mechanics*, he was able to show that the fundamental problem of this science, the calculation of planetary orbits under the influence of their mutual attraction, can by no means be solved completely and never with complete precision (and thus at best approximately). Fundamentally, it is impossible to provide a rock-solid (because exact) solution to the system of equations – which we refer to as Newton's clock to assure ourselves of its regularity – if too many elements are in motion and influencing one another within it. Then there are too many unknowns and too few equations.

In other words, the stability of the solar system cannot be strictly proven. Such stability cannot be guaranteed here below either, and a new tendency is clearly evident within contemporary theoretical physics, which Poincaré had introduced in seminal form; its key term is chaos, its central concepts non-linearity (or complexity) and unpredictability.

Physics has in fact succeeded in abolishing once again the calculability of the world proclaimed so proudly by Laplace (and not only in the 'above', as we shall see). The difference lies in the fact that while people in Laplace's time heaved a sigh of relief and felt a sense of security thanks to successfully applied rationality, no one today seems shocked by its limits. At any rate, no one reacts anxiously to the incapacities or limitations of natural science, and we tend to respond with hard-headed indifference when we learn that the world is full of dark matter and dark energy that elude our senses.

'Fear and science'

Nowadays, if people are afraid, it is no longer of potentially dangerous natural phenomena, as was the case as late as the eighteenth century, but of the natural sciences themselves and their increasing capacity to interfere in our lives.[9] Before exploring this terrain, let us return to the nineteenth century, characterized by Wolf Lepenies, the well-known sociologist and long-standing head of the Wissenschaftskolleg, Institute for Advanced Study, Berlin, as the 'age of enthusiasm for science and technology', a period that saw the 'trivialization of fear'.[10] For Lepenies, 'science and technology' began their 'triumphant progress' at the moment when 'they prevailed over magic and religion as more effective, ultimately unrivalled mechanisms for coping with fear'.

This idea seems fundamental to the topic of secularization in the wake of science-based action, because fear is one of the basic human states of mind. This remark immediately raises the question of what gives rise to this state, and the modern answer, in the context of evolutionary thought, is that feelings of fear arose as a result of selection and are among the prerequisites for the survival of our species. If, in the early days of the human race, you went about your life without fear, plunging without a second thought into dense forests, you would neither live to tell the tale nor would you leave behind any descendants to become our ancestors. Naturally, evolutionary explanations have no need to refer to God or the divine, and they made a huge contribution to secularization in the nineteenth century, as we shall be discussing in a moment.

---

[9]   One might almost be tempted to speak of a principle of conservation with respect to fear. Fear is like energy, namely indestructible, but it appears in a variety of forms. In a certain sense, in line with what was said above, this applies to God as well, who is also indestructible. Perhaps, alongside the principle of the conservation of energy with respect to matter, such a principle also applies to the soul, that is, there may be a first law of emotions as well as of thermodynamics.

[10]   Wolf Lepenies, 'Angst und Wissenschaft', in *Gefährliche Wahlverwandtschaften*, Stuttgart, Reclam Verlag, 1989, pp. 39–60.

The philosopher Peter Sloterdijk, whom we have met already, has nicely and memorably expressed the topic of fear – in allusion to Martin Heidegger's rather unfortunate and easily misunderstood remark that science does not think – by stating that 'science does not tremble'. Hence, it can function as 'a viable replacement [...] for the guarantees of order provided by theology'; in other words, scientific activities 'in the European nineteenth century [gave rise to] a kind of scientist church that consoled contemporaries by telling them that it was there to replace the pallid old faith with an energetic new one, that is, with a scientific worldview'. If, not only then, but until well into the twentieth century, people stated that 'the truth will set you free', they were no longer quoting the Gospel according to John, but laying claim to the implied possibility of autonomous action. The truth of science will set you free, from fear and worry, as people believed, from superstition and irrationality, as the founders of the California Institute of Technology, for example, believed; in the 1920s, as God-fearing physicists well-versed in the Bible, they knew these words of the Gospel and had them engraved above the entrance gate.

The point of departure for this fearful attitude towards life is the malevolence of nature, which people in the eighteenth century could experience directly throughout their lives, while we might perhaps come into contact with it as children (or TV viewers). Through the simple example of a storm, the following quotation from a novel of this era shows how people reacted to inclement weather before the consequences of secularization had made themselves felt:

> The dance was not yet ended when the flashes which we had been seeing for some time along the horizon, and which I had steadily declared to be heat lightning, began to increase greatly, and the thunder drowned out the music. Three ladies ran out of the square, followed by their gentlemen; the disorder grew general, and the music stopped. [...] To such causes I must ascribe the extraordinary contortions into which I saw several ladies fall. The smartest one sat down in a corner with her back to the window and held her ears shut. Another knelt down before her and hid her head in the first one's lap. A third pushed in between the two and embraced her dear sisters, with endless tears. Some wanted to go home; others, who were still less aware of what they were doing, did not have enough presence of mind to stave off the importunities of some of our young gourmets, who seemed to find an occupation in anticipating all the anxious prayers which were meant for Heaven, and in gathering them from the lips of the distressed beauties.[11]

---

[11]   Johann Wolfgang von Goethe, *The Sufferings of Young Werther*, London, John Calder, 1964, pp. 36–37.

My concern in relation to this scene from Goethe's *The Sufferings of Young Werther*, which appeared in 1774, is not with gender difference – only the women seem to be afraid and offer up prayers – but with the fear provoked by phenomena still inexplicable at the time, such as thunder and lightning. Naturally, without a physical explanation, they can only be alleviated by prayers. Only when people know how to protect themselves against the dangers of a storm, namely with the aid of a lightning conductor, a simple metal rod, can they calm themselves down and reassure themselves by rational means.

The lightning conductor was in fact invented and deployed during Goethe's lifetime; we should always bear in mind that it must have been difficult for the curiously simple object to hold its own in the face of the natural spectacle of thunder and lightning, which, moreover, came directly from above. Experiments with electrical discharges were carried out for the first time in France in 1752, before Benjamin Franklin popularized the lightning conductor in the New World by flying a kite (!) near thunderclouds the same year, in order to induce a spark of electricity from the cloud by means of a key attached to the end of a piece of damp string. Through this risky experiment, thunder and lightning were provided with physical causes, leaving no room for any kind of divine wrath requiring appeasement. Yet this insight did not immediately abolish the fear felt by ladies, and other people, at sinister natural forces, and it was only gradually that external nature lost its alarming or frightening characteristics, when it became possible to explain the natural phenomena it entails.

At this point, it is worth dwelling for a moment on Benjamin Franklin, not only because 2006 offered us the opportunity to celebrate his 300th birthday, but because his mastery of lightning – the heavenly fire – earned him the honorary title of the 'new Prometheus'. It was no less a personage than Immanuel Kant who described Franklin in these terms: with his kite, the co-author of the American Declaration of Independence did in fact wrest fire from the gods in very concrete fashion, placing it in the technically skilled hands of scientifically oriented human beings. What had occurred with the lightning conductor might be called undiluted secularization, that is, protecting human life had finally become an autonomous matter devoid of any residual religious associations. Furthermore, Franklin's deed entails the promise that there must be other ways of wresting from nature its tricks more or less effortlessly, in order to make them practically useful.

Just how much people trusted the analytical and rational expertise, and the plucky deeds, of the scientifically oriented man in the mid-nineteenth century is evident in an excerpt from the *Personal Recollections*, which appeared in 1902, of the industrialist Werner von Siemens; his firm Siemens, Halske & Co. was contracted in 1859 to supervise the laying of a submarine telegraph cable more than 3500 nautical miles long extending from the Red Sea to India. In mentioning these geographical locations, there is no need to underline that we are dealing here not with everyday events but major scientific adventures, as were still possible in those days and as they were perceived by the public. Siemens himself led the technologically demanding expedition, which went extremely well until shortly before it was due to end. Difficulties arose on the homeward voyage. Siemens' ship ran aground on a reef en route to Suez and began to sink. Naturally, in such a situation, fear spreads – as confirmed by the Grimms' German Dictionary, according to which fear was formerly understood to mean 'uncertainty and danger; the risks involved in transportation and delivery'. It is precisely this existential fear that is overcome by the 'prince of technology', as Werner von Siemens was described by the Prussian Academy of Science when he was admitted into its ranks. And this he manages to do by making use of nothing but the tools of his science:

> The vessel soon lay entirely on her side, and the great question, on which now the life or death of every living being on it depended, was whether it would assume a position of rest, or capsize, and hurl us one and all into the deep. I erected for myself a little observatory, with the help of which I could note the further inclination of the ship by the position of a particularly brilliant star, and proclaimed from minute to minute the result of my observations. These communications were awaited with great anxiety. The cry 'stand-still!' was greeted with short joyful murmurs, that of 'sunk further!' answered by various doleful exclamations. At last no further sinking was observable, and the paralysing fear of death gave place to energetic efforts for effecting our safety.[12]

The birth of modern science in Europe

In the nineteenth century, scientific intervention and technical action facilitated an experience of life that entailed freedom – or at least liberation from fear – and a successful search for one's own means of intervention. For some authors, this involved a tendency towards arrogance. Lepenies cites, among others, Emil du Bois-Reymond, head of Berlin University. In his lectures on 'cultural history and natural science', he poses the provocative question, 'What can touch modern culture? Where is the lightning capable of shattering this Tower of

---

[12]   Werner von Siemens, *Personal Recollections of Werner von Siemens*, London, Asher & Co., 1893, p. 195.

Babel? One's head reels at the thought of where contemporary developments will take humanity in a hundred, a thousand, ten thousand, one hundred thousand years and even further into the future. Is there anything it will be unable to accomplish?'

Similar sentiments proliferate in texts from the late 1960s, when a society with a blind faith in science felt strong enough to calculate the future. This society gave birth to a futurology that was even extolled as an exact science by some of its exponents. Before 1970, energy consumption had been calculated with apparent precision for the year 2000, without considering the dwindling of energy sources, and, as we have seen, it was thought a safe bet that religions or religious communities would no longer shape the world of the twenty-first century.

It is not only that expectations of a bright future lasted longer in the nineteenth century. The associated scientific mentality subsequently gained widespread acceptance. This mentality became a taken-for-granted aspect of the culture of Western industrial society, because it made good on the promises made at the beginning of the seventeenth century. We celebrate this era as the birth of modern science, which was ushered in from 1543 at the latest, when Nicolaus Copernicus risked a new perspective on the outside world (the heavenly cosmos) and Andreas Vesalius presented a new view of the inner world (the human body). No more than two decades later, in 1559, historians have evidence of the first use of the word 'secularization'; in the sense of *Verweltlichung* (the German term suggesting 'worldification'), it played an important role in the preliminary negotiations on the Peace of Westphalia at the latest. This brings us to the epoch in which the pioneers and promulgators of the new astronomy, new science, new methods and new Atlantis brought their work into the world. The natural sciences, as we practise them today, took shape in the years after 1600, and their founders came from more or less every part of Europe. In England, Francis Bacon recognizes that knowledge gives human beings power over divine nature; in Germany, Johannes Kepler ascertains that there are no rotating heavenly spheres above, which one must (or can) simply accept, but that there are planets moving in calculable ellipses, the cause of which must be determined. At the same time, in Italy, Galileo Galilei asserts that the book of nature is composed in the language of mathematics and geometry and that rather than having to believe, one may know what is written in it; and René Descartes presents the method of reduction, which still celebrates incredible triumphs in the form of reductionism and demonstrates to anyone who wishes to see that bodies have no souls, but consist merely of organs, tissues, cells and yet smaller units of a material nature.

The aim – 'the sole aim' – of this movement is described in the words which Bertolt Brecht puts in the mouth of the hero of his play *Life of Galileo*: 'science's sole aim must be to lighten the burden of human existence'.[13] For Brecht, this expressed a direct attack on the Church, which – in light of the Black Death for example – often stood helpless in the face of human suffering and did nothing to investigate natural causes. The scholars mentioned above took a different approach – involving experiments and inductive logic – and thus brought about the state of affairs which post-Second World War historians have characterized as the Scientific Revolution. It occurred at a time when the Thirty Years' War was raging furiously, causing widespread devastation.

Apart from the idea of progress and the derivative potential to acquire greater power over nature by understanding and utilizing its laws, the basic idea of this transformation consisted of the separation of subject and object. Nature becomes an Other, an object, to which we as subjects submit with a view to controlling it. God no longer appears within this interplay. People can even do without Him when it is moral behaviour that is at issue, for no compassionate naturalist would 'ever be guilty of the brutal ill-treatment of animals thoughtlessly committed by the devout Christian in his anthropocentric megalomania – as a "child of the God of Love"',[14] as was written in the nineteenth century.

The old division between God and the world becomes the new division between nature and human beings, who now seek out its laws – and find them. Here, it is important to be clear that what we have called the Scientific Revolution initially entailed no more than a multitude of promises which did not immediately bring improvements. Over the course of time, however, these were honoured in an almost unbelievable way, and never more than in the nineteenth century. How right Bacon was to assert that acquired knowledge can become power is evident in industrialization, which truly began to gather speed at the moment when it opened itself to science and established laboratories for basic research. And how right Galilei was to claim that the laws of nature must be expressed through mathematics was unmistakably apparent when, in the second half of the nineteenth century, a Scot by the name of James Clerk Maxwell formulated a set of equations which made it possible first to calculate and then to produce an invisible (immaterial) nature with precision. I am referring here to the electromagnetic waves with which all modern communication systems function and which clarified the nature of light for the first time (and which also enable us to understand what electricity is and how it can be produced).

We should note at this point that, rather than distancing them from God, Maxwell's equations in fact tended to bring the physicists back closer to Him. That is, until well into the twentieth century, the research fraternity showed itself so fascinated by his finding (for which Maxwell was unwilling to take

---

[13]   Bertolt Brecht, *Life of Galileo*, translated by John Willett, London, Methuen, 1986, p. 108.

[14]   Ernst Haeckel, *Die Welträtsel*, Stuttgart, Kröner Verlag, 1984, p. xii.

credit, preferring to trace it back to something within himself), that many physicists asked whether it was God who wrote these symbols. To this day one can see T-shirts emblazoned with the Maxwell equations, preceded by the words 'God spoke' and followed by: 'And there was light'.

Manifestly, God does not disappear when science succeeds and provides explanations, and this applies even to the revolution in the seventeenth century, in which the opposite occurred in the work of Kepler. When he defended the heliocentric worldview published by Nicolaus Copernicus in 1543 (making it socially acceptable for the first time), he did so not for empirical or other scientific reasons, but for religious ones. Science is worship, and in Copernicus' scheme, with the sun at the centre and a rotating earth, Kepler sees the possibility of placing the idea (the image) of the trinity in the heavens. Kepler wishes to become a theologian – rather more numerous than court astronomers – but his aim is not to teach the contents of the Bible. 'The Bible is no textbook of optics and astronomy', as he puts it in his contribution on secularization, calling on his colleagues: 'Resist misusing it in this way'. Through his reason – rather than authorities and their prescriptions – Kepler wishes to understand what happens in the world, but this does not prevent him from entering a state of 'pious frenzy' when granted the opportunity to formulate a law of nature, and he cannot thank God enough for this blessing.[15]

The question of the centre

Generally, we view the heliocentric worldview mentioned above as progress vis-à-vis the pre-Copernican conception of a cosmos with the earth at its centre. At the beginning of the twentieth century, however, Sigmund Freud saw things differently, referring to the injury being done to human beings by the new science. I mention this because Freud's absurd idea has taken root in many heads and is quoted incessantly. Yet it is utterly wrong. In the texts of the day, the central position occupied by the earth before Copernicus is identified not as a privilege but as the 'humiliation of humankind'. What Freud states and what many of us believe is in fact the opposite of the truth. '[A]ccording to the pre-Copernican world-view', as Paris-based philosopher of religion and Islamic studies scholar Rémi Brague was able to demonstrate in the last century, 'the central place of Earth is anything but a place of honor'. In the field of astronomy, 'the center is a humble place, even the humblest of all places'.[16]

---

[15]   For more on Kepler, see Volker Bialas, *Johannes Kepler – Von Wissenschaft und Philosophie um 1600*, Munich, Beck, 2004, p. 149.

[16]   Rémi Brague, 'Geocentrism as a Humiliation for Man', *Medieval Encounters*, 3.3 (November 1997), pp. 187–210, here p. 191.

It is odd that we are unwilling to acknowledge this fact and clearly do everything we can to foster an image of our 'unenlightened' medieval counterparts as idiots. Freud at least, we may hope, felt better as a result.

Newton's holy scriptures

There are good arguments for the claim that Kepler had established a so-called trinitarian physics, practised at least into the twentieth century.[17] This means, first of all, that explanations were presented and accepted within a tripartite scheme – one which, alongside the spatio-temporal dimensions and an indestructible energy, provides only for causality in order to understand and explain natural processes. Second, though, it means that the great hero of the emerging exact physics – Isaac Newton – saw himself as chosen by God, regarded space and time as emanations of God and considered attempts to come to terms with the Holy Scriptures scientifically both possible and desirable. He expected such endeavours to furnish more certainty and guarantees of the future than could the truths of science. For Newton, the notion of God and the practice of physics were so closely connected that he was quite willing not only to entrust God with the creation of the world but to expect Him to correct, through personal intervention, the instabilities which built up over the course of time as the planets moved through space.

The twentieth century, in the person of Wolfgang Pauli, made fun of Newton's God, who had to manufacture space and time all day every day, working non-stop, and all for the dubious reward of an uncertain flock of believers, the nature of whose service to Him is far from clear. What has been overlooked here is the fact that the Englishman was far more concerned with theological than with scientific issues and that he regarded those periods of his life during which he tackled the problems of optics and the cosmos as irksome interruptions that kept him from subjects of greater significance, namely those found within the Christian tradition. Newton wished to know when the apocalypse – the end of time – was going to occur, and only towards the end of his life was he prepared to revise 'his calculations of the Second Coming and [move] it to the twentieth or twenty-first century'.[18]

---

[17]   For more on this, see Ernst Peter Fischer, *Brücken zum Kosmos – Wolfgang Pauli zwischen Kernphysik und Weltharmonie*, Lengwil, Libelle Verlag, 2002.

[18]   Paolo Rossi, *The Birth of Modern Science*, Oxford, Blackwell, 2001, p. 227.

The date of Creation

Far less concerned with God was the second famous Briton who influenced the world of science, Charles Darwin. He does deal with the subject of God in the final sentence of his famous book on the origins of species from 1859, writing: 'There is grandeur in this view of life, with its several powers, having been originally breathed by the Creator into a few forms or into one; and that, whilst this planet has gone cycling on according to the fixed law of gravity, from so simple a beginning endless forms most beautiful and most wonderful have been, and are being evolved.'[19]

But it is, after all, the last sentence, and it was less a God than a Devil that Darwin had got to know through his study of nature, one who allowed or initiated agonizing death throes, insidious techniques of deception and brutal predatory attacks. Yet strangely enough, while in the case of Newton we have for almost two hundred years overlooked the fact that he was concerned more with the Holy Scriptures than with the book of nature, we are immediately struck by the fact that Darwin's ideas on evolution involved a clash with the views of the church or religious attitudes. Just a few years after the publication of Darwin's magnum opus, there was in fact a public debate between a bishop by the name of Samuel Wilberforce and the scientist Thomas Huxley, whom subsequent generations know, for good reason, as Darwin's bulldog. But this was more of a dispute over rhetoric, kicked off, unfortunately, when the bishop asked the biologist whether he was descended from an ape on his father's or his mother's side. Ever since, the impression has endured, intensified by subsequent materialistically inclined naturalists for personal rather than objective reasons, that the very idea of evolution puts paid to God as Creator of humankind. No wonder then that He has found the strangest of ways to re-enter the debate and has taken up a position to which He has no legitimate claim.

Darwin's efforts to find a causal explanation for the observable variation of life on earth can by no means deny a religious background. His aim was not to produce anti-religious – secular – explanations, but to remove from human thought its self-imposed blinkers. It was not a theologian of nature but a naturalist that he wanted to be, one who could do without 'arguments from design' and who found it silly when men of the church, 200 years after Kepler, continued to consult the Bible when they wished to know something about the natural world. If we can trust the philosopher Hans Blumenberg, which I am happy to risk here, during his voyage around the world on the *Beagle* (1831–36) Darwin took with him a Bible in which he had entered the date of Creation

---

[19]   Charles Darwin, *The Origin of Species*, London, John Murray, 6th edn, 1888.

– 23 October 4004 BC, at 9 o'clock in the morning.[20] The astounding thing here is of course the precision of the dating. As Blumenberg writes, it was clearly 'the correct date and time' that mattered to Darwin; after contemplating the entry, Blumenberg concludes: 'Suddenly, it seems, we can see how destructive this pious note was to the many pages that preceded it: the stupendous prize marks the switch to the ultimate loss – partly, and not least, because of the man who had boarded the ship carrying this holy book.'

Chance and necessity

In other words: it was not Darwin and the other naturalists of his day that ousted God from explanations of the diversity of life. It was the Bible-focused natural theologians' excessive claims which, as it were, brought their interpretation to the end of its natural life. Here, it seems, we may learn the general lesson that the cobbler really is well advised to stick to his last. In concrete terms, this means that those who exceed the bounds of, or overtax, their explanatory schemata are likely to get into difficulties (and it would come as no surprise if examples of this are to be found in the pages to come).

Should we wish to highlight one aspect of Darwin's secular interpretation of the history of life, we may point to his efforts to admit of no finality in explaining the diversity of organisms. He was concerned with cause and effect, and in scientific circles his success has left behind the impression that this programme has been implemented with universal success. This is not the case, and this fact has long since put an end to the trinitarian natural sciences in the sphere of the atom (though this often goes unnoticed). As long ago as the days of the Weimar Republic, the atomic physics that goes by the name of quantum mechanics had demonstrated that even an explanation of atomic stability is impossible solely on the basis of causality and that other factors (such as form) are needed; yet this has not yet become general knowledge, and even the experts continue to readily ignore the inadequacy of classical causality.

Darwin himself introduced a second factor. In general terms, we may state that from a history of science perspective his primary achievement was to have made a place for statistical thought within natural science. He is unable to say what exactly the effect of variation and natural selection will be in any given case. However, he can tell us that over the long term animals will adapt to, and have adapted to, their circumstances. In other words: Darwin discovered the universal and far-reaching validity of statistical thought, and gave free rein to chance.

[20]   Hans Blumenberg, *Die Sorge geht über den Fluß*, Frankfurt am Main, Suhrkamp, 1987, p. 47.

Since Darwin's time, the concept of chance has indelibly marked the biological worldview, particularly when, in the form of mutations within the genes, that which cannot be calculated on an individual basis leads to appropriate variations and these can then take up the challenge of natural selection within the struggle for survival. This is the understanding of a life science geared fundamentally towards the idea of evolution. For this science, everything arises from the interplay between *chance and necessity*, as expressed in the title of the famous book, which appeared in 1970, by French Nobel Prize-winner Jacques Monod. Before looking at this in more detail, let us return again briefly to the early nineteenth century, when Monod's compatriot, the zoologist Jean Baptiste Lamarck, became the first to discover what made Darwin famous, namely the variability of species and their adaptation. We mention Lamarck at this point because he discovered evolution not through opposition to religion, but through faith in God.

Lamarck was concerned with fossils, and he compared more than anyone else. In so doing, he was virtually forced to conclude that in the earth's past, when the geological conditions changed, some species died out. This is how we would put it today. But Lamarck saw things differently. He did not believe God capable of first creating species and then allowing them to die out, and he was able to escape this dilemma by assuming that the species had changed. It was through and in evolution itself that God's greatness was revealed. It was by means of this characteristic that He ensured the continuity of the life He had created. Rather than ousting Him, the notion of evolution takes God seriously.

But after this utterly non-secular digression, let us consider Monod's conclusion, intimated above: 'The ancient covenant is in pieces; man knows at last that he is alone in the universe's unfeeling immensity, out of which he emerged only by chance. His destiny is nowhere spelled out, nor is his duty. The kingdom above or the darkness below: it is for him to choose.'[21]

Chance has become the pre-eminent creed of evolutionary biologists, and this is nowhere more apparent than in the work of Ernst Mayr, who died in 2005 at the biblical age of 100. Throughout his life, with a radiant smile and in a state of complete contentment, he proclaimed that our presence in the world is a matter of pure chance, that our existence is no more than a coincidence. That is all. For Mayr, Darwin's idea of an evolutionary provenance and of species' continuous adaptations represents the final secularization of natural science, which can explain, without any act of creation, how life develops over time. As once applied to Laplace, the hypothesis of God is not one that Mayr and his colleagues need, and they seem not to notice the contradiction in which they daily entangle themselves. If, as Mayr and Monod assert, we owe our existence

---

[21]   Jacques Monod, *Chance and Necessity*, London, Penguin, 1971, p. 180.

to chance, then we are unable to investigate it, at least with the tools of natural science. Yet within the framework of evolutionary arguments it is precisely our existence that is under discussion, and simply by subjecting it to discussion in this way, scientists demonstrate that our presence on the earth is more than they claim it to be; more than a chance occurrence.

It is thus no surprise that there are exponents of evolutionary ideas who are far from certain how to deal with the contingency of humankind. The late American paleoanthropologist Stephen Jay Gould,[22] who enjoyed great popularity, expressed his conviction of our chance nature by suggesting that we think of evolution as a film played again from the beginning. He cannot believe that people, exhibiting our behaviour, would once again appear at the end, and he composed a brief text on this subject which 'might be chanted several times a day, like a Hare Krishna mantra, to encourage penetration into the soul':

> Humans are not the end result of predictable evolutionary progress, but rather a fortuitous cosmic afterthought, a tiny little twig on the enormously arborescent bush of life, which, if replanted from seed, would almost surely not grow this twig again, or perhaps any twig with any property that we would care to call consciousness.[23]

He has been contradicted by British evolutionary biologist Simon Conway Morris, who sees less contingency and more convergence in life and its development.[24] Convergence refers to the tendency of organisms, with the aid of mutation and selection, to come up with similar solutions despite quite different points of departure. It is simply not the case that evolution has any number of alternatives at its disposal, so that many routes may lead to the same result

---

[22] There is an anecdote about Stephen Jay Gould which fits neatly with the present topic. He played himself in an episode of the American TV series *The Simpsons* in 1997. Someone had found a fossil at a construction site – that of an angel. Gould the expert was asked whether the discovery was genuine. He conducted a careful analysis, but failed to come to an unequivocal conclusion (the evidence was 'inconclusive'). A minister of the church looking on claps his hands in joy: science has failed yet again, though the religious evidence is so overwhelming. Yet happiness continues to elude the girl who found the fossil; she simply cannot understand how the angel got there. As the episode draws to a close, someone says that from now on religion must keep at least 500 metres away from science.

[23] Stephen Jay Gould, *Dinosaur in a Haystack*, London, Jonathan Cape, 1996, p. 327.

[24] Simon Conway Morris, *Die Konvergenz des Lebens*, in Ernst Peter Fischer and Klaus Wiegandt (eds.), *Evolution – Geschichte und Zukunft des Lebens*, Frankfurt am Main, Fischer Verlag, 2003, pp. 127–46.

(what we could call a goal, if not for the fact that this is a prohibited term in biology). It is not only eyes and other sensory organs that are convergent (developing repeatedly in the same way over the course of evolution), but also an organizational form as complex as agriculture. It is found even among ants. Their 'grain' is a mushroom, which is grown in large subterranean gardens characterized by a complex internal structure, including waste disposal chambers and air vents. On closer inspection, there are striking parallels with our own methods of food production. The mushroom is grown on a bed of leaves (mulch), whose provision is organized in highly complex fashion and which has earned the ants their name: leaf-cutter ants. The ants gather arboreal foliage, bringing their harvest to the nest; intermediate storage sites may be erected along their route. Once the bed of leaves and the mushroom which is to be grown upon it are inside the ants' nest, both are tended constantly to ensure their good health. This includes eradicating weeds, the use of nitrogenous fertilizer (made from anal excretions), herbicides and antibiotics.

According to Conway Morris, it is not a priori nonsense to speak of the inevitability of humankind; even seasoned and recognized evolutionary biologists are beginning to consider whether the laws of nature do in fact involve something like an object or purpose. They are no longer content to reduce everything to random chance.[25] The physicist Wolfgang Pauli pointed out this shortcoming of any biology that proceeds on a trinitarian basis as early as the 1950s; in principle, he expounded the idea of complementarity, according to which there is an alternative to every description of reality, of equal validity, though it appears to contradict the first. Within the context of this idea, propagated especially by Niels Bohr, and also found earlier on in the work of William James, religion and science represent a *pair*, characterized by comprehensive complementarity, though I can do no more than allude to this here. In concrete terms, complementarity means that causality must be paired with another conception of equal status, and chance does not fit the bill. It is too weak. Following C. G. Jung, Pauli proposes the concept of synchronicity, through which events may be linked, even if there is no causal relationship between them. Synchronicity means something like a correspondence of meaning, though I shall not be pursuing this further here as the idea has so far failed to stir the interest of biologists.

The return of the designer

Irrespective of this, it is clear that those who preach chance in order to preclude God merely achieve His return. This is exactly what is happening, and nowhere

---

[25]   Michael Denton, *Nature's Destiny – How the Laws of Nature Reveal Purpose in the Universe*, New York, Free Press, 1999.

more so than in evolutionary biology, in which it is not the overall view of God that is changing, but merely the way in which He is referred to or in which He is incorporated into the development of the world. At present, the godless evolutionary biologists are gnashing their teeth about novel attempts by creationists and other fundamentalists, which show no signs of abating, to overturn the scientific (secular) explanation of life. In recent times, there has been a great deal of fuss about the suggestion that we leave the emergence of species and of human beings to an 'intelligent designer', to which the evolutionary biologists respond, rightly and often very wittily, by pointing to the body's (including the human body's) many organic deficiencies: if we owed our existence to a designer, we should, at best, be reproaching this being for its stupidity and carelessness; the last thing we should do is assert its intelligence.

Many biologists rightly point out that this idea is pre-Darwinist. At the beginning of the nineteenth century, the notion of a designer was still being put forward to prove the existence of God. Imagine, so the argument went, finding a clock during a stroll through the woods. This would immediately lead us to infer the existence of a clockmaker. We can thus be quite certain that there is a maker of human beings, namely God. One problem with such simple arguments is that they always evoke a God with a human consciousness, but it is precisely this which leads to the nonsense with which we are familiar from the jottings in Darwin's on-board Bible.

Anyone wishing to understand the natural world and humankind must proceed differently, and Darwin tried to do so. There is no doubt that his dangerous idea, as it is sometimes known, is also a brilliant idea which enables us to explain a very large number of phenomena of life (perhaps even all of them?) in a convincing and satisfying way in light of adaptation. But there is equally little doubt that careless attempts to trivialize our entire existence as a chance occurrence on this basis must inevitably arouse opposing forces. We are, when all is said and done, living after the *Achsenzeit* or Axial Age, and we are not only in search of laws, but also of a higher purpose and deeper meaning. We engage in both astronomy and astrology,[26] and we must make more of chance than blaming it for our existence 'as a gypsy on the edge of the universe', as Monod puts it.

Evidently – in accordance, as intimated earlier, with the principle of *yin* and *yang*, known and utilized by modern physics in the shape of the idea of complementarity – it is when God has almost disappeared that He returns and makes His presence felt. This applies not only to evolution, but also to cosmology,

---

[26]   Here, 'astrology' does not refer to the shabby 'stars' of the contemporary era, but to the age-old attempt to grasp the meaning of the stars – their *logos* – alongside their laws (astronomy).

which initially stated that the universe made (or entailed) increasingly little sense, following a period during which its capacity to explain it constantly increased. When it was thought that we had understood the beginning of the world itself, in the shape of a big bang for example, some cosmologists noticed that we cannot speak about the development of the cosmos in general – we know only of one world, and that is the one in which we live. The universe cannot be a chance occurrence; it is arranged in such a way that we were able to emerge within it. We are as we are because the world is as it is, as one sometimes reads, and this understanding of the cosmos, anchored in our nature as human beings, reflects what is known as the 'anthropic principle'. In the words of the physicist Freeman Dyson: 'The more I examine the universe and the details of its architecture, the more evidence I find that the universe in some sense must have known we were coming'.[27] This is not to assert that some great hand is fine-tuning the details of the universe, as the strong version of the principle would claim – a version that is vehemently rejected by many physicists but which, nonetheless, refuses to die away and is constantly evoked. The overriding purpose of every endeavour of an anthropic bent is to remove from humankind its chance nature and grant it a meaningful place.

When physicists refer to chance, many people expect to hear about the dice-playing God rejected by Einstein. This God will be putting in a brief appearance here, but only on the understanding that Einstein was concerned with the world on a small rather than a large scale. His remark that he could not imagine a God that plays dice refers not to cosmology but to the new physics of the atom, which was also formulated in his day, with his help. The edifice of quantum mechanics emerging at the time revealed that there are no realities within the innermost core of the world, only probabilities. We are dealing here with contingent possibilities rather than unconditional realities, which surprised Einstein and many others besides, but which he allowed himself to express and which is still keeping the physicists busy. A new twist has now come into play, for which we chiefly have Vienna-based scholar Anton Zeilinger to thank, one which I can do no more than hint at here.[28] An important aspect of the new physics consists in the insight that the natural world has (takes on) the form which we give it, which also implies that it is near-impossible to distinguish between reality and our knowledge of it. Zeilinger suggests that we regard reality and information about it as two sides of the same coin, which means that, in a given situation, our knowledge limits that which may exist. We cannot know everything, which is why individual events appear to occur by chance. This arbitrariness shows that

---

27   Freeman Dyson, *Disturbing the Universe*, New York, Harper & Row, 1979, p. 250.

28   Anton Zeilinger, 'The Message of the Quantum', *Nature*, 438 (8 December 2005), p. 743.

we cannot determine everything. In other words, it shows that, despite all our attempts to impose form, there is in fact something 'out there' that is independent of us. I think Einstein would have liked that idea.

The neutralization of the cosmos

As stated above, with respect to the cosmos, Einstein was merely concerned with the freedom or choice enjoyed by God when He created the world. Having considered this, Einstein felt that it was possible to reflect on the world as a whole (with the famous simultaneous attribution of finiteness and limitlessness), without turning once again to the question of God. God revealed Himself to him not in the cosmos itself, but rather 'in the orderly harmony of what is', and this provoked religious feelings, as is apparent in the loveliest of quotations from his work, from 1932:

> The most beautiful experience we can have is the mysterious. It is the fundamental emotion that stands at the cradle of true art and true science. Whoever does not know it and can no longer wonder, no longer marvel, is as good as dead, and his eyes are dimmed. It was the experience of mystery – even if mixed with fear – that engendered religion. A knowledge of the existence of something we cannot penetrate, our perceptions of the profoundest reason and the most radiant beauty, which only in their most primitive forms are accessible to our minds – it is this knowledge and this emotion that constitute true religiosity; in this sense, and in this alone, I am a deeply religious man. [...] I am satisfied with the mystery of the eternity of life and with the awareness and a glimpse of the marvellous structure of the existing world, together with the devoted striving to comprehend a portion, be it ever so tiny, of the Reason that manifests itself in nature.[29]

Einstein is enchanted by his discoveries, and I have chosen this enchanting word in order to close by considering the famous phrase from Max Weber; in the same year in which Einstein's theory of relativity was being acclaimed, allowing reflection upon the entire world, Weber gave his talk *Science as Vocation* (1919), in which he refers to the 'disenchantment of the world'. This is Weber's way of expressing the process of secularization that typifies the history of technology and thus the rise of modernity as well.

The key term, found in the work of both Weber and Einstein, is the *world*

---

[29]   Albert Einstein, *Ideas and Opinions*, New York, Modern Library, 1994, p. 11.

('what stands out as the opposite of Naught', as Goethe describes 'this clumsy world' in his *Faust*), and secularization – or *Verweltlichung* – has much to do with how this word has been understood over the course of cultural history. An account of how the cosmos and people's experience of the world are connected in Western thought has now been provided by the philosopher of religion Rémi Brague in his book *The Wisdom of the World*.[30] He shows that the term 'world' never stood for a simple description of reality, but has always expressed a value judgement. The cosmos and the meaning of human life were linked in the religious sphere, until the former became ethically neutral as a result of modern science. 'The image of the world that emerged from physics after Copernicus, Galileo and Newton is of a confluence of blind forces, where there is no place for consideration of the Good.'[31] The one world disintegrates into many worlds; ours may perhaps be the best, but it can no longer be a cosmos. In the nineteenth century – 1836 to be precise – the expression 'disenchantment of the world' appears for the first time in this connection, in a text by Alfred de Musset; as a contemporary witness of secularization, he refers to *désenchantement*, and goes so far as to speak of despair (*désespérance*).[32] For Brague, the process of secularization is better described as the 'neutralization of the cosmos',[33] which now lacks a God, but in which there are laws which both constrain our freedom – and to which we are subject – and which make it possible for us to act upon the world. And this human beings have to do, because nature – the world – is no longer Good in the way it used to be, but contains the Bad that causes us to suffer, may do us harm, and which must be combated. It is nonetheless still beautiful, and we remain receptive to that which is beautiful, as is apparent in our aesthetic endeavours. Ultimately, this demonstrates 'that, without having a permanent dwelling in the world, we are not purely strangers in it; we are guests'.[34] Not on earth for ever, but guests. This may be the most appealing consequence of secularization.

Once again: fear

The fear remains. It is part of us, as I have intimated, and anyone who can combat or soothe it will find followers. First it was religion that enjoyed success, then science. Through action guided by understanding, it could protect us from the dangers of the natural world. It is less capable of protecting us against the dangers which it itself produces – nuclear bombs being a prime example – or

[30]   Rémi Brague, *The Wisdom of the World*, Chicago, University of Chicago Press, 2003.

[31]   Brague, *The Wisdom of the World*, p. 185.

[32]   Quoted in Brague, *The Wisdom of the World*, p. 261, n. 71.

[33]   Brague, *The Wisdom of the World*, p. 194.

[34]   Brague, *The Wisdom of the World*, p. 224.

which arise through the use of the products of technology on a huge scale, with environmental destruction prominent among them. 'Science doesn't tremble', we have heard. But science may cause us to tremble in fear. It may be that this will cease only if it gives up or reduces its original claim to power. The aim cannot only be to attain mastery over nature 'as a result of long, laboriously accumulated experience', as Alexander von Humboldt put it. It must also be to witness it 'from within' as 'a harmoniously ordered whole'. Then we sense God in the world, and with this we cease to tremble.

9

The Religious Situation in Europe

José Casanova

This essay is divided into three parts. First, I offer a very general and therefore somewhat superficial overview of the contemporary religious situation in Europe. In the second part, I offer a series of arguments why the paradigm of secularization is not very helpful in trying to explain the complex religious situation in Europe today, and why we need to look at the secularization of Western European societies with new eyes and with new perspectives, which can only come from a more comparative historical and global perspective. Finally, I offer some suggestions as to why the expectation that religion would become increasingly privatized and therefore socially irrelevant has not proven to be correct and why, on the contrary, we are now witnessing the fact that religion is once again becoming an important public issue in Europe.

Overview of the religious situation in Europe

First of all, it is important to emphasize that there is not one single and uniform religious situation in Europe. There are multiple, very diverse and ambiguous religious situations and trends throughout Europe which one should avoid characterizing in simple terms. I can only indicate here some of the most obvious differences. Former East Germany is by far and by any measure the least religious country of all of Europe, followed at a long distance by the Czech Republic and the Scandinavian countries. At the other extreme, Ireland and Poland are by far the most religious countries of Europe with rates comparable to those of the United States. In general, with the significant exceptions of France and the Czech Republic, Catholic countries tend to be more religious than Protestant or mixed countries (former West Germany, Netherlands), although Switzerland (a mixed and traditionally polarized country comparable to Holland) stands at the high end of the European religious scale, with rates of belief similar to those of Catholic Austria and Spain and with rates of participation and confessional affiliation similar to Poland and Ireland. In general, former communist countries in East and Central Europe, with the exception of Poland and Slovakia, have rates of religiosity lower than the European mean average, a position occupied by Britain and former West Germany. But many of the former communist countries, most notably Russia, and even more so Ukraine, which does not appear in this survey, have experienced remarkable religious growth since 1989.

In order to understand the complexity of the religious situation in Europe, it is helpful to distinguish between three different levels of analysis, namely religion at the level of individual religiosity, religion at the participatory associational level of religious communities, and religion at the confessional level of affiliation, identification or membership in churches or in imagined religious communities.

Individual religiosity

With the exception of former East Germany, where only one fourth of the population believes in God, and the Czech Republic, where the number of believers is less than 50 per cent, the majority of Europeans in every other country still affirm 'belief in God' (see Table 1). Former East Germany is actually the only country of Europe in which a majority of the population, 51 per cent, confesses to be atheist. The Czech Republic is the European country with the second highest number of atheists, but the proportion is significantly lower, reaching only 20 per cent. In any case, the range of belief and unbelief in Europe is significantly wide. At the high end, over 90 per cent of the population in Poland, Ireland and Portugal declare themselves believers. In the Scandinavian countries, France, the Netherlands and Russia, the number of believers drops to a percentage in the 50s. Britain and former West Germany, with 69 and 65 per cent respectively, occupy the European middle. But the number of those who believe in a Judaeo-Christian personal God is much lower, dropping on the average over 20 percentage points in each country.

Somewhat surprisingly, the number of those who pray several times a month and, even more so, the number of those who believe in religious miracles are in many countries higher than the number of those who believe in a 'God who is concerned'. As was to be expected, the number of those who claim to have had a personal religious experience is much lower still, but the range of variation between the most and the least 'religiously musical' populations of Europe is much smaller. Former East Germany is once again at the very bottom. Only 10 per cent of its population claims to have had some deep personal religious experience or the experience of religious transcendence. But surprisingly, this figure is not so distant from that in the majority of European countries, or even in such supposedly 'religious' countries as Ireland or Poland, where only 13 and 16 per cent respectively claim to have had a personal religious experience.

Arguably, Italy, 31 per cent of whose population claim to have had a religious experience, is the country with the most 'religiously musical' population of all

Table 1.   *Belief in God in Europe (%)*

Country	Belief in God	Theist	Not atheist or agnostic	Belief in a God who is concerned	Pray several times a month	Belief in religious miracles	Personal religious experience	Atheist
Cyprus	96	85	96	71	55	89	10	1
Republic of Ireland	95	80	95	76	84	72	13	2
Poland	94	78	94	73	79	60	16	2
N. Ireland	92	79	93	73	70	68	26	3
Portugal	91	78	95	74	62	79		2
Italy	86	73	91	56	65	69	31	4
Spain	82	65	85	44	48	46	19	9
Austria	80	52	87	41	51	65	17	6
Switzerland	73	45	83	49	52	60	23	4
Slovakia	72	57	80	57	52	53	26	11
Latvia	71	39	80	46	35	35	15	9
Britain	69	50	76	37	37	42	16	10
Former W. Germany	65	45	78	37	41	39	16	11
Hungary	65	51	75	29	37	30	17	13
Slovenia	62	39	73	27	32	53	15	17
Bulgaria	60	35	75	37	26	29	16	17
Norway	59	44	77	36	29	40	16	10
Netherlands	57	42	70	32	39	37	22	17
Denmark	57	34	70	38	21	25	15	15
Sweden	54	26	65	23	20	27	12	17
France	52	39	63	29	30	37	24	19
Russia	52	32	63	29	18	38	13	19
Czech Republic	46	31	66	23	26	32	11	20
Former E. Germany	25	17	36	14	14	39	10	51

Andrew Greeley, *Religion in Europe at the End of the Second Millennium*, New Brunswick, NJ, Transaction Publishers, 2003, p. 3.

Europe. Only in five other European countries does the proportion of those who claim a similar religious experience surpass 20 per cent. Surprisingly, in this small group of countries with the highest level of experiential individual religiosity, one finds France with 24 per cent and the Netherlands with 22 per cent, two countries that in every other respect are supposedly among the most

Table 2. *Percentage claiming no religious affiliation by country and year*

Country	1991	1998	Second generation with no religious affiliation	Loss of religious affiliation since childhood
W. Germany	11 %	15 %	4 %	9 %
E. Germany	64 %	68 %	48 %	46 %
Britain	33 %	45 %	9 %	33 %
N. Ireland	9 %	10 %	1 %	1 %
Austria	10 %	12 %	2 %	8 %
Hungary	5 %	27 %	9 %	11 %
Italy	6 %	8 %	7 %	−1 %
Republic of Ireland	2 %	6 %	0	6 %
Netherlands	55 %	58 %	22 %	43 %
Norway	6 %	10 %	3 %	6 %
Sweden		29 %	9 %	15 %
Czech Republic		45 %	33 %	5 %
Slovenia	11 %	24 %	13 %	10 %
Poland	3 %	6 %	5 %	5 %
Bulgaria	13 %	13 %	10 %	−7 %
Russia	68 %	35 %	31 %	−40 %
Spain		14 %	2 %	10 %
Latvia		36 %	26 %	4 %
Slovakia		16 %	10 %	2 %
France		47 %	14 %	31 %
Cyprus		0 %	0	0
Portugal		8 %	1 %	6 %
Denmark		12 %	4 %	2 %
Switzerland		9 %	2 %	3 %
Total		23 %	11 %	15 %

Greeley, *Religion in Europe*, p. 56.

secularized of Europe. In any case, both percentages are still higher than the number of professed atheists in both countries, which are respectively 19 and 17 per cent of the French and Dutch populations. Former West Germany and Britain occupy again the European middle ground; 16 per cent of their population claim to have had a religious experience, while those who declare themselves atheists are respectively 11 and 10 per cent.

In summary one may say that although a majority of the population in most European countries still maintains some kind of general belief in God, the depth and extent of individual religiosity in Europe is rather low in so far as those who profess belief in a personal God, those who pray with some regularity and those who claim to have had some personal religious experience are a small minority in most European countries. In this respect, unlike in the United States where one finds high levels of individual religiosity even among the unchurched, a majority of the population in most European countries can be characterized as simply secular and non-religious. On the other hand, majorities of people in most European countries, with the exception of former communist countries and Denmark, believe in 'life after death' and this belief actually appears to have increased in the last decades among the younger cohorts, arguably a clear indication of strong hope for transcendence even in secularized Europe.

Participation in collective congregational religion

Evidence of the drastic secularization, or at least of the 'Entkirchlichung' (unchurching), of most European societies is more pronounced when one looks at rates of regular church attendance, at least two or three times per month, and at the proportion of those who claim never to attend church (see Tables 3 and 4). Only in three European countries, Ireland, Poland and Switzerland, do the majority of the population claim to attend church regularly. Less than 20 per cent of the population in the majority of European countries attends church regularly, while in former East Germany, Russia and the Scandinavian countries the proportion of regular churchgoers decreases to the single digits. Inversely, the proportion of those who never attend is less than 10 per cent in Poland, Ireland, Switzerland and Portugal, while it is 50 per cent or more in ascending order in France, Britain, Russia, the Netherlands and former East Germany.

This is probably the indicator of religiosity that has experienced the most drastic and dramatic decline throughout most European societies since the 1950s. There are, however, very significant differences in church attendance between Protestants and Catholics, Orthodox Christians and Muslims in Europe (see Table 5). Catholics have the highest level of regular church attendance (43 per cent) and the lowest proportion of those who never attend (12 per cent), while Orthodox Christians have the lowest proportion of regular churchgoers (only 8 per cent) and a significantly high proportion of those who never attend (25 per cent). Among Protestants the two figures are very close: 25 per cent attend regularly and 21 per cent never attend. European Muslims have very high rates of mosque attendance (40 per cent), as well as the highest proportion of those who never attend (29 per cent), which is understandable since attendance at Friday prayers is not a traditional religious obligation for Muslims, although it is becoming increasingly customary.

The data on drastic decline in church attendance across Europe constitute the strongest evidence for the defenders of the traditional theory of secularization.

Table 3. *Church attendance by study and year:*
two or three times a month or more (%)

	EVS 1981	EVS 1990	ISSP 1991	ISSP 1998
W. Germany/Former W. Germany	19	18	15	17
E. Germany/Former E. Germany			4	(flawed)
Britain	14	14	17	17
N. Ireland	51	50	56	51
Austria			26	33**
Hungary	11	21**	19	20
Italy	32	38**	49	44*
Ireland	82	81	75	73
Netherlands	25	20*	21	18
Norway	5	5	10	7
Sweden	6	6		8
Czech Republic				12
Slovenia				23
Poland			67	61*
Russia			5	5
Spain	40	29*		36
Latvia				12
Slovakia				41
France	10	10		13
Cyprus				8
Portugal				41
Denmark	2	2		7
Switzerland				64

Greeley, *Religion in Europe*, p. 70.

EVS = European Values Study

ISSP = International Social Survey Programme

Greeley characterizes the East Germany 1991 ISSP response as 'flawed', because 'those collecting data from East Germany asked attendance figures only from those who reported a church affiliation in 1998, gratuitously assuming that those with no affiliation never went to church – *even though data from the 1991 survey indicated that some of them did*. They also broke the International Social Survey Program rule that repeat questions must be asked the same way at both points in time *and* the rule that no country in the project may unilaterally change question wordings' (Greeley. *Religion in Europe*, p. 73).

One asterisk indicates significant decreases in church attendance (at least five percentage points) from one survey to the next. Two asterisks indicate significant increases in church attendance from one survey to the next.

Table 4. *Church attendance by study and year: percentage never attending*

	EVS 1991	EVS 1998	ISSP 1991	ISSP 1998
W. Germany	23 %	23 %	21 %	20 %
E. Germany			60 %	flawed
Britain	48 %	47 %	36 %	54 %*
N. Ireland	12 %	13 %	14 %	24 %*
Austria			21 %	20 %
Hungary	51 %		32 %	30 %
Italy	22 %	16 %**	13 %	19 %*
Ireland	4 %	4 %	5 %	5 %
Netherlands	41 %	43 %	54 %	60 %
Norway	38 %	40 %	34 %	34 %
Sweden	38 %	48 %		28 %
Czech				48 %
Slovenia				30 %
Poland			3 %	4 %
Russia			67 %	55 %**
Spain	26 %	30 %*		20 %
Latvia				33 %
Slovakia				24 %
France	59 %	52 %**		50 %
Cyprus				15 %
Portugal				8 %
Denmark	45 %	44 %		29 %
Switzerland				5 %

Greeley, *Religion in Europe*, p. 71.
EVS = European Values Study
ISSP = International Social Survey Programme

Table 5. *Church attendance by religion*

	% attending two or three times a month	% never attending
Protestant	25 %	21 %
Catholic	43 %	12 %
Orthodox	8 %	25 %
Islam	40 %	29 %
None	2 %	75 %

Greeley, *Religion in Europe*, p. 72.

When compared with the very different evidence of continuing vitality in congregational, associational religion in the United States across all denominations – Protestant and Catholic, Jewish and Muslim, and now Hindu and Buddhist – it is evident that this is the fundamental difference between American and European Christianity. The voluntary associational congregation, as Tocqueville already saw clearly in the 1830s, forms the basis of the competitive system of American denominationalism, and is the foundation of the generalized and vibrant associationalism of American civil society. European Christianity, for all kinds of reasons, never made the full historical transition from territorial national churches based on the territorial parish or *Pfarrgemeinde* to competing denominations of civil society based on voluntary religious congregations, the model of the modern *Gemeinschaft*. Even in Great Britain, the European country closest to the United States in this respect, the vibrant system of religious congregations that existed within both churches and sects, across England, Scotland and Wales, basically collapsed in the 1960s, contributing to what Callum G. Brown has dramatically characterized as 'the death of Christian Britain'.

It is not processes of modernization and urbanization that explain this collapse, since British Christianity, like American Christianity, had already made a successful transition to modern, urban industrial centres by the end of the nineteenth century. Thus, as long as we continue perceiving the process of Christian European secularization as a slow, accumulative and progressive process of decline that accompanies general processes of modernization, we will fail to seek a more persuasive explanation for the drastic secularization of Western European societies since the 1960s. Along with the Netherlands, Britain presents perhaps the most dramatic example of a relatively sudden and precipitous decline of church attendance as well as of church affiliation, in contrast to the Scandinavian countries and former West Germany, which still preserve a relatively high level of church affiliation, along with very low church attendance. The high percentage of those who have lost their religious affiliation since childhood, 43 per cent in the case of the Netherlands and 33 per cent in the case of Britain, which are comparable to the high figures of the highly secularized former East Germany (46 per cent) and France (31 per cent), are evidence that the collapse was almost a single-generation phenomenon (see Table 2). But in the case of former East Germany, as also in the case of the Czech Republic, one encounters a second generation without religious unaffiliation to add to the large numbers of the previous generation brought up with no religious affiliation: 48 per cent of former East Germans and 33 per cent of Czechs. Along with France, former East Germany and the Czech Republic are the most secular of all European societies. These are the countries in which religion as a chain of collective memory is clearly disappearing. But it should be obvious that in all three cases these processes of secularization cannot be understood simply in terms of processes of modernization, but should rather be viewed in terms of the particular historical dynamics of state, church and nation. I assume few people would be inclined to attribute the higher levels of secularization of former East Germany, compared with those of former West Germany, to the fact that former East Germany is a more modern society, unless of course one is willing to argue that secularity itself is evidence of modernity.

Indeed, in order to understand the significant internal variations in patterns of secularization throughout Europe, not only between former East and West Germany, but also among other European societies which are similar in many other respects – for instance between Poland and the Czech Republic (two similar Slavic East European Soviet-type Catholic societies), or between France and Italy (two similarly modern Latin Catholic societies), or between the Netherlands and Switzerland (two highly modern bi-confessional Calvinist-Catholic societies) – it should be obvious that one should look less at levels of modernization, which explain very little, and more at historical patterns of relations between church, state, nation, and civil society.

Imagined communities: national churches, confessional states and secular civil religions

Grace Davie has characterized the contemporary European pattern of relatively high levels of individual religious belief in combination with relatively low levels of church attendance as 'believing without belonging'.[1] But the inverse pattern, namely high levels of confessional affiliation with low levels of belief and/or participation (which has been characterized by Danièle Hervieu-Léger as 'belonging without believing'),[2] is equally widespread across Europe. The Lutheran Scandinavian countries are the most dramatic illustration of this pattern, but in some respects it is also typical of former West Germany. The Scandinavian countries evince the lowest levels of church attendance in Europe, comparable only with former East Germany. Only 2 per cent of Danes, 5 per cent of Norwegians and 6 per cent of Swedes attend church with some regularity. The levels of individual belief in God, just a slight majority of the population, and of occasional prayer (in the 20 per cent range), are also among the lowest in Western European societies, comparable with those in the Czech Republic and France. Yet the Scandinavian countries show surprisingly high levels of religious

---

[1]   Grace Davie, *Religion in Modern Europe: A Memory Mutates*, Oxford, Oxford University Press, 2000, p. 3.

[2]   Danièle Hervieu-Léger, *Religion as a Chain of Memory*, New Brunswick, NJ, Rutgers University Press, 2000.

affiliation, when measured by the small proportions of those who declare no religious affiliation, which are similar to the proportions one finds in much more religious Catholic countries (Italy, Portugal, Austria, Spain) or in more religious mixed countries (Switzerland or former West Germany). Only 10 per cent of Norwegians and 12 per cent of Danes declare no religious affiliation. Curiously, the number of professed atheists in Denmark is higher (17 per cent), implying that close to one third of Danish atheists still view themselves as members of the Danish Lutheran Church. The percentage of Swedes with no religious affiliation is much higher (29 per cent), but still significantly lower than the percentages in Britain (45 per cent), France (47 per cent) and the Netherlands (55 per cent). In short, the overwhelming majority of Scandinavians consider themselves members of their national churches, despite the fact that many of them have no religious beliefs and practically never attend church.

This is the phenomenon that Grace Davie has aptly characterized as 'vicarious' religion,[3] namely the notion that religion is performed by an active minority on behalf of the wider population, who implicitly not only understand but approve of what the minority is doing. Church leaders and churchgoers, the 'religiously musical' as it were, perform rituals as well as actually believing on behalf of others. Moreover, national churches are still viewed as public goods to which every citizen should have the right of access, when occasionally needed, for high festivities, rites of passage and especially in times of national crisis or disaster. This is particularly the case in the Scandinavian countries or in former West Germany, countries in which a majority of the population still voluntarily pay a relatively high church tax. But the same pattern of strong identification and low participation is found across Orthodox societies. The Catholic pattern is more mixed. One finds, on the one hand, the paradigmatic pattern of Poland and Ireland that combines very high identification with the national church along with very high participation. On the other hand, there is the Latin pattern, exemplified by France and Spain, in which the Catholic church itself becomes not so much the symbolic institution of national integration confronting an illegitimate foreign state, but actually the institution allied with an illegitimate national state and thus the catalyst of a profound national cleavage between embattled and highly mobilized clerical and anti-clerical national camps. Other Catholic societies fall somewhere in between the two extremes, while Italy actually partakes of both. Due to the particular belated process of national unification and the role first of the Papal States and then of the Vatican, some regions of Italy retain a resemblance to the Irish-Polish model, while others are closer to the Latin model.

Even these few references to various national patterns should serve to illustrate

---

[3]   Davie, *Religion in Modern Europe*, pp. 36–81.

the fact that the variations in levels of religiosity across Europe can be explained better in terms of the very diverse and historically changing patterns of fusion and dissolution of religious, political and national communities, that is, of the imagined communities of church, state and nation, than in terms of indices and levels of modernization, that is, of socio-economic development, or of levels of urbanization, education, and so on. Nonetheless, there is also a strong correlation between levels of modernization and levels of secularization. That is, some – but not all – of the most secularized countries of Europe are also among the most modern. This explains the tendency of the secularization theory to explain patterns of secularization in terms of levels of modernization, as if secularization necessarily followed modernization, in the sense that modernization itself is the cause or precipitator of secularization. Such an assumption, which is already problematic in terms of the internal variations we have examined within Europe, becomes even more untenable the moment one adopts a global comparative perspective.

European secularization from a global comparative perspective

From a global comparative perspective it is becoming increasingly evident that European patterns of secularization are exceptional, rather than being the model that other societies are likely to resemble as they modernize. There has been an extraordinary reversal in the debates on secularization in the last decade. Until very recently, most discussions of secularization had assumed that European religious developments were typically or paradigmatically modern, while the persistence of religion in modern America was attributed to American 'exceptionalism'. America was the exception that confirmed the European rule, a convenient way of not having to put into question the European rule. Progressive religious decline was so much taken for granted that what required an explanation was the American 'deviation' from the European 'norm'.

Under conditions of globalization it has become increasingly evident that the Eurocentric view that modern Western European developments, including the secularization of Western Christianity, are general universal processes is no longer tenable. The more one adopts a global perspective, the more it becomes obvious that the drastic secularization of Western European societies is a rather exceptional phenomenon, with few parallels elsewhere other than in European settler societies such as New Zealand, Quebec or Uruguay. The collapse of the moral authority and of the plausibility structures of some of the national Christian churches in Europe is so extraordinary that we need a better explanation than simply referring to general processes of modernization. By offering a pseudo-general explanation of a particular historical development, we impede the possibility of developing a more convincing explanation of what is indeed a truly significant and undeniable phenomenon, namely the increasing secularization of many Western European societies since the late 1950s.

But the alternative theory being promoted by American sociologists of religion is also rather unpersuasive. It turns the American paradigm of free competitive religious markets into a general rule, claiming that free religious markets in and of themselves are the independent variable and the primary explanatory key to religious growth and vitality everywhere. Consequently, the theory explains the secularization of European societies as the result of monopolistic or oligopolistic religious markets. But the American paradigm of free religious markets is also unable to explain the internal variations of religious vitality within Europe; for instance, the persistence of high religiosity under monopolistic conditions in Poland and Ireland, or the drastic decline in religiosity under relatively free and competitive conditions in Wales or in other parts of Britain. In my view, the American paradigm cannot even offer a very convincing explanation of the peculiar and rather exceptional system of American denominationalism. Instead of offering a comparative historical explanation, it tries to generalize its valid insights concerning American religious patterns into a universal theory of religious markets.

There is a sense in which both European secular developments and American religious developments are unique and exceptional. In this respect, one could certainly talk, as Europeans have done for decades, of 'American exceptionalism', or one could talk, as has become fashionable today, of 'European exceptionalism'. But both characterizations are highly problematic, if it is implied, as it was in the past, that America was the exception to the European rule of secularization, or if it is implied, as it often is today, that secular Europe is the exception to some global trend of religious revival. When it comes to religion, there is no global rule. All world religions are being transformed radically today, as they were throughout the era of European colonial expansion, by processes of modernization and globalization. But they are being transformed in diverse and manifold ways.

Analytically, therefore, there can be no substitute for serious comparative historical analysis. One should begin by recognizing and exploring the multiple and diverse patterns of secularization within Western European Christianity. Only then can one proceed with the task of contrasting these Western European Christian developments with other non-Western, non-European, or non-Christian developments. This essay is obviously not the place to attempt such a gigantic task. This is rather the task collectively addressed by the contributors to this volume, and by the conference in which it originated, with the kind of accumulated historical, civilizational and interdisciplinary expertise which no single scholar could possibly dream of achieving. I would only like to stress, against the simplifications of my own discipline, sociology, that we can only hope to make sense of the complex religious situation of Europe today by freeing ourselves from the assumptions of the traditional theory of secularization and by looking at the European experience of secularization with fresh eyes and with a comparative, historical and global perspective.

Let me simply offer a series of programmatic statements in this respect:

a) It has been generally recognized that the historical patterns of secularization in Western Europe are themselves somehow related to internal dynamics of institutionalization and transformation of Western European Christianity. At the very least, one must recognize that the category of the *saeculum* itself is a medieval Christian theological category, which itself served to structure the discourse and the institutional dynamics of European Christendom first and of European secularization later. Such recognition is important, irrespective of whether one sees the dynamic of secularization as the internal transformation or transvaluation of Christian theological categories into secular realities or alternatively one sees the dynamic patterns of secularization as the triumphal and legitimate emancipation of these secular realities from theological and ecclesiastical control. I am not interested at this point in evaluating the greater or lesser validity of the competing perspectives, Hegelian, Nietzschean, Weberian, Schmittian, Parsonian, Voltairian, Comtean, Blumenbergian or Habermasian, but simply to point to the particular Christian–*saecular* dynamic. Other world religions and other axial civilizations had different patterns of institutionalization or dynamic tensions between religion and world, or between immanence and transcendence.

b) By referring to Western Christendom, I want to emphasize that such a dynamic of secularization is not a dynamic intrinsic to Christianity as a religion, or to the Judaeo-Christian tradition, whatever this may mean, or to some Judaeo-Christian-Graeco-Roman synthesis, since one cannot find such a dynamic in older Eastern forms of Christianity (Alexandrian, Antiochean, Byzantine, etc.) which could claim a deeper continuity with more primitive forms of Christianity or with the Graeco-Roman civilization. Socio-historically speaking, Western Christendom only became institutionalized in the eleventh century with what Harold Berman has analysed as the 'papal revolution'.[4] This means that it is a dynamic intrinsic to Latin, but not to Eastern Orthodox, Christendom. The Investiture Conflicts are the manifestation and crystallization of this particular dynamic tension, which will repeat itself in other secular spheres, such as in the

---

[4]   Harold Berman, *Law and Revolution: The Formation of the Western Legal Tradition*, Cambridge, MA, Harvard University Press, 1983.

medieval universities, and in economic ethical debates. One does not encounter such dynamic tensions or conflicts in Eastern Christianity.

c) If the institutional, theological and discursive legacy of medieval Christendom is shared by all Western European, i.e. Catholic and Protestant, societies, internally the dissolution of the system of medieval Christendom associated both with the Protestant Reformation and with the emergence of the European system of sovereign territorial states will serve to open up new multiple and diverse patterns of secularization across Western Europe. Here, one can fortunately build upon the classic comparative analysis initiated by David Martin in his *General Theory of Secularization*.[5] Protestantism itself in its various confessional forms, diverse patterns of state formation, diverse patterns of state–church–sect relations, and the ensuing religious markets (monopoly, duopoly, pluralist, etc.) are some of the independent variables which contribute in manifold ways to diverse patterns of secularization across Europe.

d) To this one should add, again following David Martin, the crucial relevance of the Enlightenment and of the various socio-political and ideological-cultural movements deriving from it. It is, however, imperative to view the Enlightenment not as a single and uniform movement but as multiple and diverse movements. In its relation to new patterns of secularization, it is important to distinguish at least between the British, French and American Enlightenments as well as to distinguish the related yet separate and long-lasting tradition of the German *Aufklärung* as it became institutionalized in German philosophy and theology and in the *Geisteswissenschaften*.

Nevertheless, one could argue that what makes the general European situation unique and exceptional when compared with the rest of the world is precisely the triumph of secularism as a teleological theory of religious development that has its origins in the Enlightenment critique of religion. The ideological critique of religion developed by the Enlightenment and carried out by a series of social movements throughout Europe from the eighteenth to the twentieth century has informed European theories of secularization in such a way that those theories have come to function not only as descriptive theories of social processes, but also and more significantly as critical-genealogical theories of religion and as normative-teleological theories of religious development that presupposed religious decline as the telos of history.

Three dimensions of the Enlightenment critique of religion were particularly relevant: the cognitive critique of religion as a primitive, pre-rational worldview to be superseded by the advancement of science and rational thought; the political

---

[5]   David Martin, *A General Theory of Secularization*, New York, Harper & Row, 1978.

critique of ecclesiastical religion as a conspiracy of rulers and priests to keep the people ignorant and oppressed, a condition to be superseded by the advancement of popular sovereignty and democratic freedoms; and the humanist critique of the very idea of God as human self-alienation and as a self-denying other-worldly projection of human aspirations and desires, a critique which postulated the death of God as the premise of human emancipation. Although the prominence and pertinence of each of these three critiques may have changed from country to country, each of them in various degrees came to inform modern European social movements, the political parties associated with them and European theories of secularization.

In this respect, theories of secularization in Europe have functioned as self-fulfilling prophecies to the extent to which a majority of the population in Europe came to accept the premises of those theories as a depiction of the normal state of affairs and as a projection of future developments. The premise that the more modern and progressive a society becomes the more religion tends to decline assumed in Europe the character of a taken-for-granted belief widely shared not only by sociologists of religion but by a majority of the population. The postulate of progressive religious decline has become part of the European definition of the modern situation, with real consequences for church religiosity.

In my view, this is one of the key factors in explaining the drastic and precipitous decline of religious practices in post-Second World War Europe, a decline that should not be understood as simply the final cumulative effect of a long-term process of progressive decline correlated with processes of modernization. The forced secularization from above instituted by communist regimes is an altogether different phenomenon, although the Marxian critique of religion is of course itself closely related to the Enlightenment critique. The other equally influential factor was probably the institutionalization of welfare states across Western Europe, insofar as these entailed a transference of collective identification from the imagined community of the national church, or of the confessional community in multi-confessional contexts, to the imagined community of the nation-state. This is perhaps the most plausible explanation for the two most dramatic cases of decline, namely Britain and the Netherlands. In the case of Britain we have a clear transference of identification from the churches of England, Scotland and Wales to the United Kingdom. In Holland the drastic secularization is undoubtedly related to the collapse of the polarized secular/religious multi-confessional life-worlds. Though perhaps less dramatically, the same process took place in former West Germany. Outside Europe, Quebec offers equally dramatic evidence of this transference from the Catholic Church as the traditional carrier of Quebecois national identity to modern secular separatist nationalism. The cantonal structure of Switzerland and to a certain extent its neutrality and somewhat provincial isolation from the rest of Europe have probably protected the Swiss churches from similar secularizing consequences.

The culture of the 1960s itself and the critique of all types of institutional authority, as a general global modern phenomemon, was probably an additional crucial contributing factor to the drastic processes of European secularization. But it is instructive to compare the different effects that similar processes had in secular Europe and in religious America. All the processes and movements of the 1960s – the counter-culture, the student rebellion, the revolution in gender/sexual roles and norms – were certainly as radical and, probably, even more anti-establishment in puritan Protestant America than anywhere in Europe. The close association of those movements with the anti-Vietnam War movement and with the Civil Rights and Black Power movements makes the 1960s one of the most radical and transformative decades in the history of the United States, comparable only to the Revolution and War of Independence and to the Abolition movement and the Civil War. Yet, as so often happens in American history, all these movements were intimately associated with and even carried by religious movements and groups. Unlike in Europe, where such movements contributed to further secularization, in the United States they contributed not so much to secularization as to a new radical transformation of American religion, which has been likened to a new Great Awakening. To exemplify this one only needs to enumerate the explosion of new religious movements of all kinds, the proliferation of 'invisible religions' of self-expression and self-realization along with the triumph of the therapeutic and the institutional professionalization of all kinds of pastoral care of the soul, the dimensions of the New Age movement, the increasing Islamization of the African-American community along with the incorporation of immigrant Islam as an American religion, the Protestantification of American Latinos and the Latin Americanization of American Catholicism, the increasing presence of immigrant Buddhism and immigrant Hinduism as parts of the normal American religious environment, and of course the public re-emergence and the public mobilization of Protestant fundamentalism.

By the end of the twentieth century, an increasing number of Americans, roughly 20 per cent, had rejected organized 'religion', but not by converting to secularity as in Europe, but rather in the name of a broader, more eclectic and more ecumenical 'spirituality' which is supposed to offer a surer and more authentic path to the inner self and to the sacred. It is a movement from 'denomination' to 'individual mysticism', not to irreligion. This fifth of the population forms the new self-denominational category of 'spiritual but not religious'. One can safely assume, moreover, that an even larger number of Americans experience similar spiritual journeys while still belonging to traditional denominations or by joining all kinds of new religious communities. Not accidentally, the 'baby boomers' have been rightly characterized as a generation of 'seekers' who have brought a further vanishing of the boundaries between religion, spirituality and secularity within as well as outside religious denominations. Such a phenomenon has actually always been somewhat typical of American religion. Indeed, it has led many European observers and defenders of the theory of secularization to dismiss the phenomenon of American religious vitality as irrelevant and as invalid counter-evidence to their theory, because by their European ecclesiastical standards it is no longer 'authentic' religion.

It is true that similar religious trends have existed throughout Western Europe since the 1960s, with new processes of religious individuation, as well as new 'invisible religions' of self-expression: the same new religious movements and cults, the presence of Eastern religious traditions and spiritualities, the New Age and reinvented pagan religions. Moreover, institutional religion in Europe, Catholic as well as Protestant, is also in flux and in motion. As Danièle Hervieu-Léger has shown, 'the pilgrim' and 'the convert' are also prominent 'seekers' in the European religious landscape.[6] Yet all these religious phenomena have a much weaker presence and public resonance in Europe than in the USA. A majority of Europeans have converted to modern secularity and tend to look down upon those who are still, or newly, religious. There is an element of at least implicit conversion in the process of secularization insofar as it is a conversion to modernity, the will to be modern enlightened Europeans. In this respect, it entails the semi-conscious affirmation of secularity and the abandonment of traditional religion as something that modern mature Europeans have overcome and outgrown.

This is in my view the explanatory key in accounting for the exceptional character of European secularization. It also explains why churches and ecclesiastical institutions, once they ceded to the secular nation-state their traditional historical function as community cults, that is, as collective representations of the imagined national communities and carriers of the collective memory, also lost in the process their ability to function as religions of individual salvation. Crucial is the fact that individuals in Europe, once they lose faith in their national churches, do not bother to look for, or actually look disdainfully upon, alternative salvation religions. In a certain sense, the explanation lies in the fact that Europeans continue to be implicit members of their national churches even after explicitly breaking away from them. It is this peculiar situation that explains the lack of religious demand and the absence of a truly competitive religious market in Europe. The culprit is not so much the monopolistic laziness of the churches protected by state regulation, as the American supply-side theory of religion tends to argue, but the lack of demand for alternative salvation religions among

---

[6]   Danièle Hervieu-Léger, *Le pèlerin et le converti. La religion en mouvement*, Paris, Flammarion, 1999.

the unchurched, even in the face of new enterprising yet generally unsuccessful religious suppliers.

A post-secular Europe? The return of religion to the public sphere of European societies

If my interpretation is correct, it would explain why religion has again become a contested public issue in Europe. It is perhaps premature to speak of a post-secular Europe, but certainly one can sense a significant shift in the European *Zeitgeist*. This volume and the conference from which it emanates are themselves indications of new currents in intellectual and public opinion. When, over a decade ago, I first developed the thesis of the de-privatization of religion as a new global trend, the thesis did not find much resonance in many parts of Europe, certainly not in Germany. The privatization of religion was simply taken too much for granted both as a normal empirical fact and actually as the norm for modern European societies. The concept of modern public religions was still too dissonant and religious revivals elsewhere could simply be explained, or rather explained away, as the rise of fundamentalism. But in the last years, there has been a noticeable change in attitude and attention throughout Europe. Even Jürgen Habermas speaks now of 'religion in the public sphere',[7] and every other week one learns of a new conference or of the establishment of a newly funded research project on 'religion and politics' or on 'religion and violence' or on 'conflict and dialogue' between the world religions.

The terrorist attacks of 11 September 2001 and the resonance of the discourse of the clash of civilizations have certainly played an important role in focusing European attention on issues of religion. But it would be a serious error to attribute this new attention solely or even mainly to the rise of Islamic fundamentalism and the threats and challenges which it poses to the West and particularly to Europe. Internal European transformations have also contributed to the new public interest in religion. General processes of globalization, the global growth of transnational migration and the very process of European integration are presenting crucial challenges not only to the European model of the national welfare state, but also to the different kinds of religious–secular and church–state settlements that the various European countries had achieved in post-Second World War Europe.

The process of European integration, the eastward expansion of the European Union and the drafting of a European constitution have triggered fundamental questions concerning both national and European identities and the

---

[7]   Jürgen Habermas, 'Religion in the Public Sphere', *European Journal of Philosophy*, 14.1 (2006).

role of Christianity in both identities. What constitutes 'Europe'? How and where should one draw the external territorial and the internal cultural boundaries of Europe? The most controversial, yet rarely openly confronted – and therefore most anxiety-producing – issues are the potential integration of Turkey and the potential integration of non-European immigrants, who in most European countries happen to be overwhelmingly Muslim. But the eastward expansion of the European Union, particularly the incorporation of an assertive Catholic Poland, and the debates over some kind of affirmation or recognition of the Christian heritage in the preamble of the new European constitution, have also added unexpected 'religious' irritants to the debates over Europeanization.

There is a certain irony in the whole debate, since the initial project of a European Union was fundamentally a Christian-Democratic project, sanctioned by the Vatican, at a time of a general religious revival in post-Second World War Europe, in the geopolitical context of the Cold War when 'the free world' and 'Christian civilization' had become synonymous. But this is a forgotten history that secular Europeans, proud of having outgrown a religious past from which they feel liberated, would prefer not to remember. 'Religious' issues serve as irritants to secular Europeans precisely because they serve to fuel 'the glimmering embers' of Christian identity, while at the same time confirming the widely shared assumption that it is best to banish religion from the public sphere in order to tame the passionate conflicts and irrational attitudes which religion is assumed to bring into politics.

It is indeed astounding to observe how widespread throughout Europe is the view that religion is intolerant and the source of conflict. The overwhelming majority, over two thirds of the population in practically every Western European country, agrees that religion is 'intolerant', and a majority in every Western European country, except Norway and Sweden, shares the view that 'religion creates conflict'. Interestingly enough, the Danes distinguish themselves clearly from their fellow Lutheran Scandinavians in both respects. They score higher than any other European country, as high as 86 per cent, on the view that religion creates conflict, and score the second highest (with 79 per cent), after the Swiss and tied with the British, on the belief that religion is intolerant. Given their high scores on most religious indicators, the Swiss response is also interesting.

Along with most other former communist countries, the Poles score well below the Western European average on both issues. It is not surprising, therefore, that the evangelical task which Pope John Paul II assigned to his fellow Poles, to join the European Union with the mission of re-Christianizing secular Western Europe, is viewed differently in Poland and in the rest of Europe. The Polish Episcopate has accepted enthusiastically the papal apostolic assignment and has repeatedly stressed its goal of 'restoring Europe for Christianity'. While it may sound preposterous and irritating to Western European ears, such a message has found resonance in the tradition of Polish messianism.

Western European observers are accustomed to discount manifestations of Polish religious effervescence and Polish messianism as annoying and hopelessly anachronistic, if not reactionary, expressions of the Polish romantically heroic, yet desperate, penchant for resisting the march of history. It happened during the nineteenth-century Polish uprisings and it happened during the period of the Solidarity movement. Polish and Western European developments appeared seriously out of synch. Yet in both cases the Poles confounded the prevailing *Zeitgeist*. The rise of Solidarity and its role in the eventual collapse of the Soviet system radically altered the march of history and global geopolitical configurations. The repeatedly demonstrated power of renewal of Polish Catholicism, which should not be confused with a residual and recessive tradition, has confounded sceptics and critics before. It could happen again.

Given the loss of demand for religion in Western Europe, the supply of surplus Polish pastoral resources for a European-wide evangelizing effort is unlikely to prove effective. But Poland could still have an important role to play by simply showing that a modern and fully integrated European country can still continue to be a deeply religious one and thus proving the secularization thesis wrong on European soil.

While the threat of a Polish Christian crusade awakens little fear among secular Europeans confident of their ability to assimilate Catholic Poland on their own terms, the prospect of Turkey joining the European Union generates much greater anxieties among Europeans, Christian and post-Christian alike, but of the kind which cannot be easily verbalized, at least not publicly. The paradox and the quandary for modern secular Europeans, who have shed their traditional historical Christian identities in a rapid and drastic process of secularization that has coincided with the success of the process of European integration, and who therefore identify European modernity with secularization, is that they observe with some apprehension the reverse process in Turkey. The more 'modern', or at least democratic, Turkish politics become, the more publicly Muslim and less secularist they also tend to become. In its determination to join the EU, Turkey is adamantly staking its claim to be, or its right to become, a fully European country economically and politically, while simultaneously fashioning its own model of Muslim cultural modernity. It is this very claim to be simultaneously a modern European and a culturally Muslim country that baffles European civilizational identities, secular and Christian alike. It contradicts both the definition of a Christian Europe and the definition of a secular Europe. Turkey's claim to European membership becomes an irritant precisely because it forces Europeans to reflexively and openly confront the crisis in their own civilizational identity, at a moment when the EU is already reeling from a series of compounded economic, geopolitical, administrative, fiscal and legitimation crises.

The spectre of millions of Turkish citizens already in Europe but not of Europe, many of them second-generation immigrants, caught between an old country they have left behind and their European host societies unable or unwilling to fully assimilate them, only makes the problem the more visible. *Gastarbeiter* can be successfully incorporated economically. They may even gain voting rights, at least on the local level, and prove to be model or at least ordinary citizens. But can they pass the unwritten rules of cultural European membership or are they to remain 'strangers', ultimately *Fremdarbeiter*?[8] Can the European Union open new conditions for the kind of multiculturalism that its constituent national societies find so difficult to accept? The question of the integration of Turkey in the EU is inevitably intertwined, implicitly if not explicitly, with the question of the failed integration of Muslim immigrants, and, in turn, the way in which Europe resolves both questions will determine not only Europe's civilizational identity but the role of Europe in the emerging global order.

What makes 'the immigrant question' particularly thorny in Europe, and inextricably entwined with 'the Turkish question', is the fact that in Europe immigration and Islam are almost synonymous. This entails a superimposition of different dimensions of 'otherness' that exacerbates issues of boundaries, accommodation and incorporation. The immigrant, the religious, the racial, and the socio-economic unprivileged 'other' all tend to coincide. Moreover, all those dimensions of 'otherness' now become superimposed upon Islam, so that Islam becomes the utterly 'other'. Anti-immigrant xenophobic nativism, the conservative defence of Christian culture and civilization, secularist anti-religious prejudices, liberal-feminist critiques of Muslim patriarchal fundamentalism, and the fear of Islamist terrorist networks, are being fused indiscriminately throughout Europe into a uniform anti-Muslim discourse which practically precludes the kind of mutual accommodation between immigrant groups and host societies that is necessary for successful immigrant incorporation.

Finally, the debates over the new European constitution also revealed that religion has become a public contested issue accross Europe. From a purely legal positivist point of view, modern constitutions do not need transcendent references. But insofar as the main rationale and purpose of drafting a new European constitution appeared to be an extra-constitutional political one, namely to contribute to European social integration, to enhance a common European identity and to remedy the deficit in democratic legitimacy, the

---

[8]   A controversy has erupted in Germany because Oscar Lafontaine, the left Socialist leader, dislikes the euphemism *Gastarbeiter* (guest workers) and prefers to call immigrant workers *Fremdarbeiter* (foreign workers), the term used during the Nazi period.

confronting of issues of common European values and common European identities was inevitable.

Who are we? Where do we come from? What constitutes our spiritual and moral heritage and the boundaries of our collective identities? How flexible internally and how open externally should those boundaries be? Addressing such complex questions through an open and public democratic European-wide debate would under any circumstance be an enormously complex task that would entail addressing and coming to terms with the many problematic and contradictory aspects of the European heritage in its intra-national, inter-European and global-colonial dimensions. But such a complex task is made the more difficult by secularist prejudices that preclude not only a critical yet honest and reflexive assessment of the Judaeo-Christian heritage, but even any public official reference to such a heritage, on the grounds that any reference to religion could be divisive and counterproductive, or exclusionist, or simply violates secular postulates.

I am not trying to imply that the European constitution ought to make some reference either to some transcendent reality or to the Christian heritage. But one should certainly recognize that any genealogical reconstruction of the idea or social imaginary of Europe that makes reference to Graeco-Roman antiquity and the Enlightenment while erasing any memory of the role of medieval Christendom in the very constitution of Europe as a civilization evinces either historical ignorance or repressive amnesia.

The inability to openly recognize Christianity as one of the constitutive components of European cultural and political identity could also mean that Europeans are missing the historical opportunity to add a third important reconciliation to the already achieved reconciliations between Protestants and Catholics and between warring European nation-states, by putting an end to the old battles over Enlightenment, religion and secularism. The perceived threat to secular identities and the biased over-reaction of excluding any public reference to Christianity belie the self-serving secularist claims that only secular neutrality can guarantee individual freedoms and cultural pluralism. What the imposed silence signifies is not only the attempt to erase Christianity or any other religion from the public collective memory, but also the exclusion from the public sphere of a central component of the personal identity of many Europeans. To guarantee equal access to the European public sphere and undistorted communication, the European Union would need to become not only post-Christian but also post-secular.

Finally, the privileging of European secular identities and secularist self-understandings in the genealogical affirmation of the common European values of human dignity, equality, freedom and solidarity may not only impede the possibility of gaining a full understanding of the genesis of those values and their complex process of societal institutionalization and individual internalization, but also preclude a critical and reflexive self-understanding of our own European secular identities. David Martin and Danièle Hervieu-Léger have poignantly shown that the religious and the secular are inextricably linked throughout modern European history, that the different versions of the European Enlightenment are inextricably linked with different versions of Christianity, and that cultural matrices rooted in particular religious traditions and related institutional arrangements still serve to shape and encode, mostly unconsciously, diverse European secular practices.

The purpose of this argument, as noted above, is not to imply that the new European constitution ought to make reference either to some transcendent reality or to the Christian heritage, but is simply to point out that the quarrels provoked by the possible incorporation of religious reference into the constitutional text would seem to indicate that secularist assumptions turn religion into a problem, and thus preclude the possibility of dealing with religious issues in a pragmatic and sensible manner.

10

The Religious Situation in the USA

Hans Joas

Even for those who visit the USA only occasionally and lack deep historical knowledge of the country, its religious pluralism and vitality are probably impossible to miss. While the German village often seems to be built around its only church, its American counterpart generally features a large number of churches, often lined up along a single street – a reflection of the great variety of religious faiths. In Europe on the other hand, despite all the changes wrought by industrialization and urban growth, flight and expulsion, the principle that there can be just one religion in one territory is still much in evidence geographically. American churches are often provided with large car parks, and these regularly fill up on Sundays, when services are held, but also throughout the day on weekdays, because a large number of activities are organized within the parishes and congregations. After the Second World War, when settlement structures changed radically as increasing numbers of town dwellers moved into homes in the country, giving rise to the vast 'suburbs', it sometimes seemed that the new malls in the open countryside were taking the churches' central place in social life. But before long, numerous new churches and synagogues were also constructed in these suburbs, and it is arguable[1] that the average American suburban family continues to attend church more often than it goes to the mall. In the cities, the (often enormous) historic church buildings remain, the congregations now often consisting entirely of African-Americans or new immigrants. In impoverished areas of large cities, plagued by violence and drugs, you will often come across mosques of an almost extravagant appearance; built with Middle Eastern money, these generally serve African-American converts rather than Muslim immigrants. Any visitor to the country who turns on the television is likely to be astonished at the variety of religious programmes, featuring fiery revivalist sermons and offers

---

[1]   Jon Butler, 'Jack-in-the-Box Faith: The Religion Problem in Modern American History', *Journal of American History*, 91 (2004), pp. 1357–78, esp. p. 1375.

of advice and support around the clock; some will be struck by the fact that even these programmes, like many congregations, appear to be divided by race. Even the Catholic Church has now followed suit by establishing a TV channel. This, however, rather than preaching awakening, imparts knowledge of church history and theology in a way intelligible to the ordinary citizen, covering church services and papal journeys in visually attractive fashion.

Since Alexis de Tocqueville's famous journey through the USA in the 1830s and publication of his brilliant account of it, commentators have never ceased to make similar observations. The more secularized large parts of Europe became, the more exotic the religiosity of the USA seemed to European observers. Even from a distance, the religiously coloured rhetoric of American political life is perceived as rather shocking by Europeans. Many overlook the fact that this rhetoric is found in all parts of the political spectrum. If the government's justification for war has religious undertones, we should not forget that the peace movement also asks God for forgiveness for the nation's arrogance. Slavery and racism were often justified in religious terms, but the resistance to them, up to and including the civil rights movement of the 1950s and 1960s, was also nourished by religious motives and its organizational structures drew on religious networks. There are of course regional variations and more strongly secularized milieux. In the north-eastern USA and the Pacific Coast region, the country's religious vitality is certainly less visible, and the members of some intellectual milieux orient themselves towards secular models from Europe, in opposition to American traditions. Fundamentally, though, it is widely accepted that the USA is far more religious than practically any comparable European state.

This finding, drawn from everyday experience, is confirmed by controlled social scientific research. It is clearly very difficult to record religiosity precisely and reliably in quantitative terms. This is easiest when we cite figures produced by social reality itself, by attempting to record, for example, the number of those attending Sunday church services or the number of members of churches and religious communities. It is far more difficult if we wish to ask people directly about their religious attitudes, because all the standardized questions, about belief in God or life after death for example, not only intrude on a highly intimate stratum of personhood, but also come up against the variety of forms of belief and a whole range of quasi-theological interpretive possibilities. All data in this field must therefore be treated with great caution. Opinion surveys and detailed sociological research do, however, regularly suggest a picture that confirms everyday observations. Taking the figures produced by the best-known polling institute (Gallup) on the question of belief in God, 94 per cent of interviewees answered in the affirmative in 2001. For the period since 1947, for which we have the results of numerous analogous surveys, this value has always been similarly high. The same source reveals that around three quarters of all

Americans believe in some form of life after death. It is meaningless to compare these values to a European average; the internal heterogeneity of Europe, that is, the diversity of national religious cultures, is far too great. But if we compare individual countries[2] with the USA, it quickly becomes apparent that the latter exhibits the highest values. These findings have certainly provoked methodological objections. The number of those attending church, for example, seems to be systematically overestimated if we rely on what interviewees say rather than counting the number of churchgoers. Interviewees in the USA are generally quick to assume that one *wants* them to profess their faith in a religion – just as, conversely, Europeans tend to be ashamed to openly profess their faith. But even this 'social desirability bias', which probably tends to exaggerate the quantitative differences between the USA and Europe, helps confirm the present chapter's point of departure. The USA is a modern society characterized by a high degree of religious vitality.

The first part of this brief overview of the religious situation in the USA asks how we are to explain this. This is an attempt to shed light on historically persistent peculiarities of the USA with respect to religion. The second part then attempts to characterize the present.

I

Precisely because of its religious character, the USA was long considered a special case in need of explanation. Those who assumed that processes of modernization – however defined in detail – inevitably lead to secularization (in the sense of the decreasing importance of religion) were confronted with a puzzle. European countries such as Poland and Ireland, to which this rule also appeared not to apply, could be described simply as insufficiently modernized; they were still to undergo genuine modernization, and in that framework secularization would eventually occur. But the USA? Who seriously wished to dispute that we are dealing here with an economically and technologically modern society, indeed, perhaps the most modern of all?

Two explanatory models suggested themselves to all those who thought in this way, their thinking based on the unconscious assumption that European history since the eighteenth century foregrounded the ultimate fate of the entire world – in the event, that is, of successful development. One model, which seemed to have proved its worth with reference to the European exceptions, could also be applied to the USA. If the Poles and the Irish remained exceptionally religious

---

[2]   These data are easily accessible in Pippa Norris and Ronald Inglehart, *Sacred and Secular: Religion and Politics Worldwide*, Cambridge, Cambridge University Press, 2004, pp. 89ff.

because the only way for them to defend their national identity and independence was through their Catholicism, then the religious vitality of the USA might also be down to the fact that its national identity had been religiously imbued from the outset. The explanation they had been looking for was thus the legacy of Puritanism.

It is in fact entirely correct that the USA has a pronounced national mythology[3] in which the early Puritan emigrants play a major role, but which is also moulded in its innermost structures by the application of Old Testament notions of the covenant with God and of the chosen people to America; this was used to justify expansion and mission. But the terms 'Puritanism' or even 'Protestantism' are far too imprecise to truly do justice to the religious currents in the USA over the last few centuries. Another objection to this supposed explanation is, however, far more compelling. Precise quantitative studies of the USA[4] have shown that there was an almost continuous and substantial increase in the number of members of religious communities over the course of the nineteenth and twentieth centuries. Commentators have spoken here of 'the churching of America'. Again, we must bear in mind that membership is no sure indicator of faith. But given that other indicators point in the same direction, there are compelling empirical reasons to reject the interpretation of US particularism as a kind of delayed secularization, as implied in the notion of the Puritan legacy. It is not that the same process has played itself out as in Europe, just more slowly or at a later point. What we are seeing here is a different process with a different trajectory.

Rather than a 'legacy', the second obvious – but also ultimately untenable – explanation privileges something that immigrants have supposedly 'brought along with them'. It might be assumed that the USA remained so religious or even became more religious because it absorbed a ceaseless flow of new immigrants, whose religiosity, inculcated in them in their home countries, acted as a guide for them and their children even after emigration. On this view, in brief, the Poles and Irish were responsible not only for the exceptions in Europe, but also for the exception of the USA. A rich array of research also exists on this question. To summarize its findings: we can by no means self-evidently assume greater religiosity *prior to* emigration. Often, emigrants from the same countries who went to countries other than the USA were by no means conspicuously religious. In fact, it seems that – to put it very cautiously – something in the

---

[3]   An excellent overview of the extensive literature is provided by Michael Hochgeschwender, 'Religion, nationale Mythologie und nationale Identität. Zu den methodischen und inhaltlichen Debatten in der amerikanischen "New Religious History"', *Historisches Jahrbuch der Görres-Gesellschaft*, 124 (2004), pp. 435–520.

[4]   See Roger Finke and Rodney Stark, *The Churching of America, 1776–1990*, New Brunswick, NJ, Rutgers University Press, 1992.

circumstances of the USA attracted and continues to attract immigrants to religious communities, creating bonds and influencing them religiously.[5]

Against both these apparent but untenable explanations, another view has taken hold within the sociology of religion over the last few decades. Although many of its details are also contested,[6] there is broad consensus on many points. This is the idea that the decisive particularity of the USA vis-à-vis Europe is that since the eighteenth century the former has known no state-backed territorial religious monopoly of the kind characteristic of Europe since the end of the post-reformatory wars and civil wars. Both elements of the formula are important here. The absence of a monopoly facilitates pluralism; the absence of state support allows free competition between plural religious forces. By stipulating 'free exercise' and 'no establishment', the American constitution guarantees comprehensive freedom of religion on the one hand and the separation of state and church(es) on the other. At the level of the individual states, as late as the eighteenth century there were attempts to form territorial religious monopolies, but these failed to endure or truly take hold because of federal regulations. This separation of state and religious communities must, however, be understood quite differently than in the case of France, where the state sees itself as 'laicist' or secularist and takes a sceptical view of all religions. In the USA, meanwhile, the prevailing historical tradition is an encouraging relationship with religion on the part of the state. This does not mean that this is the only tradition; intense political and legal controversies about the exact nature of the separation of state and church have also arisen frequently in the USA, particularly during the present era.

This rich pluralism of religious communities[7] is thus not only extant, but politically desired and culturally legitimized. I propose that we distinguish between *plurality* as a mere empirical fact and a *pluralism* endorsed by certain values. Hence, all explanations of the religious vitality of the USA which, influenced by the conceptual models of supply-side economics, take account only of the plurality of the supply itself or even the market-like nature of religious competition, fall

---

[5]   This was of course the thesis put forward by Will Herberg, *Protestant-Catholic-Jew*, Garden City, NY, Anchor, 1960, one confirmed by numerous studies. A very good (though older) survey is provided by Timothy L. Smith, 'Religion and Ethnicity in America', *American Historical Review*, 83 (1978), pp. 1155–85.

[6]   Of the extensive literature, I would mention R. Steven Warner, 'Work in Progress toward a New Paradigm for the Sociological Study of Religion in the United States', *American Journal of Sociology*, 98 (1993), pp. 1044–93; and Mark Chaves and Philip Gorski, 'Religious Pluralism and Religious Participation', *Annual Review of Sociology*, 27 (2001), pp. 261–81.

[7]   For an overview, see for example Peter W. Williams, *America's Religions: Traditions and Cultures*, Urbana, IL, University of Illinois Press, 1998.

short. The crucial rupture pointing towards America's specific historical path in fact precedes the constitution by more than one hundred years.[8] It occurred in the 1630s, when the Puritan preacher Roger Williams, in protest at the religious tyranny of emigrant Puritans in Massachusetts, left the colony and established a new one in Rhode Island that guaranteed religious freedom for *all* Christians, but also for 'Jews, heathens and Turks', in other words Jews, native Americans and Muslims. A notion of religious freedom arising not from indifference or scepticism towards religion, but which was itself deeply motivated by religion – the idea being that the individual must be free to develop his relationship with God – thus became the 'first freedom'. For all the differences that characterized the position of religion in the American Revolution, this has rightly been seen as the nucleus of the American constitutional organization of religious life and of human rights in general.

None of this should be taken as a naive idealization of American political and religious life. A history of conflict, racism and extreme social inequality, violence and ethnic tension has hardly seen the exclusive application of noble principles. But it is on this level that we will find the explanation for the enduring religious vitality of the USA. In America, there has always been a tendency for those who cannot identify politically or theologically with their religious community to move *within* the religious sphere rather than leave it. This applies above all to Protestant Christians. Catholics traditionally tend to move closer to or further away from the church which is usually the only one in question for them. There certainly are Catholics who give up their religion – by switching to the Pentecostalist churches for example as at present – but again, they tend to remain within the ever-changing plural religious spectrum.

II

Having briefly reviewed the key religious characteristics of the USA, our task now is to diagnose the contemporary situation. To gain initial purchase on this vast and confusing field, I draw on a set of concepts proposed by the Protestant theologian Ernst Troeltsch in the years leading up to the First World War and in his constant dialogue with Max Weber.[9] He distinguishes between three main organizational forms of Christianity; we must leave to one side for the moment the question of whether this concept is at all applicable to non-Christian religions.

---

[8]   See Hans Joas, 'Max Weber and the Origins of Human Rights', in Charles Camic et al. (eds.), *Max Weber's 'Economy and Society': A Critical Companion*, Stanford, CA, Stanford University Press, 2005, pp. 366–82.

[9]   Ernst Troeltsch, *The Social Teaching of the Christian Churches* (1912), London, Allen & Unwin, 1931; the following citations are from p. 993.

The first type is referred to as 'church'; this means institutions administering treasures of salvation and grace, which aim to attract a mass membership and which are generally able to adapt to reality, 'because, to a certain extent, [the church] can afford to ignore the need for subjective holiness for the sake of the objective treasures of grace and of redemption'. In much the same way as Max Weber, Troeltsch contrasts the 'church' with the 'sect', by which he means organizations structured as free associations of believers, which thus generally have fewer members and which emphasize strict compliance with precepts rather than God's grace. In contrast to Weber, Troeltsch also identified a third type, which he calls 'mysticism'; here, 'the world of ideas which had hardened into formal worship and doctrine is transformed into a purely personal and inward experience'. He is aware that this form of religiosity allows for 'the formation of groups on a purely personal basis, with no permanent form'. Some have therefore rejected the idea that we can speak of a type of social organization here in the first place. Others, meanwhile, see this as a particular strength of Troeltsch's conceptual apparatus with respect to the analysis of religion under conditions of individualization,[10] and this is the view espoused by the present author.

An account of contemporary American realities in light of this typology turns up a number of important characteristics:

a) While the type 'church' is characteristic of Europe, this does not apply to the USA. We can therefore categorize the USA as the only North Atlantic society characterized by the type 'sect' (Seymour Martin Lipset). It is only logical that the term loses its negative connotation as a result. In describing the USA, rather than referring to churches on the one hand and sects on the other, all religious communities are typically treated equally in terms of how they are designated. Reference is made to 'denominations', that is, religious communities based on voluntary membership of equal legal status. However embedded it may be in global structures, even that religious community which prototypically embodies the type 'church' across the world – the Catholic church – must present itself as a 'denomination' within the USA.

b) For a long time, there were weighty theological differences between the individual Protestant denominations and a virtually insurmountable distance between Protestantism as a whole and Catholicism, which was considered alien, indeed un-American, on account of its international character and many cultural

---

[10]   Karl-Fritz Daiber, 'Mysticism: Troeltsch's Third Type of Religious Collectivities', *Social Compass*, 49 (2002), pp. 329–41. He points out that the concepts developed by Troeltsch and Weber were already influenced by the motif of a relativization of Europe in light of the experience of the USA as well as by the books of William James.

characteristics of Catholic immigrants, with respect, for example, to their relaxed relationship to alcohol. Among the most important developments in the period after the Second World War was the decreasing significance of theological differences, particularly within American Protestantism.[11] The USA has never been a country characterized by a broad dissemination of religious knowledge or a culture of popular theological debate. But over the last few decades, theological differences have been overlaid by other differences to such an extent that this too has made it easier to switch allegiance within the Protestant spectrum. However, the flip-side of this increasing indifference towards theological issues is that as a result other issues – of a political or cultural nature for example – are becoming key to membership and are exercising a homogenizing effect on the individual denominations.

c) Because the state is neither in alliance with a particular church nor derives its self-image from its emancipation from one, it is unable to obtain its legitimacy from a church or from its opposition to a church. As a consequence, forms of 'civil religion' have developed in the USA, classically expressed in the inaugural addresses given by presidents on assuming office as well as in speeches on national holidays.[12] This civil religion cannot be identifiable with any specific religious community, but must offer points of contact to many. In contrast to the attempts which have been made to describe this civil religion as a fixed structure, I would assert that it is more of a 'discursive space' than a 'structure', that is, a spectrum of possibility for the justification of political opinions, including contrary ones. Since President Woodrow Wilson's initiative for a League of Nations, the development of international institutions for the peaceful settlement of conflicts has been anchored within this horizon, just as was President George W. Bush's brazen declaration of the irrelevance of such institutions in the run-up to the Iraq War of 2003.

But this civil religion not only provides a space for the delivery of political rhetoric; an interreligious dialogue on values is also developing within it. There can be no disputing the fact that the civil religion of the USA was originally largely Protestant in character. Through a wide variety of efforts to come to terms with Catholicism, extending far into the twentieth century, this civil religion was repositioned on a generally Christian foundation. In the twentieth century, particularly as a result of the struggle against Nazi Germany and the experience of the Holocaust, this foundation was expanded, taking on a Judaeo-Christian character. At present, however politically charged the debate on Islam

---

[11]   The key text is Robert Wuthnow, *The Restructuring of American Religion: Society and Faith since World War II*, Princeton, NJ, Princeton University Press, 1988, esp. pp. 71ff.
[12]   See Robert Bellah's classic essay on this subject, 'Civil Religion in America', *Daedalus*, 96 (1967), pp. 1–21.

may be, there are good reasons to be optimistic that this foundation is becoming even broader, incorporating this religious tradition as well, which would allow us to refer to an 'Abrahamic' civil religion. The immigration of Hindus and Buddhists and the intensive reception of Buddhism among the American educated classes show the direction in which this process of value generalization will have to go in future.

d) A particularly attractive feature of Troeltsch's conception is its inherent potential to take seriously trends towards the individualization of religiosity. These are incontrovertible, especially in the USA. For many people, the significance of fixed religious truths, which are also anchored institutionally within a religious community, has undoubtedly diminished in favour of the aspiration to be guided by one's own 'spiritual' experience in matters of faith and to measure all doctrinal and institutional claims in this light. But this aspiration, which is to some extent democratic and anti-authoritarian in character, can have a number of different consequences. It would be very one-sided to assume that the only possibility here is a purely narcissistic-egocentric attitude which simply links together all one's own proclivities in eclectic fashion, ennobling them with the title of unique spirituality: 'I'm religious but in my own personal way. I always say that I have a Cindy Crawford religion – it's my own'[13] – as supermodel Cindy Crawford is supposed to have said. A plethora of critical terms have been coined to capture this kind of pseudo-religiosity: religion à la carte, patchwork religiosity, kaleidoscopic or 'pick and choose' religion.[14] Exponents of secularization theory see in this phenomenon confirmation of their expectation that the inevitable modern loss of faith is merely hiding behind a false characterization as religion. Other commentators counter this by arguing that there are quite different, far more serious forms of spiritual search and that many of these are in fact taking place within the major religious communities or on their margins. A spiritual search may result from experiences that inspire a desire for theological interpretation and institutional tradition; but conversely, it may also arise from the need to bring about the spiritual revitalization of the teachings of one's own religious community and of the life of this community. It would also be quite wrong to equate this individualization with the complete privatization of religion. Particularly in the USA, faith is not withdrawn into individuals' inner life, but remains the motif and object of a wide variety of forms of social life. It thus seems appropriate to classify self-organized Bible study groups, for example, or self-help

[13]   Cited in David Yamane, 'Secularization on Trial: In Defense of a Neosecularization Paradigm', *Journal for the Scientific Study of Religion*, 36 (1997), pp. 109–22, esp. p. 116.

[14]   See Karel Dobbelaere, *Secularization: An Analysis at Three Levels*, Brussels, P.I.E.-Peter Lang, 2002, p. 176.

groups in which anyone can participate whatever their religious affiliation, as the expression of a lively and sustained 'societal conversation about transcendent meaning'[15] within the USA rather than as evidence of secularization.

e) The religious pluralism in the USA has market-like characteristics to some extent. This is not, as is often assumed, self-evident. Religious communities may coexist without individuals perceiving them as offering them a range of options. But the fluid boundaries between the Protestant denominations and the waves of revivalist movements throughout American history have encouraged entrepreneurial behaviour with the aim of assimilating and mobilizing believers. Such behaviour is based on the willingness to deploy the latest technologies and media to further one's aims and to keep organizational structures flexible rather than keeping them in line with theological dogma. As far as immigrants are concerned, attempts to attract new members have tended to result in active efforts on their behalf whenever their interests seemed compatible with a given religious community. In a market like this, it is fairly easy to found a new church. It is thus no coincidence that so many of the new religions (such as Mormonism) that have managed to spread throughout the world emerged in the USA in the nineteenth and twentieth centuries.

Just as bureaucratization represents an ever-present threat to the type 'church', so does an excessive market orientation threaten the denominations within a market. So-called 'church shopping', that is, a consumeristic choice between the range of possible religious communities on offer, when a person moves house for example, seems unproblematic because in the main this occurs only within the sphere of the Protestant denominations, whose theological differences, as already noted, have lost much of their significance. More striking of course is the tendency, particularly in the so-called Megachurches, to go to such lengths to attract all kinds of potential 'customers' that what they are offered is convenience, variety and theological vagueness. Here, it stands to reason to link religious phenomena with mass culture and consumer culture in general.[16] At times, religion is even extolled as a means to an end – as a way of achieving preconceived, thoroughly worldly goals. If faith is understood in such instrumental fashion, as a kind of 'positive thinking' that helps you to be strong, successful or rich (or 'Slim for Him!'), it loses the very spur to transcendence which religion has had since the Axial Age, that is, since notions of transcendence emerged. Rather than decentring the individual, leading her away from herself,

---

[15]   Kelly Besecke, 'Seeing Invisible Religion: Religion as a Societal Conversation about Transcendent Meaning', *Sociological Theory*, 23 (2005), pp. 179–96.

[16]   Robert Laurence Moore, *Selling God: American Religion in the Marketplace of Culture*, New York, Oxford University Press, 1994.

she is seduced by a kind of autosuggestive, neo-magical practice. Like Alan Wolfe,[17] we may then refer to the danger that even politically conservative forms of religion in the USA may be lived in a culturally narcissistic way.

III

These remarks were intended to bring out some of the key characteristics of the contemporary religious situation in the USA. This could only be done in a selective way; many aspects of this hugely heterogeneous country had to be left out of account. To conclude, however, I would like to contemplate future developments, presenting two possible scenarios, which perhaps mark the extreme ends of a spectrum. The reality is likely to lie somewhere in between.

A pessimistic scenario, which seemed plausible to many in the first years of the presidency of George W. Bush, predicted a profound cultural split within the USA as a result of the triumph of Protestant fundamentalism within the political sphere. On this view, such a triumph would inevitably bring together all those unable to feel at home in an exclusively 'Christian' nation in this narrow sense. Within the framework of this resistance, a quasi-European secularism might spread and attain hegemony for the first time. As a result, cultural conflicts of a religious hue would be aggravated over the long term.

However, there have always been serious objections to this prognosis. Critics claim that the enormous polarization of the political camps that has occurred since the election of George W. Bush reflects political strategies and mechanisms rather than the actual attitudes of the American people, who can by no means be divided sharply into two clear-cut milieux. On this view, the political influence of Protestant fundamentalism is also vastly overestimated; while religiously motivated voters are taken into account in election campaigns, political decisions themselves are made on a very different basis. Even within the generally conservative Protestantism in the USA, these commentators argue, there is a great deal of political diversity. This camp is in fact far from uniform and rigid. In many areas (such as environmental protection) Christian motifs (concerning the preservation of Creation) are increasingly opposed to the political tendencies of the Republican Party. The Congressional elections of autumn 2006 and the Presidential elections of autumn 2008 seem to suggest that the critics of the pessimistic prognosis are right.

The optimistic scenario assumes that American Christianity in all its diversity will see the fulfilment of the very thing that Ernst Troeltsch dreamt of: a creative synthesis of the three organizational principles of church, sect and mysticism – or

---

[17]   See his wonderfully vivid book *The Transformation of American Religion: How We Actually Live Our Faith*, New York, Free Press, 2003.

perhaps we should say, a plethora of creative syntheses. Advocates of the optimistic scenario hope that the peaceful coexistence of all religious communities within a democratic culture will set an example for the entire world. And, in fact, all the major religions of the world have a substantial presence in the USA. Given that, as a result of modern communications technology and transportation, immigrants generally no longer lose contact with their countries of origin, it is possible that this will have repercussions on the religious life in those countries.[18] The religious life of the USA, in all its variety, thus influences the religious life of the entire globe. Processes of this kind would have a salutary effect, disrupting the ties binding a particular religion to a particular milieu again and again. Reality would begin to correspond with the state of affairs expressed so well in the motto of a (my) Catholic parish in Chicago (St Thomas the Apostle): 'God's people in extraordinary variety'.

---

[18]   I have José Casanova to thank for this idea.

11

The Religious Situation in East Asia

Joachim Gentz

To write about the religious situation in East Asia within the context of a book on 'secularization and the world religions' presupposes that the reader understands a number of points. I would like to begin by reflecting briefly on these.

East Asia is taken here to mean China, Japan and Korea. China will be a key focus of attention because it represents the largest and most influential cultural area in East Asia. The term 'religious' covers both major global religious traditions and specifically national and local religious forms that dominate the religious situation of individual regions. Alongside older religious traditions such as Daoism, Confucianism and Shintoism, this includes the new religious movements.

The opposite of *religiosus* is *saecularis*. Secularization presupposes an original unity and subsequent separation of religious and non-religious spheres. Otherwise, there is no room for this movement from one to the other that constitutes the meaning of the term. The concept of secularization highlights the relationship between modern European history and the Christian tradition.[1] The separation of church and state and the development of a plurality of perspectives and worldviews, which ended the state's monopoly on orthodoxy, and the emergence of a civil society, are key components of secularization within the process of European modernization. In countries in which religion and the state have for centuries had a very different kind of relationship, it is not meaningful to speak of a process of secularization. For example, rather than a specific feature of modernity, the nationalization of the property of religious institutions, characteristic of secularization in Europe in its original sense within the context of ecclesiastical law,[2]

---

[1] See Hans-Wolfgang Strätz, 'Säkularisierung', in Otto Brunner, Werner Conze and Reinhart Koselleck (eds.), *Geschichtliche Grundbegriffe – Historisches Lexikon zur politisch sozialen Sprache*, vol. 5, Stuttgart, Klett-Cotta, 2004, p. 827.

[2] See Strätz, 'Säkularisierung', and Giacomo Marramao's article 'Säkularisierung' in Joachim Ritter and Karlfried Gründer (eds.), *Historisches Wörterbuch der Philosophie*, vol. 8, Darmstadt, Wissenschaftliche Buchgesellschaft, 1992, col. 1133–34.

has been a key element of national religious politics in East Asia for more than a thousand years. The coexistence of a number of state-supported religions, moreover, makes both the separation between religions and the state and a plurality of worldviews indigenous elements of East Asian tradition. This does not mean that the state itself operated in secular fashion or that plurality as a concept was ever subject to reflection in the way characteristic of modernity in both Europe and Asia.[3] The fact that, in line with the internationally established European model, the state in East Asia is justified in secular terms in the twenty-first century changes almost nothing about its relationship to religions,[4] and the fact that the topic of plurality is contemplated in Asia in the European way does not necessarily lead to pluralism and democracy.

A particularly wide variety of new religious movements have developed since the late nineteenth century in Japan,[5] but also in Korea.[6] One of a series of new religious formations since the Ming period (1368–1644),[7] they were transformed in the Republican era (1911–1948),[8] destroyed by the Communist Party of China in the 1950s, and have once again become a central feature of the religious situation in China since the 1990s. The concept of secularization is as incapable of analysing or explaining this wealth of new religious movements in East Asia as in Europe. It explains the disappearance of religion from political institutions, but it explains neither the continued existence of traditional religious institutions within modernity nor the re-emergence of a variety of religious movements in

---

[3]   See Joachim Gentz, 'Die Drei Lehren (sanjiao) Chinas in Konflikt und Harmonie. Figuren und Strategien einer Debatte', in Edith Franke and Michael Pye (eds.), Religionen nebeneinander. Modelle religiöser Vielfalt in Ost- und Südostasien, Münster, Lit, 2006, pp. 17–40.

[4]   See the discussion of this paradigm of continuity in Vincent Goossaert, 'State and Religion in Modern China: Religious Policies and Scholarly Paradigms', http://www.mh.sinica.edu.tw/eng/download/abstract/abstract3–4–1.pdf (1 July 2005), pp. 11–13.

[5]   An overview of the extensive research literature is provided by Peter Bernard Clarke, Bibliography of Japanese New Religions: with Annotations and an Introduction to Japanese New Religions at Home and Abroad, Richmond, Curzon, 1999. On Western scholarship, see also H. Byron Earhart, The New Religions of Japan: A Bibliography of Western-Language Materials, Tokyo, Sophia University, 1970; and Johannes Laube, Neureligionen: Stand ihrer Erforschung in Japan. Ein Handbuch, Wiesbaden, Harrassowitz, 1995, for Japanese materials.

[6]   See Ro Kil-myung, 'New Religions and Social Change in Modern Korean History', The Review of Korean Studies, 5.1 (2002), pp. 31–62.

[7]   See Barend J. ter Haar, The White Lotus Teachings in Chinese Religious History, Leiden, Brill, 1992; Hubert Seiwert and Ma Xisha, Popular Religious Movements and Heterodox Sects in Chinese History, Leiden, Brill, 2003.

[8]   See Zhong Guofa, 'A Survey of Newly Emerged Religious Sects in the Republican Era', China Study Journal, 13.3 (1998), pp. 22–32.

modern contexts. Hence, the term 'secularization' hinders the development of theoretical approaches to explaining modern religion capable of accounting for religion as an entirely normal feature of modernity.

It is evident empirically that the influence of religion on modern societies has in fact declined markedly worldwide. At present, no one expects religious considerations to exercise a decisive influence on technological or political developments in modernity. Even in the sphere of private morality, religion no longer plays the leading role. Yet this form of empirically verifiable secularization is just one of the possible responses of religion to modernity. Religion has developed in other ways that point in a very different direction. Religion not only plays an important role within modernity as a factor in modernization; modernity has also given rise to new forms of religion, which have led to a typically modern blossoming of the religious landscape on an entirely unexpected scale. Thus, modernity has brought about the withering of certain types of religion or religious organization and commitment, but it has generated new ones which have, in their own way, displayed tremendous social dynamism. Thomas Luckmann for example states, 'what are usually taken as symptoms of the decline of traditional Christianity may be symptoms of a more revolutionary change: the replacement of the institutional specialisation of religion by a new social form of religion'.[9] It is hard to define these new forms of religion, typical in East Asia even before the modern period, with a terminology thoroughly marked by the European division into religious and secular.

If we define the decline of traditional religion as does Luckmann and, as sociologist Michael Ebertz puts it, work on the assumption of a 'dispersion of the religious',[10] then, to remain with the material metaphor of dispersion, which describes the thin spread of a material, the decline of religion would not mean a loss of substance. This decline would merely involve a change in the material of religion from a compact, institutionally organized form to one identifiable as 'traces' in many places, a form traditionally widespread in East Asia. On this view, rather than being destroyed, religion seems dispersed within the everyday world by the disintegration of religious institutions. The idea here is that, rather than simply ceasing to exist, religious traditions are broken up into countless splinters, in which form they continue to have an effect — one that often goes virtually

---

[9]   See Thomas Luckmann, *The Invisible Religion: The Problem of Religion in Modern Society*, London, Macmillan, 1967, pp. 90–91.

[10]   See Michael Ebertz, 'Die Dispersion des Religiösen', in Hermann Kochanek (ed.), *Ich habe meine eigene Religion*, Zürich, 1999, pp. 210ff., cited in Michael Nüchtern, 'Die Weihe des Profanen — formen Säkularer Religiosität', in Reinhard Hempelmann (ed.), *Panorama der neuen Religiosität. Sinnsuche und Heilsversprechen zu Beginn des 21. Jahrhunderts*, Gütersloh, Gütersloher Verlagshaus, 2001, p. 21.

unacknowledged. Religious scholars have attempted to capture this new field of the formation of the religious, associated with modernity in the case of Europe, through a number of new concepts such as 'civil religion', the 'consecration of the profane' or 'sacred secularity',[11] but so far none of these concepts has really taken hold, presumably because they speak to a field of discursive tension still marked entirely by a Christian understanding of religion. As Michael Nüchtern states, two facts above all make the identification and definition of the religious difficult at present: the appearance of quotations from and symbols of classical religion in an obviously profane (i.e. non-sacred) context, and the taking over of the functions of classical religion by profane spheres of life.[12] This blending of the religious and secular in a context in which, to some extent, the religious becomes secular and the secular religious, complicates the application of a term like 'secularization', within this second horizon of dispersed religiosity, to the point of inapplicability. Here, the inflation of multicultural religious symbols, meaningful only to ever smaller sub-groups, helps bring about a situation in which a phenomenon such as individual religiosity is increasingly defined by the obligation either to recognize all symbols as of equal value or to opt for one tradition through a profession of faith, rejecting all others. In East Asia, this polarization of secularity and fundamentalism has not developed only in the modern period; as differing religious traditions have come to terms with one another, it constitutes a centuries-old pattern with its own discursive tropes and strategies.[13]

East Asian religions have often been studied and analysed through the lens of the secularization paradigm.[14] However, as a result of the focus on a secularization aggressively imposed from above by the state and its consequences, forms of secularization not driven by the state (such as the spontaneous and autonomous transformation of temples into schools at the local level) in East Asia have been little studied and we know little about them. Even the signs and fragments indicative of a new postmodern form of dispersed religiosity have so far been investigated only in the context of party political propaganda (see below), but not yet in the context of everyday life in East Asian cultures, particularly in comparison with traditional forms of dispersed religiosity. In what follows, in order to present the religious situation in East Asia in rather more detail, we

---

[11]   On 'civil religion', see the introduction to the dissertation by Thomas Hase, *Zivilreligion. Religionswissenschaftliche Überlegungen zu einem theoretischen Konzept am Beispiel der USA*, Würzburg, Lit, 2001; and Janez Perčič, *Religion und Gemeinwesen. Zum Begriff der Zivilreligion*, Münster, 2004. On the latter two concepts, see Nüchtern, 'Die Weihe des Profanen', pp. 24ff.

[12]   See Nüchtern, 'Die Weihe des Profanen', p. 22.

[13]   See Gentz, 'Die Drei Lehren (*sanjiao*) Chinas'.

[14]   See Goossaert, 'State and Religion in Modern China', pp. 8–11.

shall be looking individually at the three major national entities of China, Japan and Korea, before coming to a comparative conclusion with respect to the issue of secularization in East Asia.

China

The process of European modernization has developed in the form of an *histoire croisée*,[15] that is, a global process characterized by its mutual entanglements and the crossing of national boundaries. This has affected China and its religious landscape as it has all other modern nations. In the wake of modernization, the Chinese empire, which was based on an agrarian economy, a monarchical regime and the ideology of Confucianism, was transformed into a modern nation state with an industrial economy and republican constitution anchored in communist ideology. As such, China now plays an increasingly important role in the global economy and in the political sphere. The People's Republic of China is a centrally governed state with a current population of more than 1.3 billion people. About a third of them live in cities, some of whose populations are several times that of entire European countries (cities such as Beijing, Shanghai or Chongqing, for example, have three times as many inhabitants as Sweden or Switzerland). In contemporary China there are five religions recognized by the state: Daoism, Buddhism, Islam, Catholicism and Protestantism, represented by the seven affiliated religious associations;[16] many local forms of Chinese popular religion; the religions of the national minorities and finally a new, highly dynamic field of new religious movements that has undergone explosive development in China since the late 1980s and early 1990s. This tense relationship between established, officially recognized religions, popular religious traditions, minority religions and new, frequently syncretic and millenarian religious movements has characterized China for many hundreds of years.

In China's case, the assessment of the relationship between modernization and secularization depends crucially on whether we classify Confucianism as a religion or as agnosticism. The debate on whether Confucianism is a religion or not, which began with the rites controversy in the late seventeenth century and has raged for hundreds of years, remains unresolved and, because it has significant consequences for the evaluation of Chinese cultural history, continues to be hotly contested by the representatives of various ideologies.

---

[15] On this concept, see Michael Werner and Bénédicte Zimmermann, 'Vergleich, Transfer, Verflechtung. Der Ansatz der Histoire croisée und die Herausforderung des Transnationalen', *Geschichte und Gesellschaft*, 28 (2002), pp. 607–36.

[16] See Karl-Fritz Daiber, 'Les associations des cinq religions officiellement reconnues en République populaire de Chine', *Social Compass*, 51.2 (2004), pp. 255–71.

That the debaters have such different things to say has to do with the fact that Confucianism in China confronts us with something which, in its specific mixture of religious practice, religious criticism and religious politics, is not compatible with any kind of Western ideology, whose religiosity was always defined via the orthodoxy of institutionalized religion. Hence, a term like 'secularization' cannot be applied here with any analytical success. The debate on orthodox (zheng: correct) and heretical (xie: crooked) teachings carried on in China by Confucian officials for more than 2000 years revolves not around the European concern to establish what is true religion or religiosity, but essentially around the issue of what constitutes correct state doctrine. Religions play a marginal role here. They are of interest in as much as they may create something like a broad moral foundation among the people resulting in social and political stability. Otherwise, they are considered potentially dangerous because, as functions of the social structure, they may disturb order within the empire, as numerous incidents in Chinese history verify.[17] Consonant with this, the Chinese state's traditional approach to religions has been characterized by policies which merely prescribe formal structures rather than content, which control the symbolic level of religious representation rather than the faith of the religious and which espouse non-intervention as long as the required ritual forms are observed.[18] It is clearly apparent in imperial edicts on religions that these were judged and disciplined not in accordance with their content but in response to their political impact.[19] This reflects the Confucian attitude towards religion as something about which nothing can be said, which one ought to respect, but from which one should keep one's distance.[20] The regulations thus argue at a merely formal level with reference to notions of social and political order. Within the religious landscape of China, this combination of state indifference to theological content on the one hand and severe restrictions on politically engaged religion on the other led to a structure made up of a number of small, powerless religious groups that mirrored and reproduced the imperial model

---

[17] See David Ownby, 'Imperial Fantasies: The Chinese Communists and Peasant Rebellions', *Comparative Studies in Society and History*, 43.1 (2001), pp. 65–91.

[18] See James Watson, 'Standardizing the Gods: The Promotion of T'ien Hou ("Empress of Heaven") Along the South China Coast, 960–1960', in David Johnson, Andrew J. Nathan and Evelyn S. Rawski (eds.), *Popular Culture in Late Imperial China*, Berkeley, University of California Press, 1985 (repr. Taipei, 1987), pp. 292–324, here p. 323.

[19] See Yang Ch'ing-k'un, *Religion in Chinese Society*, Berkeley, University of California Press, 1961, 1967 (repr. Taipei, 1991, 1994), edict from 1724, p. 194; Seiwert and Ma, *Popular Religious Movements*, pp. 99–101, 140, 163.

[20] See Confucius' oft-cited statements on the subject in the *Analects of Confucius* (*Lunyu*) 5.12, 6.22, 7.20, 11.11.

of order in their social organization, religious notions and practices.[21] State criticism of religions and steps taken against religions related not to religious concepts, but to the violation of prescribed measures. State prohibitions were short-lived, religious organizations and institutions were destroyed, refashioned and refounded, but traditional policies on religion featured no strict control of the faith of particular religions; the doctrinal boundaries between individual religions were too nebulous.[22]

This attitude changed as a result of the encounter with the West. Now that the concept and the term 'religion' had appeared in China for the first time, Chinese intellectuals began to reflect on the concept towards the end of the nineteenth century. The new constitution of 1912 formulated the concept of religious freedom (*zongjiao ziyou*) on the Western model for the first time. The adoption of the Western concept of religion, however, required the adoption of the Western distinction between true religion and superstition.[23] As a result, the first two decades of the twentieth century saw the wholesale persecution and destruction of all traditional religious institutions that did not fit the definitional model of Western religion and were therefore branded backward superstition.[24] Because traditional religion also mirrored and reproduced dynastic hierarchies of order, the destruction of the old imperial political legacy of feudalism and the destruction of feudal superstition were often mentioned in one breath. Secularization was deployed as an instrument of the restructuring of religiously based, traditional power relations; it did not occur as a process of the gradual decline of religious faith.[25] In order to comply with the new conception of religion and protect themselves from persecution, religious traditions adopted the new prevailing political symbolism and rhetoric.[26] From 1912 on, Buddhism,

---

[21]   See Barend J. ter Haar, 'Local Society and the Organization of Cults in Early Modern China: A Preliminary Study', *Studies in Central & East Asian Religions*, 8 (1995), pp. 1–43.

[22]   On these issues of content and form, see Joachim Gentz, 'Envisioning Conflicts: Aesthetic Representations in Negotiations between State and Religion in China', unpublished talk given on 29 September 2005 at the University of Leiden. This text will appear as a chapter in a forthcoming book.

[23]   See Goossaert, 'State and Religion in Modern China', pp. 2–5.

[24]   See Vincent Goossaert, 'The Beginning of the End for Chinese Religion?', *The Journal of Asian Studies*, 65.2 (2006), pp. 307–35.

[25]   See Prasenjit Duara, 'Knowledge and Power in the Discourse of Modernity: The Campaigns against Popular Religion in Early Twentieth-Century China', *The Journal of Asian Studies*, 50.1 (1991), pp. 67–83, here pp. 75ff.

[26]   See Poon Shuk Wah, 'Refashioning Festivals in Republican Guangzhou', *Modern China*, 30.2 (2004), pp. 199–227, here p. 222.

Daoism, Islam and Christianity developed as overarching national religious institutions on the model of Western churches, separate from the institutions of popular religion, which were now viewed as superstition. Daoism, because it was traditionally associated with communities of local cults whose practices were considered superstitious, was often compelled to defend its status as religion. With its 'atheistic' philosophy extending over much of Asia, it was much easier for Buddhism to portray itself as an international religion compatible with science and modernity, with a global orientation and opposed to superstitious notions and practices. With the modernization of China, Chinese Buddhism, which had formerly been in decline, received fresh impetus and underwent a revival driven primarily by the laity. Rather than the secularization of Buddhism, modernization led to an international revival.[27] This did not apply to Daoism; on account of its local manifestations and cleavage into traditions, it was less easy to slot into the programme of modernization in a standardized form. Moreover, it lacked a laity actively pursuing its revival.[28]

Because religion had to organize itself into national religious institutions in the 1910s in order to gain legitimacy, religious institutions developed an officially sanctioned, internal institutional hierarchy for the first time.[29] As a consequence of this transformation and redefinition of Buddhism and Daoism, Daoist and Buddhist communities that did not fit the modern concept of religion and which were linked with local cults, along with their associated temples, could be more easily destroyed: they were impossible to integrate into the newly formed umbrella organizations and thus no longer had any basis for legitimacy as religion. Lacking the new attributes of religion such as their own church-like institutions, a hierarchically organized priesthood, holy scriptures, etc. (and lacking their own military force),[30] the local religions had no chance to establish themselves in the modern religious sphere and were largely eliminated through several waves of anti-religious movements.[31] These movements peaked in 1922 through the efforts of the 'Great Federation of Anti-Religionists', founded early the same year, when it was announced that the 'World Student Christian Federation' would meet in Beijing in April. The

---

[27]   See Hubert Seiwert, 'Religious Response to Modernization in Taiwan: The Case of I-Kuan-Tao', *Journal of the HK Branch of the Royal Asiatic Society, Royal Asiatic Society of GB and Ireland, HK Branch*, 21 (1981), pp. 43–70.

[28]   Vincent Goossaert, 'The Quanzhen Clergy 1700–1950', in John Lagerwey (ed.), *Religion and Chinese Society II: Taoism and Local Religion in Modern China*, Paris and Hong Kong, Chinese University Press, 2004, pp. 699–771.

[29]   See Daiber, 'Les associations des cinq religions officiellement reconnues'.

[30]   See Ownby, 'Imperial Fantasies'.

[31]   See Duara, 'Knowledge and Power', p. 79–80.

proclamations of the Great Federation cast scorn on the 'poison' of religion and were initially aimed at Christians. Though it was Christians that constituted the movement's primary target from 1922 to 1927, on a theoretical level it came to the more general conclusion that religion is a product of primitive peoples, that it is based on superstition, is dogmatically intolerant and stands in the way of human progress. It was thought to hinder individual development and social improvements and was seen as hypocritical. On this view, the origins of morality lie in human nature and are not dependent on religion. It was through the arts and sciences that the people's lot would be improved.[32] Meanwhile, following the 'European barbarism' of the First World War, representatives of the religions took up arguments found in European cultural criticism, contrasting the materialistic culture of the West with the superior spiritual culture of Asia. China thus negotiated a European contradiction existing between, on the one hand, the often fundamentalist missionary movements with their critique of a modern society considered to be 'materialistic, atheistic and inhumane', and the modernizers with their 'scientific' critique of religion on the other. The theological critique of materialistic culture thus became one of the bases of the spiritual model of Asian culture, while the scientific critique of religion formed one of the foundations of the critique of 'superstitious' tradition.[33] Between 1913 and 1929, a whole series of new religious laws were enacted, formalizing certain elements of the religious practice of the Qing dynasty. These no longer merely provided general guidelines, but precise lists detailing the specific features of correct religions, lists which formed the basis for determining whether local religions should be destroyed or preserved.[34] Religious traditions that lacked these features had to redefine themselves in secular terms as tradition, custom, folklore, self-cultivation or Qigong in order to survive.[35]

But alongside these new religious laws, it was three factors above all that destroyed the social bases of many traditional forms of religion:

---

[32]   See Wing-tsit Chan, 'The Historic Chinese Contribution to Religious Pluralism and World Community', in Edward J. Jurji (ed.), *Religious Pluralism and World Community: Interfaith and Intercultural Communication*, Leiden, Brill 1969, pp. 113–30.

[33]   See Robert N. Bellah, 'Epilogue: Religion and Progress in Asia', in idem (ed.), *Religion and Progress in Modern Asia*, New York, Free Press, 1965, pp. 168–229, here p. 205.

[34]   Vincent Goossaert, 'Le destin de la religion chinoise au 20ème siècle', *Social Compass*, 50.4 (2003), pp. 429–40, here p. 435. See also Goossaert, 'State and Religion in Modern China', referring to Rebecca Allyn Nedostup, 'Religion, Superstition, and Governing Society in Nationalist China', PhD thesis, Columbia University, 2001, pp. 196–211.

[35]   Poon Shuk Wah shows this in detail with reference to two religious festivals in his 'Refashioning Festivals in Republican Guangzhou'.

1. Festivals and rites, which were bound up with the agricultural cycle, lost significance and decreased in number as a consequence of *industrialization*.

2. The *urbanization* that accompanied industrialization shattered the social and spatial realities characteristic of the villages. Here, community and religious community were almost identical, their unity based on the village temple. Social communities saw themselves as part of the locality and its resident forces and ancestral graves. New social relations developed in the city, and these were no longer identical with the neighbourhood community. Traditional religious life, which was a part of the community, thus lost its social and spatial basis.

3. *Cultural contact with foreign countries* led to Westernization. From the perspective of modern Western science, traditional Chinese religion was superstition. Traditional Chinese culture now no longer represented the sole aesthetic arsenal of the Chinese lifestyle, but was joined by Western ways of life and values. On this basis, people also turned against traditional religion, which was suddenly located within an aesthetic cultural context no longer self-evident to young city dwellers. In these times of rapid change, traditional rituals appeared bereft of meaning to the youth of the cities; ties to the ancestors no longer seemed binding. Rather, on the Western model, based on Western urban values, smaller families developed, as did a more individual worldview in which the social forms of traditional religion no longer had any place.

After the Chinese Communists seized power in 1949, religion was viewed in true Marxist style as a reflection of unresolved class contradictions; it would disappear when these were resolved. It therefore seemed absurd to fight against religion, and people were granted the freedom to follow one; only the five officially permitted religions were and are considered to be religions. A statement made by Mao Zedong shows that he considered Chinese Marxism the religion of the people,[36] and visual propaganda produced by the Communist Party of China shows with particular clarity that the party drew very heavily on the traditional popular pictorial arsenal of Chinese religion to promote communism. This developed into nothing less than an iconographic orthodoxy during the Cultural Revolution,[37]

---

[36]   Donald E. MacInnis, *Religion im heutigen China. Politik und Praxis* (orig. *Religion in China Today: Policy and Practice*, Maryknoll, NY, Orbis, 1989), German translation edited by Roman Malek, Nettetal, Steyler, 1993, p. 26.

[37]   See John Gittings, 'Excess and Enthusiasm', in Harriet Evans and Stephanie Donald (eds.), *Picturing Power in the People's Republic of China: Posters of the Cultural Revolution*, Lanham, Rowman & Littlefield, 1999, pp. 27–46, here pp. 30–31; Stefan R. Landsberger,

one which lays bare how traditional religious functions such as the worship of idols, public rituals, sacrifices and martyrdom, redemption, a cosmic world order, morality, exorcism, final judgement and true knowledge were transmitted through the medium of visual propaganda.[38]

As a consequence of Deng Xiaoping's Open Door policy, launched in 1979, Document No. 19 was circulated by the Central Committee of the Communist Party of China in 1982. Here, for the first time, it was accepted that religion could survive and grow under socialism. The right to propagate atheism was removed from the constitution the same year, replaced by a prohibition on forcing anyone to believe or not to believe in something.[39] A few years later, the subject of religious studies was reintroduced in the major universities of China. The key concern of research on religion was no longer with demonstrating a materialist and atheist tradition in China, as had been the case with research on atheism decades earlier, but with new questions relating to the possible function of religion in the development of a socialist society in China and religious policies reoriented in accordance with this. On this view, by means of its ethics, religion should help to create good socialist citizens and to produce social stability and unity. Churches and temples were reopened, and religious practice was widely tolerated again.[40] This resonated so profoundly that commentators spoke of a

---

'Role Modelling in Mainland China during the "Four Modernizations" Era: The Visual Dimension', in Huang Chun-Chieh and Erik Zürcher (eds.), *Norms and the State in China*, Leiden, Brill, 1993, pp. 359–76, here pp. 369, 376.

[38] See Stephan Feuchtwang, *The Imperial Metaphor: Popular Religion in China*, London, Curzon, 2001, ch. 8; Barend J. ter Haar, 'China's Inner Demons: The Political Impact of the Demonological Paradigm', *China Information*, 11.2–3 (1996), pp. 54–88, here pp. 60, 79–84; Joseph M. Kitagawa, 'One of the Many Faces of China: Maoism as a Quasi-Religion', *Japanese Journal of Religious Studies*, 1.2–3 (1974), pp. 125–41; Geremie Barmé, *Shades of Mao: The Posthumous Cult of the Great Leader*, New York, Sharpe, 1996; Joachim Gentz, 'The One Discourse that Pervades All: Concurrent Constructions of an Ideal Order in the Fight Between the CCP and the Falun Gong', unpublished talk given in Heidelberg on 27 August 2004, to appear as a chapter in a forthcoming book. On the religiosity of the modern-day Communist Party in China, see also Anthony C. Yu, *State and Religion in China: Historical and Textual Perspectives*, Chicago, Open Court, 2005, p. 145.

[39] See Merle Goldman, 'Religion in Post-Mao China', *The Annals of the American Academy* 438.1 (1986), pp. 146–56, here p. 150.

[40] See Monika Gänßbauer, *Parteistaat und Protestantische Kirche. Religionspolitik im nachmao-istischen China*, Frankfurt, Lembeck, 2004, esp. 'Religionsverständnis im nachmaoistischen China' (pp. 213–45). On the case of Daoism, see Lai Chi-Tim, 'Daoism in China Today, 1980– 2002', *The China Quarterly*, 174 (2003), pp. 413–27; on the case of Buddhism, see Yoshiko Ashiwa and David L. Wank, 'The Politics of a Reviving Buddhist Temple: State,

rampant religious fever. At the same time, there was a mushrooming of unofficial popular religious traditions and unregistered religious institutions across the country, such that the Chinese government felt obliged to take serious measures to restrict illegal religions and cults. To avoid contradicting its own new religious policies, it pursued a twin strategy: on the one hand, it granted the registered religions greater recognition, freedom of action and tolerance. On the other, it implemented strict measures against unregistered, illegal religious activities. In 1993, Jiang Zemin became the first high-ranking politician to speak positively about religion in a socialist society. In his famous 'Three Represents', he insisted that religion must be practised within the framework of clearly defined laws. As a result, the religious laws were tightened up markedly in 1994.[41] Shortly after the 'Three Represents' had been reformulated in an even more diluted form in 1999, a major demonstration was held by the Falun Gong movement, in which around 10,000 devotees gathered in front of the seat of government in Beijing; this came as a shock to the Chinese government. This event changed religious politics in one fell swoop, showing that the changes which had occurred in religious policies and legislation in the 1980s must be understood as a form of state tolerance of religion rather than religious freedom in the modern sense. The new religious movements have been dealt with far more harshly since then.

A complex and confusing landscape of new religious movements developed in the PRC in the 1980s and 1990s. Scholars are unable to provide a neat empirical account of these core groups, let alone all their off-shoots, because most of them must remain underground if they wish to survive.

These groupings can in principle be differentiated into those which pick up the thread of indigenous Buddhist, Daoist or Qigong traditions and those based chiefly on Christian elements. Christian and Chinese elements are, however, almost always combined in varying proportions, and it is possible to discern numerous elements of Western esotericism in many of these groups, from psychological elements through ufological concepts to European notions of Eastern spirituality.[42] One of the key motives for joining such groups is the belief

---

Association, and Religion in Southeast China', *The Journal of Asian Studies*, 65.2 (2006), pp. 337–59.

[41]   See Gänßbauer, *Parteistaat und Protestantische Kirche*, pp. 257–66. See also Tony Lambert, 'The Present Religious Policy of the Chinese Communist Party', *Religion, State & Society*, 29.2 (2001), pp. 121–29, here pp. 124–125.

[42]   See Kristin Kupfer, '"Geheimgesellschaften" in der VR China: Christlich inspirierte, spirituell-religiöse Gruppierungen seit 1978', *China Analysis*, 8 (2001) published by the Center for East Asian and Pacific Studies, Trier University, Germany, http://www.asienpolitik. de/working_papers.html (pdf file); Tony Lambert, 'Modern Sects and Cults in China', *China Study Journal*, 13.3 (1998), pp. 6–9. See also the subsequent articles in the same issue

in their healing powers. This applies to the Qigong movement and local cults, to the Christian congregations, most of which are Pentecostalist in character, and to Falun Gong.[43]

The Chinese government became aware of these groups and their huge following at an early stage. The problem, however, was that the government was more likely to inspire social unrest than social peace by taking harsh measures against so many millions of practitioners. But if the Bureau of Religious Affairs had officially included these many groups in a new, expanded definition of religion, the number of believers would have grown to such an extent that, in its existing form, the Bureau would no longer have been able to deal with them administratively; it would have required significant expansion, at considerable cost.

Among the larger groups, 15 have so far been officially designated 'heretical teachings' (xiejiao) and prohibited. In addition, there are at least five so-called harmful groups, all of whose origins lie in the field of Qigong. At least 30 such groups, which were founded after 1978 and were active for a number of years, are known to have existed. 18 of these groups are still in existence. The years between 1983 and 1993 were the golden age of the foundation of new religious movements. The tensions of religious politics, along with the typical structure of new religious movements, with their loose institutional organization and fixation on a charismatic leader, cause these groupings to splinter and be renamed on a regular basis. This makes it difficult to determine precisely the origins and development of the individual movements. The spread of these groups ranges from individual provinces to the national and international levels. It is extremely difficult to determine the number of adherents because most of them are unregistered and make no official profession of their faith. According to official estimates, the total number of adherents of new religious movements in the PRC is 1.5 million, while other estimates assume a figure of up to 80 million. This would be around 5.3 per cent of the total population.[44] The number of members probably lies between a few thousand and a few hundred thousand per group, a small number of larger groups extending into the millions. Falun Gong (FLG), which used to have 70 million followers, is an exception here.

---

by Lu Yunfeng, 'Report on an Investigation into the Illegal Organisation, the "Disciples Sect"', pp. 9–16, and by Luo Weihong, 'The Facts about the Activities of the Heterodox Sect "The Established King"', pp. 17–21. See also Deng Zhaoming, 'Recent Millennial Movements on Mainland China: Three Cases', Inter-Religion, 34 (1998), pp. 47–57.

[43]   See Claudia Währisch-Oblau, 'Healing Prayers and Healing Testimonies in Mainland Chinese Churches: An Attempt at Intercultural Understanding', China Study Journal, 14.2 (1999), pp. 5–34; Fan Lizhu, 'The Cult of the Silkworm Mother as a Core of Local Community Religion', The China Quarterly, 174 (2003), pp. 359–72, here pp. 365ff.

[44]   See Kupfer, '"Geheimgesellschaften" in der VR China'.

We know the Falun Gong movement because of the meditators, often clothed in yellow garb, or the small groups performing traditional Chinese dances, both of which can be seen in the pedestrian areas of Western city centres, their activities intended to raise awareness of the repression and torture suffered in China by this new Chinese religious movement. It was founded in 1992 as a lay movement by Li Hongzhi (born 7 July 1952 or 13 May 1951) and is representative of a religious dynamic that developed subsequent to the Qigong fever of the 1980s in China. Li, the charismatic leader of this movement, sees FLG as a path of perfection leading to the highest possible levels of physical and spiritual cultivation. This includes a whole series of Qigong exercises as well as a doctrine centred on the three concepts of truthfulness (*zhen*), compassion (*shan*) and forbearance (*ren*). These three concepts are considered to be moral principles and at the same time characteristics of the cosmos present in its smallest elements. According to the teachings of the FLG, by refraining from every kind of desire and all forms of individual wilfulness, one's spiritual nature becomes cultivated to such an extent that, first of all, one attains supernatural powers and one's body is transformed; eventually, one's individual cells and molecules consist purely of cosmic energy. The Falun Law Wheel, which according to Falun Gong doctrine is inserted into the abdomen of the practitioner by Li Hongzhi's transcendental Law Body, is helpful here. According to Li, it is a high-energy, intelligent rotating body consisting of matter, which has the same properties as the cosmos and thus represents a cosmos in miniature. It continuously collects energy from the cosmos and, even during sleep, brings about a permanent transformation, automatically converting it into cultivating energy.[45]

According to Li Hongzhi's teachings, the world is morally corrupt, which is due in part to the influence of harmful beings from other worlds, which have brought modern science to this world in order to make people dependent on them and thus subjugate them. Li Hongzhi sees himself as the only one who knows and embodies the cosmic principles and who has therefore attained such a high level of cultivation that only he is capable of saving the world from ruin, of changing it back into a good world.

Li Hongzhi describes his own system as part of the Buddhist school, but underlines that Falun Gong has nothing to do with Buddhism as a religion. He is also very keen to ensure that no religious terminology is used in translations of his works. But the FLG doctrine entails many elements from the religious traditions of Chinese Daoism and Buddhism. It bears all the typical hallmarks of popular lay religious movements since the Ming era (1368–1644): it has its

---

[45]   See Li Hongzhi, *Zhuan Falun* (the complete teachings of Falun Gong), Gloucester, MA, Fairwinds, 2001; idem, *Das Große Vervollkommnungsgesetz des Falun-Buddha-Gebotes*, Bad Pyrmont, Ost-Zhou-Verlag, 1998.

own scriptures, cultivates a sophisticated body discourse concerned with the healing or rejuvenation of the body through moral or technical practice, while the adherents believe in limitless human potential and supernatural abilities and transformation of the body, above all through morality. They also believe in the notion that human beings have been cast out from a blissful original state, the aim being to return to this state. There is also a belief in a living Buddha who embodies the highest truth, and, finally, the associated belief that one may take short cuts to redemption through external help such as the Law Wheel, in other words, beliefs of a kind associated with the tradition of Mahayana Buddhism.[46] At the same time, modern concepts are integrated into the doctrinal system to a striking degree. Alongside Buddhist and Daoist content, the teachings express a worldview which, up to and including specific lines of argument, is strongly imbued with pseudo-scientific and ufological elements of new Western religions in the same vein as Erich von Däniken's ideas. The teachings of FLG thus represent a syncretic blend of indigenous traditional religion, modern science, esoteric doctrine and ufology quite typical of twentieth-century new religious movements around the world.

In response to the FLG mass demonstration held by around 10,000 adherents (of around 60 to 70 million FLG practitioners at the time) on 25 April before the seat of government in Beijing, FLG in China was prohibited as a 'heretical cult'[47] on 22 July 1999. The group is accused of causing unrest and social instability, spreading superstition and heretical ideas and of deceiving the masses – all of them accusations characteristic of Chinese religious politics for centuries, some of them using an identical form of words. As a consequence, a new religious law was enacted in October 1999, featuring more stringent criteria for the prohibition and prosecution of 'heretical cults', whose activities could now be punished as criminal acts for the first time.

Since the mid-1990s, Li has been living in the USA in an unknown location. The FLG movement is defending itself against party propaganda with massive counter-propaganda and lays claim to the party's key spheres of legitimacy such as true knowledge, correct morality and correct leadership, using the same tools of propaganda as the party, mirroring its approach in perfect symmetry.[48] In contrast to the brutal deployment of physical violence against FLG followers on the part of the Chinese state, such violence has not yet been used by the FLG.

---

[46]   See David Ownby, 'A History for Falun Gong: Popular Religion and the Chinese State since the Ming Dynasty', *Nova Religio*, 6.2 (2003), pp. 223–43.

[47]   The traditional Chinese term *xiejiao* refers to illegitimate teachings and is now understood as equivalent to the American term 'heretic cult', which is also used to translate it.

[48]   See Gentz, 'The One Discourse that Pervades All'.

One consequence of this clash is the enactment of far stricter laws on religion since 1999. All the important religious laws of the last six years may be related to the FLG. Apart from the latter, however, they are directed at all new religious movements, Qigong groups, all of which were removed from the official register and therefore lost legitimate status, and the underground Christian churches.[49] Furthermore, the global discourse on terrorism subsequent to 11 September 2001 serves the Chinese regime as a new, politically correct justification for the persecution of religious groups in China, particularly the Muslim minorities in the province of Xinjiang.[50]

Since the early 1950s, the Chinese government has built up an elaborate bureaucratic supervisory structure intended to ensure that religion serves political objectives, and which essentially continues to exist today. The Bureau of Religious Affairs has divisions at every level of the state bureaucracy and is active politically at the provincial, municipal, district and county level. Each of the five officially recognized religions has a 'patriotic association' that regulates the relationship between religion and state and sees to it that state directives are implemented at the local level and that all relevant information from the association arrives at the centre. The structure of these patriotic associations parallels that of the Bureau of Religious Affairs.

Essentially, the Bureau's responsibilities consist in registering, monitoring and regulating membership, places of religious gathering and practice, religious education, selection of clergy, publication of religious material, financing of religious activities, etc. It undertakes annual checks on registration and imposes prohibitions and punishments on 'illegal' organizations and activities. Registration-related work is one of the Bureau's key tasks, representing the Chinese state's most important tool for controlling and monitoring religious organizations, as registration requires religious groups to give up their power to reach autonomous decisions on their clergy, financial affairs, programmes, religious materials, education and more besides; this power passes to the Bureau, which keeps an eye on these areas and is involved in decision-making.[51] Services may be monitored; in a Christian context, for example, certain topics such as the Second Coming, Judgement Day and the biblical creation story may be censored. All baptisms must be reported and applied for in triplicate. One form goes to the Bureau of Religious Affairs, one to the appropriate Patriotic

---

[49]   See Gänßbauer, 'Religion (zongjiao) versus üble Kulte (xiejiao)', ch. 11.3 in *Parteistaat und Protestantische Kirche*, pp. 257–66.

[50]   See the 115-page report from Human Rights Watch 'Devastating Blows: Religious Repression of Uighurs in Xinjiang', vol. 17, no. 2 (C), April 2005, http://hrw.org/english/docs/2005/04/11/china10447.htm.

[51]   See Human Rights Watch/Asia, *China: State Control of Religion*, New York, 1997.

Association and one to the applying parents' place of work. Legal recognition of a baptism depends on the consent of all three entities.[52]

In 1994, the formerly typical legal regulations, which were of a general and flexible character, were replaced by a large number of detailed regulations governing registration procedures. As the state begins to base its religious policy far more strongly on the law, it is evident that we are dealing here with something like secularization in the legal sense of the consolidation of a system of justice that is secular because it no longer has a purely ideological foundation. Since then, the condemnation of religious practice has increasingly been justified with reference to specific offences rather than counter-revolution and other ideological principles. The law on religion, which has been tightened since 1999, relates to all religious groups classified as illegal; alongside followers of FLG, who have faced outright persecution, this applies in particular to the underground Christian churches; organizations such as ChinaAid report encroachment by the state on a weekly basis in the form of persecution, arrests and torture. In this respect, the Internet as a medium of information facilitates an entirely new and in some cases shocking transparency, of a kind unthinkable in the past.

Of key importance here is the state's distinction between the practice of religion and criminal activity, on which the state's understanding of religious freedom rests. Consonant with this, the official line is that no one is prosecuted or punished on account of his or her faith, but only for engaging in illegal activities in the form of criminal offences, which recalls traditional religious policies. According to the new laws, all religious activities which are not officially registered are considered criminal offences. The interpretation of religious activities on the part of the Communist Party generally differs markedly from the self-image projected by the religious communities.[53]

Alongside the Ministry of Public Security, the Ministry of State Security and other government departments, three organizations have been established specifically to monitor new religious movements:

1. The Central Leading Group on Dealing with FLG and so-called 610 Office, which has overall responsibility for dealing with FLG. The 'Falun Gong Surveillance Team', established on 10 June 1999 and thus generally known by the abbreviated form '610 Office', is the most important response from an administrative point of view to the mass demonstration carried out by the FLG in April 1999. This institution takes its orders directly from the central government; on this basis, it operates autonomously on all political

---

[52]   See Gänßbauer, *Parteistaat und Protestantische Kirche.*

[53]   See the in-depth study by David Ownby, 'Imperial Fantasies'.

and administrative levels, across all administrative, local and juridical boundaries.[54]

2. The Office for Prevention and Handling of Heretical Teachings, which coordinates the day-to-day operation of state religious policy.

3. The China Anti-Cult Association, concerned largely with propaganda and research.

The Minister for Public Security, Zhou Yongkang, described the FLG and other ethnic-religious activities as the two greatest threats to the social stability of China.

To place these organs of surveillance, conceived by the central government, within the context of their pragmatic deployment at the local level, I will refrain from examining here the many dreadful arrests and cases of torture regularly reported by missionary societies and human rights organizations. While this perspective must be taken very seriously, it is nonetheless geared selectively towards the activities of these organs, which tell us little about the relationship between politics and practice in the religious field, which is, in all, far more complex. In what follows, I shall therefore look at the near-daily ritual occurrences that are a key characteristic of the popular religion so strong in southeast China and which illustrate very well the complexity of the relationship between state and religion at the local level. It is hard to fathom these ritual events with the criteria typical of European definitions of religion. Southeast China is home not to hierarchically organized religious institutions, but to a complex network of local temples dedicated to a rich pantheon of local divinities. Rather than a hierarchically organized priesthood, there are local leaders who are endowed with responsibility for organizing local communal rituals on an alternating basis through rotation procedures or divination. Daoist, Buddhist

---

[54]   The most detailed account yet of this institution is found in the first volume of the inquiry report on the persecution of Falun Gong; see Zhuicha pohai Falun gong guoji zuzhi (World Organisation to Investigate the Persecution of Falun Gong) (ed.), *Zhuicha pohai Falun gong guoji zuzhi diaocha baogao ji* (Investigation Reports on the Persecution of Falun Gong) vol.1, Hyde Park, MA, USA, http://upholdjustice.org/, 2004, pp. 18–19, 42–53. A translation of the book into English (472pp) is available as pdf-file at: http://www.upholdjustice.org/English.2/WholeBook.pdf (21.04.09), for e-book format see http://www.zhuichaguoji.org/en/index2.php?option=content&task=view&id=103&pop=1&page=0. According to the introduction to the first volume (p. 16), the second volume will deal exclusively with the government institutions, elaborating in more detail on the functioning of the 610 Office. See also the diagram in the version of the *Diaocha baogao* from 15 August 2004 at http://www.upholdjustice.org/NEWS/ZC-all.pdf, p. 6 (16 August 2004).

or Confucian ritual specialists are employed, mostly from outside the villages, to carry out specific rituals. Local spirit mediums are often possessed by the divinities of the village temple, perform religious acts and say powerful words during the ritual. But all these acts are too diverse and specific to constitute a particular doctrine or to express specific religious beliefs. They thus fail to tally with the Communist Party's official concept of religion, which is geared towards definitional criteria such as doctrine, literature, organized institution, hierarchical priesthood, rituals which express religious beliefs, etc. – criteria, in other words, which were developed in light of European religious history and which are of little use in describing Chinese popular religion as practised by hundreds of millions of Chinese in southeast China.

According to Kenneth Dean, the popular religion of southern China is better described as a 'syncretistic field'.[55] Most of the thousands of villages have at least one temple, often more, dedicated to a community divinity. Since the destruction of the Cultural Revolution, many of these temples have been rebuilt over the last 20 years. The life of the temples is highly active and is organized by temple committees. Events are held there several times a week, ranging from processions of gods within the village through processions between villages or to holy sites and a variety of rituals, to performances of traditional opera, puppet theatre and even films. A procession may involve up to 100 villages and last up to a week. In this way, stable local networks are created and continuously strengthened. This extremely dense network of local temples sometimes takes on a large number of local administrative tasks, thus forming a kind of unofficial second level of local government. This restoration of the traditional temple networks in southern China can, therefore, also be seen as the continuation of a particular kind of politics that has increasingly taken hold over a period of 400–500 years, namely the transferral of tasks and duties of the central government to the localities, which are organized institutionally through these temple networks and thus gain some degree of local autonomy. Here, local autonomy does *not* mean the separation of religion from the state, but the downwards distribution of responsibility for local affairs to a local managerial elite, whose institutional basis lies in temples, lineage associations and similar local institutions. These

---

[55]   Kenneth Dean, *Lord of the Three in One: The Spread of a Cult in Southeast China*, Princeton, Princeton University Press, 1998. My account also draws on Dean's *Taoist Ritual and Popular Cults of Southeast China*, Princeton, Princeton University Press, 1993, and his article 'Local Communal Religion in Contemporary South-east China', *China Quarterly*, 174 (2003), pp. 338–58. See also his 'China's Second Government: Regional Ritual Systems of the Putian Plains', in *Shehui, minzu yu wenhua zhanyan guoji yantaohui lunwenji* (Collected Papers from the International Conference on Social, Ethnic and Cultural Transformation), Taipei, 2001, pp. 77–109.

constitute a dense and well-organized religious infrastructure used concurrently for other purposes. But this does not mean that the religious structures are straightforwardly secular; we can merely observe that the boundaries of our analytical concepts are seemingly not drawn so strictly in practice. It is important to how we evaluate these phenomena that the newly emerging temples and rituals are not merely a rigid revival of a lost past. Above all, they are arenas in which the forces and themes of modernity are actively negotiated. It is precisely modern traditions and motifs that are being actively grappled with, integrated and adopted in the context of local culture; what we are seeing here is the absorption and adoption of technological and political innovations within the indigenous cultural symbol system, whether it is portraits of Mao in processions or the exchange of CD-ROMs, featuring the latest ritual innovations, between the temple committees. The three main actors in this field are the clergy of the local temple, national religious associations under the aegis of the state and the Bureau of Religious Affairs. Resources and meanings are constantly being negotiated between these three key actors. Confrontations between them are played out within the institutional framework of the religious laws laid down by the state, laws whose specific interpretation is constantly negotiated by all sides through mutual discursive exchange. The national religious associations play a dual role here: they both supervise and protect the local religious communities and have a mediating and translating function between state and local interests. It is their task to ensure that the local institutions retain the greatest possible degree of autonomy without infringing the state's religious laws, while asserting their own autonomy as much as possible vis-à-vis both parties.[56]

Hence, these examples at least clearly refute the thesis that modernization brings detraditionalization and secularization in its wake. But despite this revival, religious life in the People's Republic of China is very different from that which pertained before the ravages of the twentieth century, which have markedly diminished the religious sphere as a result of the long period of repression and the economic restrictions that accompanied it. However, in those places where the local economy is reviving, the reconstruction of the old traditions is also proceeding much more rapidly, in Fujian on the southeast coast of China for example, which has close ties with Hong Kong and Taiwan, from which it receives a great deal of financial aid. But religious life was most damaged by the decline of the lineage as the centre of socioeconomic and ritual life. Because the clan associations no longer have estates or central financial administrations, they are no longer able to keep up their clan rituals on a large scale. The temples

---

[56]   See the detailed case study by Ashiwa and Wank, 'The Politics of a Reviving Buddhist Temple', which provides a very clear account of the individual camps' options for action.

of the local divinities and associated rites, on the other hand, have been very well preserved and reconstructed since 1979. Some were prohibited, others were frozen in the form of museums, while others managed, by involving old retired party cadres for instance, to grow, thrive and become rich, emerging as significant cultural centres in which community events took place, in much the same way as sometimes occurs in the parish hall in rural Germany. But apart from the waves of anti-religious campaigns, to which smaller local temples have repeatedly fallen victim, regulations have been increasingly bureaucratized since the 1990s, severely curtailing many temple activities. The *Far Eastern Economic Review* (6 June 1996) reported that in the province of Zhejiang between February and June 1996, at least 15,000 unregistered temples, churches and graves were destroyed by the police; the city of Ningbo alone lost 3,000 temples. On 12 December 2000, *Agence France Press* reported the destruction of 1,200 temples in the region of Wenzhou alone, carried out partly with dynamite. A failure to register them properly was claimed to be the reason.

On the whole, however, simply because of their own limited means, the state institutions in this extremely large and diverse country must still leave plenty of gaps in the systems of control and administration. These are then filled by local, autonomous forms of collective organization that create their own order, forms which are often not only tolerated by the state, but on which it in fact depends. This very often entails recourse to pre-modern modalities which express a particular way of life, the regional tradition and particular cultural values, which flourish anew on the basis of a mutual understanding between representatives of local religion and the state. This, though, is possible only to the extent that these local forms do not become too powerful and continue to observe the official rituals of regular reports and contact with the political centre. The ritual events in southeast China constitute temporary autonomous zones, in which local communities express themselves and are given form, zones which are constantly in motion and of a kind which can only ever exist through such movement. In the north of China, local cults develop less in the context of a religious infrastructure organized on a large scale than around powerful religious personalities, who then bring about the development of individual religious structures[57] or as places in which, in a kind of local public sphere, the power of local elites is articulated vis-à-vis or together with the local representatives of state power; these sites link various institutions, all of which benefit from the religious activities in various ways and therefore support them.[58]

It is of relevance to the present topic that these temple activities have certain

---

[57]   See Lizhu, 'The Cult of the Silkworm Mother'.

[58]   See Adam Yuet Chau, 'The Politics of Legitimation and the Revival of Popular Religion in Shaanbei, North-Central China', *Modern China*, 31.2 (2005), pp. 236–78.

traits of civil society associations and clearly contradict the thesis that modern religion involves a withdrawal into the private sphere.

According to Goossaert,[59] it is possible to identify three basic state measures in China relating to religion in the twentieth century, which also shed light on our topic of secularization. First, the state replaced the traditional distinction between orthodoxy and heterodoxy, which related to the imperial, canonically based ethical-cosmological system, with the Western distinction between religion and superstition, which involved entirely new criteria and led to the identification of five officially recognized religions. Second, the state attempted to reform these five religions and to bring their teachings and practices into alignment with state ideology. Third, it incorporated some elements of the religions into its own secular programme. Thus, secularization appears here mainly as a programme of new classifications within a new system of order, within whose categories religious traditions had to reinvent themselves as 'religion', or, if they failed to exhibit the defined characteristics, as 'sciences', 'medicine', 'folklore', 'philosophy', 'ethics' or 'sport'. In this context, then, secularization must also be understood as the redefinition of traditional teachings and practices within a new conceptual system. Here, the place reserved for 'religion' was so greatly diminished that the continuity of religious traditions could be ensured only under a secular banner.

Japan

Japanese religious history is marked by constant state intervention in religious affairs and constant wrangling over authority in religious activities. The role of the state has constantly changed, as Kitagawa has convincingly shown.[60] In the Japanese context, an inquiry into secularization must focus in particular on the state functionalization of religion to political ends, which dominated Japanese religious politics long before the modern period, beginning in the Meiji era, and which has remained one of its key features.

During the Tokugawa shogunate (1615–1868), religions were kept under strict surveillance, stricter than was ever possible in China. In order to clamp down on the prohibited new Christians, from 1635 all citizens were required to become members of Buddhist temples and have themselves registered in Buddhist temple registers. The Buddhist temples thus became divisions of the state administration, in which births, marriages, adoptions, deaths, changes of residence, occupation and other data were recorded. The temples also functioned as schools, in which

---

[59]   Goossaert, 'State and Religion in Modern China', p. 5.

[60]   See Joseph M. Kitagawa, 'Some Reflections on Japanese Religion and its Relationship to the Imperial System', *Japanese Journal of Religious Studies*, 17.2–3 (1990), pp. 129–78.

reading and writing as well as Confucian ethics were taught. But while every citizen had to become a Buddhist, documents of the period show no evidence at all of an increase in the citizens' interest in Buddhism. Buddhist priests thus became state functionaries and bureaucrats, and Buddhism as a religion developed little during this period. This integration into the state apparatus initially led to a reduction in religious-spiritual activity and thus to secularization. In the Meiji period, from 1868 on, this situation changed through the encounter with the West and the intense Westernization that set in as a result. Shintoism developed, together with the plethora of new religions, as a countermovement to a Buddhism perceived as hollowed out. The Meiji regime, led once again by the emperor after many hundreds of years, transformed this general antipathy towards Buddhism into harsh persecution, which peaked in the 1870s under the slogan 'Eliminate Buddhism' with temple closures, the expulsion of Buddhist priests and monks and the destruction of Buddhist religious objects. Popular discontent and foreign protests led to alleviation of the persecution and ultimately to formal freedom of religion and the separation of church and state. At the same time, an attempt was made to cleanse Shintoism of all Buddhist elements and to transform it into a state religion on the Western model, to which end the Meiji government formulated new criteria, which often had little in common with local Shinto practice.[61] The idea of a state Shintoism was abandoned again in 1872, and a Ministry of Religion was established which held jurisdiction over Buddhism and Shintoism. The personnel of both religions were now urged to spread nationalism and to teach religion and morality with an emphasis on loyalty to the ruler and state.

In 1873, Christianity was permitted again, which immediately led to the establishment of a large number of Christian organizations. In 1882, the state recognized the many newly founded Shinto schools as independent groups in their own right and now distinguished officially between sect-Shinto, which was financially autonomous, and shrine-Shinto, which received support from the state. In 1884, the separation between religion and the state was officially codified. The Administrative Bureau for Religious Affairs was dissolved, and from now on the state-backed shrine-Shintoism was no longer regarded as a religion but as a national cult. It was therefore divested of the authority to carry out funerals, which had become a Shinto prerogative during the period of persecution of Buddhism. In 1889, a new constitution extended freedom of religion to the entire population and banned religious education in public schools. But it allowed shrine-Shintoism broad scope for non-religious activities, making patriotism into a national cult. Veneration of the emperor and other Shinto divinities, all

---

[61]   See Gaynor Sekimoni, 'Paper Fowl and Wooden Fish: The Separation of Kami and Buddha Worship in Haguro Shugendô 1869–1875', *Japanese Journal of Religious Studies*, 32.2 (2005), pp. 197–234.

of which were declared national divinities, now became part of the syllabus of public schools and the patriotic duty of citizens of all ages. In this way, traditional religious politics was now carried on in supposedly modern nationalist-secular fashion. From the turn of the century onwards, it is evident that representatives of Japanese Buddhism also responded to the Western understanding of religion by incorporating the conceptual standards of Christian religion into their own self-portrayals, in which experiences of transcendence, for example, now appear as a significant feature of Japanese Buddhism for the first time.[62] In the years leading up to the Second World War, we can discern a power struggle between the state's efforts to organize and control religions on the Western model, and countervailing religious forces, which also asserted their religiosity on a Western model; as a result, the state organs of surveillance changed constantly. The state tried to use the leaders of individual religious schools to control religion in a general sense. It delegated surveillance to the religious groups, which were forced to merge to form larger entities in 1941 and 1942, enabling the state to monitor them very closely. The 56 Buddhist branches were reduced to 28; Christians, Buddhists and sect-Shintoists were forced to take part in shrine worship; religious leaders who resisted this were browbeaten, punished and locked up; religious groups which resisted were repressed, so that no opposition to speak of could get off the ground. Religions were entirely subject to a totalitarian regime.

In 1945, subsequent to Japan's defeat in the Second World War, shrine-Shintoism was abolished as a national cult, the emperor officially revoked his divine status, and freedom of religion was proclaimed under a new constitution that reduced state control of religion. A Department for Religious Affairs was established within the Ministry of Education to monitor this. The original 56 Buddhist branches separated again, which meant that, together with all the splinter groups now approved, a total of 260 Buddhist corporations existed in 1950; this figure was reduced to 170 by the law on religious corporations of 1951. This splintering weakened the Buddhist centres financially and politically.[63] Social groups that formed around particular shrines were often identical with so-called neighbourhood associations (chônaikai), which were state-decreed and state-controlled initiatives. A similar intermediate institutional status was enjoyed by the so-called corporations of public interests (kôeki hôjin), which enabled the state to monitor civil activities since their codification in Article 34 of the Meiji civil law of 1896. After 1945, the form of state intervention into civil affairs changed, primarily taking the form of very precise bureaucratic regulations.

---

[62]   See Isomae Jun'ichi, 'Deconstructing "Japanese Religion": A Historical Survey, *Japanese Journal of Religious Studies*, 32.2 (2005), pp. 235–48, here pp. 238–39.
[63]   See Edward Norbeck, *Religion and Society in Modern Japan: Continuity and Change*, Houston, Tourmaline Press, 1970.

Specific laws were made for the administration of all types of corporation, including religious ones, but all these corporations are subgroups of these state corporations of public interests. These corporations have to report regularly to a ministry and may be investigated and prohibited by it. The corporations, including the religious variety, must hand over lists of their annual activities, assets, membership figures, expenditure, accounts, planned activities, etc., which limits their autonomy. Often, an understanding exists that former administrative employees from state institutions are to be appointed on a preferential basis, so that the groups' membership also tends to list stateward. Not all religious groups, however, have been incorporated into such corporations, or have been incorporated only after many years. When the law on religious corporations came into effect in 1951, the Religious Affairs Section (*Shûmuka*) of the Agency for Cultural Affairs (*Bunkachô*), which was tasked with administration of the law, kept track of unincorporated religious organizations, and their number was published annually in the Yearbook of Religions (*Shûkyô nenkan*) between 1947 and 1960.[64] In this period, the number of unincorporated groups grew from 13,300 in 1947 to 40,000 in 1960. It is, unfortunately, impossible to determine how many of these groups exist today. At 178,603, the number of religious corporations has been astonishingly stable since 1951, with a maximum deviation of just 3 per cent.

Buddhism continues to be the strongest religion in Japan. Because it is also regarded as the normative religion on account of its continuity, there are almost no studies on contemporary Buddhism in Japan, despite the fact that around half of all Japanese take part in the practices of traditional Buddhism.[65] It is hard to keep track of Buddhist organizations. They are organized around so many different activities within civil society that they are often scarcely identifiable as religious groups. Traditional practices are being modernized, and contact is being made with Buddhist organizations abroad; some get involved in politics, while others play an active role in the provision of social welfare, carry out missionary work abroad or attempt to strengthen patriotism. Since the 1880s, a large number of Buddhist teaching associations and lay associations have developed. Many new groups have been founded over the last 120 years, and time and again great efforts have been made to unite these groups with the established Buddhist schools, for the big schools are very closely monitored by the Home Ministry, which requires them to obtain state agreement for all major projects and all changes. Since 1974,

---

[64]   For an evaluation, see David Reid, 'Statistics on Religious Organisations in Japan 1947–1972 (I)', *Japanese Journal of Religious Studies*, 2.1 (1975), pp. 45–64 and in the eight following issues, up to no. 4.4 (1977).

[65]   See also the introduction by the two editors of the special issue on contemporary Buddhism in Japan: Stephen G. Covell and Mark Rowe, 'Traditional Buddhism in Contemporary Japan', *Japanese Journal of Religious Studies*, 31.2 (2004), pp. 245–54.

however, the Buddhists have established a large number of new organizations outside the sphere of state influence, of which the NGO (non-governmental organization) network founded in 2002 is undoubtedly the most important. It now comprises more than 40 NGOs, of which the largest manages an annual budget of around 6.5 million euros, has around 183 employees and branches in three countries.[66]

As with traditional Buddhist institutions, it is impossible to provide a precise account of the foundation of new Shinto organizations. Up to 1945, Shintoism in Japan was divided into three main organizations, out of which the Shinto Shrines Association (*Jinja Honchô*) developed to unite the Shinto world after the war. So far, no Shinto NGOs have emerged. The preservation of a small unit of around 8,000 Shinto priests under the leadership of the Central Authority of the Shinto Shrines Association clearly takes priority over the dissemination of Shintoism within society through specific projects.

Alongside the established traditional religions, Japan is famous for its many new religions: these were first founded towards the end of the Tokugawa era, from the early to the mid-nineteenth century, during the upheavals that led to the emergence of modern, industrialized Japan. The Tokugawa government, however, prohibited the establishment of new religious groups beyond the 13 Buddhist schools already approved. After the Meiji restoration, these new religious movements were permitted to set themselves up as 13 new Shinto schools, triggering a second wave of new religions in the form of Shinto sects in the early to middle Meiji period, in other words between 1870 and 1890. Some of these religions were institutionalizations of nationalist Shinto movements, while others were popular religious groups which had formed above all around mountain hermits. A third wave began in the 1920s, a period of political repression at the hands of a military government. The fourth and largest wave followed the removal of state control of religion after 1945. The last wave of the so-called 'new new religions' runs from the 1970s to the present day. In total, we have evidence of the foundation of around 400 new religions in Japan, a figure that includes only those religions that made some public impact and whose existence has been reported. Approximately twice as many new Christian groups have been founded.

The new religions are generally characterized as follows: 1) Their teachings place emphasis on ceremonies and revealed holy scriptures. 2) The founders are usually charismatic figures promising salvation and often come from unsophis-ticated, impoverished families. 3) They are mostly syncretic and entail various mixtures of Buddhist, Shinto, Christian and shamanistic elements. 4) In terms

---

[66]   See the account by Jonathan S. Watts, 'A Brief Overview of Buddhist NGOs in Japan', *Japanese Journal of Religious Studies*, 31.2 (2004), pp. 417–28.

of doctrine and ritual, the new religions are very simple in form. Rarely based on innovative ideas, they draw on the religious-historical arsenal characteristic of their immediate context with varying emphases. They are very easy to understand and thus spread quickly among the population at large. 5) Adherents are promised worldly success; material gain is highly valued and is a key component of preaching. 6) Physical wellbeing and healing thus play a major role. 7) Most new religions are strongly eschatological in character and point to a happy life in the near future. 8) Enthusiasm and individualism mark out the new religions from their traditional counterparts. 9) Many new religions reject any hierarchy that distinguishes between lay people and specialists; most members are involved in the performance of holy rites. 10) While maintaining a clear distance from the old religions, the new religions are nonetheless emphatically Japanese and make reference to old Japanese traditions. 11) The new religions include many popular religious elements, magical practices, shamanistic rites and ancestor worship. 12) At the same time, modern elements are also incorporated; women, for example, play an important role and enjoy a new, equal status.[67]

From 1921 to 1933, around twice as many new religions were founded as in the previous 20 years. There was a pronounced peak in 1940, a decline during the war, and another surge after it. After the war, some of the new religions became real mass organizations. While some of the groups, which achieved memberships of more than one million after 1945, such as the Sôka Gakkai, the Reiyû kai Kyôdan or the Risshô Kôseikai, had already been founded before the war, their growth had been held in check by state restrictions until 1945; they subsequently underwent truly explosive expansion. From 1965 on, we can again discern a clear slackening in the new religions' developmental dynamism. At the same time, the post-1945 period saw the substantial development of Christian groups. Alongside the Christian churches, the Christian Yearbook for 2004 lists a wide range of charitable, evangelical and other groups. Of these, we can identify around 1,000 different groups that still exist. The developmental dynamic of Christian groups differs from that of the new religions. Up to 1900, Christianity showed strong development, but in the period between 1900 and 1945 it was regulated and

---

[67]   See the chapter 'Characteristics' in Clark B. Offner and Henry van Straelen, *Modern Japanese Religions*, Leiden, Brill, 1963, pp. 28–38, which provides a detailed account of the specific characteristics with reference to numerous examples. Ichiro Hori summarizes this chapter through a list of eleven points; see *Folk Religion in Japan*, Chicago, University of Chicago Press, 1968, paperback Chicago, 1974, p. 224. See also the eight characteristics identified by Harry Thomsen in *The New Religions of Japan*, Rutland, VT, and Tokyo, Tuttle, 1963, 1969, pp. 20–29. He mentions three additional characteristics: they are centred on a place of pilgrimage, emphasize the unity of religion and life, and endow their members with a sense of importance and dignity.

restricted by the military government; after 1945 it resumed its vigorous growth. The growth rates of Christian organizations are truly remarkable in light of the fact that Japanese Christians, who number around one million, make up no more than one per cent of the Japanese population. Thus, compared with the new religions, some of which have millions of members, these groups are very small. According to the figures for temples, shrines, churches and new religions listed in the Japanese yearbooks on religion, there are around 180,000 religious corporations in post-war Japan.[68]

In all, though, despite the increasing number of new religions, religious faith declined by more than half from 1946 to 1950. Between 1970 and 1980 it diminished further to 30 per cent of the population. The shock incurred by the 1994 gas attack on the underground rail system by the Aum sect, in which 27 people were killed, led to a further decline in religious faith to 20 per cent. Nonetheless, during the period when the number of believers stood at around 30 per cent, the number of those taking part in religious rituals was double that of believers, according to national surveys. And even when the numbers of believers fell further in the 1970s, there was no discernible decrease in the numbers of those taking part in the rituals. In 2005, the number of those visiting temples and shrines during the three-day new year festival even climbed somewhat (770,000 more than in the previous year) to a total of 89,660,000. It is true, as Peter Köpping has shown, that it is above all Japanese tourists who attend the village festivals, which have acquired a quite new 'staged' character in the broken-up village community of today,[69] but this does not straightforwardly clarify the relationship between these new productions and the old with respect to their religiosity. For to measure the adherents of a religion according to their belief rather than their participation in rituals conforms to a typical Christian-European perspective, which has taken hold in Japan only under the influence of Christianity. In this sense, the category of a-religious or non-religious Japanese has existed only since the category of religious faith became established within internal Japanese discourse. Thus, secularization as measured through Western religious statistics is spreading in the shape of a Western religious discourse within Japan, and not necessarily in the form of changes in Japanese religious practices.[70]

---

[68]   See Helen Hardacre, 'Religion and Civil Society in Contemporary Japan', *Japanese Journal of Religious Studies*, 31.2 (2004), pp. 389–415, here pp. 400–401.

[69]   See Peter Köpping, 'Die Umkehrung des Blicks. Zur Akkomodierung von Inauthentischem in festlichen Inszenierungen in Japan und Indien', in Erika Fischer-Lichte and Isabel Pflug (eds.), *Inszenierung von Authentizität*, Tübingen, Francke, 2000, pp. 1–23.

[70]   See Satsuki Kawano, *Ritual Practice in Modern Japan*, Honolulu, University of Hawaii Press, 2005, p. 13.

It is no easy task to determine religious affiliation among the Japanese. It is frequently stated that, because of multiple answers, questionnaires indicate that far more than 100 per cent of Japanese are affiliated to a religion. There are estimates suggesting that around 50 per cent of all Japanese can still be described as Buddhists, while other sources state that only 30 per cent of Japanese have any religious ties at all, most of them to new religious movements. In a 1976 article on secularization in Japan, Jan Swyngedouw proposed that, in light of the many coexisting religions in Japan, we should regard the 'religion of Japanese-ness' as the entity vis-à-vis which something akin to secularization is taking place.[71] Max Eger has an even more critical take on application of the theory of secularization to Japan. As he sees it, secularization occurred in Japan earlier than in Europe and independently of modernity. In sharp contrast to Europe, according to Eger, with the host of new religions, modernity in Japan has in fact brought about a resacralization of the country.[72]

Korea

As in China and Japan, Korea's religious history also features two cultural encounters that have exercised a lasting effect on the country's religious landscape: the encounter with Buddhism in the fourth century and that with Christianity in the seventeenth and nineteenth centuries. Only so-called shamanism, whose origins are unknown, can be described as an indigenous Korean religion.[73] However, Buddhism, Confucianism, Christianity and a new Korean religion, Ch'ondogyo ('doctrine of the heavenly way'), founded in the nineteenth century, can be described historically. In different phases of Korean history, different religions had a particularly close relationship with the ruling court and were promoted and given preferential treatment: Buddhism came to Korea in the fourth century and had the status of state religion during the Shilla and Koryo

---

[71]   See Jan Swyngedouw, 'Secularization in a Japanese Context', *Japanese Journal of Religious Studies*, 3.4 (1976), pp. 283–306, here pp. 294, 297. On the theory of secularization in Japan, see also idem, 'Reflections on the Secularization Thesis in the Sociology of Religion in Japan', *Japanese Journal of Religious Studies*, 6.1–2 (1979), pp. 65–88. See also the following article by Tamaru Noriyoshi on pp. 89–114, 'The Problem of Secularization: A Preliminary Analysis'.

[72]   See Max Eger, '"Modernization" and "Secularization" in Japan: A Polemical Essay', *Japanese Journal of Religious Studies*, 7.1 (1980), pp. 7–24.

[73]   See Cho Hung-Youn, *Koreanischer Schamanismus: Eine Einführung*, Hamburg, Hamburgisches Museum für Völkerkunde, 1982. See also Kang Wi Jo, 'Indigenous Tradition of Korean Religions', *Shinhak nondan*, 14 (1980), pp. 189–219; and Kim Chol-choon, 'Native Beliefs in Ancient Korea', *Korea Journal*, 3.5 (1963), pp. 4–8.

kingdoms (from 668 to 1392).[74] Under the Yi dynasty (from 1392 to 1910), when it was the turn of Confucianism to function as state religion,[75] Buddhism, which had by then become politicized and secularized, was subject to significant restrictions.[76] Temples to Confucius were erected, and society was organized according to Confucian hierarchies, headed by scholar-officials and soldiers with a Confucianist education, with butchers, shamans and Buddhist monks making up the lower end of the spectrum. All religious groups stood in a state of powerless opposition to state Confucianism.[77] Some of them engaged in political resistance and were consequently persecuted to a greater or lesser extent – the former applying to the Christian communities founded in the late eighteenth and the early nineteenth century.

In 1895, Japan invaded Korea, annexed it fully in 1910 and governed it as a colony until 1945. The Confucianist system was abolished, Western teachings were introduced and Christian missionaries were allowed to carry out their work. As a consequence of the modernization forced upon the country by the Japanese invasion, a large number of new religions emerged between 1890 and 1910 as protest movements against penetration by things Western,[78] whose political dominance led to a politicization and secularization of the religious field.[79] In opposition to the powerful new Western influences, a new liberation movement developed in the second half of the nineteenth century, which initially took the name 'Eastern Teaching' (Tonghak), thus defining itself as the opposite of 'Western teaching', which meant Catholicism. This Eastern Teaching united Confucian, Buddhist, shamanistic and – despite its xenophobic and anti-Christian stance – Christian-humanist elements, making this a typical example of a neo-religious

---

[74]   See Lewis R. Lancaster, Kikun Suh and Chai-shin Yu (eds.), *Buddhism in Koryo: A Royal Religion*, Berkeley, Center for Korean Studies, Institute of East Asian Studies, University of California, 1996.

[75]   See Key P. Yang and Gregory Henderson, 'An Outline of Korean Confucianism', *Journal of Asian Studies*, 18 (1958), pp. 81–99, 259–76.

[76]   See Keel Hee-Sung, 'Buddhism and Political Power in Korean History', *The Journal of The International Association of Buddhist Studies*, 1 (1978), pp. 9–24. On Buddhist survival strategies, see Robert E. Buswell, Jr, 'Buddhism under Confucian Domination: The Synthetic Vision of Sosan Hyujong', in JaHyun Kim Haboush and Martina Deuchler (eds.), *Culture and the State in Late Chosôn Korea*, Cambridge, MA, Harvard University Press, 1999, pp. 134–59.

[77]   See Boudewijn Walraven, 'Popular Religion in a Confucianized Society', in Haboush and Deuchler (eds.), *Culture and the State in Late Chosôn Korea*, pp. 160–98.

[78]   See Kil-myung, 'New Religions and Social Change'.

[79]   See Kang Wi Jo, 'The Secularization of Korean Buddhism under the Japanese Colonialism', *Korea Journal*, 19.7 (1979), pp. 42–47.

national doctrine. In response to the increasing influence of the revolutionary Tonghak ideology, the movement's founder, Choe Che-U (1824–64), was executed in 1864 along with 20 of his followers. The movement, however, lived on, and formed the underpinnings of a series of peasants' revolts, of which the uprising of 1894 led to full-blown civil war, which was ultimately put down with the aid of Japanese troops. In 1906, the movement was re-formed under the new name of Ch'ondogyo, again played a key role in the movement opposing the Japanese occupation in 1919, but then lost significance before coming to life again in the Christian Minjung theology of the 1970s and 1980s. Significantly, both the early political leaders of South Korea and their contemporary counterparts, many cabinet members, most members of the Liberal Party and around a quarter of the present-day National Assembly belong to this Christian community. Hence, Christianity has been granted political privileges since the end of the Korean war in 1953, in part because it is intended to function as a bulwark against communist North Korea.

In parallel to this, the Korean economy underwent a profound transformation from the 1960s on, turning from a traditional agrarian economy into an industrial one and prompting a major urbanization of society, a society now concentrated around a small number of cities. This period saw the emergence of charismatic churches with huge numbers of followers, churches bearing the unmistakable hallmarks of traditional shamanism.[80] At the same time, the Christian churches increasingly cooperated with European churches, prompting them to oppose the authoritarian leadership style of General Park Chung-hee, who came to power as a result of a putsch in 1960, and to work towards a democratic, humane, open society. It was, therefore, often priests who led the nationwide pro-democracy movements. However, church activities and institutions were banned by the regime towards the end of the 1960s. In 1972, a constitutional amendment effectively abolished the separation of powers and allowed Park to govern as a dictator. The Christian groupings responded in a variety of ways, ranging from cooperation to vehement opposition, and in line with this, Park dealt with them in differing ways, through cooptation, exclusion and persecution. After Park's murder at the hands of the head of the secret service and another putsch, students carried out mass demonstrations, culminating in 1980 with a massacre and a wave of arrests. The opposition movement that developed out of this united old popular religious traditions, Buddhism and Ch'ondogyo into a messianic-political movement called Minjung (oppressed, suffering people). The Korean Christians took up this idea and created out of it a Minjung theology that brought together messianic elements

---

[80]   See Hong Young-gi, 'The Background and Characteristics of the Charismatic Mega-Churches in Korea', *Asian Journal of Pentecostal Studies*, 3.1 (2000), pp. 99–118, here p. 108.

of the Korean religions combined with the Christian theology of suffering to make a Koreanized Christian theology; its simplistic radicalism helped make it hugely successful as a political opposition, and it played an important role in changing Korean society.[81] In 1987, after further student unrest on a massive scale, a new constitution was adopted, in which the separation of powers was reinstated.

The opposition movement, strongly motivated by Christian impulses, played a key role in this transition to democracy, a role which it subsequently lost. This plunged the churches into a crisis, amplified by the fact that the economic situation had by now improved so much that – even within Christian circles – an increased interest in personal advancement pushed interest in religion into the background.[82] The religious institutions of Korea responded in very different ways. Some Christian groups, with their radical theological vision of a heavenly kingdom, remained outside political structures in the fundamentalist opposition, while others focused their attention on the bourgeoisie emerging in the new Korean democracy, formed parties and got involved in politics and in thousands of civil society organizations; these emerged in the 1990s and saw themselves as a kind of 'third power' between state and capital that wished, as critical observers, to open up a public debate on socio-political topics (environment, transport policy, industrial law, women, historical guilt, political division) in the interests of the common good.[83] The churches too took up these subjects as well as building worldwide networks through the World Council of Churches. In the Buddhist sphere, a Minjung Buddhism drawing on Minjung theology developed in the 1980s in the wake of an intellectual movement inspired by liberation theology. This began in the 1960s with the aim of reviving Buddhist consciousness, in the sense of Mahayana Bodhisattva compassion, in order to alleviate suffering and achieve liberation. On the one hand, this Minjung Buddhism opposed the two great conservative movements of the patriotic communities (of monks and lay people), which, with their nationalist demands, it accused of wishing only to retain power and estates and thus of pursuing a purely secular agenda. On the other hand, it opposed the fusion of popular Buddhist practices of Amitabha veneration and traditional shamanistic rites, practised

---

[81]   See Lee Sang Taek, *Religion and Social Formation in Korea: Minjung and Millenarianism*, Berlin, de Gruyter, 1996; and Ryu Tongshik, 'Religion and Socio-Cultural Transformation in Korea Today', *Asian Cultural Studies*, 12 (1981), pp. 61–72.

[82]   See Park Yong-Shin, 'Protestant Christianity and its Place in a Changing Korea', *Social Compass*, 47.4 (2000), pp. 507–24, here pp. 519–20.

[83]   See Christine Lienemann-Perrin, 'Religion und staatliche Macht in Korea. Eine Skizze mit Beispielen aus Geschichte und Gegenwart', in Peter Schalk (ed.), *Zwischen Säkularismus und Hierokratie. Studien zum Verhältnis von Religion und Staat in Süd- und Ostasien*, Uppsala, University Library, 2001, pp. 143–67, here p. 163.

mainly by women, which supposedly ensured a long life and worldly wellbeing. Again, it objected to these practices on the grounds that they were concerned solely with secular goals.[84] Thus, in twentieth-century Korea, Buddhism too incorporated the impulse against secularization that formed the basis for the development of new religious movements.

In much the same way as in Japan, with respect to society and politics as well as in their relations with each other, religions in Korea occupy a field of tension involving very different endeavours. First, they advocate traditional-conservative stances, on the basis of which they often attempt to serve politics in a nationalistic fashion. Second, they involve themselves in the political opposition which, in sharp contrast, conceives of religion as fundamentally opposed to politics. Furthermore, religious groups engage in civil society in an active attempt to introduce their religious ideals to society. Finally, new religions emerge. Within the unlimited field of global multicultural impulses, these religions attempt to forge new, coherent religious identities from the rubble of their own fragmented tradition.

Practically nothing is known about the religious situation in the north of Korea. According to the Christian missionaries best informed about it, there is theoretical freedom of religion, but, in the shape of the ephemeral state-controlled North Korean Christians' Association, all that exists in reality is an ersatz church with three churches in Pyongyang, to which only carefully selected members are sent. As in China, the religious communities are organized in state-controlled organs. Since 1946, Protestants have been brought together in the Korean Christian Federation (KCF), Catholics, since 1988, in the Korean Catholic Federation, and other members of religious groups, since 1989, in the Korean Religionists' Council. According to estimates, around 10,000–12,000 of the 24 million North Koreans are Christians, compared with up to 18 million out of 44 million in South Korea, that is, rather more than 40 per cent. According to official figures, there are 10,000 Buddhists in North Korea, and there is universal religious freedom. However, as the communist ideology of North Korea is atheistic, despite the god-like status of its political leader and the quasi-religious personality cult that surrounds him, we must assume that religions are strictly controlled and probably subject to extensive repression, even after the 1992 removal of the clause in the constitution explicitly prohibiting religious activities.

Following this rough sketch, I shall conclude by drawing some conclusions about secularization in East Asia.

---

[84]   See Shim Jae-ryong, 'Buddhism and the Modernization Process in Korea', *Social Compass* 47.4 (2000), pp. 541–48, here pp. 542–43. See also Henrik H. Sorensen, 'Buddhism and Secular Power in Twentieth-Century Korea', in Ian Harris (ed.), *Buddhism and Politics in Twentieth-Century Asia*, London, Pinter, 1999, pp. 127–52.

Conclusion

Taken together, East Asian religions appear Janus-faced: the servants and allies of the state on the one hand and its opponents and enemies on the other. In all three countries, a limited number of specific religious traditions have been permitted by the state; these have been used to further the state's secular goals and have, at different times, been favoured or repressed. In this connection, it is possible to discern the secularization of religious traditions in East Asia long before the dawn of the modern age. Further, all three countries – and here their traditions differ from the Christian traditions of Europe – have absorbed and integrated several foreign religions over the course of the last two thousand years. Consonant with this, through the encounter with Europe, all three have developed numerous new religious movements that closely resemble one another in their basic features (syncretism, charismatic leaders, simple dogma, millenarian focus on salvation, etc.). As a result, in all three countries the old religious traditions have also changed greatly and, in light of the Christian-Western concept of religion, have often renewed themselves behind the shield of secular concepts, which suggests continuities with East Asian forms of religion and Western processes of secularization. Finally, very much in keeping with contemporary global developments, all three currently feature an extremely wide range of religious diversity and their religions currently enjoy broad appeal.

The question of whether secularization has occurred in the individual East Asian countries always demands a dual answer, one positive, the other negative. With respect to China, we might answer, positively, as follows:

- Yes, since 1911 there has been no Son of Heaven, his rule legitimized by a heavenly mandate; the state has a secular foundation and there is a strict legal separation between religion and the state.

- Yes, the everyday religious routine has been lost in most parts of the country. Most people do not regularly take part in religious activities. It is the exception rather than the norm to be religious in China; religion has suffered a marked loss of significance.

- Yes, the concept of religion has been introduced and with it the critique of religion. As a rule, the world is explained without recourse to gods and spirits. Practically no religious socialization occurs, while perspectives critical of religion are promoted. Thus, religion does not constitute a fundamental system of reference; across most of China, it is a private matter.

- Yes, over the last hundred years, throughout the country, religious institutions have suffered acts of destruction – long since irreversible – on a massive scale. Certainly, temples have been reconstructed and ordinations performed, but even tens of thousands of temples with hundreds of thousands of clergy are a mere drop in the ocean in this context, and religious institutions have thus declined markedly as well.

- Yes, in those places where religion has a secure place, this is entirely due to the understanding that it relieves the state of order-maintaining functions at the local level, making it akin to a secular and civil society-based institution. The five officially recognized religions act in conformity with the secular expectations that the state has of them. They stand outside social life, as institutions endowed with a religious character that exist within a secular context.

One might counter:

- No, the Communist Party certainly promotes the idea that it is atheistic, but has always made use of religious concepts and images in cultivating its image. Besides, it makes theological decisions on orthodoxy and heresy, on true religion and superstition. Thus, religion and the state are not truly separate.

- No, while the everyday religious routine has vanished for the time being as a result of temporary political repression, in those places where it is developing most strongly at present, in the southeast of China, it is already playing an important role in public life, and is thus by no means slipping away into the private sphere.

- No, there are countless local cults, hundreds of new religious movements and the major religious traditions are growing year on year. Temples are being built everywhere, while monks and nuns are being ordained in their thousands. With increasing economic growth, the country will again be dotted with countless temples, and an intact religious landscape will again take shape over the long term.

- No, in some fields the religious infrastructure is so vital to local life and local politics and administration that it is impossible to separate the religious from the secular. The fact that the state has begun to transfer state functions even to the official religions over the last decade shows that they too have a solid political basis. Thus, religion will become increasingly important, and without it, it will no longer be possible to maintain the sociopolitical order at the local level.

With respect to Japan, we can answer positively as follows:

- Yes, on 1 January 1946 the Tenno officially renounced his divine status; the constitution states explicitly that religion and the state are separate.

- Yes, the concept of religion has been introduced and with it the critique of religion. As a rule, the world is explained without recourse to gods and spirits.

- Yes, the number of believers has declined markedly, by more than half from 1946 to 1950, down to 30 per cent between 1970 and 1980 and to 20 per cent following the gas attack on Tokyo's underground rail system by the Aum sect in 1994.

- Yes, the Buddhist temples increasingly offer rituals with a worldly orientation (concerned with prosperity, security, etc.) that no longer have anything to do with their old religious-spiritual meanings.

- Yes, Shintoism has been emptied entirely of its religious content and has been secularized into nothing more than a state cult.

- Yes, the many new religious movements are an expression of the fact that religion has disintegrated into discrete, highly individualized spheres that primarily pursue secular goals.

- Yes, the institutionalized religions are all heavily involved in civil society; they too primarily pursue secular goals.

- Yes, the village communities have suffered such shattering transformation that more tourists than villagers now attend rural religious festivals.

On the other hand:

- No, Japan is full of temples and shrines. Both in the cities and in the countryside there are religious establishments on every corner that are actively maintained and have a full roster of events.

- No, public rituals are a common occurrence in which many people, increasing numbers in fact, participate. The everyday religious routine is largely intact; regular participation in religious events is a cultural norm and defines Japanese religiosity far more profoundly than religious faith.

- No, the new religious movements are so numerous and active that religion continues to be a key topic for many different social classes, giving it an important role in public discourse. Religion is not, therefore, a purely private, personal affair.

With respect to Korea, the positive answers are:

- Yes, the constitution codifies the separation of state and religion.

- Yes, the concept of religion has been introduced and with it the critique of religion. As a rule, the world is explained without recourse to gods and spirits.

- Yes, in the face of the overriding interest in economic development in Korea, religions are either meaningless or involve themselves in the pursuit of worldly salvation and in political and civil society-related affairs.

On the other hand:

- No, there is no indication that the religions are declining or losing importance. They are growing steadily and are a lively presence in public and social life.

- No, creative religious work is being done and there is clear evidence of internal religious debates; both lead to religious innovation.

- No, religious education is a widespread phenomenon, and active missionary work is being carried out all over the world. Religion continues to make a significant impact.

These answers reveal that the concept of secularization, with its associated criteria, can help us see certain realities more clearly. At the same time, it is apparent that, rather than describing fully the contemporary religious situation in East Asia, it can only reveal various aspects. Depending on the criteria we select, we can describe these as secular or not; they exist within a process of lively, mutual negotiation. It appears to be the specific fusion of these different aspects, a fusion subject to a process of constant transformation, that ultimately distinguishes these religious cultures from one another.

12

The Relevance of the European Model of Secularization in Latin America and Africa

David Martin

Secularization involves several dimensions, but refers in particular to the decreasing salience of any reference to the transcendent or to a realm beyond, above or interfusing with mundane reality. Any tension between the transcendent and the mundane is relaxed, or else taken over by the secular utopias of politics or by the myths of nationalism. This process has been seen in an enlightened perspective as the erosion of superstition by rationality or science and/or the liberation of humanity or the human as such from oppression and alienation. It has also been seen as inevitable, spreading out by degrees from its Western European heartland, with France at its epicentre, to encompass the whole world. France is frequently identified as the *secularist* country, whereas (say) Britain, Scandinavia, Holland and Germany are sources of mere *secularity*. There are serious differences here. Secularism is a doctrine promoting the secular, secularization is a process whereby a secular condition becomes progressively more dominant, and mere secularity is not so much a doctrine as a state of affairs in which the transcendent is irrelevant for most individuals and for the nation as a whole.

Secularization is more than the decline of church-going or even of Christianity. If one adopted a rigorous definition it would involve indifference to 'the spirit' and that, at least, seems not to be the case, even in Western Europe. In Germany church-going diminishes but spirituality in all its many forms appears to be on the rise.[1] Much depends, therefore, on what is covered by such an omnibus word as 'spirit'.

---

[1]   See the EKD Report, *Fremde, Heimat, Kirche*, Hanover, Evangelische Kirche in Deutschland, 1993.

For the sake of what follows I take spirituality to be some kind of anthropo-logical universal, which is channelled in different ways in different cultures. Spirituality characterizes the Western countries and the North Atlantic, but whereas in the USA it is mostly channelled through churches, in Europe that is decreasingly the case.[2] In Europe we notice a growth of individual spiritualities, put together according to personal preference. Elsewhere in Latin America and Africa we have not only spirituality, much of it channelled through churches (or through Islam), but a profoundly inspired religious landscape providing a backdrop to everything else. In Africa that includes politics.

Initially I want to take the situations in Western Europe and North America as benchmarks against which to pursue my main focus, which is the kind of secularization, or rather the conspicuous lack of it, found in Latin America and Africa. My main benchmark is the historically close relation of church and territorial state found in Western Europe, because that closeness has pushed social change into anti-ecclesiastical, anti-clerical and even anti-religious channels. That is most of all true where the Catholic Church in particular has had a national or regional monopoly uniting a territory and a people. Historically, Europe has been characterized by church–state monopolies, all of them now in a state of advanced disintegration, above all in France, and those monopolies were reproduced in Latin America up to the mid-twentieth century, at which point they too showed signs of disintegration. By contrast, North America has progressively lacked anything even approaching an institutional monopoly covering *a* people in *a* territory, and Africa south of the Sahara has historically lacked modern state development as such. It has also lacked distinct ecclesiastical institutions, let alone religious monopolies. The pluralism that Britain exported to North America it also exported to Africa; and one has to add that in much of Africa state-formation has continued to be difficult, and the problems are exacerbated where the territorial borders set by colonial powers are disputed, and ethnicity divides as much as it unifies.[3]

At this point, I want, instead of proceeding directly to the characteristics of Latin America and Africa, to make a standard observation already hinted at, and it concerns whether we treat secularization as a universal process originating in and emanating from Europe, either as Anglo-Saxon secularity or as French secularism.

My question is whether secularization is written into universal history,

---

[2]   See Robert Wuthnow, *All in Sync: How Music and Art are Revitalizing American Religion*, Berkeley, University of California Press, 2003; Christopher Partridge (ed.), *Encyclopedia of New Religions* (Section on 'Modern Western Cultures'), Oxford, Lion, 2004, pp. 357–416.

[3]   See Paul Gifford, *African Christianity: Its Public Role*, London, Hurst, 1998.

conceived as the triumph of rationality and rationalization, and/or as the triumph of the privatization and individualization of religion whereby it falls into social and political irrelevance. It is this question that generates the debate about 'exceptionalism', that is, how we identify who exactly is out of step with universal history. Originally the United States was treated as exceptional because nobody could gainsay its status as a quintessential modern state, rational, scientific and technically advanced, yet one in which religion neither declined nor fragmented into social insignificance. In the United States modernity, progress and faith marched in tandem, and moreover Americans thought that was normal and just as it should be. But then observation of Latin America showed that it too differed from Europe, in particular from Latin Europe, whence it derived, because secularization in the French style was largely confined to the elite. The exceptions were in places like Uruguay, where European migrants arrived at a time of maximum tension in the sending countries between church and state.

Africa was also sui generis, though secular elites in the West might dismiss it as merely pre-modern and religiously backward. The black elites of the newly independent states were mostly nurtured by Christian missionary education, and often invented national religions out of traditional and Christian materials. Kwame Nkrumah, for example, did not have great success with his invented national ideology for Ghana, but his slogan 'Seek ye first the political Kingdom' successfully exploited a Christian resonance.

Yet further observation suggested that the left-wing and/or secularist movements in Islam, in Africa and elsewhere, were yielding place to Islamism. That allowed the philosopher-anthropologist Ernest Gellner to postulate 'Islamic exceptionalism'. Again, we might dismiss Islamic revival as just a phase, like 'fortress Catholicism' from 1860 to 1960, but the situation was clearly paradoxical. With North America, Latin America, Africa and Islam all characterized as exceptions, it did not take long for sociologists, notably Peter Berger, to argue that the real exception was Europe. In *The Desecularization of the World* Berger suggested that the rest of the world was very far from travelling along the path charted by France or Scandinavia.[4] Indeed in his view it remained as vigorously religious as ever. So the universality of the process of secularization, hitherto assumed, was called into question. There were even revivals in Christian Europe, notably in post-communist Russia and possibly in Orthodox Greece and Romania. The ethno-religious faiths of Greece and Romania, as well as Poland, turned out to be remarkably resilient.

So much for exceptionalism. I want now briefly to discuss the role of the

---

[4]   See Peter Berger (ed.), *The Desecularization of the World: Resurgent Religion and World Politics*, Grand Rapids, Eerdmans, 1999, pp. 1–18. See also Grace Davie, *Europe: The Exceptional Case*, London, Darton, Longman & Todd, 2002.

Jews in representing what is a key dialectic for my purposes between religion as part of the ethnic and territorial sacred and religion as a portable identity, and as promoting the secular over against the ethnic and territorial sacred represented by Christendom. The Jews can be seen as having invented the sacred nexus of land, city, temple, people and faith. Of course, primitive Christianity subverted the ethnic and territorial sacred by universalizing the faith and spiritualizing the city and the temple as transcendental goals for all peoples, but the original nexus of the sacred returned, though modified, in what became Christendom. Within Christendom the Jews became universal nomads bound by a very particular religion. Many centuries later when Jews emerged from the ghetto they encountered a Christianity which had reverted to the sacred union of land, temple, city and nation initially characteristic of themselves. The dialectic of locality and universality had almost reversed itself, above all in holy Russia.

In Russia the Jews quickly became urbanized and educated, as well as held together in their wanderings and their role as middle-men by webs of ethnicity and faith. As Yuri Slezkhine argues, they could advance by adopting the culture of the nation and repudiating the ghetto.[5] They adopted Pushkin, just as in Germany they adopted Goethe and Schiller. If patriarchal religion held them back, parricide would bring them out of the particular ghetto and into the universal enlightenment. Once that was achieved the attenuated universalism of Christianity could be undermined by the universality of reason and then of secular revolution. There is thus a Jewish contribution to secularization from Spinoza to Bela Kuhn.

Those Russian Jews who did not follow the revolutionary path either went to Israel or to the other Promised Land in the United States. In the USA the nomads had joined a country of nomads, and, like the Armenians and Lebanese, they rapidly rose to the top. Jews became disproportionately represented in the most prestigious and secular echelons of the United States. Moreover, just as Marxism had become the secular religion of Bolshevik intellectuals, so Freudianism was adopted as an ancillary faith to Christianity by middle-class Judaeo-Protestant America. When the sixties brought a wave of intellectual radicalism, Jews were again to the fore, not only in the USA, but even in Europe, as is shown by the evidence assembled by Yuri Slezkhine and Seymour Martin Lipset.[6] In only one

---

[5]   See Yuri Slezkhine, *The Jewish Century*, Princeton, Princeton University Press, 2005; and David Hollinger, 'Jewish Intellectuals and the De-Christianization of American Public Culture in the Twentieth Century', in Harry Stout and D. G. Hart (eds.), *New Directions in American Religious History*, Oxford, Oxford University Press, 1997, pp. 462–86.
[6]   See Slezkhine, *The Jewish Century*; S. Martin Lipset, personal communication. Cf. Arthur Liebman, *Jews and the Left*, New York, Wiley, 1979; and Tony Judt, *Post-War: A History of Europe since 1945*, London, Heinemann, 2005.

country outside the North Atlantic sphere was there anything remotely resembling the American adoption of psychoanalysis. Argentina has both the largest Jewish community in Latin America and nurtures a widespread psychoanalytic culture on a North American scale. Nowadays Argentina is distinguished by a large-scale efflorescence of neo-Pentecostalism.

My object is, following Slezkhine, to underline the way Jews by virtue of their nomadic status, and by being nurtured in specific occupational niches such as commerce, media, the academic world and 'the knowledge class' generally, pioneered a more general modern condition: a transnational identity which in the Jewish case was based on a network of ethnic and familial connections, though in its Christian versions it can be based on a quasi-familial brotherhood and sisterhood without any ethnic connections. That is the plausible essence of Slezkhine's argument, and it points to portable identity, whether ethnic or religious or both, as characteristic of our time. It links up with the shift away from the unity of people, land, city and temple, to the kind of global migrations we observe today and to their religious manifestations. Putting it aphoristically, we are now all of us wandering Jews, rather like the earliest Christians wandering all over the Roman empire, before they settled down in new sacred territories and built new sacred cities, such as Rome, Constantinople and Cologne.

Perhaps I should recapitulate elements of the argument so far. I have distinguished between Anglo-Saxon secularity and French secularism. Then I have indicated the different ways in which spirituality is channelled, beginning with Europe where spirituality moves outside the churches in the context of territorial and more or less established churches, and America where spirituality moves inside the churches in the context of non-establishment and pluralism. In Latin America there is an all-encompassing spirituality, and church–state alliances are now under strain in a way that opens up a space for a religion of the Holy Spirit to pour in. In Africa there is an all-encompassing spirituality and a traditional pluralism open to the pluralism of Pentecostalism, especially where the historic churches exercise some state functions, as de facto NGOs. Finally, I have set out a permanent dialectic between religions of territory and sacred place, and religions which provide a portable identity. In a way, Judaism was a pioneer of both, though Christianity originally represented a portable identity (which is now revived by Pentecostalism in contemporary conditions of global mobility), while Judaism perforce adopted a portable 'nomadic' identity until it partly returned to its original specified territory in Israel.

Islam has, of course, also become part of the massive contemporary global migration. A world-wide faith, initially as geographical as Judaism, but also imperial and expansionist, has been activated through modern global media and the stimuli provided by colonialism, by the power of oil and the fact of Israel. Islam is in diaspora in Europe, while throughout its heartlands in North

Africa, the Middle East and South Asia, it takes part in the great trek to the cities. There is also, I would add, a parallel trek of Christians to the cities in sub-Saharan Africa, and a black diaspora in Europe, including migration from the West Indies.[7] We therefore see a black Christian minority in Europe alongside the Muslim minority, and the religious landscapes of European cities, in particular London and Amsterdam, are marked by the buildings of these two minorities.

The most startling case of this global migration of souls (and bodies) is the egalitarian, transnational faith in a personal possession by the Spirit and reformation of life represented by Pentecostalism and its charismatic penumbra. Pentecostals are a barely noticed minority in Europe, and even in the USA they are much less visible than evangelicals, but so far as the vast incursion of Protestantism in Latin America is concerned, they are the majority, and in sub-Saharan Africa they number well over a hundred million. The fastest growing element in Christianity today in Latin America, Africa and Asia (including China) is Pentecostal and includes perhaps some quarter of a billion people, one in five of all Christians.[8]

Pentecostals are disciplined, aspiring and hard-working, as befits the spiritual heirs of German Pietism, Anglo-American Methodism and black revivalism. They combine awakenings of the spirit such as occurred in the United States, especially on the frontier, with a mobilization of themselves as 'imagined communities' across national borders. Like Muslims, Pentecostals are part of a network making the trek to the megacity where in their latest manifestation they congregate in megachurches. Where they differ, and differ crucially, from both Jews and Muslims is in being part of a voluntary association based on choice, rather than an organic ethnic entity, whether or not that entity is infused with a faith. This is in keeping with the origins of Christianity and in keeping with their own more proximate origins as voluntary groups separated from the state. Today they contribute to and represent a global move towards lay, conscientious, participatory, pluralist, decentralized and voluntary religion. Pentecostalism worldwide, and particularly in Latin America and Africa, constitutes a non-violent mobilization of the poor, especially the black female poor, seeking a respectable place in a shared modernity. Because they are participatory and aspiring, they should in principle contribute to a democratic and economically disciplined ethos. Certainly their

---

[7]   See Roswith Gerloff, 'The African Diaspora in the Caribbean and Europe from Pre-emancipation to the Present Day', in Hugh McLeod (ed.), *Christianity: World Christianities c. 1914–c. 2000*, Cambridge, Cambridge University Press, 2006, pp. 219–35.

[8]   See David Martin, 'Evangelical Expansion in Global Society', in Donald Lewis (ed.), *Christianity Reborn*, Grand Rapids, Eerdmans, 2004, pp. 273–94. Cf. Alan Anderson and Edmond Tang (eds.), *Asian and Pentecostal*, Oxford, Regnum, 2005.

origins in the Protestant culture of voluntary association and persistent fission make it unlikely that they will attempt to take over as the sole or dominant religion of the state, even though in some African countries, such as Zambia, Ghana, Nigeria, Zimbabwe and even Uganda, they exercise considerable political power. 'Big men' and 'big women' appear among the Pentecostal leadership and in that respect carry forward an old African tradition.

Here I want to turn specifically to Latin America and to Catholicism, which is, alongside Pentecostalism, the other great expansive arm of contemporary Christianity.

Like all religions, but especially Christianity, Catholic Christianity is potently ambiguous, able to legitimate conquest and resistance. Thus the Spanish and Portuguese in Latin America could represent mass conversion as a crusade while those who resisted and even rebelled, such as the Tupac-Amaru, could substantiate from the Scriptures of the conquerors their claim to understand the real meaning of the faith. That is always the case: the colonized select from the Christian repertoire according to their needs and situation. An exodus from oppression to a promised land, and the arrival of a better kingdom, have perennial appeal. Faith can help the oppressed both to accommodate and to protest.[9]

Independence in Latin America, like colonialism, came much earlier than in Africa, but in both continents Christianity showed its capacity to mean diverse things to diverse people. For the Peninsulares and the upper clergy religion meant the Hispanic imperium, for the creole elites that took over the new nations it could mean independence and certainly meant taking over control of the Church. Given that Spanish colonialism, unlike British, meant a wholesale package of Catholic Church and state, the classic Latin European conflict of clerical and anti-clerical was played out a second time in Latin America. It came to a climax in the 1920s and 1930s in Mexico, and relations between the Vatican and Mexico were only restored in 1992. It is hardly a dead issue even today.

Popular Catholicism is a distinctly female domain. A more self-conscious Catholicism is the product of middle- and upper-class schooling, with the result that movements such as Catholic Action, Christian Democracy, Liberation Theology and Opus Dei have an upper-class leadership and following. Opus Dei is an attempt to modernize under authoritarian auspices; Liberation Theology and Charismatic Catholicism are explicitly attempts to pre-empt both Marxism and Pentecostalism in order to retain the traditional role of the Catholic Church. I am not saying that these movements lacked intrinsic ethical and political ideals,

---

[9]   See Gustavo Benavides, 'Christianity in Central and South America', in *International Encyclopedia of the Social and Behavioral Sciences*, vol. 16, Oxford, Elsevier, 2001, pp. 1764–67.

only that they had other aims as well. With the arrival of global communication in Latin America, and the great trek to the megacities, especially the service sector, the old agrarian, ritual, hierarchical and sacramentalized society began to collapse. Pentecostalism poured into the fissures and into the vacant spaces.

It was able to do this in Latin America and not in Europe because the elites, however much influenced by the French model, lacked a centralized state with which to secularize the great mass of the people. In Gustavo Benavides' formulation, the result was half-enchantment rather than disenchantment.[10] Latin America remained inspirited, though not so inspirited as Africa. At least in Latin America religion could be distinguished from politics whatever the power exercised by religious influences. But then, Latin America gradually shifted from the French model of elite secularization to the Anglo-American model of religious pluralism and voluntarism.

That was as much an indigenous development as the result of diffusion from North America. Whatever the impact of missions from North America and Scandinavia, a religion of the Holy Spirit rapidly became indigenous in an inspirited continent and acted as a vehicle for the autonomous mobilization of the poor. With time and social mobility that mobilization extended to large sections of the new middle classes, above all in Brazil. Brazil is the largest Catholic country in the world, but it also includes some 25 million Protestants, mostly Pentecostals. I should add that Rio de Janeiro is the nearest approach in Latin America to the kind of secular sector found in Europe or the relatively irreligious west coast of the USA. As Berlin is to the northern heartland of secularity in Europe, and Los Angeles and San Francisco are to California, so Rio and Montevideo, perhaps Caracas too, are to Latin America. What visitors to these cities in Latin America do not see is the vast network of Pentecostal churches among the poor in city sectors and favelas only a walk away from the luxury hotels.

It is not possible to trace how the Catholic Church has become not just a fact of Latin American life but affected by self-conscious mobilizations, both on the modernizing right through Opus Dei and on the modernizing and political left derived from Catholic Action and Liberation Theology. Everyone knows that the base communities were sponsored by the Church as ginger groups, simultaneously devotional and politically committed, and above all effective as sources of resistance in the periods of military government in Brazil and Chile. They have now been largely neutralized by the local churches and by Rome, but Catholicism, particularly in its charismatic form, and through the media, has experienced its own revival alongside Pentecostalism. Perhaps the denominations most taken aback by Pentecostalism were the 'historical Protestants', whose schools and welfare agencies had for decades exercised major influence. For them, as for

---

[10]   See Benavides, 'Christianity in Central and South America'.

nationalists in the elite, it was easy to regard the mobilization of the poor as an extension of the American supermarket into the religious sphere, though that was only plausible with respect to a later wave of neo-Pentecostalism, preaching a gospel of prosperity in places such as Guatemala City, São Paulo and (latterly) Buenos Aires.

Here I want to emphasize the contrasting models of autonomous mobilization represented by Pentecostalism and its considerable charismatic penumbra, and the sponsored mobilization represented by the Catholic Church and its mobile international priestly intelligentsia. The two kinds of mobilization offer different advantages and suffer different constraints but can be seen as complementary and overlapping.

The Catholic Church is well placed to pursue sponsored mobilization, because it has long-standing experience of political engagement and theories of the relationship between church and state, spiritual and political power. It also has, particularly since Vatican II, a programme for peace and justice. Whether that programme is implemented, and whether it mainly involves clerical intellectuals or a well-informed laity as well, depends on how close the links are between church and state, and between church and elite strata, including the military. For example, in Argentina the Church, though it had episodes of tension with the state, was to a large extent complicit with the military regime.[11] Even where the Church adopts a liberationist approach, as in Chile and Brazil, it still has institutional interests it wishes to conserve. Certainly it wishes to retain control of base communities, to make sure mobilization does not get out of hand. Given that part of the object is to pre-empt Marxism and/or Pentecostalism, one does not want to be so politically radical that radicals take over, nor does one want to generate a quasi-Pentecostal fervour that strains the authority of the Church.

Pre-emption is always institutionally risky if taken beyond a certain point. Again, the institutional interests of the Church in society require the maintenance of some degree of communication with the forces in the state against which it is protesting. Thus in Chile the period of confrontation with the Pinochet regime was followed by a period of negotiation, and in Brazil the Church held secret dialogues with devout Catholics in the military regime to keep the lines of communication open.[12] These are constraints, and furthermore the Church seeks to retain its ability to influence the state after the period of dictatorship to implement Catholic norms with respect to (say) the family. That is increasingly

[11]   See Anthony Gill, *Rendering Unto Caesar: The Catholic Church and the State in Latin America*, Chicago, University of Chicago Press, 1998.

[12]   See Kenneth Serbin, *Secret Dialogues: Church–State Relations, Torture and Social Justice in Authoritarian Brazil*, Pittsburgh, Pittsburgh University Press, 2000.

difficult to achieve in the contemporary world, including places such as Chile, given that the Catholic Church even in Latin America is becoming more like a voluntary pressure group.

Once the crisis is over, other institutions take over from the base communities, except in rural areas; the radicals have no need of the shelter they afforded; the radical foreign priests give place to local priests more integrated into local power structures.[13] Moreover, in Chile and elsewhere the Catholic elite chooses schools, such as those run by Opus Dei or the Legionaries of Christ, which encourage an ethos of paternal social service in the context of a market economy rather than a challenge to the structures. This kind of moral conservatism based on family and service is in one sense like Pentecostalism, except that the elite are large entrepreneurs and the Pentecostals independent people in the informal economy.[14]

There are therefore spaces the Catholic Church cannot easily fill when it comes to *fully* autonomous mobilization. Sociologically speaking, the Catholic Church can be seen as complementary, as well as rivalrous, to enthusiastic Protestantism. Consider the situation of Pentecostals and their penumbra of free-floating charismatics and evangelicals. They offer a buried intelligentsia of the poor in pursuit of respectability a chance to run their own show outside the status structures of which any established church is bound to be a part. After all in Chile, though Pentecostals make up 14 per cent of the total population, in the lowest stratum they make up 21.4 per cent. Those who lead and those who follow draw social boundaries around a capsule of mutual help and moral security, combining release, and renewal for the spirit, with a discipline for everyday life. The believers, especially women scarred by the consequences of machismo, see that in the church they count, and that collectively they may even begin to count in the wider society. They acquire skills in negotiating with that society, learn to accept organizational roles, and are buoyed up by assurance of Providence not the decrees of fortune. If they do not immediately engage in politics it is because they see it as a corrupt arena in which they will be the lowest participants and more likely to lose their integrity than snuff out corruption.[15] They prefer to address local issues such as water supply, but that can also be true of the base

---

[13]   See Manuel Vasquez, *The Brazilian Popular Church and the Crisis of Modernity*, Cambridge, Cambridge University Press, 1998.

[14]   See M. Angelica Thumala, 'Chile's Business Elite: The Role of Catholicism in Rebuilding an Ethos', unpublished PhD thesis, University of Cambridge, 2005, now published as *Riqueza y Piedad. El catolicismo de la elite economica chilena*, Santiago, Arena Abierta, 2007.

[15]   See John Burdick, *Looking for God in Brazil*, Berkeley, University of California Press, 1993.

communities. In any case they are nurtured on the Bible, with whose characters they identify, and the Bible has more to say about prosperity than about the relationships of church and state, concerning which they have no experience. So if there are constraints affecting the Catholic Church, there are different constraints affecting Pentecostals.

I return here to the dialectic between sacred place, temple and people and the portable identity of people on the move as migrants or nomads. The Catholic Church both sponsors mobilizations among those on the move and reinforces sacred emplacements from which to address whole peoples, Urbi et Orbi. The vast new cathedral to Our Lady Queen of Brazil and the new cathedral of Our Lady of Guadalupe in Mexico City are venues constructed to include and address a whole people. At the same time, the Pentecostal faith (like para-Christian movements such as the Mormons) concedes something to the spatial principle, though for the most part its buildings are utilitarian, and often just tiny shelters run by 'the little people' in society.

Pentecostalism appeals in some areas to indigenous peoples, for example in Bolivia, Peru and Ecuador, or the Maya in Central America and the Mapuche in Chile, where whole segments of society may fall away to embrace the new faith. In Guadalajara, Mexico, an indigenous group called La Luz del Mundo, with roots in the nationalist passions of the Civil War, has colonized a whole area of the city to create a temple at the centre of its New Jerusalem.[16] Rather like Ethiopian Christianity it contains strong Jewish elements and more than a hint of Christian Zionism. In Latin America, as in Africa, reading the whole Bible easily generates a Christian Zionism and even stimulates the creation of a new sacred landscape. In the vast temple of La Luz del Mundo in Guadalajara one sees the impact of creative imagination in spatial and architectural terms, parallel in its way to the Mormon creation of Salt Lake City and its temple in North America. The Jewish model is present simultaneously as sacred territory and as a nomadic or migrant portable identity. In Africa likewise landscapes are sacralized, and new independent churches can create their own versions of African Zion, or of Ethiopia, or even build a New Jerusalem as the followers of Simon Kimbangu did in the Congo. These are sacred 'new creations'.

Thus far I have discussed in the context of Latin America a tension between the Catholic Church with roots in sacred place, and so embedded in the social world it tends to sponsored mobilization, and Pentecostalism, a movement based on autonomous mobilization, but also tending again to sanctify place and people. In turning to Africa I want to indicate not only a sequence of social change but also changes in the way that sequence has been understood. The

---

[16]   See Renee de la Torre, *Los Hijos de la Luz*, Guadalajara, ITESO, 1995.

gist of the matter turns on the different chronology of the cultural revolution wrought by Pentecostalism in Latin America and Africa. Had the change in Africa occurred in the 1950s and 1960s as in Latin America, rather than two decades later, Western understanding of it would still have been dominated by Marxist views of appropriate development and the 'colonization of consciousness' by religion, as well as by Weberian notions of development as rationalization, and by a functionalist anthropology in alliance with ideas about what was and was not 'authentic' and properly traditional. In any case, in Latin America there was bound to be some transfer of Latin European intellectual notions, with a Marxist (and liberationist) component. That was less influential in Anglophone Africa, and in Africa as a whole it is not as if Marxist leadership in Zimbabwe or Ethiopia has proved reassuring.

In relation to Pentecostalism in Latin America I was myself part of a process of reassessment qualifying, even reversing, the early hostility of cultural nationalists, Catholic conservatives and historical Protestants.[17] I also became all too aware of the way North Americans saw this global revolution in terms of their own cultural wars between liberals and 'fundamentalists'. Our understanding of changes in Africa has been similarly distorted, as well as affected by the negative view of missions popular in the radical sixties. Since then, the emphasis among anthropologists has changed, in particular because many of them now stress the empowerment of Africans, the way they select from the Christian repertoire, as well as the pre-eminent role of Africans in Christian expansion, before, during and after the colonial period. One might go further to suggest that missionaries were those dislodged from secure status in Europe, including in particular women, who allied themselves to those who were marginal and apt for change in Africa.

Historians have also made massive contributions to the reassessment of mission, for example Adrian Hastings and Terence Ranger, and in the younger generation David Maxwell. In discussing Africa I am primarily deploying the work of the German anthropologist working in Amsterdam, Birgit Meyer, and that of David Maxwell.[18]

---

[17]   See Humberto Lagos Schuffeneger, *Sectas Religiosas en Chile: Fe o Ideologia?*, Concepcion, IAR, 1987; and idem, *La Religion en las Fuezas Armadas y de Orden*, Concepcion, IAR, 1987.

[18]   See Birgit Meyer, 'Christianity in Africa: From African Independent to Pentecostal-Charismatic Churches', *Annual Review of Anthropology*, 33 (2004), pp. 447–74; David Maxwell, *African Gifts of the Spirit*, Oxford, James Currey, 2006; idem, 'Decolonisation', in Norman Etherington (ed.), *Missions and Empire*, Oxford, Oxford University Press, 2004, pp. 285–306; and idem, 'Post-Colonial Christianity in Africa', in McLeod (ed.), *Christianity*, pp. 401–21.

Anthropologists and historians also work on Islam in Africa. The eight hundred million or so Africans are now divided roughly half and half between Christians concentrated in the south, the centre, and the western coastal countries, such as Ghana and southern Nigeria, and Muslims concentrated in the north and in the eastern coastal countries, with some inland penetration, for example in parts of Ethiopia. A 'clash of civilizations' occurs along the frontier, most notably in Sudan and Nigeria.

Islam has expanded in Africa, shifting across the Saharan divide for well over a millennium, and has been linked to trade and the formation of states. In East Africa Muslims in the mercantile states on the coast mixed with Africans in the Bantu interior, and Swahili was the result. Throughout there was a layer of orthodox Islam, sometimes advancing by jihad, and a layer of customary Islam characterized by spirit-possession and religious brotherhoods. Spirit mediums played an important role in the recent civil wars in both Liberia and Zimbabwe.

In the nineteenth century Islam spread like Christianity by imitation. Where the two religions met, for example in Buganda, there could be civil war, in that case won by the Christians. The British, with their policy of indirect rule, and the Germans likewise, used Muslims for administration in Muslim areas; by contrast, in East Africa chiefs and the British promoted Christianity as part of progress and education, combining traditional and colonial authority. Colonial and indigenous authorities were inclined to see African-inspired Christian movements, including Pentecostalism, as subversive.

In post-independence Nigeria Muslims inserted themselves positively, even aggressively, in the state, in particular to prevent secessions in the Christian south, where oil resources were situated. Muslim reformism in Africa was initially latitudinarian, but grew sterner and more Puritan, especially with respect to women, and to secularism, including Darwinism. The Muslim Brotherhood and similar para-military youth organizations were ideologically fuelled from Egypt, Saudi Arabia and Pakistan, as well as stimulated by colonialism, the Iranian revolution against a modern state, and the existence of Israel. The great trek to the cities resulted in an army of migrants, some slum-dwellers, others intellectuals, many of whom found in militant Islam an international resource for identity and the politics of identity. Islam also served as an ideology to undermine the modern secular state, in particular by establishing Sharia law, as has happened in some states of northern Nigeria. Many of the states of north Africa, for example Algeria and Egypt, are riven by tensions between nationalist elites and Islamists.[19] Sub-Saharan Christian Africa is by no means free of conflicts,

---

[19]   See Peter Clarke (ed.), *Islam*, London, Routledge, 1988; and idem, 'Islam: Sub-Saharan Africa', in *International Encyclopedia of the Social and Behavioral Sciences*, vol. 12, pp. 7927–30.

for example the genocidal war in Rwanda where Christians were prominent in war-making and peace-making, and the Lord's Resistance Army in northern Uganda, fuelled by a government with a southern base not unwilling to see chaos and mayhem in the north. But there is no equivalent of jihadism or attempt at theocracy, however much 'Big Men' and 'Big Women' such as President Chiluba, President Mugabe and his wife, and Janet, the wife of President Museveni, have sought born-again legitimacy.

What has been the sequence of change in sub-Saharan Africa over the past half century as seen through the varying lenses of anthropology and history? The central fact, obvious whatever lens you employ, is that Christianity has taken off post-independence to the point where the global centre of Christian gravity is moving south. It has been suggested that today the average Anglican is a 24-year-old black woman.

Initially it seemed as though the future of Christianity in Africa lay with the African indigenous churches (AICs), because they could be welcomed by nationalist elites (and by anthropologists) as authentic forms of inculturation, as 'resistance', and as proto-political. The Aladura movement in Nigeria, the Kimbanguist Church in South Central Africa, and the Zionist churches in South Africa came into this category, though the Zionist movement also contained some genes from early Pentecostal progenitors. Nor is it alone in that.[20]

However, a new phase opened in the appropriation of Christianity with the astonishing expansion of Pentecostal and charismatic churches, in particular megachurches in megacities run by charismatic leaders, many of them with a flamboyant modern lifestyle. The Pentecostal movement spread across frontiers, creating transnational 'imagined communities', affecting mainline Protestant churches at the same time and, with the onset of democratization and liberalization, spreading to Francophone Africa in Togo, Benin and Cameroon. This development was disliked by neo-traditionalists in the national elites, and by those in the older churches pressing for 'inculturation', as well as not appealing to anthropologists interested in authenticity. What was needed, therefore, was some kind of examination of Western notions of tradition and authenticity, some appreciation of the (selective) search for modernity and the empowerment acquired by mastering modernity. Also needed was a better understanding of the real continuities between Pentecostalism and the African past, which it at least took seriously enough to demonize. This was inculturation in a different mode, and those elements found least acceptable by outside observers, such as exorcism as a new version of witchcraft eradication, the power of 'Big Men', and religion viewed as bringing 'goods' of every kind, were also the most African.

---

[20] See Alan Anderson, 'The Pentecostal and Charismatic Movements', in McLeod (ed.), *Christianity*, pp. 89–106.

Critics neglected the ability of Pentecostalism to pick up local issues in its basic narratives, the freedom it gave from gerontocracy to women and young men, its moralization of wealth and work, its attack on wasteful consumerism and the 'spirit of poverty' as demonic and destructive, and its emphasis on personal conscience as exercised alike by men and women in long-term familial relationships. Jane Soothill in particular stresses the role of women, whose access to spiritual power enables them to redeem male victims of spiritual manipulation. Like Bernice Martin she challenges any notion that Pentecostalism revives patriarchy.[21]

No doubt, the modernizing and individualizing motifs can be overstressed, as well as the escape from restrictive family and tribal networks, and the dangers of leaders cosying up to the powerful are real, but the impact on everyday life is positive, as is the shift in priorities. Millions of people have acquired a 'portable identity' in an 'imagined community' reinforced by modern media and capable of sustaining them in exploring global networks of the like-minded. That was particularly the case among the educated young in West Africa.

It was ethnography, and sometimes female ethnography, for example the work of Birgit Meyer, which accented the positive and could translate the idiom of the demonic and the way the old forms functioned in the body of the new.[22] It was history that could discern the impact of vernacular Christianities made available through translation, as well as opening on to the near-universal Anglosphere. Historians also understood how the biblical narrative could be selectively seized upon by the African imagination to build up selfhood, and to create nationhood.[23] While the older churches were moving as NGOs into the vacant spaces in health, education and development left by failed states, and even acting as political arbiters, particularly in Catholic Central Africa, the Pentecostal and charismatic churches were creating a shared idiom and cultural capital along classic pluralistic, transnational and voluntary lines.

One of the most interesting cases concerns the spread of charismatic practices in the ancient Coptic churches which preceded Islam and were partly or completely overwhelmed in Egypt and Nubia. During the reign of the Emperor Haile Selassie in Ethiopia, born-again churches were illegal, and then under the

---

[21]   See Jane Soothill, *Gender, Social Change and Spiritual Power: Charismatic Christianity in Ghana*, Boston and Leiden, Brill, 2007; Bernice Martin, 'The Pentecostal Gender Paradox', in Richard K. Fenn (ed.), *The Blackwell Companion to the Sociology of Religion*, Oxford, Blackwell, 2001, pp. 52–66.

[22]   See Birgit Meyer, *Translating the Devil: Religion and Modernity among the Peke Ewe in Ghana*, Edinburgh, Edinburgh University Press, 1999.

[23]   See John Peel, *Religious Encounter and the Making of the Yoruba*, Bloomington, Indiana University Press, 2000.

'Red Terror' from 1978 to 1991 they were persecuted, along with the Coptic Church. During that period an underground movement developed which affected all churches, for example the Lutheran Mekane Jesus Church, but according to Jörg Haustein[24] of Heidelberg University there are now 250 denominations, concentrated in the south west, comprising 13 per cent of the population and in some areas a majority. Though its origins may lie in Scandinavian and American missions, the movement was effectively generated by prayer meetings in Addis Ababa, in particular among students, rather along the lines found in Nigeria and indeed parts of East Africa.

The expansion of Catholicism has also been dramatic. In a way, the organic nature of Catholicism resonated with the collectivism of the new states, but whereas Protestant missions had produced the new elites rather than a highly educated black clergy, the Catholic Church had created an educated black clergy and hierarchy rather than an educated lay elite. That enabled it to acquire black leadership at an early stage though, in common with all the other historic churches, it formally Africanized in an atmosphere clouded by anti-colonial suspicion. After a period when Christian leaders had to tread carefully, the time came when the Catholic Church and the other historic churches had acquired roots in African soil deep enough to protest against the exploitation, violence, cults of personality, and corruption engaged in by the new elites. Hierarchy and international contacts, and personnel in the religious orders help in such conflicts. In Mozambique NGOs, religious and secular, 'called the shots', according to David Maxwell, and the Vatican brokered the eventual peace there.[25] Earlier the churches of Mozambique had suffered repression under Frelimo, but in 1982 under President Machel the government had to turn to the churches as allies. Interestingly, in Portuguese territories such as Angola the old alliance of Catholic Church and political establishment meant that Protestants were concentrated among the insurgents.

One of the paradoxes of inculturation in the Catholic Church was its 'top-down' character, analogous to the sponsored mobilization noted in Latin America. The international priestly intelligentsia ignored the resonance an older Catholicism might acquire in Africa, only to discover that the resistance to a modernized liturgy and the downgrading of traditional devotions came from African Catholics. Occasionally African Catholics went too far with their own inculturation, as when Archbishop Milingo carried the practice of 'deliverance' to the point where he was permanently called to Rome. There is quite a chasm between Catholics, Anglicans, Lutherans and liberal Protestants in North America and Europe, and the fruits of the spirit in Africa. Globalization can emphasize

---

[24]   On the new Global Pentecostalism website, http://www.glopent.net.

[25]   See Maxwell, *African Gifts of the Spirit*, chapter 6.

differences between cultural contexts to the point of threatened schism, and as a result a conservative minority in the North Atlantic churches has linked up with a majority in the global south.

One difference which is not straightforwardly aligned with the liberal/ conservative divide turns on how one reads the Bible. The Western churches have since the Middle Ages laid stress on redemptive suffering, whereas the primitive tradition, and now the African tradition, laid stress on victory. Allied to that there is an Afro-Jewish evaluation of prosperity. African Christianity is realized in dance and story rather than propositions, and it proclaims a Jesus who is victor over evil and death rather than a lamb brought to the slaughter. The slogan 'Go for gold!' says it all. There is also perhaps a female element in Christianity, symbolized among Protestants by the predominance of women in the missionary force for over a century, and among Catholics by devotion to the Blessed Virgin, which runs counter to the Third World validation of maleness and reproduction. At any rate, the message of Christianity is received by Third World women. Even if males are in ultimate control, it speaks to their condition, in particular by bringing the man back into the family and, in a continent ravaged by AIDS, by stressing male self-discipline. Of course, Catholic opposition to contraception has dire consequences for women where that discipline breaks down.

By way of a postscript one might add that it has been widely held by missionaries and anthropologists alike that Christianity does not 'take' among hunter-gatherer societies (sometimes called 'first peoples'), whether in North America, Amazonia, Africa or Australia. According to recent evidence, that seems to be breaking down, and in Terence Ranger's formulation a crucial variable seems to be whether Christianity is brought in a missionary package, as part of Western overlordship, even if that includes welfare and education, or can be left to the initiative of indigenous carriers.[26] That is also the lesson of Christianity in contemporary Africa and, to some extent, of changes in contemporary Latin America. The key is indigenous appropriation rather than the so-called 'civilizing mission' of the past, though insofar as civilization meant education and (later) health, the good achieved was unequivocal.

Overall, I am suggesting that secularization, on either the Anglo-Saxon or the French model, is not inevitable in Latin America or Africa. It is clearly important to mark the difference between Islamic and Christian, in particular Pentecostal, excursions into politics, the one pressing towards a regulated religious, perhaps theocratic, political order, the other towards competition.

[26]   See Terence Ranger, 'Christianity and the First Peoples: Some Second Thoughts', in Peggy Brock (ed.), *Indigenous Peoples and Religious Change*, Leiden, Brill, 2005, pp. 15–32. For further discussion cf. David Martin, 'Mission and Empire', *Journal of Religion in Africa*, 36.2 (2006), pp. 224–36.

Above all, the experience of church–state relations in Europe is no guide to the future of such relations in Africa, given the patrimonial character of most African states, and given the extent to which political culture is inflected by a profoundly pluralist religious field in an inspirited continent. After all, Pentecostalism in Africa in part succeeds because it simply adds to a fissionable pluralism. Pluralism and competition are compatible with economic advance and democratization, and if Big Men and Women seek a combination of spiritual and material power there are alternatives available at least to pose a challenge. Sir Bob Geldof, though an atheist, is right to stress that you cannot understand Africa without understanding religion; and the time is past when whole books can be written on development in Latin America without paying attention to its religion and culture.

13

The Desecularization of the Middle East Conflict: From a Conflict between States to a Conflict between Religious Communities

Hans G. Kippenberg

The Charter of the United Nations disapproves of a practice long a standard feature of human history, one often glorified by history books and religions. Article 2 stipulates:

> 3. All Members shall settle their international disputes by peaceful means in such a manner that international peace and security, and justice, are not endangered. 4. All Members shall refrain in their international relations from the threat or use of force against the territorial integrity or political independence of any state, or in any other manner inconsistent with the Purposes of the United Nations.

On this view, when Alexander the Great acquired territories 'with the spear', deriving from this the right to rule without limitation, he would, according to contemporary law, have to reckon with a war crimes trial. The settlement of land by the tribes of Israel or the conquest of the Middle East by Islamic armies are also violations of current law, though they are transfigured and idealized in religious writings. 'Conquest no longer constitutes a title of territorial acquisition', as Graf Vitzthum sums up the modern-day conception of the law in the volume *Völkerrecht* ('international law').[1] I would like to look into a case which demonstrates how

---

[1]   Wolfgang Graf Vitzthum (ed.), *Völkerrecht*, Berlin, de Gruyter, 2004, p. 26 (translation by the author).

great, even today, the tension can become between this international prohibition on violence and religious claims to a territory, bringing out the political turbulence to which this gives rise. The case considered here is virtually the flip-side of what, by modifying a formulation of Ernst-Wolfgang Böckenförde, we might refer to as the desecularization of state action: 'At the mention of secularization in the context of the emergence of the state, most people think of the [...] declaration of neutrality with regard to questions of religious truth'.[2] It is the aspiration to neutrality that has increasingly been abandoned in the Middle East conflict. The development of this conflict is practically a yardstick of the growing strength of religions in the present era. But it is also a case that enables us to see how elusive the power of religions within modernity is.

Religions and the prohibition on violence under international law: the case of the territories occupied by Israel in 1967

It all began with a minor imprecision. Following Israel's military victory in the 1967 Six Days' War, the UN Security Council confirmed in Resolution 242 that it is impermissible to acquire territories through war. In order to achieve a just and lasting peace in the Middle East, all states must first recognize one another. Second, the UN called for the 'withdrawal of Israeli armed forces from territories occupied in the recent conflict'. In French, which has equal status with English in the UN, this reads a little differently: 'retrait des forces armées israéliennes des territoires occupés lors du récent conflit'. Should Israel merely leave occupied territories or *the* occupied territories as a whole?[3] This linguistic imprecision became politically explosive when, in the 1970s, it became bound up with a power shift within Israel.

Despite the clear legal position, the Labour government annexed East Jerusalem immediately after the military victory. However, the government made no move to allow the Arab population of East Jerusalem to vote on this new status or to give them Israeli nationality, as occurred to a limited degree in the case of the Arabs living in the territory of Israel in 1948. Now even

---

[2]   Ernst-Wolfgang Böckenförde, 'The Rise of the State as a Process of Secularization', in idem, *State, Society and Liberty: Studies in Political Theory and Constitutional Law*, New York, Berg, 1991, pp. 26–46; the cautious way in which Böckenförde expresses himself is worthy of note. In terms of Europe's historical reality, the state has never been neutral with respect to religions.

[3]   On the resolutions, see John Quigley, *The Case for Palestine: An International Law Perspective*, Durham, NC, Duke University Press, revised and expanded edn, 2005, pp. 170ff.

the democratic society of Israel was convinced that it was acceptable to act in line with principles requiring no agreement from the affected population or the international community, according to Meron Benvenisti,[4] who sat on the Jerusalem city council in the 1970s and collected and published reliable data on developments in the occupied territories for many years.[5]

Most members of the government saw the former territories of the British mandated area as possible objects of exchange in the sense of land for peace, but wished to come to a decision about which areas to return only in the event of a peace treaty with the neighbouring Arab states. Yigal Allon, general and minister, developed a plan to exclude additional territories around Jerusalem and the Jordan Valley from being returned and to populate them with Jewish settlers for reasons of military security.[6] The 1970s saw a quite new development. Religious Zionists began to resettle those areas once part of the biblical land of Israel.[7] When the Likud party took power in 1977, the new government aligned itself entirely with the settlers' movement and took charge of further settlement itself. It can only be forbidden to annex foreign land, not one's own, declared Israel's new prime minister, Menachem Begin; it was in Judaea and Samaria, he stated, that Israel came into being.[8]

The attitude of the USA to the settlement of the occupied territories also changed over the same period. It was still disapproving under President Jimmy

---

[4]   See Meron Benvenisti, *Intimate Enemies: Jews and Arabs in a Shared Land*, Berkeley, University of California Press, 1995, p. 34. The entire chapter 'City of Strife' (pp. 1–51) is a vivid account of the tensions in the violently reunified city, in which, for example, the eastern portion was blatantly discriminated against in the city budget.

[5]   See Meron Benvenisti, *The West Bank Data Project: A Survey of Israel's Policies*, Washington, American Enterprise Institute Studies (vol. 398), 1984; idem, *Demographic, Economic, Legal, Social and Political Developments in the West Bank*, Jerusalem, Westview, 1986.

[6]   See Benvenisti, *The West Bank Data Project*, pp. 51ff.; idem, *Intimate Enemies*, pp. 51ff.

[7]   The extent of biblical land fluctuates in the Jewish texts. *Eretz Yisrael* might be the 'Promised' Land of Canaan referred to in the story of the Patriarchs; it might refer to the area actually settled by Israelites or the land defined by the Halakha; it reaches its greatest extent in Gen. 15:18–21: God promises Abraham that He will give his descendants all the land from the Nile to the Euphrates. The land of Israel was holy in the Jewish tradition because it was in the possession of God. God is the possessor of the territory, and the land cannot be sold: Lev. 25:23. In this sense, *Eretz Yisrael* is a 'geotheological' concept, as Gudrun Krämer puts it in *A History of Palestine: From the Ottoman Conquest to the Founding of the State of Israel*, Princeton, Princeton University Press, 2008, pp. 5–10; 19–22; 23–26.

[8]   See Quigley, *The Case for Palestine*, p. 176.

Carter. As late as 1978, an internal legal report produced for Congress by the State Department stated that Israel was occupying these territories (Gaza, the West Bank, the Golan Heights and Sinai).[9] Such territory, the report declared, has a special status under international law. The occupying power is prohibited from settling its own people in the territories under its control. The report referred to the Fourth Geneva Convention, to which Israel was a signatory and which stipulates in Article 49: 'the Occupying Power shall not deport or transfer parts of its own civilian population into the territory it occupies'.[10] In 1980, in a subsequent resolution, 465, the UN Security Council confirmed this provision for the Israeli occupied territories: Jewish settlements, the resolution stated, are unlawful and represent a violation of the Fourth Geneva Convention; the settlements must be removed. The conflict was aggravated by the First Additional Protocol to the Geneva Convention of 8 June 1977, in which it was agreed that the rules of the Geneva Convention apply not only to wars between states, but also to a case previously left out of account: armed conflicts in which people 'are fighting against colonial domination and alien occupation and against racist regimes in the exercise of their right of self-determination, as enshrined in the Charter of the United Nations'. In line with this, Palestinian resistance organizations also had a right to be treated in accordance with the Geneva Conventions, provided that they themselves complied with their rules.

Let us return to the attitude of the USA to the Middle East conflict. In 1981, the newly elected American President, Ronald Reagan, suddenly assessed the situation differently from his predecessor. Two weeks after taking office, he declared, 'I disagreed when the previous administration referred to them [settlements] as illegal – they're not illegal'.[11] Certainly, the settlements were an obstacle to peace, but they were not illegal. Israel, as well as the Palestinians, had legitimate claims to these territories. As a result of this new conception, the USA no longer supported the UN in its efforts to enforce its resolutions against Israel. The government of the USA abandoned its neutrality towards Israel's religious pretensions until, in 2004, George W. Bush finally declared, during a visit to Washington by prime minister Ariel Sharon, that the annexations of parts of the occupied territories by Israel were irrevocable and the return of Palestinian refugees was out of the question.[12]

---

[9] This may be found on the website of the Foundation for Middle East Peace under: Documents, Opinion of the Legal Advisor, Department of State, 4–21–78 (http://www. fmep.org/documents/opinion_OLA_DOS4–21–78.html).

[10] Adam Roberts and Richard Guelff (eds.), *Documents on the Laws of War*, Oxford, Oxford University Press, 2000, p. 318.

[11] *New York Times*, 3 February 1981.

[12] 'Statement by the President' of 14 April 2004, http://www.whitehouse.gov/news/

When, after twenty years of martial law, the Palestinians rose up against Israel in the Intifada of 1987, the secular liberation movement of the PLO acquired an active religious competitor. Prominent members of the Muslim Brotherhood in Gaza were unwilling to leave the organization of the rebellion to the PLO and its United National Command (UNC) and brought Hamas into existence in December 1987 – its name an acronym of the Arab term for Islamic resistance movement (*harakat al-muqawama al-Islamiyya*) meaning 'zeal'. Just as religious Zionists claimed the occupied territories as the land of Israel, the supporters of Hamas demanded a whole Palestine, undivided, stretching from the Mediterranean to the Jordan. This is the land which the early Muslims handed down to the later generations until the day of resurrection.

The present chapter deals with this shift in the interpretation of the Middle East conflict. To understand this shift, including in a conceptual sense, we may usefully draw on sociological action theory. Every action entails a definition of the situation, which, however, does not necessarily arise from the circumstances themselves.[13] This does not mean that every situation can be interpreted arbitrarily; actors remain dependent on external conditions. Yet the interpretation is not prescribed by these conditions. Hence, it is a key element of all action that actors define the situation in which they find themselves. This framing of reality provides an outline of a sequence of events – a social script. Viewed from this perspective, the problem arises of when and why the parties to conflict ceased to interpret the Middle East conflict in a secular way and adopted a religious perspective, and how this impacted on their actions. Even a secular conflict can be 'framed' religiously. In making this statement, I follow Max Weber, who saw

---

releases/2004/04/20040414–2.html: 'The goal of two independent states [...] remains a key to resolving this conflict. [...] It seems clear that an agreed, just, fair and realistic framework for a solution to the Palestinian refugee issue as part of any final status agreement will need to be found through the establishment of a Palestinian state, and the settling of Palestinian refugees there, rather than in Israel. [...] As part of a final peace settlement, Israel must have secure and recognized borders, which should emerge from negotiations between the parties in accordance with UNSC Resolutions 242 and 338. In light of new realities on the ground, including already existing major Israeli population centers, it is unrealistic to expect that the outcome of final status negotiations will be a full and complete return to the armistice lines of 1949. It is realistic to expect that any final status agreement will only be achieved on the basis of mutually agreed changes that reflect these realities.'

[13]   See Hartmut Esser, *Soziologie. Spezielle Grundlagen*, vol. 1: *Situationslogik und Handeln*, Frankfurt, Campus, 1999, p. 63. A concise summary of this analytical model can be found in idem, 'Die Definition der Situation', *Kölner Zeitschrift für Soziologie und Sozialpsychologie* 48.1 (1996), pp. 1–34.

religion as a case of action by a whole community and whose special features he wished to understand and explain in light of the 'meaning' which subjects give to their actions.[14] Religion as the expectation of salvation is not an independent class of actions, but may become attached to a variety of actions, giving rise to specific forms of collective religious phenomena.[15]

In line with this, the key evidence that a conflict between states has become a conflict between religious communities is that the parties to conflict now interpret their actions primarily in terms of religion rather than international law. It is this shift with which we are concerned here. My analysis concludes with the thesis that processes of establishing religious communities have played an increasingly powerful role within society since the 1970s and that this has had consequences for the policies pursued by Israel, the USA and the Palestinians. I begin with Israel.

Israel's wars of redemption

From its beginnings in the nineteenth century, Zionism, which aimed to establish a Jewish nation state in Palestine, inspired objections from orthodox Jews, for whom the ending of the exile was solely a matter for the Messiah. Those who attempt to resettle the Promised Land now are succumbing to the temptations of Satan and wish to 'force the end'.[16] A Jew in the land of Israel is permitted only to pray and study the Torah. To this day there are Jews, including some in Israel, who therefore see their situation as one of ongoing exile.

There was, however, a rabbi in this camp of the so-called ultra-orthodox who developed a religious reading of the foundation of the secular state of Israel: Rabbi Abraham Isaac Kook (1865–1935).[17] From 1921, he was chief rabbi of the Ashkenazi Jews as well as being a devotee of Hasidic mysticism. This mysticism enabled him to interpret the secular Zionist project through the prism of a

---

[14]   See Max Weber, *Economy and Society: An Outline of Interpretive Sociology*, ed. Guenther Roth and Claus Wittich, Berkeley, University of California Press, 1978, vol. 1, chapter VI: 'Religious Groups (The Sociology of Religion)', pp. 399–634.

[15]   See Hans G. Kippenberg, 'Religious Communities and the Path to Disenchantment: The Origins, Sources, and Theoretical Core of the Religion Section', in Charles Camic, Philip S. Gorski and David M. Trubek (eds.), *Max Weber's Economy and Society: A Critical Companion*, Stanford, Stanford University Press, 2005, pp. 164–82.

[16]   As described by Aviezer Ravitzky, *Messianism, Zionism, and Jewish Religious Radicalism*, translated from the Hebrew by M. Swirsky and J. Chipman, Chicago, University of Chicago Press, 1996, pp. 40–78 (chapter 2: '"Forcing the End": Radical Anti-Zionism').

[17]   See Ravitzky, *Messianism, Zionism, and Jewish Religious Radicalism*, pp. 79–144 (chapter 3: '"The Revealed End": Messianic Religious Zionism').

particular philosophy of history. The progress of messianism, he asserted, occurs regardless of actors' intentions. In the 1930s, his attempt to bring the secular and the religious together under the roof of a mystical messianism enjoyed little success. This changed with his son Zvi Yehuda Kook (1891–1982),[18] who simplified but also coarsened his father's philosophy of history. His standing was derived from one event in particular. On the national holiday of 1967, three weeks before the Six Days' War, while giving a sermon, he suddenly broke into a lament about the fact that Hebron, Sichem, Jericho and Anathot had been torn away from Israel as a result of the United Nations' partition plan and the subsequent war of 1948. Just three weeks later, Israeli troops corrected this disaster, conquered these very cities in almost miraculous fashion and placed them under martial law. This conquest had been endowed with a religious meaning in advance by Rabbi Kook. The Six Days' War was a 'war of redemption'; the biblical 'Land of Israel' was 'redeemed' from the unbelievers. The younger Rabbi Kook had this sermon to thank for his reputation as a prophet of almost biblical proportions, though what had occurred was in fact more a ritual lament than a prophecy. Every account of the history preceding the religious settlers' movement mentions this event.[19]

Students and rabbis at the Kooks' Talmudic school became the avant-garde of the religious settlers' movement and organized the occupation of the promised inheritance of Judaea, Samaria and Gaza in opposition to a hesitant and internally divided Labour government.[20] When territories that had been part of the biblical land of Israel were lost in the Yom Kippur war of 1973, they interpreted this as a punishment of secular Zionism, which trusted only in its own policies rather than in God. In response to this setback, which they interpreted as the 'birth pangs of the Messiah', Kook's followers formed the *Gush Emunim*, the 'bloc of the faithful'.[21] Its historical theology legitimized its taking charge of the settlement of the occupied territories. The settlers' movement was driven by a simple and stirring core idea: 'Redemption is underway – Eretz Yisrael is holy and cannot

[18]   See Gideon Aran, 'The Father, the Son, and the Holy Land: The Spiritual Authorities of Jewish-Zionist Fundamentalism in Israel', in R. Scott Appleby (ed.), *Spokesmen for the Despised: Fundamentalist Leaders of the Middle East*, Chicago, University of Chicago Press, 1997, pp. 294–327.

[19]   See Gershom Gorenberg, *The Accidental Empire: Israel and the Birth of the Settlements, 1967–1977*, New York, Henry Holt, 2006, pp. 21–23.

[20]   See Samuel C. Heilman, 'Guides of the Faithful: Contemporary Religious Zionist Rabbis', in Appleby (ed.), *Spokesmen for the Despised*, pp. 328–62.

[21]   On Gush Emunim, see Gideon Aran, 'Jewish Fundamentalism: The Bloc of the Faithful in Israel (Gush Emunim)', in Martin E. Marty and R. Scott Appleby (eds.), *Fundamentalisms Observed: The Fundamentalism Project*, vol. 1, Chicago, University of Chicago Press, 1991, pp. 265–344.

be shared with Gentiles – there is an inherent link between settlement of the holy land and hastening the coming of the Messiah – international law does not apply'.[22]

This religious Zionism inspired a whole generation of young Jews. Above all else they wished to be more national than the ultra-orthodox and more religious than the Zionists. In this spirit, they forged ahead with the settlement of old biblical areas and towns. Israeli martial law in these territories and the disunity of the Israeli government in this matter bolstered their plans.[23] It was the prevention of a new partition of the land of Israel rather than Israel's need for military security that dictated the settlers' actions. By 1977, they had established almost 80 settlements in the occupied territories, home to around 11,000 inhabitants; in East Jerusalem and its new districts there were another 40,000.[24] After 1977, the number of settlers grew to 42,000 in 1985 and to 76,000 in 1990, as illustrated in a table produced by Robert A. Pape. By 2002, the figure was 226,000.[25] Martial law in the occupied territories enabled the expropriation of properties, confiscation of uninhabited land, and construction of Jewish settlements and roads featuring Israeli checkpoints.

One consequence of these settlement activities was conflict with the Palestinians living in these territories. Israeli scholar Ehud Sprinzak counted 3,000 cases of communal conflicts between settlers and Arabs from 1981 to the beginning of the First Intifada in 1987.[26] These included bomb attacks on the mayors of two Arab cities in revenge for a Palestinian attack on the Talmudic school of Beit Hadassah in Hebron that cost the lives of six Jewish students. In 1983, settlers attacked an Islamic seminary in Hebron, killing a number of students. Both these acts of violence were approved by rabbis. Following the two Oslo Accords of 1993 and 1995, the settlers' shock and resentment grew. It first found expression in a massacre carried out in 1994 by a doctor, Baruch Goldstein, originally from the USA, in the burial chamber of Machpela at Hebron, during which he was killed by incensed Muslims.[27] Goldstein's funeral was attended by

---

[22] See Ehud Sprinzak, *The Ascendance of Israel's Radical Right*, New York, Oxford University Press, 1991, pp. 110–24; in addition, on the principles, see Jamie Rosenman, 'The Apocalyptic Ideology of Gush Emunim', 2004. www.jjay.cuny.edu/terrorism/TheApocalyptic.pdf.

[23] See Gorenberg, *The Accidental Empire*, p. 206.

[24] Figures from Gorenberg, *The Accidental Empire*, p. 358.

[25] See Robert A. Pape, *Dying to Win: The Strategic Logic of Suicide Terrorism*, New York, Random House, 2005, p. 49. The table is based on official Israeli data. East Jerusalem is not included.

[26] See Sprinzak, *The Ascendance of Israel's Radical Right*, p. 148.

[27] For analyses of these events and of the heroization of the perpetrator, see Mark

more than a thousand settlers; his grave became a place of remembrance; friends erected a gravestone with an inscription hailing him as a saint and martyr:

> Here lies the saint, Dr. Baruch Kappel Goldstein, blessed be the memory of the righteous and holy man, may the Lord avenge his blood, who devoted his soul to the Jews, Jewish religion and Jewish land. His hands are innocent and his heart is pure. He was killed as a martyr of God on the 14th of Adar, Purim, in the year 5754.[28]

The use of violence was central rather than marginal to the settlers' movement, concluded Ehud Sprinzak in a study of the subject.[29]

Another factor contributed to the aggravation of the conflict with the Palestinians. The protocol to the Geneva Convention that acknowledged that combatant members of Palestinian liberation organizations also had a right to protection inspired a furious backlash. In 1979 and 1983, Benjamin Netanyahu, later prime minister of Israel, organized two conferences on terrorism for the Jonathan Institute, one in Jerusalem and one in Washington. Benjamin Netanyahu's brother Jonathan, after whom the Institute was named, was the officer in charge of freeing the Jewish hostages at Entebbe airport in Uganda in 1976, an event during which he lost his life. Both conferences had the declared aim of mobilizing the West to fight against terrorism and rejected 'absolutely the notion that "one's man terrorist is another man's freedom fighter"'.[30] The Western media had rashly taken the reasons for their actions from the terrorists themselves and presented them as resistance fighters, wrote Netanyahu. 'This is precisely what the terrorists would like us to believe.' In reality, he asserted, they mutilated and murdered innocents intentionally and with full awareness of what they were doing. The 1979 conference in Jerusalem therefore came up with a different definition of terrorism: 'Terrorism is the deliberate and systematic murder, maiming, and menacing of

---

Juergensmeyer, *Terror in the Mind of God: The Global Rise of Religious Violence*, Berkeley, University of California Press, 2000, pp. 49–59; and Ehud Sprinzak, *Brother against Brother: Violence and Extremism in Israeli Politics from Altalena to the Rabin Assassination*, New York, Free Press, 1999, pp. 1–4, 238–43, 258–66.

[28]   Source: http://www.fact-index.com/b/ba/baruch_goldstein.html.

[29]   See Ehud Sprinzak, 'From Messianic Pioneering to Vigilante Terrorism', in David C. Rapoport (ed.), *Inside Terrorist Organizations*, New York, Columbia University Press, 1988, pp. 194–216, esp. p. 213.

[30]   Benjamin Netanyahu (ed.), *Terrorism: How the West Can Win*, New York, Farrar, Straus, Giroux, 1986, p. 3.

the innocent to inspire fear for political ends'.[31] On this view, terrorists have no right to call themselves resistance fighters or guerrillas, because they attack weak and helpless civilians. The battle against terrorism can be won only if the public and media in the West relinquish their misconceptions. This removed the air of ambivalence surrounding Palestinian combatants, the sense that they were fighting for a legitimate cause with reprehensible means. The good and the bad, the chosen and the depraved, now faced one another across a clear dividing line.

Among the Israelis, existing differences of opinion about how to resolve the conflict were also aggravated. The geotheology of Gush Emunim endowed the imperative of settling the 'Land of Israel' with a value overriding all other values, one which demonstrated that one truly was one of the people of Israel and showed true faith in the Torah. This view, which did not go uncontested (even by some devotees),[32] justified a willingness among convinced settlers to use violence even against fellow Jews. This was aroused above all at times when the government of Israel yielded to international pressure and returned biblical territories. For many settlers, exchanging 'land for peace' was tantamount to apostasy. When the second Oslo Accord of 1995 extended Palestinian autonomy to a further seven towns and hundreds of villages, the association of rabbis in the occupied territories sounded the alarm. To vote to return the land – including military installations – was equivalent to declaring your brother to be a thief. A rabbinical tradition was circulated: anyone who 'delivered' (moser) Jews to this fate or 'persecuted' (rodef) them must be killed if necessary.[33] A group of activists gathered before the residence of prime minister Yitzhak Rabin and carried out the most terrible ritual of damnation known to Judaism: pulsa di nura (Aramaic, literally 'flame of the fire').[34] A Talmudic student at Bar Ilan University, Yigal

---

[31]   Netanyahu (ed.), Terrorism, pp.8–9.

[32]   Sprinzak describes such a controversy in The Ascendance of Israel's Radical Right, pp. 153–55. Rabbi Yehuda Amital, graduate of Kook's Talmudic school, accused Gush Emunim of overstating the importance of 'land' at the expense of 'people' and 'Torah' within the process of salvation.

[33]   Ronald C. Kiener has compared this type of assassination with that of Anwar al-Sadat: 'Gushist and Qutbian Approaches to Government: A Comparative Analysis of Religious Assassination', Numen, 44 (1997), pp. 229–41.

[34]   See Sprinzak, Brother against Brother, pp. 274ff. In October 2004, when Ariel Sharon announced his plan to withdraw from Gaza, the Middle East Web Log reported: 'One rabbi offered to conduct a medieval Pulsa Di Nura ceremony on PM Ariel Sharon, to cause his demise by magic means. Security experts including GSS (Shabak) chiefs, warn that we are only one step away from an actual planned assassination attempt, and perhaps worse, that there are Jewish groups planning to destroy the mosques on the Temple

Amir, considered himself authorized by rabbinical statements to take action and murdered the prime minister in 1995 during a peace rally.[35]

Over a twenty-year period, the essence of the Middle East conflict had changed: from a territorial conflict between the state of Israel on the one hand and the states of Egypt, Lebanon, Syria and Jordan on the other, it had become a conflict between Israelis and Palestinians over the legitimacy of their religiously grounded claims to the land and hence also a conflict *among* Palestinians and Israelis.

Agitating for the land of Palestine as Islamic endowment (*waqf*)

We find competing framings of the conflict among the Palestinians. On one side stood the Palestinian Liberation Organization, founded in 1964, which claimed to act on behalf of all Palestinians regardless of their religious affiliation, that is, including Arab Christians. When the PLO adopted a charter in 1968, it justified resistance in terms of the struggle of the Arab peoples against imperialism.[36] An independent Arab Palestine was to be established, and would be achieved through the solidarity of all Arab states; Arab unity and Palestinian liberation went hand in hand. Zionism was considered a regional variety of imperialism. The partition of Palestine by the UN in 1947 and the foundation of Israel were unlawful; in reality, the Jews were a religion, not a nation. The aim must be to liquidate the Zionist presence, in other words the state of Israel (Article 15).

On the other side stood the Muslim Brothers, who framed the conflict with Israel differently. In view of the decline which Islam had undergone since the dissolution of the Ottoman empire, they believed that the time for armed struggle against the state of Israel had not yet come. Islamization of Arab society must take precedence over anti-imperialist armed struggle. For years, the Muslim Brothers pursued the idea of gradually building an Islamic order. The government of Israel left them alone because it saw them as a welcome counterweight to the PLO. The driving force of the Islamization of Gaza in the 1970s was Sheikh Ahmad Yasin, who had risen to the status of dominant

---

Mount in order to bring about the last messianic war and the establishment of the Third Temple.' http://www.mideastweb.org/log/archives/00000305.htm.

[35]   See Sprinzak, *Brother against Brother*, ch. 8: 'To Kill a Prime Minister' (pp. 244–85).

[36]   English text, 'The Palestinian National Charter', in Walter Laqueur and Barry Rubin (eds.), *The Israel-Arab Reader: A Documentary History of the Middle East Conflict*, Harmondsworth, Penguin Books, 6th revised edn, 2001, pp. 117–21.

spiritual leader among the Muslim Brothers.[37] In 1973, he founded the Islamic Centre (*Mujamma' al-Islami*) as a bulwark against the unbelievers; Israel officially recognized the institution in 1979. The obligation to engage in *jihad*, to 'strive' for the establishment of an Islamic order, did not only consist in a readiness to carry out warlike acts; doing one's best to promote justice and the common good (*maslaha*) of the community was of equal importance. Driven by an ethic of brotherliness, Muslims created social institutions and networks. By the mid-1980s, the Centre had developed into the most powerful institution in Gaza, featuring mosques, libraries, nursery schools, businesses, schools, clinics and a university. Responsibility for this social work required that the Muslim Brothers be circumspect about conflicts with Israel's military power; hence their restraint with respect to direct armed struggle as practised by the PLO and demanded by others.

Following the devastating military defeats suffered by the Arab states in 1967 and the associated loss of respect suffered by Arab nationalism, the PLO also lost credibility. Palestinians increasingly sought in Islam the strength needed to cope with the two 'catastrophes' (*al-nakba*) – the partition of Palestine in 1948 and the occupation of the Palestinian territories by Israel in 1967.[38] In the late 1970s, when the Revolution in Iran shook the Islamic world, a new generation of Palestinian Muslims rejected the official line of the Muslim Brothers that the time for an uprising against Israel was not yet ripe. They were no longer prepared to accept the catch–22 of embracing either secular political activism or Islamic quietism. Islamic traditions and role models would now serve to interpret the situation of the Muslims in Palestine and as a guide to revolutionary action. This ushered in a period of vigorous development for Palestinian Islamist groups.[39]

This was the state of play in 1987. In association with the First Palestinian Intifada, a well-matched revolutionary religious competitor rose to challenge

---

[37]   His father was a farmer in the Gaza Strip who became a refugee as a result of the war of 1948. Ahmad Yasin, born in 1936, grew up in a mosque run by the Islamic Brotherhood. At the age of sixteen, he broke his neck while playing and was almost entirely paralysed from then on. On the life and work of Sheikh Ahmad Yasin, see Ziad Abu-Amr, 'Shaykh Ahmad Yasin and the Origins of Hamas', in Appleby (ed.), *Spokesmen for the Despised*, pp. 225–56.

[38]   See Ziad Abu-Amr, *Islamic Fundamentalism in the West Bank and Gaza: Muslim Brotherhood and Islamic Jihad*, Bloomington, Indiana University Press, 1994, pp. 90 and 106; on the two 'catastrophes', see the website http://www.alnakba.org.

[39]   See Reuven Paz, 'The Development of Palestinian Islamic Groups', in Barry Rubin (ed.), *Revolutionaries and Reformers: Contemporary Islamist Movements in the Middle East*, New York, SUNY Press, 2003, pp. 23–40. The text is also available online.

the PLO. The uprising was triggered on 6 December 1987 by an accident which Palestinians interpreted as deliberate revenge for the death of a Jewish businessman in the Gaza Strip. Yet this was merely the apparent reason. The uprising had been preceded by a series of clashes between Palestinians and settlers, whose numbers had steadily risen. Palestinians protested against martial law in the occupied territories and its negative consequences with campaigns of civil disobedience such as the flying of Palestinian flags, shouting Palestinian slogans, burning tyres at road junctions, throwing stones at the cars of Jewish settlers, closing shops without authorization and various other measures. The response of the Israeli army was severe and bloody. To coordinate these spontaneous disturbances, the PLO appointed a supreme command. The head of the Islamic Centre in Gaza, Sheikh Ahmad Yasin, seized the initiative and consulted with the key members of the Centre, including Dr Abdul Rantisi. The group decided not to leave coordination of the uprising to the PLO and its United National Command and to found their own organization. It was to be called the Islamic Resistance Movement (*harakat al-muqawama al-Islamiyya*), whose contracted form *hamas* also means 'zeal' in Arabic.[40] The foundation of Hamas as a distinct organization within the Brotherhood was also intended to protect the network of the Muslim Brothers in the Gaza Strip from direct confrontation with Israel and its armed forces. If these institutions or their representatives were attacked by Israel, the organization responded with deadly violence.

On the Palestinian side, the conflict was initially carried on with the tools of civil disobedience and the leaflets of the UNC only gradually called on the people to use violence; Hamas, though, considered violence a component of the conflict from the beginning.[41] Those shot dead by the Israeli army were martyrs on the divine path, as an early communiqué of 14 December 1987 put it.[42] Their

---

[40]   The history of Hamas has been appraised by Khaled Hroub, *Hamas: Political Thought and Practice*, Washington, Institute for Palestine Studies, 2000; and by Shaul Mishal and Avraham Sela, *The Palestinian Hamas: Vision, Violence, and Coexistence*, New York, Columbia University Press, 2000.

[41]   A selection of communiqués by the UNC and Hamas during the first few years of the First Intifada has been published by Shaul Mishal and Reuben Aharoni, *Speaking Stones: Communiqués from the Intifada Underground*, Syracuse, NY, Syracuse University Press, 1994. In the chapter 'Paper War: The Intifada Leaflets', the authors examine this literary genre and compare the contents of both organizations' leaflets (pp. 25–49); a comparison of the two camps with respect to calls for violence is found on pp. 39–42. This is proceeded by the chapter 'The Road to the Intifada' (pp. 1–23), in which the authors deal with the growing importance of young people to the social institutions in the West Bank, pointing to the Israeli policy of occupation as an explanation (pp. 18–21).

[42]   English translation in the appendix of Hroub, *Hamas*, pp. 265ff.

death was an expression of the spirit of self-sacrifice of the Palestinians, who loved the eternal life more than their enemies did the earthly. A people with no fear of death cannot die. On this view, the uprising represents a rejection of the occupation and its pressures, of land confiscation and the creation of settlements, of the Zionist policy of subjugation. It also awakens the conscience of those left gasping after what were viewed as a sick peace, empty international conferences and treasonous partial agreements such as Camp David. The Intifada shows that Islam is the solution and the alternative. The Jewish settlers would be left in no doubt: the Palestinian people know the path of sacrifice and martyrdom and are very generous in this respect. 66 acts of violence against Israelis in the first three years of the Intifada, often carried out with knives, showed how serious this threat was.[43]

In August of the following year, 1988, Hamas published its charter, its manifesto, putting forward a consistently Islamic interpretation of the uprising.[44] It was a wing of the Muslim Brothers (Article 2) and wished to raise the banner of God over every corner of Palestine (Article 6). The Islamic Resistance Movement believes that the land of Palestine is an Islamic land entrusted to the Muslim generations until Judgement Day. Following the conquest, the Caliph had decided that this land should remain in the hands of its inhabitants, but that its revenue must be used for the public welfare for ever more (Article 11). With this interpretation, Hamas took up a concept that attained its contemporary meaning only in the twentieth century, through the process of coming to terms with Zionism.[45] The institution of the *waqf* as such, it is true, dates back to the time of the Prophet. He advised a comrade-in-arms to transfer conquered territories to the needy as alms, thus making it impossible to sell them. But the application of this notion to Palestine as a whole is of more recent vintage. In the 1930s, Islamic scholars spoke out against the sale of Palestinian land to Jews, until the Mufti of Palestine, Amin al-Husaini, finally claimed Palestine as property entrusted (*amana*) to the Muslims in a fatwa in 1935, condemning

---

[43]   These figures are taken from Mishal and Sela, *The Palestinian Hamas*, p. 57 and n. 6 on p. 209.

[44]   English translation in the appendix of Hroub, *Hamas*, pp. 267–91; excerpts in German in Andreas Meier, *Der politische Auftrag des Islam. Programme und Kritik zwischen Fundamentalismus und Reform. Originalstimmen aus der islamischen Welt*, Wuppertal, Hammer, 1994, pp. 384–93.

[45]   See Krämer, *A History of Palestine*, pp. 249–54; on the legal institution of the *waqf*, see Jan-Peter Hartung, 'Die fromme Stiftung [*waqf*]. Eine islamische Analogie zur Körperschaft?', in Hans G. Kippenberg and Gunnar Folke Schuppert (eds.), *Die verrechtlichte Religion. Der Öffentlichkeitsstatus von Religionsgemeinschaften*, Tübingen, Mohr Siebeck, 2005, pp. 287–314, esp. pp. 298–303.

those who sold land as apostates. In analogy to the Jewish idea of the 'salvation' of the land, Muslims too called for it to be 'saved'.

By incorporating an old Islamic legal institution into the interpretation of the situation, Palestinian nationalism was anchored in Islam. 'Nationalism (*wataniya*) [...] is part and parcel of religious ideology', the charter continues in Article 12. The struggle against the occupation is the fulfilment of an old commandment. There could be no peaceful solutions. 'There is no solution to the Palestinian problem except through jihad' (Article 13). 'When an enemy usurps a Muslim land, then the jihad is an individual duty on every Muslim' (Article 15). The justification for interpreting the land as *waqf* added a social dimension to nationalism. The movement prided itself on promoting social solidarity and looking after the needy. Islamic society is a cooperative society (Articles 20 and 21). Hamas valued and respected other Islamic movements, as everyone has the right to interpret Islam in his own way (*ijtihad*) (Article 23). The PLO was a close companion, but had made the mistake of adopting the idea of the secular state, which was inconsistent with religion and must be rejected. 'The Islamic nature of the Palestine issue is part and parcel of our religion.' If the PLO were to adopt Islam as its programme, Hamas would be the fuel for its fire – the charter thus impressed upon the Palestinians that their land would be liberated only by creating an Islamic order.[46]

Suicide bombings/martyr operations

In 1991, Hamas created a brigade whose task was to engage in armed struggle and which was to lead this struggle against Israel in a calculated way. The phased model of the brotherhood was realized and modified through the founding of a distinct organization. This armed wing was named after Izz al-Din al-Qassem and thus continued a tradition which began in the 1930s. As a member of the Egyptian brotherhood and imam of an old-town Jerusalem mosque, Izz al-Din al-Qassem combined reformist sermons with social engagement and called on young Muslims to return to the Islamic order and take up armed struggle against the British and the Jews. With the slogan 'This is jihad, victory or martyrdom [*istishhad*]', he established under his command a force of several hundred voluntary fighters (*fida'iyyin*) to engage in armed struggle against the infidels. He died in 1935 during a clash with a British patrol. As a martyr, his memory lived on.[47] During the First Intifada,

---

[46] On patriotism within Palestinian Islamism, see Jean-François Legrain, 'Palestinian Islamisms: Patriotism as a Condition of their Expansion', in Martin E. Marty and R. Scott Appleby (eds.), *Accounting for Fundamentalisms*, Chicago, University of Chicago Press, 1994, pp. 413–27.
[47] See Krämer, *A History of Palestine*, pp. 259–63.

it was not only the leaflets distributed by Hamas that invoked him, but those of the UNC as well.[48]

The brigade achieved notoriety chiefly because of its suicide attacks. These were inspired by experiences in Lebanon. Israel unintentionally helped pass on these experiences in 1992 when it expelled hundreds of Islamists from the occupied territories, among them Abdul Rantisi; Lebanon refused them entry. They were stranded in no-man's-land for months, where they were looked after by members of Hezbollah, who, among other things, helped them to appreciate the special advantages of suicide attacks. Years later, in conversation with Mark Juergensmeyer, Abdul Rantisi explained that initially Hamas's military operations were targeted solely at soldiers in the occupied territories. This changed only when the Israeli police bloodily dispersed a demonstration by Palestinians before the al-Aqsa mosque on Temple Mount in 1990 and the Jewish settler Baruch Goldstein massacred Muslims in the Cave of the Patriarchs at Hebron in 1994. Only then were civilians in Israel attacked.[49] This assertion is amenable to verification.

Robert A. Pape has classified all suicide attacks worldwide by date, type of weapon, aim, number of dead and campaigns.[50] The list itself shows that suicide attacks are not specifically Islamic. They occur in territories occupied by democratic states and in places where the people are too weak to resist militarily. Hence, we should not blame their spread in the Middle East on an inherently violent Islam; they are linked with the ongoing occupation of Palestinian territories by Israel. On the surface, these acts look like acts of individuals. In fact, though, a suicide attack is not the work of an individual, but requires a team, which justifies the act, determines the goal and instructs the perpetrator. The latter is usually not an uneducated believer, but is often a member of the educated middle class, and by no means particularly easy to manipulate. The more one learns about the sequence of events and the profile of the perpetrators, the clearer it becomes that what we are seeing here is a selfless death to the benefit of a community – an altruistic suicide, to use Emile Durkheim's conception, or an act of violence rooted in an ethics of conviction, in Max Weber's sense.

---

[48]   See Mishal and Aharoni, *Speaking Stones*, p. 33: leaflet no. 2 by the UNC and leaflet no. 31 by Hamas.

[49]   See Juergensmeyer, *Terror in the Mind of God*, pp. 69–78 ('Abdul Aziz Rantisi and Hamas Suicide Missions').

[50]   See Pape, *Dying to Win*, Appendix II, 'Suicide Terrorist Campaigns, 1980–2003', p. 263; the phenomenon is dealt with in a similar way by Ami Pedahzur, *Suicide Terrorism*, Cambridge, Polity, 2005, pp. 241–53, Appendix, 'Suicide Bombings (December 1981– June 2005)'. I am unable to go into the differences between the two here.

Hamas's first campaign took place on 6 and 13 April 1994. Forty days had passed since the massacre by Baruch Goldstein in the Cave of the Patriarchs, when a suicide attack, resulting in deaths and injuries, was carried out on a school bus in the city of Afula (northern Israel) – tying in with the usual commemoration of a martyr forty days after his death. A week later, a bus in Hadara in Israel was the target of an attack, and again there were a number of deaths and many injuries. Another campaign by Hamas and Islamic Jihad followed from October 1994 to August 1995.[51] During the Second Intifada from 2000, when Ariel Sharon demonstratively desecrated the Islamic sites on Temple Mount, another campaign of suicide attacks began. It struck Israeli civilians in Israel and triggered retaliatory measures by Israel. The suicide attack as a technique had now crossed the boundary with the nationalists. The PLO established its own al-Aqsa Brigade, which operated in the same way.[52] Here, we must bear in mind opinion polls among Palestinians. They show growing approval of this kind of fighting as a response to Israeli repression: from 29 per cent in 1995 to 73 per cent in 2001 and 61 per cent in 2003.[53]

Violence in the *Heilsgeschichte*

The violence of Hamas was embedded in a script shaped by a *Heilsgeschichte*. The charter invoked a *hadith*, handed down from the Prophet, relating to the end times:

> The Final Hour will not come until Muslims fight against the Jews and the Muslims kill them, and until the Jews hide behind rocks and trees, and a stone or tree would say: O Muslim, servant of God, there is a Jew hiding behind me, come on and kill him! But the tree of Gharqad would not say it, for it is the tree of the Jews.[54]

David Cook has shown that with the defeats of 1967, a renaissance of apocalyptic ideas began in the Arab world. *Heilsgeschichte* could render comprehensible something which remained a mystery to the normal, rational individual: how puny Israel was able to beat the more powerful Arab states of Egypt, Syria and

---

[51]   See Pape, *Dying to Win*, Appendix II, 'Suicide Terrorist Campaigns, 1980–2003', pp. 253–64.

[52]   The explosion of violence is apparent in the overview by Pape, *Dying to Win*, pp. 260–62.

[53]   See Pape, *Dying to Win*, pp. 49–51.

[54]   Hroub, *Hamas*, p. 272; on this tradition, see also Anne Marie Oliver and Paul F. Steinberg, *The Road to Martyrs' Square: A Journey into the World of the Suicide Bomber*, Oxford, Oxford University Press, 2005, pp. 19–24 ('The Gharqad Tree').

Jordan militarily and take the endowed land of Palestine from the Muslims. In the Islamic conception of eschatological history, the appearance of the Mahdi is preceded by the rule of the Dajjal, the Islamic 'Antichrist'. Only after his destruction will the Mahdi fill the world with justice, as it is now filled with tyranny and injustice.[55] To this traditional end-times scenario was added the anti-Semitic conspiracy theory of the 'Protocols of the Elders of Zion'. In addition, Islamic theorists of the Apocalypse borrowed from American pre-millenarianism the expectation that the 'Antichrist' would establish his bloody regime of terror in Israel at the end of times.[56] Graffiti, videos and leaflets produced by Hamas, which Anne Marie Oliver and Paul F. Steinberg have collected and published, presuppose this connection. They demonize the Jews as 'sons of apes and pigs', depict their end in sadistic fashion, revel in the notion of the fear that will grip their hearts at the sight of a 'living' martyr.[57] The index finger raised to heaven, which stands for the uniqueness of God and his Prophet, is celebrated as the finger pulling the trigger of a machine gun.[58] A single drop of blood shed by a Muslim secures his redemption and his place in paradise. A martyr's funeral is really his wedding.[59]

These attacks represent a serious violation of the Fourth Geneva Convention. A leaflet produced by the American organization Human Rights Watch on this topic recapitulates the legal regulations in armed conflicts and condemns suicide attacks on civilians as crimes against humanity and war crimes.[60]

American pre-millenarianism and Israel

The transition to war between religious communities has also affected the USA. It is particularly disastrous that efforts to establish links with the Bible have had an impact, especially on its foreign policy. The idea of *eretz Yisrael* mobilizes understanding and loyalty, the word *waqf* nothing but irritated responses. The precedence given to Israel's claims over those of the Palestinians and the exorbitant military and financial aid with which the USA furnishes the state

---

[55] For a recent study of the apocalyptic traditions in Islamic history, see David Cook, *Studies in Muslim Apocalyptic*, Princeton, Darwin, 2002; on the Dajjal, pp. 93–120.

[56] See David Cook, *Contemporary Muslim Apocalyptic Literature*, Syracuse, NY, Syracuse University Press, 2005, pp. 13–58 ('Building a New Vision of the Future in the Wake of the Six Days' War').

[57] See Oliver and Steinberg, *The Road to Martyrs' Square*, pp. 76–80.

[58] See Oliver and Steinberg, *The Road to Martyrs' Square*, p. 77.

[59] See Oliver and Steinberg, *The Road to Martyrs' Square*, pp. 72–76.

[60] *Erased in a Moment: Suicide Bombing Attacks against Israeli Civilians*, New York, Human Rights Watch, 2002, pp. 43–61.

of Israel can hardly be put down solely to the influence of a Jewish lobby;[61] their roots also lie in the view of history characteristic of a particular strand of Protestantism, which has become a significant force in American society. It dates back to the nineteenth century, when countless Jews were forced to flee from Russia. Even before the First Zionist Congress of 1897, American Protestants petitioned their president to allow the displaced Jews to return to their homeland of Palestine.[62] The reason for their engagement was a specific eschatological scenario.[63] They did not believe that the biblical promises to the people of Israel had been transferred to Christians and thus to the Church, a widely held view in Christian theology, but rather that they continue to apply to the Jewish people. In accordance with the still unfulfilled prophecies, the process of restoring Israel had begun in the present age; the final millennium would soon commence. A particularly striking feature of this theology, invented by John Nelson Darby (1800–82), was the doctrine of the rapture of the righteous. Before the time of suffering begins, the chosen or the 'Church' will be delivered to the Lord (1 Thess. 4:17), thus escaping the horrors of the end of history. This view of history is therefore also known as pre-millenarianism. After the rapture, seven years of tribulation will begin for all those left behind (Mt. 24:21). During this time, the Antichrist, based in Jerusalem, will unleash a reign of terror over the world. The Jews, who have returned to Palestine, will reach an agreement with him to rebuild the Temple. Finally, though, the Antichrist, together with the heathens and the Jews, unless they embrace Jesus, will be wiped out in the battle of Armageddon in Palestine. In this process, God has given the USA a similar role to that played by the Persian king Cyrus, who helped the Jews return from their Babylonian exile to Palestine and was thus described as 'anointed by the Lord' by the prophet Isaiah (Isa. 45:1).

As increasing numbers of Jews moved to Israel over the course of the twentieth century, this process in turn had an impact on the pre-millenarian Protestants' attitude to politics: 'For the first time [they] believed that it was necessary to leave the bleachers and get onto the playing field to make sure the game ended according to the divine script'.[64] Protestants were no longer content to play the role of onlookers; they sought active involvement. Before their (inner)

---

[61]   See the controversial article by John J. Mearsheimer and Stephen M. Watt, 'The Israel Lobby and U.S. Foreign Policy', http://www.lrb.co.uk/v28/no6/print/mear01_html.

[62]   On this petition, see Yaakov Ariel, *On Behalf of Israel: American Fundamentalist Attitudes towards Jews, Judaism, and Zionism, 1865–1945*, New York, Carlson, 1991, pp. 70–72.

[63]   For an account of this theological current and its relationship to Israel, see Timothy P. Weber, *On the Road to Armageddon: How Evangelicals Became Israel's Best Friend*, Grand Rapids, MI, Baker Academy, 2004.

[64]   Weber, *On the Road to Armageddon*, p. 15.

eyes, the *Heilsgeschichte* played itself out: from the Balfour Declaration of 1917 through the proclamation of the state of Israel on 14 May 1948, the Suez war of 1956 and the Six Days' War of 1967 to the occupation of the old town of Jerusalem by the Israeli army on 8 June 1967 and the occupation of the West Bank. As one of the next steps, these American Protestants expect the restoration of the Jewish Temple. Some of them openly affirm that the Islamic Dome of the Rock would have to be destroyed first.[65]

This conception of history has had an impact far beyond religious communities. Hal Lindsey helped popularize the end-times scenario with his 1970 book *The Late Great Planet Earth*.[66] The final era of the fulfilment of the biblical end-times prophecies was fast approaching. A sure sign of this was the restoration of Israel in the Holy Land in 1948. The theatre of war was being made ready. The time had come of which Jesus said:

> From the fig tree learn its lesson: as soon as its branch becomes tender and puts out its leaves, you know that summer is near. So also, when you see all these things, you know that he is near, at the very gates. Truly, I say to you, this generation will not pass away until all these things take place. (Mt. 24:32–34)

Now that Israel had been restored, the seven-year age of tribulation would begin within no more than one generation, in other words by 1988 at the latest.[67]

The war of 1967 and the annexation of the old town of Jerusalem to the state of Israel created the conditions for the rebuilding of the Temple.[68] The geopolitical alliances which clash in the Battle of Armageddon are, according to Lindsey, already discernible (chapters 5–9). The threats to Israel from the Soviet Union in the north and Egypt in the south and the return of the Roman empire in the shape of the European Community are part and parcel of the last days of humankind. Next, the followers of Christ would be removed from the Earth. Eye-witness accounts illustrate how we are to imagine this process. For example: as I was driving along the motorway, there was sudden pandemonium; cars were zigzagging around because the drivers had been transported to heaven. There are further brief accounts of how people are suddenly removed while going about

---

[65] See Gershom Gorenberg, *The End of Days: Fundamentalism and the Struggle for the Temple Mount*, Oxford, Oxford University Press, 2002.

[66] Hal Lindsey with Carole C. Carlson, *The Late Great Planet Earth*, Grand Rapids, MI, Zondervan, 1970.

[67] Lindsey, *The Late Great Planet Earth*, pp. 53ff. (interpretation of the parable of the fig tree).

[68] Lindsey, *The Late Great Planet Earth*, pp. 54–57.

their work and the world then descends into chaos.[69] The rapture of the righteous is followed by the period of great suffering for those left behind. The Antichrist promises to give the world peace, and Israel makes a pact with him: 'It is through an ingenious settlement of the Middle East problem that the Antichrist will make good his promise to bring peace to a world terrified of war'.[70] After this, though, the Lord arrives (Lindsey's chapters 11–13). A nuclear Armageddon destroys this world; Jesus Christ establishes the Kingdom of God.

When the fundamentalist or evangelical current which propagated this view of history took on a political form as the 'Moral Majority' and coalesced around the Republican Ronald Reagan towards the end of the 1970s, Hal Lindsey produced another book: *The 1980s: Countdown to Armageddon*.[71] Here he furnishes us with a gloomy account of the three possible fates of the USA: a Communist takeover, preceded by a surprise nuclear strike by the Soviet Union, or dependency on the ten states of the European Community. Yet he sees a glimmer of hope: the USA can be saved by a political programme which curbs the welfare state and bureaucracy, rejects the SALT treaties and turns America into a military superpower. What was in reality Reagan's election manifesto became a means of proving one's faith in the battle against the forces of the Antichrist. When the Soviet Union was no more, Lindsey wrote a new book, *The Magog Factor*, but the apocalyptic drama featured a new villain. Now it was Islamists who took on the role of the Antichrist and his followers.[72]

Hal Lindsey's success with *The Late Great Planet Earth* beggars belief. 35 million copies had been sold by 1990.[73] This book did more than any other to popularize the pre-millenarian conception of history.[74] Yet even this success was to be surpassed by a series of novels written by Tim LaHaye and Jerry Jenkins, entitled *Left Behind*. Tim LaHaye, born in 1926, was a graduate of Bob Jones University and founding member of the Moral Majority. He too maintains the doctrine of the rapture before the beginning of the time of tribulation. Intent on popularizing this end-times scenario through the novel, he found a gifted co-author in the shape of Jerry Jenkins. The first novel, *Left Behind: A Novel of the*

[69] Lindsey, *The Late Great Planet Earth*, pp. 136ff.

[70] Lindsey, *The Late Great Planet Earth*, p. 152.

[71] Hal Lindsey, *The 1980s: Countdown to Armageddon*, New York, Bantam, 1981.

[72] See Stephen D. O'Leary, *Arguing the Apocalypse: A Theory of Millennial Rhetoric*, Oxford, Oxford University Press, 1994, pp. 172–93 ('Apocalyptic Politics in the New Christian Right').

[73] See Weber, *On the Road to Armageddon*, p. 191.

[74] Paul S. Boyer has produced a comprehensive account of the popularity of the pre-millenarian current in the USA: *When Time Shall Be No More: Prophecy Belief in Modern American Culture*, Cambridge, MA, Harvard University Press, 1992.

Earth's Last Days, appeared in 1995; the latest, *Kingdom Come: The Final Victory* in April 2007. The series is not only found in religious bookshops, but has also sold in vast quantities in Barnes and Noble, Borders and Wal-Mart. With an estimated 60 million copies sold, it has far surpassed Hal Lindsey's book. The publisher, Tyndale House, disseminated the series still further by creating other product lines such as comics, audio cassettes, websites, videos and DVDs.[75]

The story is based on a small theological revision of the notion of the rapture with significant dramatic potential. While Darby's work leaves those left behind with no prospect of evading their fate, this series opens up the possibility that they might yet escape damnation by converting. This modification gives rise to the series' basic plot, which drives the action in every scene.[76] The left behind can still prove their faith – the men, of course, primarily through heroic and courageous struggle against the Antichrist and his soldiers. At the centre of the action is flight captain Rayford Steele, who is piloting his Boeing 747 from Chicago O'Hare to London Heathrow when passengers and cabin staff suddenly make the terrible discovery that dozens of passengers have disappeared. All that remains on their empty seats is their articles of clothing and jewellery. Steele is ordered back to O'Hare, where he finds a world in chaos. Aircraft without pilots have crashed the world over. Arriving home, he finds his house and marital bed empty. His wife, a born-again Christian, has also been transported. Rayford Steele bands together with others to form the 'Tribulation Force' to counter the forces of evil. They enter into battle with Nicolae Carpathia, the UN secretary general, who is really the Antichrist. His peace treaties with Israel are merely intended to secure his dominion. For the sake of truth, there can and must be no peace, only violence, during the seven years of his reign. In this period, the left behind still have one final chance to prove themselves and become combatants in the drama of the end times.

This plot rouses readers' imagination and imparts a view of history and model of action: it is the faithful rather than any political institutions that represent the true America; the United Nations is an instrument of the Antichrist. The more time goes by, the faster the moral, religious, military and economic decline. Promises of peace, disarmament, environmental protection and international

---

[75] For information on the series, see Weber, *On the Road to Armageddon*, pp. 192–96; Bruce David Forbes and Jeanne Halgren Kilde (eds.), *Rapture, Revelation, and the End Times: Exploring the Left Behind Series*, New York, Palgrave Macmillan, 2004; here, see 'How Popular Are the Left Behind Books … and Why?' by Bruce David Forbes on pp. 5–32. The figure of 60 million copies sold is on p. 7.

[76] Jeanne Halgren Kilde, 'How Did Left Behind's Particular Vision of the End Times Develop? A Historical Look at Millenarian Thought', in Forbes and Kilde (eds.), *Rapture, Revelation, and the End Times*, pp. 33–70, esp. p. 60.

treaties are the work of the Antichrist.[77] The success of this series brings to light something which otherwise tends to remain hidden: a religious subculture that is entering the political mainstream; the matrix of an American popular culture that is creating specific views of history and politics. These are pervaded by a Manichaean structure. Evil is not something that comes from our world, but from beyond it. People are not both good *and* evil; they are *either* good *or* evil. The solution to the existence of evil is not meekly to tolerate it, but to destroy it by force; the good guys win in the end.[78] This basic structure, also familiar from Hollywood films, comics and science fiction, has a lengthy history in the USA.[79] The popular fascination with this type of masculine violence is taken up by *Left Behind* and turned to religious ends. The idealization of violence is transformed from 'religious half-product' to the content of subjective religiosity.[80] Today, forty to fifty million Americans sympathize with such an end-times scenario and make up a huge block of potential voters, mobilized by the Republicans under Ronald Reagan and George W. Bush.

The linkage of religious history and foreign policy in the New Christian Right is not a direct one, but may be particularly effective for that very reason. The effect exercised by pre-millenarianism on US politics consists of a religious aggravation of political differences. A quotation from a televangelist, cited by Grace Halsell is a typical example: 'There'll be no peace until Jesus comes. Any preaching of peace prior to this return is heresy; it's against the word of God; it's Antichrist.'[81]

The semantics of the terms 'freedom fighter'/'terrorist'

George P. Shultz, American secretary of state from 1983 to 1989, took part in the second conference of the Jonathan Institute and adopted the new definition of terrorists. Terrorists are enemies of democracy. Their violence does not serve the

---

[77]   See Amy Johnson Frykholm, *Rapture Culture: Left Behind in Evangelical America*, Oxford, Oxford University Press, 2004; idem, 'What Social and Political Messages Appear in the Left Behind Books? A Literary Discussion of Millenarian Fiction', in Forbes and Kilde (eds.), *Rapture, Revelation, and the End Times*, pp. 167–95.

[78]   Forbes, 'How Popular Are the Left Behind Books?', pp. 22–29.

[79]   See Robert Jewett and John Shelton Lawrence, *Captain America and the Crusade against Evil: The Dilemma of Zealous Nationalism*, Grand Rapids, MI, Eerdmans, 2003.

[80]   The concept of the 'religious half-product' comes from Georg Simmel and his book *Sociology of Religion* (1922), New York, Philosophical Library, 1959.

[81]   Grace Halsell, *Prophecy and Politics: Militant Evangelists on the Road to Nuclear War*, Westport, CT, Lawrence, 1986, p. 16. See also Forbes' remark in 'How Popular Are the Left Behind Books?', p. 28.

goal of winning over others to a just cause; they act out of hate for civilization. If you have understood this, Shultz stated in 1983, it is not difficult to distinguish between terrorists and freedom fighters. Those fighting in Afghanistan or the Contras in Nicaragua for example do not kill innocents and are therefore genuine resistance fighters rather than terrorists.

This formation of a new concept shows in exemplary fashion how, through the act of speaking, a term is infused with judgements, giving rise to a semantics which is in turn capable of legitimizing actions. Following Tomis Kapitan, I would describe this semantics as follows:[82] those who refer to terrorists remove from their listeners any desire to learn something about the reasons for the actions of those thus designated; they divert attention away from the question of whether one's own policies may possibly have contributed to the development of such phenomena; they imply that it is absurd to negotiate with such people.

The term 'terrorists' confronts us with a metaphysical concept which separates an act of violence from any kind of understandable explanation, leaving the elimination of the perpetrators as the only adequate solution to the problem. Terrorists are moral nihilists and stand outside the legal order. They must be annihilated through war. The US State Department draws up an annual list of terrorist organizations. If we turn from this semantics to how it is applied, inconsistencies emerge. Let us return to George P. Shultz's assertion that it is crystal-clear who is the resistance fighter and who the terrorist and to his two examples. The Contras, supported by the USA, killed around 3,000 civilians in Nicaragua in the 1980s, to say nothing of the atrocities of the anti-Soviet fighters in Afghanistan. In retrospect, it is apparent not only that both examples were unfortunate choices, but that the rhetoric of 'terrorism' is dominated by the political friend/enemy schema. At the moment of its application, the term automatically becomes identical with one's political enemies. A recent example illustrates this point. After invading Iraq, the USA agreed a truce with an Iranian opposition group, the Mujahedin-e Khalk, which had for years been readying itself for the violent overthrow of the Iranian regime; they were allowed to hold onto their weapons so that they could use them against possible invaders from Iran. In order to do so, however, the group had first to be removed from the State Department's list of foreign terrorist organizations. Daniel Pipes, who reports these events in a newspaper article entitled 'A Terrorist U.S. Ally?', concludes that there could be no objection to this. The group no longer represented a threat to the security of the United States.[83]

---

[82]   See Tomis Kapitan, 'The Terrorism of "Terrorism"', in James Sterba (ed.), *Terrorism and International Justice*, New York, Oxford University Press, 2003, pp. 47–66.

[83]   See Daniel Pipes and Patrick Clawson, 'A Terrorist U.S. Ally?', *New York Post*, 20 May 2003.

Let us return to the issue of the definition of terrorism. In 1983, the same year that the conferences of the Jonathan Institute took place, the US State Department committed itself to a definition of terrorism: 'The term "terrorism" means premeditated, politically motivated violence perpetrated against non-combatant* targets by sub-national groups or clandestine agents, usually intended to influence an audience'.[84] This definition brands every kind of violence practised by non-state groups against non-military targets as terrorism – regardless of whether or not it is an act of resistance against an occupation. The asterisk is particularly worthy of note. We are informed that 'civilians' includes military personnel who are not on duty at the time.

When President George W. Bush declared war on terror, he signed an internal memorandum in February 2002:

Subject: Humane Treatment of al Qaeda and Taliban Detainees.

The Commander in Chief and Chief Executive of the United States determines as follows: '... none of the provisions of Geneva apply to our conflict with al Qaeda in Afghanistan or elsewhere throughout the world because, among other reasons, al Qaeda is not a High Contracting Party to Geneva'.

Of course, the memorandum goes on, our values require us to treat humanely even those detainees who are not legally entitled to such treatment. Subsequently, the Commander-in-Chief reaffirmed an order issued by the Secretary of Defense, 'requiring that the detainees be treated humanely and, to the extent appropriate and consistent with military necessity, in a manner consistent with the principles of Geneva'.[85] Without this qualification, the practices in the prison camps of Guantánamo and Abu Ghraib would not have been possible. Seymour M. Hersh has researched debates within the government on torture in Guantánamo. The unanimous view was that not all cruel, inhumane or degrading practices cause sufficient pain and suffering to come under the prohibition on torture. Besides, by virtue of the constitution of the United States, the president has the right to suspend the Geneva Convention with respect to Afghanistan, though he did not at present wish to make use of this right.[86]

---

[84]   US Department of State, Counterterrorism Office, Releases, Patterns of Global Terrorism 2000, Introduction. http://www.state.gov/s/ct/rls/pgtrpt/2000/2419.htm.

[85]   See Mark Danner, *Torture and Truth: America, Abu Ghraib, and the War on Terror*, New York, New York Review of Books, 2004, pp. 105–106.

[86]   See Seymour M. Hersh, *Chain of Command: The Road from 9/11 to Abu Ghraib*, New York, HarperCollins, 2004, pp. 1–20.

Conclusion: an unfamiliar chapter
of contemporary religious history

To look closely at the religious interpretation of the Middle East conflict is to open a new chapter in the religious history of modernity. But we also notice how difficult it has become for us to understand religion; we have become religious illiterates. I would therefore like to conclude by summarizing what we can learn by examining this case.

Historically, the assumption that there can no longer be any belief in a *Heilsgeschichte* in modernity is wrong. Alongside the belief in a progress which human beings could bring about themselves through mastery of nature and social reform, the expectation of a time of salvation at the end of all history has remained in place. There are thus two distinct ways to conceptualize the future. The future may be sketched out from the perspective of the present; this renders it an open space that may be planned and created by human beings. Sketched out from the perspective of the end of time, however, the future may also be understood as a time of salvation in which humanity is delivered from its suffering and all absurdities – here, the future is understood as the fulfilment of the salvation promised to Abraham and his descendants. Both constructions – history as a secular sphere of planned progress, and as the scene for the manifestation of salvation – have remained equally valid.

Actors may still frame a conflict in terms of *Heilsgeschichte* without necessarily being uneducated fanatics. In the case of the Middle East conflict, this has undoubtedly been an aggravating factor. If the settlement of an occupied territory or resistance to it are interpreted in terms of *Heilsgeschichte*, solutions within the framework of international law appear to be impossible. Yet this is not necessarily the case. The ultra-orthodox rejection of the foundation of a Jewish state has not disappeared with the emergence of religious settlers. Even today, ultra-orthodox Jews still live, as they see it, in a double exile: not only in a time without the Messiah, but also in a religiously illegitimate Jewish state. This finds particularly vivid expression in the fact that one member of the delegation of Palestinians with whom the government of Israel carried out negotiations within the framework of the Oslo accords was an ultra-orthodox rabbi. He saw himself as a Jewish Palestinian contributing to the establishment of a non-Jewish state in Palestine. The idea that a Jew cannot force the end to come has remained part of the Jewish tradition and may therefore become binding again at any time. The authority of religious traditions is not inherent in those traditions; it is something that believers endow them with. In the same way, two options are built into the salvation-based interpretation applied to the conflict by Islamists: alongside a warlike ethics of conviction which demands armed struggle for the community there exists an ethics of responsibility which, in light of existing social institutions and the people dependent on them, calls for the exercise of patience. It is true that there can never be peace with Israel from this perspective; but it is quite possible to imagine a truce. Even interpretations of conflict based on *Heilsgeschichte* do not necessarily end in violence. It is thus incorrect to state that such interpretations always aggravate conflict and are therefore bad. They may equally demand of believers that they 'live with difference', in other words, they expect salvation without changing the present order through violence. The characterization of entire organizations as terrorist regardless of this ambivalence, and the desire to eradicate them, ignores this ambivalence and itself becomes a source of violence.

Religious networks and communities have been spreading dramatically for several decades. The explosive spread of Protestant congregations in Latin America and the Pacific is as worthy of mention here[87] as the surge in the foundation of mosques in Europe and the USA.[88] Clearly, globalization is fostering the development of religiously based communities. With the advent of economic and political orders of a rational, modern character, religious communities have become increasingly important – because of their ethic of brotherliness. This is in particular demand in critical situations in which the individual fails to receive, either from neighbours or kin or from the state, sufficient protection and security against growing risks and threats to his or her existence. The ethic of brotherliness may take on various forms in these circumstances. In situations in which its networks were threatened from outside, Hamas has promoted a belligerent ethics of conviction; when the threat diminished, it has demanded an ethics of responsibility. I suspect that all attempts to destroy Hamas (or Hezbollah) are doomed to failure and only ever give rise to new manifestations of belligerence.

In a study of the struggle over Temple Mount,[89] Gershom Gorenberg has pointed out that politicians are not blameless with respect to the way the Middle East conflict has changed: 'The problem is the ease with which political leaders

---

[87]   We have British sociologist of religion David Martin to thank for the soundest empirical studies of this subject: David Martin, *Tongues of Fire: The Explosion of Protestantism in Latin America*, Oxford, Blackwell, 1990; idem, *Pentecostalism: The World their Parish*, Oxford, Blackwell, 2002 (see also his contribution in the present volume).

[88]   Olivier Roy (*Globalized Islam: The Search for a New Ummah*, New York, Columbia University Press, 2004) examines this process from an Islamic Studies perspective. Empirical material must be garnered from studies of individual countries. For Germany, see Ursula Spuler-Stegemann, *Muslime in Deutschland. Informationen und Klärungen*, Freiburg, Herder, 2002; for Europe, see Grace Davie, *The Sociology of Religion*, Los Angeles, Sage, 2007, p. 168.

[89]   See Gorenberg, *The End of Days*, p. 244.

seek the support of religious figures while discounting the potential impact of their views'.[90] We must demand consistent policies of our politicians: that they cease to tolerate, in one-sided fashion, Jewish movements that disregard international law and that they discontinue their equally one-sided wars against Islamic networks. The ambivalence of religious communities offers sufficient bases for a policy of de-escalation on both sides. For the sake of peace, we need a state which defends the existing legal order against all religious claims; and we need politicians who deal constructively with the power of religious communities for the common good.

---

[90]   Gorenberg, *The End of Days*, p. 195.

Afterword

Klaus Wiegandt

While the natural scientific conferences of my Foundation bore the imprint of Ernst Peter Fischer, the scientific advisor at my Foundation, those within the field of the social sciences and humanities bear the unmistakable signature of Hans Joas. The book arising from the third conference, 'The Cultural Values of Europe', which he directed, has now run to four editions and appeared in English in 2008.

The fifth conference, 'Secularization and the World Religions', was also planned and realized by Hans Joas in exemplary fashion. I would like to express my personal thanks to him both for this and for his editorship of the present volume.

Attentive readers of the Forum für Verantwortung series may wonder what has become of the planned activities of my Foundation aimed at informing and mobilizing civil society with respect to the topic of sustainability. Guided by the motto 'The courage to achieve sustainability', this initiative has now taken on clear forms. I first asked renowned scholars to provide an account, comprehensible to the general reader, of the state of research and possible options for action with respect to twelve topics crucial to the future of our planet, with one book devoted to each topic. The twelve volumes originally appeared in German in 2007. They are now published in English by Haus Publishing and tackle the following topics: *Our Planet: How Much More Can Earth Take?* (Jill Jäger); *Feeding the Planet: Environmental Protection Through Sustainable Agriculture* (Klaus Hahlbrock); *The Earth: Natural Resources and Human Intervention* (Friedrich Schmidt-Bleek); *Climate Change: The Point of No Return* (Mojib Latif); *Water Resources: Efficient, Sustainable and Equitable Use* (Wolfram Mauser); *Energy: The World's Race for Resources in the 21st Century* (Hermann-Josef Wagner); *Overcrowded World: Population Explosion and International Migration* (Rainer Münz and Albert F. Reiterer); *Our Threatened Oceans* (Stefan Rahmstorf and Katherine Richardson); *Costing the Earth: Restructuring the Economy for Sustainable Development* (Bernd Meyer); *The New Plagues: Pandemics and Poverty in a Globalized World* (Stefan Kaufmann).

In order to continue the initiative begun with these books on a broad basis in the coming years and to obtain suitable teaching material for the comprehensive educational activities necessary to this end, the ASKO EUROPA-STIFTUNG foundation commissioned the Wuppertal Institute for Climate, Environment and Energy to didacticize all twelve volumes. Against the background of the authors' key ideas and the interconnections between the topics dealt with in the books, the first communicative modules have already been developed. These are being used in courses and workshops on sustainability at the European Academy in Otzenhausen. We are reaching civil societies throughout the German-speaking world, not least by disseminating digital media and teaching materials and through long-term cooperation with a large number of prominent figures. The key aim of these educational activities is to impart knowledge that both guides understanding and provides a basis for action, to nurture the powers of discernment and competence of every individual in a globalized world and to motivate civil societies and their actors to take a proactive stance.

I would like to invite anyone interested in further information about our educational initiative or who wishes to make a contribution to our debate on sustainability to contact Dr Hannes Petrischak of the ASKO EUROPA-STIFTUNG foundation (Pestelstraße 2, D–66119 Saarbrücken, fax: +49 (0)681/92674–99, email: h.petrischak@asko-europa-stiftung.de).